Praise for

Allegiance

"An exciting new approach . . . People of a different stripe dominate here as in a novel, and [he] gives them life, character, and
unforgettable meaning. . . . A wealth of new information. The
presentation reads with the ease of a good novel. In short, it is
historical reporting at its best."

—*Richmond Times-Dispatch*

"A must for Civil War buffs . . . A tale of passion and deception,
politics and bravery."

—*Star-Observer* (Hudson, WI)

"Detzer puts human faces on a major historical event and adds personalities, color and texture to our understanding of the first shot
of the Civil War."

—*Post & Courier* (Charleston, SC)

"A narrative with a fast-beating pulse, packed with striking anecdotes and intimate details that give new life to an old story. It is
history at its finest: soundly researched, skillfully utilizing that
background in the service of a vital, exciting chronicle. I haven't
read a more entertaining book of history in recent years."

—*Columbia State* (SC)

"With such incredible, significant detail, Detzer . . . makes the six
months surrounding the Fort Sumter crisis come alive. . . . Detzer
is to be commended, for he incorporates not only the great men of
history, but the lesser people as well."

—*The Decatur Daily* (AL)

"Vividly recreates the people and politics of the day . . . Illuminates the passions and delves into the personalities of the decision makers, the risk takers, and the ordinary citizens as they went about the business of life, that was soon to become the business of death for so many of them. A history of a pivotal moment in American history."

— *The Advocate* (Los Angeles, CA)

"Detzer knows how to explain history. . . . Ambitious, interesting."
— *Civil War Book Review* (Nashville, TN)

"Has all the elements of a military epic: a divided nation, trigger-happy politicians, unruly crowds, dedicated soldiers, a change in presidential administrations. A superb popular history is the result, bringing to life the men (on both sides) who were responsible for the first shots of the Civil War. Its immediacy, engagement and basis in fact are unquestionable."
— *Publishers Weekly*

"With a novelist's gift for storytelling and an artist's eye for detail, the author brings new drama and insight to the well-worn narrative of the 'firing of the first shot' of the war. . . . A gripping account of how many earnest men lost control of events."
— *Library Journal*

"A riveting and moving narrative."
— *Booklist*

"A fascinating historical account . . . Dozens of fascinating details and anecdotes keep the story flowing. . . . If you need top-notch reading material to sustain yourself while lying on the beach or lounging in your own backyard make a pledge to yourself right now to read David Detzer's *Allegiance*."
— toledotalks.com

"A highly enjoyable and easy-to-read book on the fall of Fort Sumter and the climate in Charleston and Washington in the weeks and months immediately before the Civil War . . . Riveting . . . The author is as much a storyteller as an historian."

— *The Viking Voice* (Grayson County College)

"A splendid story of people, ordinary and extraordinary, living through extraordinary experiences. David Detzer tells of the decisions in Washington and Montgomery that lit the fuse of war at Fort Sumter. But his main focus is on the soldiers and civilians in Charleston and its harbor, especially Major Robert Anderson, whose lives intersected with history. Their story has never before been told so well."

— James M. McPherson, author of *Battle Cry of Freedom*

"Well researched, dramatically yet thoughtfully written, *Allegiance* shows that events truly are driven by the people as much as by external forces, and that when and where and how the Civil War began owes as much to personality as to policy. *Allegiance* should take a place as the definitive word on the first moments of our greatest national tragedy."

— William C. Davis, author of *An Honorable Defeat*

"This is the story of Sumter and how the Civil War began, told from both sides, rich in detail, rich in understanding, rich in human drama, and richly told — all that good narrative history ought to be."

— John Waugh, author of *Reelecting Lincoln*

"Entertaining."

— Clint Johnson

Allegiance

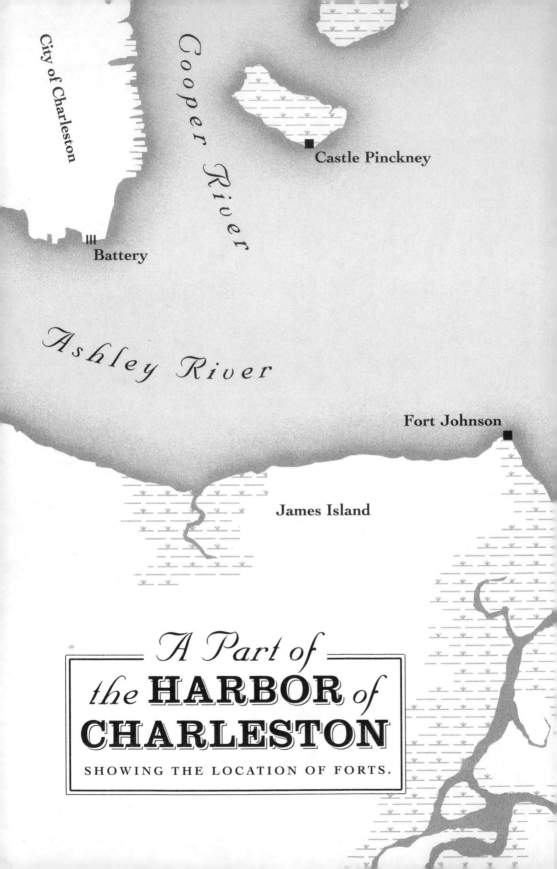

City of Charleston

Cooper River

Castle Pinckney

III
Battery

Ashley River

Fort Johnson

James Island

A Part of
the **HARBOR** of
CHARLESTON
SHOWING THE LOCATION OF FORTS.

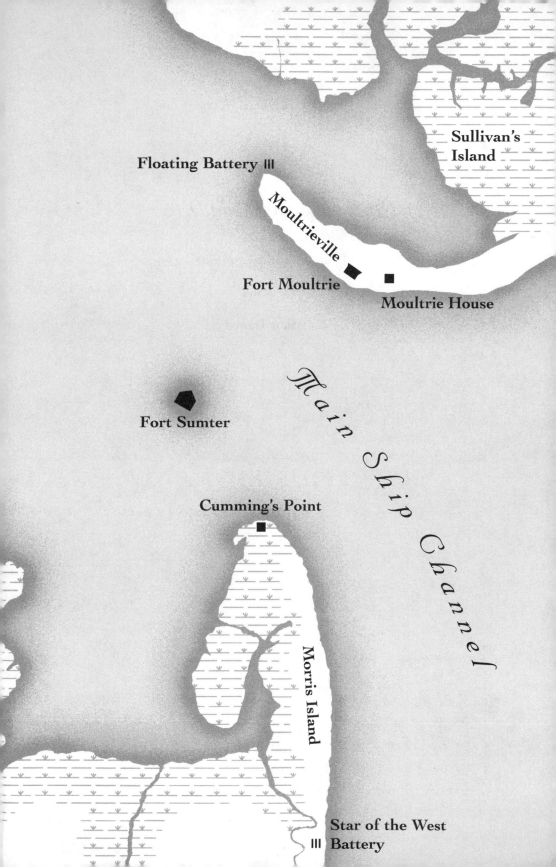

Other books by David Detzer

Thunder of the Captains

The Brink

An Asian Tragedy

ALLEGIANCE

Fort Sumter, Charleston,
and the Beginning of
the Civil War

David Detzer

A HARVEST BOOK
HARCOURT, INC.

San Diego   New York   London

www.HarcourtBooks.com

Library of Congress Cataloging-in-Publication Data
Detzer, David.
Allegiance: Fort Sumter, Charleston,
and the beginning of the Civil War/David Detzer.
p.   cm.
Includes index.
ISBN 0-15-100641-5
ISBN 0-15-600741-X (pbk.)
1. Fort Sumter (Charleston, S.C.) — Siege, 1861.
2. Charleston (S.C.) — History — Civil War, 1861–1865.   I. Title.
E471.1 .D48 2001
973.7'31 — dc21   00-050570

Text set in Cochin
Designed by G. B. D. Smith

Printed in the United States of America

First Harvest edition 2002
A C E G I K J H F D B

Mornin' time,
   'n evenin' time,
      'n summertime,
         'n wintertime . . .
            now and forever—

Melanie

The Union flag that flew over Sumter.   *Courtesy National Park Service*

"I pledge allegiance to the flag of the United States and to the Republic for which it stands, one nation, indivisible, with liberty and justice for all."

—FRANCIS BELLAMY, 1892

Contents

Foreword

Our American experiences of 1861–65 have been variously described. They have been called the War of Southern Secession and, as I observed a couple of years ago during a Virginia visit, are still sometimes known as the War of Northern Aggression. (Such was the term utilized on a Petersburg menu telling the history of a former barn in which the eatery was housed.) In the South of decades gone, it was considered most impolite to allude to the Late Unpleasantness as anything but the War Between the States; for to term it the Civil War implied that the Confederate States of America were never really a political entity, but simply a group of citizens of the United States temporarily in a mistaken insurrection. And of course in late nineteenth century romantic fashion the fighting was sometimes styled The War of the Brothers.

There was another term: The Irrepressible Conflict. Our war was indeed unstoppable. The United States required it to weld in terrible fire what had been and what might be. The end of one epoch and the birth of another could not be accomplished peacefully. It was all preordained.

Yes. But where and how everything commenced is another matter, and it is this which involves the author of this splendid book. Our country of a century-and-a-half ago possessed scores of coastline forts, most unoccupied while ready for garrisoning to repel a seaborne enemy—the British, most likely. We remember none of their names save for, perhaps, one or two near where we live. But Fort Sumter is known to all. We take this as a given, as we do our mental picture of Gettysburg, the burning of Atlanta, the assassination of Abraham Lincoln. But what for us is acknowledged fact studied in school, seen on the History Channel, read about in books, was all in the unknown future for those of the Charleston Harbor of long ago. In this book, we join those who were to bring the war on, and that we share their tensions gives David Detzer's work great value.

The author is good. An academic, he is unlike those of his brethren who when writing books retain habits formed when taking tests in the days before they became professors. What then produced good grades does not, unfortunately, produce readability. It is not a sin to stoop to being understood and exciting. (Although at times I fear it leads to unfortunate chapter headings, with Thirteen's "Takes Two to Tango, But One Can Do the Twist All Alone" particularly wince-producing.) And we don't need to know everything. We want to be told a story. David Detzer gives us that.

Some of this storyteller's recitations made my eyebrows rise. I often turned to the source notes in the back to check documentation for truly outlandish, indeed astonishing, text revelations. Was it really possible that a state governor in office for a few weeks saw himself as conducting foreign policy when he negotiated with the government of the United States, even as he issued orders to the South Carolina navy? Even today, when of course we know about the war and states' rights, it seems incredible. For some people that was the case back then; and at least one officer wept when firing upon the flag under which he had long served. But to most people, we learn, it was all quite acceptable. So was it, apparently, that the issue of war or peace be left entirely in the hands of the governor who was a ninny—a favored David Detzer word—and the U.S. Army major who commanded Fort Sumter, Robert Anderson.

We meet a fifty-five-year-old career soldier from Kentucky, a former slave holder married to a Georgia woman. Unlike the

Charleston militia unit dandies and teenage cadets from the Citadel who menace him, he knows battle—he's seen plenty of it against the Indians in Illinois and Florida and in the Mexican War. He thinks it abominable, dreadful. But to his horror he finds that war unsurpassed for America is in his hands. He is given virtually no guidance from Washington as the outgoing and incoming Presidents of the time vie for fecklessness in this regard. The author doesn't hesitate to give us his opinions on that. "Lincoln was covering his backside." That is not our accustomed picture of our premier leader. But this author's got the right to be judgmental. He's earned that right. He's got the facts, he knows what happened, and he's here to tell us.

Through the author's narrative we follow Anderson through purgatory on his two-and-a-half-acre windswept island mound with a complement of eighty-six enlisted men and a handful of officers. His government sends a supply and reinforcement ship. South Carolina's batteries fire. The ship comes about and races back to New York. The major and his command are isolated and alone and entirely without instructions for weeks on end. What in God's name is he to do? Fire on the South Carolinians? Run down his flag, turn over everything, and get out of town, as is happening elsewhere? He cuts rations and as firewood and oil for the lamps dwindle, he sits. Drummers on shore threateningly beat the long roll, and emissaries, some self-appointed free-lancers, sail or row up to Fort Sumter to offer demands and suggestions. Washington is silent. It is a measure of the author's narrative talent that we almost wonder what the end game is going to be.

Then David Detzer shows us, not tells us, through cited sources of diaries, newspapers, letters, previous works, what happened in the Charleston Harbor of long ago. The Irrepressible Conflict was coming. It might have begun elsewhere at an earlier or later time. But it was given to Fort Sumter that at this moment the storm broke and Americans called upon the God of Battles, the Lord of Hosts, as *Allegiance* so vividly describes.

Gene Smith
January 3, 2001

Allegiance

CHAPTER ONE

Asunder

"A line of enemies is closing around us."
— SENATOR JAMES CHESNUT

In the autumn of 1860 a train rattled over the damp, mostly desolate landscape just north of Charleston, South Carolina; then, with no genteel preliminaries, it entered the outskirts of the city, pulled into a rambling station, and stopped. Among the passengers was a slight man wearing an officer's uniform of the American army. He was a quiet, graying individual in late middle age, his posture erect, his face leathery and worn from years in the sun. He had no swagger, no charisma. When he stepped from the train he would have seemed just another military man. Few would have paid him much mind, though his coming had been deemed newsworthy enough a few days earlier that both of Charleston's major newspapers had carried brief notices about it. "In the ordinary routine of Army changes," a paper noted, "Col. Gardner has been relieved from the command of Fort Moultrie. Maj. Anderson, the next in rank, has been designated his successor." One old soldier, Colonel John L. Gardner, nearing retirement, had been replaced by another. Apparently nothing more. Thus does history move. The arrival of Major Robert Anderson to take charge of nearby Fort Moultrie would in fact become one of the crucial events in American history, a critical cog in the churning events of the next few weeks and months. In time, this mild man would alter the life of the city. But just now he passed, unnoticed, through it. Charleston herself was too busy to pay much attention to him. Its leaders, in their pride, were about to try and change the very destiny of America. They considered themselves in the forefront of the South, perhaps the world.

A city is simply a passel of people packed in a pot like pickles. It is assorted buildings where a population can eat and drink, worship God or manna, a place to amuse or be entertained. Observers often commented that Charleston seemed "exotic." It was vastly different from Richmond or Baltimore, Cincinnati or Hartford — even Boston or New York. Only Cajun New Orleans rivaled her distinctiveness, though that Louisiana city could not match Charleston's civic spirit, her pride in her many schools, her medical research, her charities. Charleston's leading citizens were rightfully proud of their more than twenty benevolent organizations. Today, little but the better edifices is left from that era, and tourists too easily conclude that antebellum Charlestonians were either very wealthy individuals or their slaves. The reality was more complicated.

Censuses tell us that Charleston's population at the time was approximately 50,000, and that almost half was black (although this percentage had been dropping due to the sale of slaves to plantations farther west). About 30 percent of the city's whites were immigrants, mostly Irish and Germans. We know that Charleston housed a Dickensian world of poor newsboys who brought home their pittance to their destitute mothers, and an Orphan House that took in the bastard children of syphilitic prostitutes and the abused progeny of drunken fathers. We know that the Alms House was an asylum for the city's insane, for broken and abandoned wives, for the indigent sick. Visitors could purchase the favors of a trollop near the docks, and the city had several major whorehouses, including Big Brick at 11 Fulton Street, a large and well-known establishment. Most prostitution, however, was centered in Dutch Town (where the majority of the city's many Germans lived). Here, pathetic slatterns earned money in unsavory rooms behind grocery stores.[1]

Charleston, in other words, was not a romantic, quaint town. Most of her money came, directly or indirectly, from commerce. The city's substance, if not her soul, lay in her wharves, nineteen of them, lining the Cooper River for two miles or more. In this region were countinghouses and mansions, seedy dives and bustling wharves, sailmakers' and coopers' shops, sailors' saloons and restaurants for every taste.

Charleston sits at the end of a south-drooping, priapic "peninsula," created by the confluence of two languid rivers, the Ashley on the western side, the Cooper on the eastern. Vessels of every sort crowded in, like animals drinking at an oasis. Old, blurred photographs show a thriving city. In all seasons goods arrived and goods went out, but the busiest time came between October and March when cotton and rice were harvested and readied for market. Then the wharves bustled. One-masted sloops and barks of various sizes arrived from upriver or the sea islands, carrying goods, dropping them off. Cotton bales, averaging more than three hundred pounds, were stacked by sweating black men onto the docks in huge, mountainous piles, awaiting steamers to take them away.[2] Wagons loaded high clattered in and out, carrying things important and trivial. Brick warehouses lined the wharves shoulder-to-shoulder. In December ships hurried in. During the first four months of each year, on any day, a Charlestonian might see fifty or sixty ships loading and unloading, hear their anxious captains shouting orders.

Charleston, however, was more than a seaport. In addition to its black stevedores and white bookkeepers, a fair percentage of its population was involved in industry. Uptown, on the Ashley River, were four rice mills, which took the raw kernels sent from the plantations and readied them for the export market. Each mill used large gangs of slaves, living in nightmarish barracks and shanties on the property. Charleston's workers, free and slave, manufactured umbrellas and shoes, carriages and stained-glass windows, turpentine, lime, and paper. In terms of total industrial output, the city stood only eighty-fifth in the nation, but it was third in the South, following Richmond and New Orleans, two much larger cities. Although many city workers were slaves, Charleston did have typical labor problems. The Typographical Union went on strike in October 1860 against the *Evening News,* which the union leaders called a "rat office," and stayed off the job for several months.[3]

Money, however, was not the city's most salient characteristic. Its leaders were proudest of the quality of their life. Charlestonians considered the enjoyment of life a worthy goal. Wealth was very nice to have, and honor and family were of critical importance, but there was a great deal to be said for a life of the senses — and the leisure time to appreciate such things. The most distinctive architectural style in the city was called the "I" house, and these homes well represented Charleston's attitude about life, for their fronts did not face the street but were turned away from the hurly-burly. To gain access to them, one first had to enter an open courtyard through a gate. The size of these courtyards depended on the owner's wealth; some were quite small, perhaps twenty feet by forty feet, others large, with a water pump and shanties for the slaves. One resident later recalled that in his grandmother's courtyard dwelled nineteen servants, plus "sundry and various children."[4] Some critics have suggested that the unusual setup of these houses and their compounds indicated a kind of anxiety, a fear of slave uprisings, but the posture of these homes seems to have grown out of the Charlestonian emphasis on individualism and privacy and pleasure. When the sun was overhead and the harbor breezes blew softly by, these courtyards could provide a circus for the senses; large or small, they would, in season, waft with the wonderful fragrances of Charleston's flora. Honeysuckle sweetened the air. In the springtime one could smell the aroma of yellow jasmine, of mock orange and phlox and gardenia, the bittersweet scent of passion flower. To pleasure the eyes, the courtyards offered the breathtaking loveliness of hydrangea and forget-me-not and periwinkle, plus rainbow shades of roses and azaleas. Among all these flowers fluttered tiny hummingbirds, and from courtyard trees came the medleys of mockingbirds. The houses, generally with two or three stories, had verandas ("piazzas," they called them in Charleston) jutting off each floor, facing the courtyard. The home's inhabitants could come out and sit, enjoy the breeze, and catch the bouquet of their own private, sensual world.

On the other hand, it was a vulgar fact that sections of Charleston often reeked. Many backyards were crowded with animals: goats, cows, chickens, horses. During the rainy season, cesspools and privies often backed up. The city, flat as cornpone, sat only a few feet above sea level. Its water table was high, and many homes had their own cisterns: the results were feculent. Late in the 1850s the city had begun building deep sewers. Graves could now be dug far deeper than they had; earlier, gravediggers had hit water as close to the surface as two feet.[5]

Life in Charleston could be quite splendid. If Charlestonians were not at their own homes or visiting acquaintances, those who were hungry could snack at the "ice-cream garden" on King Street or the Commercial Coffee House on East Bay. They could sup at the Sideboard or the French Coffee House. If thirsty, they could choose from among 92 licensed taverns and beer cellars, as well as a multitude of other unlicensed grog shops and grocery stores where they drank corn whiskey, rye whiskey, gin, rum, peach brandy, or a spectrum of wines. Rum sold for a dollar a gallon; a single drink at a tavern cost six and a half cents.[6]

For the pleasures of strolling, the city had several parks and promenades. Though most were rather seedy, even unsavory, places uptown, often with clusters of hunched-over gamblers or staggering drunks puking or brawling, the Battery was different. Down at the tip of the city where the city overlooked Charleston Harbor, the Battery was a handsome park four blocks long with graceful shade trees lining pleasant paths for promenaders and benches for those who chose to sit for a spell and observe the passing parade. In front of the park was an avenue for carriages or men on horseback, a place to see and be seen, to tip one's new beaver hat to the ladies, to show off one's latest dress, to visit while maintaining a leisurely and genteel motion, round and around, past the twenty-five-foot bronze lantern, which stood, mastlike, overlooking the harbor and its commerce.

Charlestonians of both sexes tended to dress up more than their counterparts in other cities. The most famous examples of this, remarked on by many visitors, were those African Americans who promenaded through the city on pleasant Sundays, decked in their finery, who even rode their carriages past disgruntled working-class whites. Most no doubt were from the well-to-do "brown elite" of Charleston, a city with a free black population of more than 3,200.[7] Charleston's free blacks tended to fall into one of two categories. Many were destitute individuals, "freed" by miserly owners when too old to work or too handicapped in some way. Other free blacks, however, worked as seamstresses or mantua makers, barbers or pastry cooks, cabinet makers and bricklayers. There were also men like Richard Dereef and Robert Howard, lumbermen, who employed a large staff of black laborers, as well as a black clerk and a black bookkeeper. In the city there were 131 slave-owning African Americans — virtually all of them more beige-colored than chocolate — the city's brown elite.[8]

James D. Johnson, a mulatto tailor, was a free man and a person of some substance in the city, a leading member of its African American upper class. His tailor shop on King Street was frequented by some of Charleston's wealthiest families. He was a parishioner of the Grace Episcopal Church, one of the city's more prestigious congregations. He traveled. He read. He maintained a wide circle of acquaintances, white and black, but he had little contact with slaves, outside of those his family owned. He felt little or no identification with slaves, nor did he sympathize with them. All in all, James Johnson was a confident man, with solid reasons for his confidence.

All this changed in August 1860. Charleston's free blacks had always lived in a world where they were subjected to a variety of indignities. Their movements were restricted. They were not, for example, permitted to stroll on the Battery during designated hours. They could not gather in groups of seven or more — for a birthday party, for instance, or a wedding — without the presence of at least one "responsible" white. Such laws were seldom enforced, because doing so seemed unnecessary and cumbersome, but still they represented an ominous threat. Also, free blacks were required to pay special taxes, and their education was restricted, as were their medical facilities — regulations that *were* enforced. Their vulnerability became obvious when suddenly, in mid-August 1860, city authorities went to each of their homes and demanded proof, some sort of document, that they were indeed free. Those who could not provide such documentation, even those whose status had been clear for two generations, were enslaved. James Johnson was out of town when this occurred. He had taken an extended vacation, leaving by chance on August 7, to travel to Boston, then Canada. On September 16 he wrote home from Toronto that he had heard from his son about the disturbing events in Charleston. "I regret to learn through James that things look so dark and gloomy at home. What will be the issue I fear to think. I am afraid it will come to leaving." Actually, Johnson would not leave the city, but hundreds, perhaps thousands, of the city's free blacks did flee between August 1860 and the fall of Fort Sumter in April 1861.[9]

Drastically further down the social scale were black men like Robert Smalls, his wife Hannah, and their two-year-old daughter Elizabeth — all of them slaves. Hannah worked as a chambermaid at the Mills Hotel, turning her earnings over to her owner. Robert, born in Beaufort, South Carolina, spent his early years as a house servant there, a favorite of his master. (Southern owners were careful to differentiate between their field hands and their "servants.") When Robert was twelve, however, his owner sent the boy to Charleston to find a job and deliver his pay to his owner.

Smalls's first employment in the city involved cleaning the glass panes of Charleston's new gaslights. Many of the city's slaves, like Robert, lived a semifree existence, able to move about the streets without supervision. Some worked as stevedores on the docks or firemen (many of the city's fire companies were manned primarily by slaves). Some fished, then hawked their catch in the streets. Others toted baskets of goods to sell at market. They had opportunities to earn a little money on the side, to mingle with one another, to pitch pennies, to slip into one of the city's German grog shops for a libation or two. Even, like Robert and Hannah, to meet, to date, to marry — and to dream. Once their daughter, Elizabeth, was born, the young parents took extra jobs on Sundays and in the evenings, keeping any monies they earned — as was their traditional right — saving it to buy Elizabeth's and Hannah's freedom. In time Robert Smalls became a sailor and a pilot, studying and learning the tricky currents of the region, soon sailing boats to islands far up and down the coast, using the inland waterways and even the Atlantic. It was this knowledge, this skill, that allowed him eventually to become a hero in the Civil War, when he would sail the steamship *Planter* out to join the federal blockade. He was a man of intelligence and remarkable courage. In years to come he would get to shake hands and chat with President Lincoln, serve in Congress, see a son graduate from college, and become a respected old man in Beaufort — at least a respected "colored man."[10]

The city's whites felt an emotional conflict. On the one hand most believed their slaves — their "people" — could be trusted performing tasks in the streets of Charleston. Perhaps not everyone's slaves, mind you, but certainly yours. Your butcher was likely a slave, and the barber who shaved your neck, and the boy who rowed you and your friends, all decked out in your new finery, across the harbor on an afternoon's lark. Working-class whites sometimes felt a sense of resentment at the competition for jobs, but the men who ran the city in the late 1850s showed little uneasiness — on the surface.

South Carolina had a long, repugnant history of violence. Murder, rape, assaults, dueling, and general mayhem were far too common, but in most parts of the state, so long as these actions were not done by blacks or did not involve property, grand juries tended to be rather indulgent. Lawyers successfully used the argument of "hot-bloodedness" to justify violence.[11] In 1821 the state had finally made it a felony to kill a slave — unless it was done, according to the law, "in sudden heat and passion," in which case it was deemed a misdemeanor and resulted only in a fine. State newspapers maintained a code of silence on rapes and duels, and never deigned to discuss the raping of slave women by whites. It is therefore impossible to know with any precision how bad the situation was, but there is more than enough evidence to indict South Carolina for being a land of short-tempered, coarse violence.[12] By 1860 the state still numbered gangs of highway robbers and teams of pickpockets and blacklegs who feasted off crowds gathering on militia muster days and public hangings and race weeks.

Charleston was more progressive, more "civilized," than the rest of the state. For years Charlestonians had watched the region just north of their town limits — an area called the Neck — become lawless. For decades the city's leading citizens had looked on it with tolerant shrugs, but by the late 1840s the spillage of crime and sin, to say nothing of the fact that city blacks could walk into the Neck and immediately come under less supervision, caused Charlestonians to decide that something needed to be done. In 1849–50 the city simply incorporated the Neck, making it part of Charleston. In 1860 40 percent of Charleston's population lived there, in a section that had been virtually without government or law a few years earlier.

Throughout Charleston, after sunset each day, patrolmen walked their beats, while guards on horseback clattered back and forth. They searched out crimes of every kind, but their main job was to awe and control the city's black population. Visitors to the city were struck by the omnipresence of these policemen.[13] Every evening, at ten minutes before nine o'clock — or ten o'clock, depending on the season — a drummer stood before each police station and beat the warning *rat-a-tat* indicating that curfew was about to begin. A few minutes later, while blacks scurried to shelter, the drummer beat one last time, just before St. Michael's bells tolled.

In 1860 all this emphasis on racial control was especially necessary, most white Carolinians believed, because of the prospect of the Republican Abraham Lincoln's election. Charleston's newspapers reported preposterous tales of abolitionists sneaking about the South, stirring up slaves. In October the *Courier* reported that citizens of Greenville, South Carolina, "have had reason to believe that their slaves were being tampered with by Abolition emissaries. A Vigilance Committee was formed, but owing to the cunning and dexterity of the incendiaries, it was found impossible to catch them." A week later a father and his son were seized by a

Marion, South Carolina, mob. "An informal jury," according to the newspaper, discovered they possessed various letters and arms, "which proved their guilt beyond a shadow of a doubt," and the "jury" immediately hanged them. On October 27, with the election just over a week away, the *Courier* reprinted an article from the Montgomery, Alabama, *Mail.* "The South," this article stated, "is infested with scores and hundreds of abolition agents, whose business here, it is, *to prepare our people for the rule of Lincoln.*" The *Mail* urged "Southern men everywhere to be on their guard against them."

A Charlestonian calling himself CAUTION wrote the *Courier* in October 29 that "It is well known that our city is at the present time overrun with Abolition emissaries disseminating incendiary principles among our negroes, deluding these credulous people with the belief that the election of Lincoln will be their millennium. . . . Our safety lies in extreme measures."[14] Vigilance committees prowled Charleston's streets at night, searching for dreaded abolitionists and any signs of slave unrest. Such committees were a symptom of a disease, a pathology that wracked the city, and the state, and most of the South.

By early September 1860 Lincoln's election seemed almost inevitable. A sense of foreboding permeated South Carolina. In mid-October Keziah Brevard, a steady and practical owner of 6,000 acres of plantations, a widow in her mid-fifties, told her diary, "It is time for us to show the rabble of the North we are not to be murdered in cold blood because we own slaves." Emma Holmes, only twenty-two years old, told her diary, "We have truth, justice and religion on our side & and our homes to battle for." H. Pinckney Walker wrote that Lincoln's government "will be bent on the destruction of the Southern institutions." Charleston's fire commissioner announced that presumed incendiaries lit six major fires between September 29 and November 12. Shortly after secession, Mary Chesnut crisply stated: "We separated because of incompatibility of temper. We are divorced, North from South, because we hated each other so."[15] Each of these South Carolinians firmly believed they were in the midst of a crisis, that the "North" *hated* them, and would, as soon as Lincoln became president on March

4, 1861, attempt to destroy them. They were aggressively wrong-headed. There was no "North" in 1860.

Vermont, Pennsylvania, Iowa, and California were vastly different from one another. For that matter, Philadelphia was very different from Altoona, Pennsylvania, or Gettysburg. Some few Republicans did want to destroy slavery, but they were a minority in their own party and were hardly representative of that fictive "North" that these South Carolinians spoke of, any more than the wealthy planters of South Carolina represented the hill folk of Arkansas or Kentucky, the industrialists of Richmond, the German butchers and beer brewers of St. Louis, the Seminoles of Florida — to say nothing of the three and a half million Southern slaves. South Carolinians may have been incorrect in their analysis, but their fears were genuine. And fear moves men to action.

Since 1841 every white male aged eighteen to forty-five in South Carolina could be called upon for three months' military duty. The state had dozens of militia companies, ranging from fancy, well-outfitted units like Charleston's Washington Light Infantry to "companies" in name only, without uniforms or weapons, or sometimes even members. South Carolina was in no condition to alter this situation quickly. Its arsenals were still stocked with colonial flintlocks, now pathetically out-of-date.[16] The militia companies were laughable social clubs whose members sporadically dressed up, played at soldiering, and drank heavily.

Late in September or early October 1860, South Carolinians began to create special, extra-legal military bands called "Minute Men," the name aligning them to their Revolutionary forefathers. Vigilante groups springing up in the state were different; they were neither well-organized nor efficient, and were little more than mobs, capable of hanging terrified blacks or tar-and-feathering an "abolitionist," but obviously unable to offer local regions any real protection.

The preamble to the Minute Men's constitution, written in October, was both bombastic and lawyerly. It spoke of a concern that their "dearest interests . . . must fall, in the event of the triumph of Northern fanaticism" (that is, the election of Lincoln).

They promised "to sustain Southern constitutionality in the Union," and if they failed, "to establish our independence out of it." Like the Founding Fathers and their Declaration of Independence, each Minute Man personally signed this document and pledged "our *lives,* our *fortunes,* and our sacred *honor.*" Each member also promised to give a dollar to the organization and to wear a blue cockade on the left side of his hat; also to provide himself a rifle (or something comparable) and a Colt revolver. (A. H. Colt of the Colt Company of New England spent weeks in Charleston that winter, happily taking orders.)[17]

South Carolina's politicians, perhaps not wanting to be left behind, also proposed action. On October 5, Governor William Henry Gist wrote to his fellow governors in every cotton state except Texas (where Sam Houston was well known to oppose secession), telling them that South Carolina would likely secede, and urging them to join her. A week later he ordered South Carolina's legislature to assemble on November 5, one day *before* the national election — thus they'd be ready to act if Lincoln was the victor, as seemed probable. On October 25, at the urging of Senator James Chesnut, the state's political leaders met at the plantation home of Senator James Henry Hammond, one of South Carolina's wealthiest men. Gist told them he had not yet received replies from the other governors, so the group discussed whether South Carolina should act alone or whether she should wait, to act in concert with the rest of the Deep South. After some debate they agreed that, if Lincoln was indeed elected, South Carolina must leave the Union, and not wait for the others.

In November, just before the presidential election, a huge crowd, accompanied by a band, gathered outside Janey's Hotel in Columbia. Senator Chesnut was staying within, but when they shouted that they wanted to hear him speak he came out and provided them with a peroration.

"A line of enemies is closing around us," he announced. "Should New Englanders . . . determine our affairs?"

"No, never!" the crowded screamed back, and applauded their wisdom.

"Or should Carolina be governed by Carolinians?" he asked.

"Yes, yes! Forever!" More applause.

"For myself," he concluded, "I would unfurl the Palmetto flag." And there followed, according to the *Mercury*, thunderous applause.[18]

"State sovereignty" was hardly a Southern concept. New England politicians had discussed leaving the Union during the War of 1812—a time when South Carolina's leaders had been fervently nationalistic. Most states in fact had, at one time or another, toyed with the notion. Virtually all of America's politicians, North and South, assumed that a citizen owed his state a greater loyalty than he owed to the federal government. Except for a postal service, most people had little connection to the national government; important things like education and roads and crime were handled locally.

In November 1860 Lincoln won handily, despite his name not appearing on the ballot in any Deep South state.

In Charleston one diarist noted that "This past week has been one continued scene of excitement. The city is filled with banners of every kind," though a few days later he wrote in disgust, "Torchlight this eve was a great turnout of urchins and ragamuffins, quite a Motley Crew."[19] Charlestonians were feeling rabid. When the next issue of *Harper's Weekly* appeared, with a portrait of Lincoln on its cover, the city's bookstores—according to the *Mercury*—returned all copies of the issue, and closed their account with the distributors.

Living as she did on an isolated plantation, Keziah Brevard did not learn the results of the election for several days. But on November 9 she wrote in her diary: "Oh My God!!! This morning heard that Lincoln was elected. . . . I do pray that if there is to be a crisis that we all lay down our lives, sooner than free our slaves in our midst. No soul on earth is more willing for justice than I am, but the idea of being mixed up with free blacks is *horrid*!!"[20]

Governor Gist told his legislature that they were "contending for the safety of our homes and firesides." He urged them to summon a special convention to decide South Carolina's future. As an aside, he proposed that South Carolina raise ten thousand soldiers.

Yet the legislature reacted with surprising caution. Its representatives accepted the right of secession, but many, perhaps even a majority, favored waiting for their cotton-state brethren to join them.[21] They were tipped into immediate action, however, when they learned of an incident in Charleston.

A grand jury was in session at the U.S. District Court in Charleston, Judge Andrew Gordon Magrath presiding. The jury foreman was Robert Gourdin, an extremely wealthy commercial leader of the city. Early on November 7, as telegrams arrived confirming Lincoln's election, the court began its day. Magrath opened the day's session officially asking Gourdin if the jury had any presentments to make. Gourdin rose, and in the solemn, silent courtroom he intoned that Lincoln's election had "swept away the last hope for the permanence, for the stability, of these Sovereign States." He concluded, "In these extraordinary circumstances, the grand jury respectfully declines to proceed with their presentments."

Gourdin, acting as an official of an American court, had just cut the South's first link to the federal government. Judge Magrath stood. A charming gentleman, if a bit of a windbag, he had been a federal judge the past four years. While muted sobs broke the silence, he melodramatically removed his robe and announced he was resigning his office. "As far as I am concerned," he said, "the Temple of Justice, raised under the Constitution of the United States, is now closed." Magrath thus became the first paid federal official to publicly resign his position as a result of Lincoln's election.

Word of Gourdin's and Magrath's actions at the District Court, combined with reports that Georgia might secede even before South Carolina did, apparently was enough for the legislature in Columbia. It called for the immediate election of a secession convention.

A few days later Senator Hammond posted a letter. "C'est fini," he wrote with little enthusiasm. "I have resigned. I heard yesterday that Chesnut and [Senator Robert] Toombs [of Georgia] had resigned." Hammond privately admitted, "I thought Magrath and all those fellows were great asses for resigning and have done it myself. It is an epidemic and very foolish. It reminds me of the Japanese who, when insulted, rip open their own bowels."[22]

Captain M. Berry, skipper of the steamship *Columbia,* left New York on November 17 for his regular run to Charleston. As his ship steamed past Governor's Island, Berry ordered that the United States flag be hauled down, and amidst the cheers of his crewmen a Palmetto flag was run up the stern flagstaff. Berry himself had apparently ordered this particular flag sewed, for South Carolina did not yet have an official state flag. The flag he designed included fifteen stars laid on a vermilion ground, each star representing one of the fifteen states with pro-slave laws on their books. (When the country had first been created *all* thirteen states had had slave codes, and were therefore "slave states," but in time the seven states north of Maryland adopted measures gradually eliminating it. When slavery grew into a major issue in the politics of the 1830s, it became convenient for spokesmen on either side to note whether a state was "slave" or "free" — that is, whether it still retained a group of laws protecting local slavery. Any state that did not was "free.") In the political jargon of the 1850s the fifteen American states that yet retained slave codes constituted the "South." In the overheated rhetoric of November 1860 the magic number "fifteen" was a shibboleth. Berry's flag simply took that symbol and turned it into cloth.

When the *Columbia* arrived two days later several of Charleston's leading merchants presented to the captain an inscribed cane, then trooped to the ship's saloon where they devoured a fine repast and drank to each other with champagne.[23] The matter of flags and such symbols would soon take on increasing importance.

It was this city, at this moment of excitement, that Major Robert Anderson entered.

CHAPTER TWO

A Gentle Man

During the next five months Robert Anderson would dominate events in Charleston. It was his destiny to try personally to keep America together, while buffeted by tornadolike emotions of sectionalism. Like some character out of Norse mythology he would try to hold together the fabric of the sky. Oddly, the man in question was remarkably quiet and unassuming.

Anderson, a lifetime soldier, loathed war. "I think," he said early in his career, "that killing people is a very poor way of settling national grievances."[1] Seven years after graduating from West Point in 1825, he'd had his first experience with it. An Indian called Black Hawk had persuaded several hundred warriors to join a raid on western Illinois. At first successful, shattering a poorly organized army of Illinois militiamen, they soon faced a much larger force, which hounded after them. Black Hawk's allies scattered, his mounts broke down, he ran out of food. Starvation and disease set in. His people died in droves. Second Lieutenant Anderson, given the temporary rank of colonel and placed in command of a bunch of Illinois volunteers — including gawky Illinoisan Abraham Lincoln (whom he probably never met) — was among those pursuing Black Hawk's pathetic remnants. These few months sickened the young officer. On August 3, 1832, he was present at the Battle of Bad Axe, which ended this sorry episode. Afterward, he was walking the battlefield and saw an Indian woman lying dead on the ground next to a baby, itself severely wounded by the musket ball that had killed its mother. He scooped up the child and rushed it to a dressing station where doctors saved its life.[2] Three days later, in disgust, he wrote his brother that he had observed scenes of "misery exceeding any I ever expected to see in our happy land. Dead bodies, males & females, strewed along the road, left unburied, exposed—poor, emaciated beings."[3]

Over the next several weeks Anderson and a fellow West Point graduate, Jefferson Davis, escorted the prisoner Black Hawk until they deposited him with the proper authorities.[4] Following those weeks together, Anderson and Davis remained friends.

Five years after the Black Hawk War Lieutenant Anderson had his second taste of battle, which he loathed as much as his first. The Seminole Wars form an ugly chapter in American history, growing out of the usual land disputes between spreading American settlements and resident Indians, along with an additional complication. Runaway slaves, particularly those from Georgia, had settled among the Seminoles. Georgia slaveholders, determined to eliminate this escape hatch, demanded that the federal government do something. As a result the American army stumbled around for years searching for elusive Indians, who simply retreated into the Everglade swamps. Both sides committed atrocities. Lieutenant Anderson saw action on several occasions, receiving a brevet promotion for gallantry—but he also developed fevers, which recurred for the rest of his life.[5]

Anderson's third war came in Mexico. He might easily have avoided the fighting, because of his Florida-induced fevers, but he pressed the army to send him. Once there he could have accepted a position on General Winfield Scott's staff. Anderson had served off and on for years as one of Scott's closest aides. The two had grown close, virtually father and son. During Scott's Mexican campaign the general often invited him to dinner. Anderson referred to the general, the highest-ranking officer in the army, as "my best friend," and "my most kind friend," saying that Scott "has been as kind and affectionate as ever to me."[6] Scott offered him a position on his staff, but Anderson begged off, feeling it his duty to see action.

His letters home spoke sympathetically of the Mexican people. During the siege of Vera Cruz in 1847, he expressed concern for the Mexicans inside and a worry that American soldiers might commit atrocities when the city fell. "It really goes to my heart to be compelled to do my duty when I know that every shot either injures or seriously distresses the poor inoffensive women and children, who have neither part nor lot in this War." He wished, he said, to see "this war *civilized*," with "civilities between the forces whenever they are not engaged in battle."[7]

He was mortified when his old Florida illness, fever and chills, felled him and kept him from a major battle, but he recuperated enough to fight in the Battle of Molino del Rey, one of the war's hottest actions. His orders that day involved the capture of a huge building that dominated the plain in front of the city. Inside this structure was an open quadrangle. Whichever side held this courtyard could hold the building, and with it, perhaps the whole battlefield. Anderson and his few men battered through a door and rushed into the quadrangle. They immediately came under attack from Mexican troops who stood above them on all four walls. Under this deadly fire, wounded in five places, Anderson kept his tiny command together for two hours until relieved. From his sickbed he later wrote his wife. He reported that he was first wounded in his shoulder. Blood soaked his cloak, but he continued to lead his command. He grew weak. "My wound, giving me much pain, had now rendered me less vigorous than I was." Still he kept on. "Getting a half dozen men more, I went forward and entered the enclosure under a pretty galling fire. As I passed through the passageway, a ball grazed my right leg, grazing the bone outside about three inches below my knee." He stumbled, but continued on for two more hours, until other officers arrived with reinforcements. He assured her that the wounds in his arms and leg would show scars but "are nothing," and that the ball, still in his shoulder, would, according to a physician, "do no harm." He did not tell her that when the relief force found him he was lying on the ground, holding his head up with his hands, directing the remnants of his command. As he was being carried out on a litter, he still supervised the care of his wounded.[8]

Despite his brave words to his wife, he was never quite as strong again. He was a man of middling height, 5'9", with a slender, muscular body, which he never lost. His posture would remain militarily erect till he died, but the fevers, the dysentery ("the old soldier's disease"), and these wounds took a toll on his health. He spent the next dozen years in quiet duties, shuffling papers. In a sense, although he grumbled about it, that kind of life probably suited the person he was, probably always had been.

After his graduation from West Point the army had placed him in the artillery and ordered him to Fortress Monroe's Artillery School. While there, he toyed with the notion of leaving the military. He confided to his sister that he felt "thrown on the sea of life," unsure of which "port I ought to direct my bark!" "I know not whether," he said, "it be better to leave [the army] for the more diversified life of a citizen, or to continue, content with little & little getting." He admitted to her that he felt "discontented" right now. The problem, he said, lay in his dream that someday, "I might come to something in civil life."[9]

His father had recently died, and this may have created a temporary moment of uncertainty for him. His father, Richard Clough Anderson, had been with George Washington at the Battle of Trenton, where he was wounded, the first of several times. Later he served as an aide to Lafayette during the Revolutionary War's final campaign at Yorktown. After the war he became surveyor-general of Virginia, similar to the position George Washington had held many years earlier. He married a sister of George Rogers Clark, Kentucky's most famous leader, and when she died he married a cousin of Chief Justice John Marshall. Among the guests at his home, called Soldier's Retreat, were Andrew Jackson and President James Monroe.

After his father's death Anderson accepted a position with West Point's department of artillery, where he taught for two years. Among his students during this period were several who would become his friends in years to come, William Tecumseh Sherman and Braxton Bragg, as well as a bright young student whom he personally chose to assist his teaching, Pierre Gustave Toutant Beauregard. Other students would also make their names known: Irvin McDowell, George Meade, Joseph Hooker, Jubal Early. The battlefields of the 1860s were crowded with generals whom he had once taught the rudiments of using firepower efficiently.

Before 1860 his best-known contribution to the army concerned his scholarly works on the subject of artillery. In 1839, after leaving West Point, he translated a French essay on field artillery tactics. He clarified the original French tome and provided it with elegant illustrations. Anderson's book presented clear principles about how to use and maneuver artillery pieces during battle, and it immediately became the bible on the subject for America's artillerists. One result was that the American army became more efficient, more mobile, helping it defeat the Mexicans a few years later. The army later made Anderson a member of a commission that produced in 1851 America's official textbook for siege artillery.

Anderson was never a gay person, hail-fellow-well-met. But neither was he sour, or laconic, or taciturn. He was simply a discreet, slightly restrained gentleman. He did not tolerate bawdy gossip, and he was remarkably modest in his demeanor. During the Mexican War he wrote his wife that he had met some soldiers who were quite full of themselves. "No one admires courage more than I do," he said, "but I always regret to hear the hero trumpeting his own fame." As to pushing his name forward to gain fame or promotion, he wrote, "I would cut my tongue out before I would allow it to commit so great an indelicacy." After admitting to his wife that he had purposely avoided staff duty to be where the fighting was, he said that he would never have told anyone else this, because "it looks exceedingly like *egotism*." He was so sensitive about any scent of overweening pride that he avoided even looking at Mexican soldiers who had been captured: "I was afraid they might detect something of triumph in my countenance, when I thought them so humiliated by their surrender."[10]

Beneath his gentility and self-control lay an unsuspected, almost poetic, sensitivity. "I just this moment hear a mocking-bird warbling his sweet notes," he wrote his wife from Mexico. "The Band of the 2nd [Regiment] is practicing, and this sweet bird seems answering to some notes he loves. How many, many miles do those notes bear my thoughts! They tell of home, of a beloved wife, but yet of a home I do not enjoy with her. Sing on, sweet bird, there is joy mingled with the sadness of your song. I may soon be as free as you are and return on wings of love to my own mate."[11] Perhaps not deathless prose, but still a gentle expression of loneliness and love.

Anderson had a strong nose and a full mouth; thick dark eyebrows hung over his deep-set hazel eyes. He was a quietly handsome man, but he remained unmarried for many years. A niece once wrote him that he had a reputation in the family of being "very fastidious in your opinion in regard to the other sex."[12] In his late twenties, while stationed at Portsmouth, New Hampshire, he became serious about an unnamed young woman, apparently a pretty and well-to-do girl from Boston. His letters speak of her with obvious interest, although he does not name her. But he sighs that she seems "like an icicle." A few weeks later he writes ruefully, "I failed in a love scrape," but bravely adds that "this has not discouraged me." What ended his relationship with the girl is uncertain, but in that same letter he added, "I am still satisfied with my Northern friends. They have some ideas of which I am not fond, but their politeness, kindness, and hospitality are gratifying."[13] He does not specify which "ideas" he meant, but these might have involved slavery. He wrote this letter in 1834, three years after William Lloyd Garrison began his abolitionist periodical, *The Liberator*, in Boston. Anderson's position on slavery was ambiguous. He had been born and brought up in Kentucky among slaves, and when he finally married, his wife would be a member of a Georgia plantation family. Like most soldiers of that, or any, era, he was conservative, cautious about change. He hated politics and despised politicians. As a young man he had concluded that people were pretty much the same. "I have in my pilgrimage thus far," he wrote, "found mankind nearly the same in every region. The differences in manners and customs, I have accredited as caused, principally, by education."[14]

An interesting sidelight to his unsuccessful New England ro-
mance was that he had noted that the young woman in question
was well-to-do. In that era men were often quite straightforward
about their interest in a bride with money. Anderson could also be
practical. During his first year as a professor at West Point, perhaps frustrated by his slow advancement in the army, he wrote his
mother about his financial straits. He said he was considering
doing something with some land he had inherited in Ohio, perhaps growing mulberry or silk, but the chairman of West Point's
artillery department had just retired, leaving him the sole professor of artillery at the school, and he was asked to accept a permanent position there. In that case, he said, "I may feel it a duty to my
country to consider at once the propriety of taking a wife." He
closed, remarking only that if he could find a woman as good as
his mother, "I'll marry her directly, even if she had not more than
twenty thousand Dollars for her future."[15] Maybe he was only
joking, but when he did finally marry, seven years later, his bride,
Eba, did have access to the requisite "twenty thousand Dollars."

Eba Clinch Anderson was a chronic invalid. Her exact medical
condition is vague, but it had started during her childhood and
lasted throughout her life. She suffered from severe headaches, as
well as weakness and pain in her feet and legs. She spent much of
her life having — or choosing — to rest. Perhaps her ailment was a
serious neurological problem or a condition such as diabetes, or it
might have been "neurasthenia," which some medical books of the
time vaguely defined as a "functional nervous weakness or debil-
ity." More recently neurasthenia has been described as a form of
neurosis, generally accompanied by hypochondria, headaches,
dizziness, aches of uncertain origin, insomnia, and so on. Even so,
a photograph of her, standing next to her husband, taken during
the Civil War, shows a handsome, nicely rounded, middle-aged
woman, not a person wasted from disease. She was able to bear
four children and she outlived her husband. Yet whether physically or emotionally induced, Eba's health was always frail.
Throughout her life, people nursed her. By the time she was a
young woman, her Georgia father, concluding her illness seemed

to worsen in warm weather, sent her to New York City for an extended stay. Eba, a Southern belle, settled comfortably into the city, and, except for a few, relatively brief periods, it became her home. There she met Robert, a handsome officer sixteen years older, who was in New York working on a new edition of his textbook. He often visited his mentor General Scott, who maintained headquarters in the city. Scott and Eba's father were old friends, and one can assume that this was how Robert and she met. His first mention of her was in a short note to Scott, in which he noted that "Miss Clinch" would be seeing the general soon, and that she "says that she has a great deal to tell you about me," then added, "she still continues to improve."[16] A flirtation between Robert and Miss Clinch had begun.

Shortly before they married, her father, General Duncan Lamont Clinch, wrote Robert a note, approving the match, and offering an analysis of his daughter. Eba was, he said, "highly gifted by nature, and has had every advantage that I could give her." She was "affectionate & devoted in her attachments, pure, elevated and a *little proud* [he underlined this trait] in her views, sentiments, and feelings." He went on. "She has been indulged in every wish, but these wishes have always been tempered by her good sense." He would not be able to attend their wedding since she and Robert planned to wed up in New York. He told Robert that, although he would like to give the bridal couple a fine gift, he was temporarily a bit short of funds, since his rice crop had fallen "short of my expectations." As to Eba's present health, he trusted she would soon be "once more on her *little feet* & walking about her room."[17] General Clinch had three girls and five boys, yet he always maintained a special fondness for Eba, his oldest, so this note to Anderson may have carried subtle, perhaps unconscious, warnings.

Eliza Bayard Clinch — for that was Eba's full name — was born in the fall of 1821 into a prominent Southern family. Her mother was a daughter of a wealthy Georgia planter. Her father, a soldier before the War of 1812, served for twenty-eight years, often in Florida against the Seminoles. After retiring from the army, Duncan Clinch spent the rest of his life administering his large and prosperous rice plantation and dabbling in politics. He served a single term in the House of Representatives, then ran unsuccessfully for governor of Georgia.[18]

When he died, five years after Eba's marriage, he was one of the richest rice planters in America. Most of his wealth went to his sons and his young widow (who outlived him by fifty-four years), but Eba did receive from him, and also from her maternal grandparents, sufficient funds to afford a quite comfortable lifestyle — certainly better than she could have expected as the wife of a simple army officer. During the latter decades of her life she lived in a suite at the Brevoort House, a posh hotel on Fifth Avenue.

Among Eba's inheritances were a number of slaves in Georgia. In 1857 Robert mentioned in a jocular note that her wealth was growing because of "the increase of her darkies," but Eba's exact connection to the slaves remains unclear, for she seldom visited the South after 1850; apparently she and her husband sold all of them before the Civil War. According to one unverified report, Robert, in April 1860, long before he arrived in Charleston, sold twenty-nine slaves to John G. Cocks of Georgia for $1,300, Cocks providing him with a promissory note (which Cocks refused to pay a year later because, he said, of Anderson's part in the Fort Sumter crisis).[19] It would seem that neither Robert nor Eba owned any slaves on that day in 1860 when he arrived in Charleston.

Robert and Eba were married on March 26, 1842. He was thirty-six, she twenty. Winfield Scott, standing in for his friend Duncan Clinch, gave away the bride. Only half a dozen people attended the ceremony, since Robert did not, as he wrote her father just prior to the wedding, want to "run the risk of injuring darling Eliza's health by inviting such a number as will worry her or make her feel uncomfortable." He promised he would consult a physician, and was optimistic. "My dear Eliza is continuing to improve — everything gives me good hopes that ere many weeks she will have the use of her feet again."[20]

Robert's letters to Eba reveal an abiding affection for her, and his constant concern about her health. He was often urging her to rest, not to exert herself. During the Mexican War, while on an exhausting and dangerous campaign, and himself quite ill with fever, he constantly told her how anxious he was about her sickness, her exhaustion, her suffering. "You must not write me such long letters," he wrote, "one page telling me that all are well and that you are walking about and getting strong again, would give all the pleasure I can receive from any letters, particularly when I know that the effort necessary to write these long letters tires you. Let me urge you by all the love you bear me, and I know its weight and worth, to take care of yourself." He said that he was fine, and used the opportunity to cheer her up. "Do you not see how groundless were a thousand fears which have harassed and worried your life out?"[21]

From 1855 to 1859 the couple lived much apart from each other, she at the Brevoort in New York, he in Trenton, New Jersey, two hours away by train. The army had assigned him the duty of inspecting Trenton's production of iron beams used in federal building projects like the Washington Aqueduct. An important enough task, perhaps, but one that might have been performed by a lower-ranking officer with a much less distinguished reputation. Since he was quite close to Winfield Scott, the head of the army, as well as a good friend of the present secretary of war, Jefferson Davis, it seems likely this duty was intended as a sinecure. He had not fully recovered from his Florida fever, nor the terrible wounds he had received at Molino del Rey, so it was probably an act of kindness. Just the same, he found it boring, and lonely. He wrote Eba how much he missed her, and commented often about his concerns for her health: her headaches, her weariness, the problems with her legs. He spoke a great deal about his love for their daughters, Eliza, Sophie, and Maria. (Their fourth child, a son named Robert, Jr., was conceived on one of his visits to New York.) Their three daughters did not at that time live with Eba. Each, although quite young, attended boarding school in New Jersey. It may have been that the physicians, or Eba, had concluded that the stresses that went with child-rearing might prove too much for her, but it may explain a coolness the girls later evinced toward their mother.

One of his notes to her is poignant. He had just participated in the confirmation ceremony of their eldest daughter, Eliza, at a church in Philadelphia. "She knelt by my side," he said, "and we were the last two of about thirty who were confirmed." In the same note he also informed Eba, as an aside, that little Eliza was now attending a school run by a Mrs. Gardel, a fact his wife obviously had not known.[22] Here Eba was at the Brevoort while her oldest child participated in an important rite of passage, one that could just as easily have been performed a few blocks from the hotel's front door. Perhaps Eba was, at that moment, more ill than usual.

By the late 1850s Robert had accepted obscurity, perhaps embraced it. In 1857 he wrote Eba from Trenton that he been contacted by some land agents in Iowa who were urging him to buy some farmland there. He playfully suggested that maybe they should move out to that desolate region. "What do you say to our moving out to, and settling on, our principality? I think it would sound so well — not in history, for I fancy we shall not have much ink wasted on us — but in the voices of our g.g.g. children, to have them say, this piece of property was won by our g.g.g. grandpapa — who was an officer in one of our wars. 'Yes,' cries out little _____, who knows everything, 'it was in the Revolutionary War and he fought under Genl. Washington. I saw his name in my history.'"[23] Robert had come to consider himself just another military bureaucrat, undistinguished and dull. Although he loved his army, he felt for it a kind of disdain. Once, when he learned that Eba's brother Duncan had joined the army, he said that he was sorry to hear that the young man "chose the profession of arms. He might have done much better."[24] Robert knew too well the constrictions of the profession.

By 1860 he had made the army his life, but at least he could take satisfaction that he had put fighting behind him. Years earlier, halfway through the Mexican War, he had written Eba, "This will, I hope, be the last war I shall take an active part in. I think after the declaration of peace, I may safely promise that I will go 'a-soldiering' no more." Then he reiterated his hatred for all wars. "I think that no more absurd scheme could be invented for settling national difficulties than the one we are engaged in — killing each other to find out who is in the right." A few weeks later he wrote optimistically, "The impression in high quarters is that a treaty will be concluded," and he added what soldiers often say, "and then for home, never, never, no never, to leave my beloved land to fight again in foreign lands."[25] As it turned out he was half wrong. He would once more "go a-soldiering," though the next time, unfortunately for him, the war would not be "foreign."

During the summer and fall of 1860 Anderson was a member of a small commission, along with his friend Senator Jefferson Davis, examining the curriculum of West Point, and its system of discipline. It was the kind of duty the army gave to its favored older officers. Major Anderson was fifty-five now, his brown hair graying along the temples. His health was uncertain, and he may have been contemplating retirement. A dozen years later, a reporter, after interviewing several who knew him, concluded that early in 1860 he had been offered the job to lead Fort Monroe's Artillery School. It would have seemed a perfect fit, but he had apparently turned it down. The reporter concluded that the major, in ill health, had been about to resign from the army.[26]

He was not exactly an old man, but his weakened constitution made him feel a trifle fragile and ancient. He was really a gentle sort, as considerate and well-mannered as Robert E. Lee—and, like that famous Virginian, a dutiful husband to a woman of dubious health, a good father to his children, a loyal servant of the army, a man of unexpectedly deep-rooted principles. Had the Civil War not plucked him from his obscurity, he would, like the old soldiers of the song, have faded away . . . and disappeared.

Events in Charleston Harbor, however, altered Major Anderson's existence. Whatever might have been his inclinations, his quiet life was about to change—dramatically. On November 15 he received an official, written order:

> Major Robert Anderson, First Artillery, will forthwith proceed to Fort Moultrie, and immediately relieve Bvt. Col. John Gardner, lieutenant-colonel of First Artillery, in command thereof. . . .
> By command of Lieutenant-General Scott.[27]

The reasons for this appointment were simple. The situation in Charleston had become sticky. Anderson, unlike Gardner, had been born in a slave state and was, moreover, married to the daughter of a famous Georgia politician and soldier. He had once even been stationed at Fort Moultrie and still knew some people in the city. He was a friend of powerful Southerners like Jefferson Davis and Senator John J. Crittenden of Kentucky, and was well respected in the army, with close ties to General Scott and other high-ranking officers. He had a reputation as a military scholar and was a distinguished war hero. Had anyone cared to ask him, Anderson would have indicated a vague sympathy for the South and the concern of its white leaders about the status of slavery. As to secession, he opposed it, but he was not inclined to fight about it. He was a man of peace. Unfortunately, he was arriving in a society hurtling toward something else altogether. Charleston was on the edge of revolution. He had of course heard of events in Charleston but, as was his wont in political matters, he had paid little attention. Yet powerful figures in Washington had reviewed their options and concluded that Major Robert Anderson was perfect for the delicate assignment at the small military base of Fort Moultrie.

CHAPTER THREE

Salad Days

> "They were big strong days — our young days."
> — WALT WHITMAN, ON THE YEARS
> JUST BEFORE THE CIVIL WAR

If you stood on the Battery and looked east toward the Atlantic, five or more miles away, Charleston's harbor lay before you as a great basin. Its upper and lower jaws were created by interlocked islands reaching toward the sea. You could imagine the harbor a gaping mouth, with Charleston its tongue. Several of these islands held military fortifications, the oldest being Fort Moultrie on Sullivan's Island, which stretched along the harbor's northern side.

During the lingering, late summer of 1860, as heat waves rose from Sullivan's Island's dunes and sand fleas searched for victims, Fort Moultrie paused in lethargy. Civilians traipsing through its open gate on an evening's promenade might think her imposing. They would have been mistaken. Her walls seemed solid enough, almost sixteen feet thick, with sides of brick exterior and a top capped with stone, but the interior of these walls was only packed earth. The fort was strong enough to sustain a barrage from enemy ships, but it had profound weaknesses. Even a civilian like Edmund Ruffin could spot them.

During a trip to Charleston Ruffin, an elderly Virginian who had long and fervently believed in secession, visited Moultrie. He was a farmer and agronomist who had made no study of war, but after his brief visit he told his diary that he knew how to take it. The fort, he said, sat on a narrow strip of land and was bordered on both sides by civilian properties. South Carolina could erect an earthwork several hundred yards away, hiding it beyond some cottages, and place there a battery of guns that could prevent ships from bringing Moultrie more provisions, thereby starving out the garrison. He told his idea to three members of the state legislature's Military Committee, and they thought it interesting but unnecessary. If they ever wished to grab Moultrie, they told him, the fort could "easily be taken by the militia."[1] She was indeed pathetically vulnerable to attack by men on foot.

Winds had pushed the island's sands so high against its walls that grazing cows could walk up the gentle sand slopes and stumble through her embrasures, ending up within the fort's parapet.[2] Even if Moultrie's garrison found some way to evade disoriented cattle, they still needed to correct the fort's basic vulnerability. On its west side, cottages huddled nearby as if to use it to protect themselves from Atlantic gales. On its eastern side were a few more houses, plus, more ominously, tall sand dunes that rose higher than the fort's walls. On its harbor side the fort was relatively formidable, if someone removed the slope of sand leaning against its wall, but the north side was terribly weak. Sullivan's Island's only road meandered past the fort a few feet from its unguarded main gate. An assault force, coming at night, could land by boat either east or west of the fort, then simply creep, unseen, up the road. Outside Moultrie's gate were the garrison's small hospital, its church, and a half dozen shacks that served as quarters for Moultrie's "camp women." Attackers could seize these convenient structures and use them to assault the gate. Or, led even by officers of debatable competence, a force could simply surround the fort at nighttime, using the cottages and dunes as shields, and fire inside from commanding positions. If the commander of the garrison put his men around the parapet, spacing them equally, he would be able to place a soldier only every seventeen feet, which would be bad enough during daylight and absurd at night. Congress had not allocated any funds for refurbishing the fort in the previous five years, and Moultrie was showing inevitable signs of neglect.[3]

During the colonial period Sullivan's Island had had no regular settlement, though it was used as a way station for incoming slaves (a sort of Ellis Island for Africans), but in the 1790s the state legislature began selling half-acre lots there, and the island developed into a summer resort. Some of Charleston's most respected families—the Hugers, the Pettigrus, the Ravenels—owned cottages there. During summer's high season, when sweet ocean breezes cooled the air, the ferry to the island was packed. People tumbled gaily onto the island's wharf with their bags and picnic baskets. A single, sandy lane stretched from the wharf up the length of the island, through a cluster of mostly gray, one-story resort cottages, called Moultrieville, passing through Fort Moultrie's reservation, eventually arriving at a large two-story hotel called the Moultrie House, whose 284 feet faced the beach. One of the South's most famous resorts, this exclusive and expensive hostelry had a billiards room, a bowling alley, and a shooting gallery.

Moultrie House offered entertainment, with dancing of an evening, and horses to ride, and games. On balmy evenings Fort Moultrie's regimental band provided the islanders with musical entertainment, and in fact were occasionally hired to play at civilian parties.[4] The fort's young officers, in their fine uniforms, made quite acceptable dancing companions for the daughters and nieces of the residents, or of the guests at the hotel. In South Carolina's upcountry, plain folk danced reels or "walked the cake," but here on Sullivan's Island the tone of musical encounters was more sedate, more formal, more artful. In the 1840s and '50s the cotillion had become fashionable, but for those hotel guests willing to perspire in August evenings, Moultrie House sometimes offered the schottische, the galop, the polka, and the waltz. The fort itself served as one of the island's chief attractions. One officer noted, "The principal and only general amusement among the people is to come into the garrison and listen to the Band which plays every evening."[5] During daylight hours a stroll through the fort was always appropriate and pleasant for islanders and their visitors. To them, Fort Moultrie was more a public park than an actual fortification. (Such attitudes were true throughout America. In 1834 Lieutenant Robert Anderson, stationed at a New Hampshire fort, wrote his sister: "You must know that military posts are generally considered fashionable places to visit."[6])

When the season was over and the days grew short, when the breezes off the Atlantic quickened and chilled the skin, servants closed up the cottages, guests at the Moultrie House dwindled, laughter no longer echoed on the dunes. The owners of the island's small saloons, places where a thirsty man could purchase spirits without paying Moultrie House's exorbitant prices, boarded their windows for the winter. Finally even the great hotel itself closed down.

By mid-autumn the men of Fort Moultrie and their families were almost entirely alone with the chill briny air and the squawking gulls. Their days, then, even their hours, moved slowly. It was like this in October 1860, just before the secession crisis rolled over the fort. To understand what was about to occur, it is necessary to visualize the fort and, more specifically, its garrison.

The enlisted men's barracks stood at attention on Moultrie's Charleston side, with the officers' quarters directly across an open parade ground. A few enlisted men had wives and children, but these families lived outside the fort in a row of tiny houses just beyond the main gate. Some wives worked as official "laundresses," which allowed them to receive a food ration and bedding straw. Other wives earned their keep as servants — maids or cooks — for the families of the officers. Almost nothing is known about their daily lives. Part of the explanation is the matter of class — the life of a "washerwoman" hardly seemed worthy of notice.

Married officers sometimes lived outside the fort, renting one of the island's nearby cottages. In 1860 the colonel of the garrison, John Lane Gardner, lived with his wife and daughter, Caroline, down the road. Born in 1793, when George Washington was in his second term, Gardner was sixty-seven. He had entered the army during the War of 1812, found his niche, and stayed. The army offered no retirement program, so an officer generally found it financially prudent to remain in his traces till he died. Lieutenant Colonel Gardner had had a relatively distinguished career. He had performed well in the Mexican War, and had served with some distinction against the Seminoles in Florida. But now he was tired. Let the younger officers run the daily routine; he would show up when occasion required — if he were not elsewhere, on one of his extended leaves. When faced with difficulties he tended to whine and shunt off responsibility. His officers — apparently, universally — felt contempt for him. One of the fort's brightest officers, Lieutenant Theodore Talbot, wrote his sister in 1860 that Gardner was "utterly incompetent to command a post under the most favorable circumstances."[7] Life at Moultrie hardly noticed Gardner's usual absence.

Mornings for the garrison, following army practice, began with the drumbeat of Reveille, at 6 A.M. The men donned flannel shirts and dark blue uniforms. The garrison at Moultrie was part of the army's First Regiment of Artillery, so their uniforms had red decorative facing. If they had been in the cavalry, the facing would have been yellow; other specialties used other colors. In summer months the garrison's men wore lighter uniforms, though still much too heavy for the semitropical Carolina climate. In winters they shrugged into long, thick greatcoats.

At 6:30 came the drumbeat that signaled breakfast — "peas upon a trencher," they often called it. A soldier could expect to eat salt pork or salt beef, beans, peas, or boiled "desiccated" vegetables, hard bread or biscuits, and coffee. That was pretty much it. If the commissary officer on a base was energetic or merciful, he could also provide the enlisted men some local specialties. Western garrisons might dine on venison; at Fort Monroe in Virginia they sometimes ate crabcakes. Soldiers at some western garrisons actually spent more days tending cattle than they did soldiering.

In a world with little access to clocks and watches, drum signals provided important guidance. There were drum calls for drill and for lunch, there was "retreat" at sundown, and then, at the end of the day, tattoo. "My time," Lieutenant Talbot wrote, "is pretty fully occupied with parades, drills, and the other minutiae of military routine in a garrison. Not enough to keep me fully oc-cupied but too much to allow of devoting myself seriously to any-thing else, in consequence of the frequent interruptions. I might perhaps best define it as busy idleness."[8]

The routine of army life could be tedious and emotionally sap-ping. Alcoholism was a problem. So was desertion. In an average year the army lost 28 percent of its enlisted men—some due to discharge and death, many to desertion. In 1856 out of an army of about 13,000 enlisted men, 3,223 deserted.[9] Officers learned to be especially watchful every other month, right after the army pay-master brought his strongbox of hard currency from which he paid the men.

Army pay was a complex morass, based on various factors, involving a soldier's specialty and rank and longevity. Congress had been notoriously frugal with the military. Many Americans considered soldiers a disreputable breed. They must be lazy louts or drunken ne'er-do-wells; how else could one account for a man's willingness to linger in the ranks when the nation offered so many better opportunities? Some politicians expressed a purse-lipped concern about the apparent conflict between the existence of a military and the innocence of democracy. Historical examples were readily available. There was the Roman Empire and Crom-well's England, and the always-favorite numerous bad examples provided by the French. To this way of thinking, West Point itself seemed more than suspicious. Some Americans wondered sourly whether their tax dollars were paying to create a dangerous, and rather alien, elite. During the Jacksonian era, with its romantic af-fection for amateurishness and its suspicions of anything smack-ing of expertise, the Military Academy on the Hudson was almost forced out of business.

Many Americans mistakenly believed any military victories their soldiers won had resulted simply from the hardy character, the *civilian* valor, of "common people." Most American history books that spoke of their revolution preferred to focus on Lexing-ton and Bunker Hill, for example—and not the patient profes-sionalism of the armies of Horatio Gates and George Washington and the Comte de Rochambeau.

It is hard to grasp now, but pressures before the Civil War on army personnel to pinch every penny were staggering.[10] If an enlisted man's clothes wore out too quickly, his commander could be held responsible and would personally have to pay for the uniform in question. Even the condition of a unit's flags was subject to scrutiny. Army regulations expected a flag — raised every morning, flown all day in all sorts of weather — to last two years. If an officer felt it necessary to request a new flag, he had to justify his reasons in writing, and at excruciating length A standard "storm flag," used at Fort Moultrie, cost $17 at this time. If, in 1860, the army's Quartermaster Department refused to pay for a new one, Lieutenant Samuel Breck, the garrison's assistant quartermaster, would have had to pay for it himself, costing him one-third of his monthly base salary. Lieutenant Breck was, accordingly, careful about such matters.[11]

The rates of pay for America's soldiers actually rose a bit in the 1850s, perhaps mainly due to the support of Secretary of War Jefferson Davis, a graduate of West Point. Officers had their base salaries, plus additional funds to cover rations and "servants," which usually meant either maids to clean their quarters or male servants who cooked meals and served at mess. Lieutenant Colonel Gardner had a base pay of $95 per month. In addition he received $117 to cover his rations and servants.[12] The total — $212 per month, or $2,544 a year — would hardly have made him seem a wealthy man, especially by the standards of Charleston's well-to-do, but such an income was no longer shamefully low (according to one estimate, about the same as that of a Harvard professor).[13] An artillery captain, like Abner Doubleday, earned $115.50 per month ($1,386 a year), and Assistant Surgeon Samuel Crawford earned $170.50 per month ($2,046 a year).

Promotion among officers in the regular army came *solely* by seniority. As a result, deserving officers lingered in rank for decades. Robert E. Lee remained stuck in his rank into his sixth decade, simply because the men in front of him refused to have the good grace to get out of his way. In 1860 the army had only *nineteen* regimental colonels; eleven of these were veterans of the War of 1812. Fifteen had more than forty years' service. In the artillery's own First Regiment the unwillingness of John Gardner to retire — or die — meant that every officer below him in the regiment was stuck on his rung of the ladder. This meant that Major Robert Anderson, on assignment in New York and Washington, one of the best officers in the army, had been unable to get a well-deserved promotion. The whole of the officer corps was circumscribed in this way. In a sense the system was democratic, since it diminished the sometimes revolting necessity of boot licking, but the arrangement had obvious unhealthy side effects. Among them was the fact that many good officers grew impatient and left the service, while deadwood remained.

As to enlisted men, recruits were supposed to be at least twenty-one years old, but never older than thirty-five. Birth certificates, however, were virtually unknown and recruiting sergeants were quite capable of fudging a date or two. (One famous case involved Edgar Allan Poe, who was only eighteen when he joined the army in 1827, but a considerate recruiter simply added four years to his enlistment papers, making him more than old enough. As it turned out, Poe was not an especially good soldier, but he did serve at Fort Moultrie, and the experience was vivid enough for him later to write "The Gold Bug," one of his more famous stories, which is set on Sullivan's Island.)

Theoretically a new recruit must stand at least 5'3". The requirement was probably more the result of the army's need to have soldiers who would fit into the standard-sized uniforms then available. A physician who examined hundreds of recruits said they averaged 5'7" and 147 pounds.[14] Soldiers of that era were therefore slightly above average height for an American male, and beefier, not the emaciated alcoholics, the sweepings of the cities' gutters often portrayed by cost-cutting politicians.

Other studies tell us more about them. Many were illiterate, though the term "literacy" is often vague. One analysis reports 25 percent could not *read*; another concludes that a quarter of the recruits could not sign their names.[15] But by most definitions a large percentage of Americans were illiterate — certainly more than one out of four. About two-thirds of enlisted men in 1860 were immigrants, half of them Irish. When one takes into account the level of literacy in Ireland at that time — to say nothing of large sections of the South—we can conclude that the military's educational level was in fact better than one would expect.

In 1860 the First Artillery Regiment was made up of ten understrength companies, scattered across the United States, less than 400 soldiers. A man could spend his entire adult life in the regiment and never see more than a few of its companies, since it was virtually never gathered together at one time. Two of the regiment's companies spent four years in the wilderness of Oregon; the rest moved from one barracks to another in the South: Texas, Virginia, Louisiana, Florida, and South Carolina's Fort Moultrie.

The entire army consisted of 198 line companies; 183 of these were on the frontier, scattered over 79 isolated, dusty posts. This left only fifteen companies of about thirty men each—therefore about 500 soldiers—to guard the Canadian border, the entire eastern seaboard from Maine to New Orleans, and to maintain and guard 23 federal arsenals. In 1860 the First Regiment maintained two companies at Moultrie: Company E and Company H.

Company E was rather typical of the First Regiment, and of the U.S. Army itself.[16] It numbered thirty-two enlisted men: four sergeants, four corporals, twenty-one privates, a designated "musician" (responsible for the company's various drumbeats), and two men whose official rank was *artificer.* (An artificer's specialty was the construction or repair of the wooden carriages that cannon sat on. There were only a few of these carpenter-specialists in the entire army.) The military records of the men of Company E show that three quarters were born outside the United States; one was from England, two from Scotland, seven from Germany, and fourteen from Ireland. The names of those born *in* the United States indicate that many of these were of recent Irish or German extraction; one can assume that as many as half of these men were the children of immigrants. Their listed ages ranged from twenty-one to forty-two, most either twenty-six or twenty-seven. Their average service time was four years, making them, therefore, "professional soldiers," though few had seen combat. Each had signed up for a five-year hitch.

Enlisted men in the 1850s, portrayed by civilians as lazy sots, often were. Moultrie had its share with problems but, when taken altogether, they do not seem nearly as disreputable as their reputation. Maybe the source of the problem was that most people who wrote about them were educated Americans, with either class or cultural prejudices, and most soldiers were immigrants or simple laborers, or both.

What, then, can we piece together about this particular band of men in 1860, as they prepared to face their next enemy, the secessionists? Private Lewis Schroeder, a short German born in Prussia, served as Company E's tailor. Privates James McDonald, once a hatter, and James Digdam were clearly buddies from long before. Each was in his mid-twenties, had been born in Westmeath, Ireland, and had volunteered in New York City on the same day. The two men looked almost like twins: the same height and build, each with light eyes and ruddy, fair complexion. They both had the same disposition toward trouble. Private Digdam spent two months during the summer of 1860 in confinement. Then, from October 31 to December 31, 1860, both Digdam and McDonald were in confinement, on bread and water—two stock characters from some bad vaudeville routine about brawling Irishmen. Company E also had a Private Daniel Hough with diagnosed emotional problems.

A few of the enlisted men were married, most were not. Some had relatives in the city, most did not. A few were skilled craftsmen, but most represented the desperate flight of Ireland's poverty-stricken masses. All in all, the company seem to mirror quite accurately the army of that period. As to their deportment, an 1860 army report noted that thirteen of the garrison's enlisted men out of sixty-four (20 percent) were being confined for some infraction, not a good reflection on their leadership.[17]

At Moultrie a hundred feet of sandy parade ground divided the enlisted men's barracks from the officers' quarters. Those few score yards constituted a social chasm, maintained by class prejudice and military protocol.

Since Colonel Gardner lived outside the fort, the highest-ranking line officer living in the officers' quarters was Captain Abner Doubleday, promoted to that rank in 1855.

Early in the twentieth century, long after Doubleday's death, a committee anxious to promote the sport of baseball examined its origins and claimed that he had invented it in 1839—which was and is absurd. The game's roots went back to eighteenth-century England—and, depending on how one defined it, perhaps long before. But the committee preferred to think it was dealing with "the great *American* pastime." Their main justification came from a Denver mining engineer who recalled that Doubleday, seeing some local boys playing a game, suggested some rules for them. Oddly, this myth—never claimed by Doubleday himself—remains the most famous thing about him.[18]

He was born in Cooperstown, New York, June 26, 1819. West Point was only a hundred miles from home, and free. His father had the necessary political connections to get him his appointment. Doubleday's record there was second-rate, at best.[19] Academically, he consistently ranked as a middling student. The Academy had a classroom ranking system that was highly competitive. A student was *precisely* ranked in every course he took, so the school could determine *exactly* how he compared with his classmates. Doubleday graduated in the middle of his class, twenty-fourth in a class of fifty-six students—about how he ranked in most of his courses.

Cadets were also ranked in matters of behavior. They were given demerits for a variety of infractions, from minor ones involving neatness or tardiness to mildly heinous activities. Many students piled up demerits for smoking in their rooms or slipping out to "Benny's" for a nightcap. Not Doubleday. He was neither a drinker nor a smoker. More remarkable for that era, neither was he a chewer and spitter. He was, however, lazy and sloppy, traits he never entirely outgrew. His West Point records are a bit muddled; one source states he earned 187 demerits; another, 247. In either case his demerit-record was undistinguished. The year he started there, 1838, a young man named Pierre Gustave Toutant Beauregard, whom he would later face in battle, graduated with only 14 demerits. While numbers of demerits hardly provide a completely accurate picture of a student's behavior, they do suggest something about how a cadet comported himself. During Doubleday's last year at West Point the school had a student body of 217 cadets; his conduct rating, based on the 132 demerits he received that year, when he was twenty-two years old, was 181st. A classmate, a few months after he died, recalled Doubleday's cadet years. "He enjoyed a good anecdote," the classmate said. "He was rather averse to outdoor sports and retiring in his manner."[20] Perhaps Doubleday was simply a rather lazy young fellow who preferred the *rap-tap-tap* of his own indolent drummer. During the Civil War he acquired the nickname "Twenty-four Hours," due to his dilatory tendencies.

On graduation the army assigned West Point graduates to a specialty, based primarily on their class standing. The best students were made Engineers. The next level, men like Doubleday, were put into the Artillery. The worst students were assigned to the Infantry or Cavalry.

Shortly after graduation Doubleday was sent to Fort Moultrie in Charleston Harbor, his first experience this far South. He was unimpressed. "As all manual labor was done by slaves," he would write about that time, "the inhabitants of South Carolina always seemed to be at leisure."[21] Doubleday's fellow officers were a fascinating group, many of whom would one day become generals — on one side or the other — in the Civil War: William Tecumseh Sherman, John F. Reynolds, George H. ("Pap") Thomas, and Braxton Bragg. These men had just returned from fighting the Seminoles in Florida, and told him they much preferred, he recalled, "the elegant hospitality of Charleston."[22] A few months later the army ordered Doubleday to a post in Maine. The people there, he noted appreciatively, were industrious, as well as being book readers (unlike the population of South Carolina, he thought).[23] This sudden respect for hard physical activity is ironic.

Following a tour of duty with Zachary Taylor in the Mexican War, he married Mary Hewitt, daughter of a Baltimore lawyer. Mary Doubleday, unlike most military wives, preferred to accompany her husband to all of his posts. During the Civil War she would be with him even at Antietam, when the two armies fought the bloodiest day of the war. A fervent nationalist, Mary in 1860 felt contempt for those who toyed with notions of secession, and fury at those who practiced it. During the Civil War she would be a frequent visitor at the White House and would sometimes drive with President and Mary Todd Lincoln.[24] All in all, she was, perhaps, the most interesting thing about her husband.

Abner Doubleday tended a bit toward self-righteous moralism. In 1859, while on an extended leave in Washington, Doubleday watched some congressional debates. Afterward, his diary spoke angrily of Southern intransigence and he concluded that war was inevitable.[25] As the secession crisis developed in 1860, Moultrie's other officers felt some sympathy for the South, but Abner Doubleday was the only officer to support the Republicans. His stance on slavery was clear: he firmly opposed it. He remained undiplomatically candid on these subjects, and he was quite open about his support of Lincoln's candidacy and his disdain for the entire Southern "cause." During the coming crisis Doubleday, tall and tending a bit toward portliness, served as the thick lightning rod for Charleston's ire. Local newspapers wallowed in their loathing for him.

Lieutenant Jefferson C. Davis was second-in-command of Company E. No relation to the famous Confederate leader with the same name, Lieutenant Davis suffered as the butt of many a bad joke about possible connections. He was, in fact, not a good man to make sport of. A brawny fellow with receding hair and a great shaggy beard, he was a natural scrapper. Born in Indiana in 1828, he volunteered for a local militia unit when the Mexican War loomed, and became a war hero at nineteen. Doubleday later dubbed him "the boy sergeant of Buena Vista."[26] Offered an appointment to West Point, Davis turned it down. At twenty, still too young even to enlist in the regular army as a private, his commanders thought so much of his fighting abilities they chose to bypass the academic route and appointed him a lieutenant of artillery. During the Civil War he would rise to the rank of major general and was one of Sherman's most pugnacious fighters. In 1860 he felt no antagonism toward slavery, but he loathed secession.[27] Oddly, Davis took leave from Moultrie during the early fall of 1860. When he returned in mid-October, apparently oblivious to the tensions wafting through the Carolina air, he brought with him his young sister, Annie, whom he enrolled at a Charleston girls' school.[28]

Brevet Captain Truman Seymour commanded Moultrie's other company, Company H.[29] One of the only true Yankees at the fort,

Seymour was born in Burlington, Vermont, the oldest son of a
Methodist minister. At fifteen he enrolled at Norwich Academy, a
local military school, stayed two years, then entered West Point in
the summer of 1842. One of his classmates later recalled young
Seymour as being quite shy, not "aggressive in forming acquaintances."[30] In 1846 he graduated, 19th in his class of 59, now an artillery officer, just in time for the Mexican War, during which he
distinguished himself for his energy and courage. Shortly afterward he was appointed an assistant professor of drawing at West
Point. (During the coming crisis at Fort Sumter Captain Seymour
would earn extra money on the side, selling some of his drawings
to *Harper's Weekly.*[31]) A broad-shouldered, stocky individual of average height with a thick dark-brown beard, a mountain climber,
an artist, son of an impoverished Yankee preacher, fond of poetry
and music, a hardened soldier, Seymour was an intriguing man.

Lieutenant Theodore Talbot, Seymour's second-in-command,
was in his mid-thirties and unmarried. A professorial type, he was
just a trifle prissy.[32] Hundreds of Talbot's letters from this period,
collected at the Library of Congress, show him to have been perceptive, sardonic, and intelligent. He cared deeply about his wid-
owed mother and spinster sister. In his letters he often gossiped
about the officers at Fort Moultrie and the girls he encountered at
the island's soirées — many of whom he described as less than
pretty. He liked to dance and socialize, and he always looked forward to the island's high season.[33]

At some point in his life Talbot had contracted tuberculosis.
Although slight and small in stature, as a young man he had been
quite hardy. He had accompanied John C. Frémont's first expedition across the Rockies, where several members, including Frémont himself, had grown seriously ill in the high altitudes while
Talbot showed no ill effects. But by 1860 his consumptive cough
had grown noticeable. His mother sent him medicines. In January
1861 he wrote her, "My cough continues about the same. I have
found the tar syrup beneficial. . . . With better weather I hope to
improve."[34] He did not. A month later he wrote her again. "I am
pretty well," he told her, adding that the fort's new commander,
Major Anderson, "will not let me do any guard duty until the

weather is quite fair & settled because he says he might need my services for more important duty, and he does not choose that I should undergo any unnecessary fatigue in the meantime."[35]

Lieutenant Norman Hall, twenty-three years old, was the youngest officer at Fort Moultrie. His record of demerits at West Point was worse even than Doubleday's, but his infractions indicated only a certain boyish immaturity. By his last year at West Point, he seems to have grown up. Another cadet later recalled Hall in his last year at the Military Academy as "a mature, scholarly-looking man, with a large, broad, clear forehead, chestnut hair, and quiet, unassertive manner."

He graduated in 1859, 13th in a class of 21, and was sent shortly thereafter to Moultrie.[36] As the youngest and newest officer, he was assigned the post's two most thankless tasks, garrison quartermaster and commissary officer. A quartermaster is responsible for housing and transportation, for clothing and fuel, even for providing stationery. The commissary's job involved supervising the fort's food supply: doing inventories of beans and biscuits, purchasing beef and peas. Undramatic tasks, generally rather unimportant, their significance was about to change, drastically.

Not counting Lieutenant Colonel Gardner—who was perhaps not worth counting—these five were Moultrie's line officers: Doubleday and Davis, in charge of Company E; Seymour and Talbot with Company H; and Hall, the new boy, in charge of the garrison's mundane matters.

The fort also housed Samuel W. Crawford, officially Moultrie's Assistant Surgeon. (The Surgeon of the fort, a Dr. Simons, was an older man who lived off the post with his wife.) Most of Crawford's responsibilities involved tending the health of civilian laborers. In the long run, his story would be one of the fort's most interesting.

Captain Samuel Wylie Crawford—"Wylie" to his friends—would eventually write a history of these days: *The Genesis of the Civil War: Fort Sumter, 1860–1861.* The book was a remarkable achievement for its time. Not only did Crawford draw from his own observations, highlighted by notes he'd taken during the crisis, but he also spent twenty years after the Civil War doing research, gathering documents from both sides of the conflict, interviewing participants, and corresponding with individuals around the country. Although he did not publish his history until 1887, he actually began the project during the crisis as a way to make extra money. "I have a secret to tell you," he wrote his brother. "I have kept close notes of all our doings since the disturbance began. Why should I not write them out carefully and print them. It will be a book eagerly sought after, I think, and would certainly pay. Two different firms have applied."[37] Additional income seemed a worthy goal to Crawford; during the crisis he, like Captain Seymour, sold sketches, at $25 a piece, to *Harper's Weekly*.

Although he put his medical career aside during the war, rising to the rank of major general (by brevet), and fought in some of the war's bloodiest battles, Crawford was able afterward to reconnect with Southern friends from the antebellum years. They remembered his warm feelings toward the South, and his disdain for the Republicans. On the day Lincoln had been inaugurated, Crawford wrote that "The South in her position stands by the Constitution which in spirit and in letter has been violated by the aggressive power now in power." Crawford was a native Pennsylvanian and, though he strongly opposed secession, he despised Lincoln. "A vulgar, third-rate politician," he called him, "a man without anything to entitle him to the position he holds, an uncouth Western Hoosier."[38] In this judgment Wylie Crawford, like many people of his time, and most Southerners, assumed that Lincoln would be a mouthpiece for the abolitionists. Crawford hated—and feared—abolitionism. The next step after ending slavery, he understood, would be a move toward equality. "Any proposition to lift the Negro to the social level of the *white man* is to me monstrous and insane."[39]

While such opinions may make Crawford seem an antediluvian bigot, he was in fact quite complex. With his triangular face, high forehead, and full mustache he looked remarkably like Edgar Allan Poe. He was intelligent and had a broad, even scientific, curiosity. His devotion to medicine was probably shallow—he certainly left it easily enough—but his voluminous notes reveal a mind interested in many things, from weather patterns to food preservatives.

There were others at Fort Moultrie. There was a regimental band, consisting of a sergeant, a corporal, and six privates. Each regiment of the U.S. Army had its own "band," whose primary duty was to entertain. The musicians at Moultrie performed occasionally for the island's residents; they also played songs on many evenings for the troops at the fort. Moultrie also housed Dr. Crawford's medical "stewards" (corpsmen, essentially). Two of the fort's enlisted men were listed as "cooks." And in one of the cottages outside the gate lived the Reverend Matthias Harris, regimental chaplain, and his wife. More shadowy yet were the fort's black servants. One was called "Jim," a local young man, who served in one of the officers' mess units. The officers did not realize it, but "Jim"—whose name was actually Thomas Moore Lynch—was in fact a slave, and this would become an issue a few months into the crisis. There were other black servants. We do not know how many, and we do not even know their names. One worked for Doubleday, who would later wax caustic at his servant's apparent cowardice during Fort Sumter's bombardment. The little we know about these servants tells us much about military protocol—and about America's racial (and class) divisions.

In the summer of 1860 Fort Moultrie was a sleepy post with an undermanned garrison and a commanding officer who was old and weak and lazy. Sand dunes leaned gently against its walls, almost as high as its parapets. Seabirds flew overhead, crying down at the garrison, and their echo melded with the sound of lapping waves. The people of Fort Moultrie—Doubleday and Hough, Talbot and "Jim," Reverend Harris and Mary Doubleday and young Norman Hall—were about to confront the crisis of secession.

CHAPTER FOUR

The Fulcrum

The garrison, of course, was well aware of the growing secessionist stir in the city. The soldiers read the local newspapers, they chatted with friends and relatives from Charleston, they spent time there shopping, socializing, doing whatever soldiers do when away from the tedium and discipline of their posts. Their letters, diaries, and reports made passing references to the coming election, but until late October they showed little anxiety about any danger to themselves. In July, one of the officers, probably Doubleday, urged the regiment's authorities to strengthen Moultrie's two sadly depleted companies. Rumors were rife that this might occur, but in October Lieutenant Davis, who had been in Washington, returned unaccompanied by any recruits, and announced they were to receive no reinforcements until, at the earliest, December or January. Talbot, in a letter to his sister, did not seem overly concerned.[1] Things at the old fort seemed about as usual, except for some refurbishing.

In August 1860 the Army Engineers had sent Captain John G. Foster to Charleston to improve Fort Moultrie, as well as to work on two other fortifications in the harbor: Fort Sumter and Castle Pinckney. No one in Washington apparently foresaw possible problems in Charleston, but the date of Foster's assignment is curious. "The reason privately assigned to this [order]," according to Abner Doubleday, "was that we were drifting into compli-

cations with England and France with reference to Mexico."
Doubleday found it hard to swallow this explanation.[2]

John Foster had graduated fourth in his 1846 West Point
class. During the Mexican War he served with General Scott's
army. In the brutal Battle of Molino del Rey, where Anderson was
so severely cut up, Foster personally led a band of foot soldiers,
not something engineers often did. He was so badly wounded in
the leg that doctors wanted to amputate it, but he persuaded them
not to. In 1860 he still walked with a noticeable limp.

Thirty-seven years old, Foster was a physically imposing man,
standing over six feet tall, his upper body thickened with muscle
and flesh. His hair had retreated but he sported a thick and bushy
beard. With his blue eyes and thick, peaked eyebrows he presented a manly appearance.

After his arrival, he set up an office in Charleston where he
kept his drawings, maps, and assorted paperwork. Foster was not
normally an affable sort but he could be genial enough, and he
soon made the acquaintance of members of Charleston's social set.
One of them, C. H. Simonton, rented Foster and his wife, Marl, a
cottage on Sullivan's Island, not far from Fort Moultrie. They
lived there, along with their daughter Annie, Foster's brother-in-
law Henry, and a black servant, Benjamin Scott. No doubt the
cottage felt cramped.[3]

Foster set out to hire civilian workers, hundreds of them. He
needed some with specialized skills in one of the building trades,
but most would simply supply muscle. He looked for workmen in
Charleston, but was unable to find enough. Since he had contacts
in Baltimore, he hired over a hundred and fifty construction men
from there, many of them masons. And his work began.

Captain Foster remained aloof from the daily activities of the
artillery companies at Moultrie. Even his food, and that of his laborers, was different. According to regulations, he and his laborers
did not draw their supplies from the post commissary. Foster was
personally responsible for purchasing food, materials, and equipment for his workmen, using separate accounts. He even had his
own boats for transporting his men and supplies. He was an intelligent man and an excellent administrator with executive ability.

After his death, a friend eulogized him: "By nature he was genial and sympathetic, manifested cordiality and affection to his companions, was an admirable raconteur with an almost exhaustless store of anecdote and story, and by his family and intimates was greatly loved."[4] Unfortunately Foster, a descendent of impoverished New England Yankees, was also a proud man, standoffish and haughty, which would create unpleasantness in the coming crisis.

Soon after he arrived it was obvious that he would need engineering assistance. In late September the army sent him First Lieutenant George W. Snyder, a native New Yorker who had graduated originally from Union College, then had gone on to West Point, where he stood first in his 1856 class. He was still there, teaching, when ordered to Charleston Harbor to assist Foster. When Snyder arrived, Foster sent him out to Fort Sumter with more than a hundred laborers to work on that empty, isolated bastion.[5] Snyder was a phlegmatic sort, with a giant riverboat-gambler mustache and an air of gravitas.

In addition to Fort Moultrie and Fort Sumter, Charleston Harbor contained two more forts. Across the harbor from Moultrie sat Fort Johnson, consisting of a few empty buildings that could be used, if needed, as barracks. Although seldom visited, this post had never been completely abandoned; Fort Moultrie kept its supply of coal there. Nearer Charleston was a small, attractive fortification called Castle Pinckney, perched on a boggy reef just outside the mouth of the Cooper River, less than a mile from the city's wharves. The army had built it as a last protection for Charleston. If an enemy fleet somehow broke through the barrier created by Moultrie's and Sumter's guns, Castle Pinckney might still save the city. It was round in shape, and it had two tiers of cannon behind its twenty-foot brick walls. In 1860 its only occupants were an ordnance sergeant, his wife, and daughter. Its water cisterns needed some repair and its barracks were not quite prepared for occupancy, but otherwise it was ready for use.

In a sense fortification is simple. Children throwing snowballs discover they are safer standing behind trees than out in the open. All else is just details. But by 1860 the details had grown complicated. In 1836 Dennis Hart Mahan published a book on fortification — a textbook studied by West Point cadets for decades. He sprinkled it with hundreds of French terms and used an inordinate layer of fairly complicated mathematics. (For example, to calculate the proper square footage of a parade ground, Mahan said, an engineer must first know the precise size of the garrison, and then apply this formula: $[X-9]^2 = 150y + s + s + s.^6$) Was it any wonder that the army chose only West Point's top graduates to become engineers and that their numbers remained low? In 1860 there were a total of only forty-six engineering officers. They were called "staff" officers and considered themselves an elite group, quite separate from "line" officers.

A person of the "line" was someone whose military expertise involved fighting. Naval line officers, for example, might serve aboard a man-of-war. In the army, a line officer might be a member of the cavalry or the infantry or the artillery. A staff person might participate in a battle, but normally his career involved filling out papers or storing or transporting men and materiel. Quartermasters were staff people, so were ordnance sergeants and mapmakers, meteorologists and engineers. Fort Moultrie housed both types of officers, line and staff. Even in a small garrison like this, their lives and focus were often far apart.

One of the first things Foster did, once he had sufficient workmen, was to dig away the sand slope against Moultrie's south wall. They pawed at it like burrowing ants. When they reached ground level they kept digging till they created a trench fifteen feet wide and several feet deep below the wall. Foster wanted this moat deeper but he had reached the island's water table. Foster used the sand they had removed from the wall to build a slope grading down to the beach, permitting the garrison a clear line of fire to the water's edge. Foster also turned his attention to the other three walls. He sealed up narrow doorways on the east and west sides. (Most fortifications had such doors—the army called them *sally ports*—designed so that soldiers within a fort could "sally" out to surprise and repel attackers.) Foster also built a *bastionette* on Moultrie's northwest corner, a sort of bump-out, designed to support an artillery piece that could aim down the road in both directions. Around most of the fort he erected a picket fence within pistol shot of the walls.

In Charleston, not everyone was happy with Foster's changes. A gentleman from the city trekked over to Sullivan's Island and reported to the *Mercury* that hundreds of men were working there, including, he emphasized, "some free negroes." A day later the *Mercury* itself groused, "Until late in the summer the defenses of Fort Moultrie have remained in an unfinished condition; the sand of the beach, piled up by the wind against the south walls, had rendered them easy accessible almost by a single leap." But things had changed, it said. The *Mercury* found Foster's renovations upsetting and barely tolerable.[7]

On Sullivan's Island tensions began to simmer. Doubleday later recalled that "a Secession meeting was held in our immediate vicinity, accompanied with many threats and noisy demonstrations." Colonel Gardner, still ensconced off base, reminded Doubleday that the captain was responsible for the safety of the fort. On November 3, at a Charleston rally, someone objected to Foster's rebuilding Fort Moultrie. Proudly wearing blue secessionist cockades, the group went all the way to the fort and tramped about inside it, inspecting the progress of Foster's work. They made themselves quite at home.[8] This incident made the garrison uneasy. Nor were men like Doubleday comforted by the fact that Moultrie was momentarily in disarray from the work being done by Foster's crew, who had strewn piles of material everywhere. Worse, Foster had actually dismounted some of the fort's cannon to reinforce their foundations. Colonel Gardner seemed frozen in uncertainty.

It was Lieutenant Snyder, the engineer in charge of Fort Sumter's ongoing construction, who took the first step. He noticed that some of his laborers had begun to wear small blue cockades. With a hundred and nine of them spending each night at the fort, it would have been easy for them to take it over in a rush. Snyder asked Washington if he might be permitted to arm a few loyal workmen, assuming he could find any. On October 31 the head of Army Ordnance wrote Secretary of War John B. Floyd about Snyder's request, saying he concurred in its wisdom. Floyd casually approved the idea, and in early November Gardner received a note from headquarters summarizing these discussions, and giving him official blessing to procure forty muskets from the federal arsenal in Charleston if he wished.[9]

The day before Lincoln's election Gardner responded to Washington's suggestion about the muskets in a carefully worded letter. He thought the notion, given "the feeling of the time," a good idea, but he did not trust the loyalty and resolve of the workers at Sumter. Most of them, he noted, were "of foreign nativity," and some had said that they would support whoever gave them the largest bribe. He was not even confident of Captain Foster's workers at Moultrie, about fifty of whom were from the Charleston region. His best advice was that the army should instead send reinforcements, some to Moultrie, and others to man Sumter and even Castle Pinckney.[10]

In Charleston the day after Lincoln's election, crowds of excited citizens surrounded the bulletin boards at the two major newspapers, reading notices coming in by wire. There was much talk of war. Remarkably, at this volatile juncture, soldiers from Fort Moultrie arrived in town to get military supplies from the arsenal. The results were inevitable.

Moultrie had been running low on ammunition due to normal usage in practice. Colonel Gardner had resisted getting supplies from the arsenal, but perhaps the demonstration at the fort on November 3 — the one that so annoyed Doubleday — swayed him. Maybe he was simply dense. He chose Election Day to order Doubleday to write out a list of their needs. Doubleday checked their stores and noted they needed more cartridges for their muskets, some hand grenades, and similar items. (Obviously, Doubleday was choosing things that could be used against mobs.) Gardner sent Doubleday's list to the man in charge of the arsenal, Captain F. C. Humphreys, to allow him time to get the materials ready.

The next day Captain Truman Seymour volunteered to go, accompanied by a few enlisted men. With the men dressed in civilian clothes, they sailed the fort's own schooner to the wharf used by the arsenal on Charleston's western edge. They thought they might go undetected. But even before Seymour and his soldiers left Moultrie, Sullivan's Island's own vigilance committee, which had been watching the garrison, spotted them. Two vigilantes crossed over to the city and told Charleston's own vigilance committee to watch for the arrival of the schooner.[11]

Seymour's boat tied at the arsenal's wharf. Corporal Costolan stayed by it while Seymour and the others went to the arsenal, a few hundred feet away, to begin the process. They piled boxes of ammunition on an arsenal cart, toted them to the boat, and hurried back for more. The tide and the few remaining hours of daylight made them rush. They got a second load, a third, a fourth. Then a well-to-do gentleman appeared and commanded them to stop. When Seymour rushed up, the gentleman (unnamed, but probably the owner of one of the two nearby rice mills) told him the wharf belonged to him and he would not permit it to be used for anything that had not approved by the "authorities." He had, he said, already sent a messenger to these authorities and they would be arriving soon. When Seymour expostulated, the man told him that, if the soldiers did not cease immediately, he himself would have to stop them. All he would have to do, he said, would be to lift his hand, and a hundred men would pounce on them. A crowd had gathered; Seymour did not want to initiate an ugly incident, so he took the ammunition back to the arsenal and returned to Moultrie.

The next morning he called on Charleston's mayor, Charles Macbeth, to ask permission to procure supplies from the arsenal. Macbeth found himself in a delicate position. The city's vigilance committee had gotten involved and clearly would not favor ammunition being moved to Moultrie. On the other hand, Macbeth could think of no legal reason to deny the request, so he signed a permission slip, which Seymour carried back to Moultrie. But Gardner ordered him not to pursue the matter any further, probably having lost his nerve; he justified his decision on his unwillingness to accept Macbeth's permission, since doing so would be to sanction the right of a local official to dictate to the federal army.[12] Gardner's stance on this issue was not absurd, but seems a bit too legalistic since the army often sought the permission of mayors or governors to move about or use private property. The entire episode smacks of military ham-handedness. If the garrison needed ammunition, or even if they wished simply to bring it to

Moultrie where it would be safer, taking it from the arsenal was a reasonable way to proceed. But to do so when they did, on the day after Charleston learned that the hated Republicans had won the election, was unwise. Then, having gone that far, not taking the crucial materials from the arsenal once they had the mayor's permission was imprudent.

Edmund Ruffin, visiting at that time, was not happy about the odor of mobocracy in Charleston on November 8. One issue was the incident at the arsenal. Another, according to Ruffin, involved a steamer from Philadelphia, which attempted to tie up at one of the wharves, and was prevented from doing so by "the boys of the city" until the ship's captain pulled down the American flag. "Popular feeling," Ruffin noted, "is very strong." He was not pleased.[13]

On November 12, four days later, Governor Gist placed a militia unit of twenty men just outside the arsenal. Captain Humphreys, in charge there, nervously wrote his superiors in Washington that Gist had "tendered" the militiamen "in view of the excitement now existing in this city and State, and the possibility of an insurrectionary movement on the part of the servile population." This explanation seems doubtful, given the confidence most white Charlestonians had in the affections of their "people." A clue to Gist's motives may be found in one of Ruffin's diary entries where he noted that he personally worried "the people will run ahead of the government," writing these words immediately following a conversation he'd had with Governor Gist. Ruffin was probably reflecting the governor's own concerns about the city's unruly guttersnipes. No doubt Gist sent militia to the arsenal to prevent a mob from arming itself. During the coming weeks South Carolina's leaders acted outraged at any hint they were not in complete control of South Carolina. "We do not act by mobs," the *Mercury* sniffed. "We are accustomed each to think and judge for himself."[14] Gist, it would seem, was not so confident.

One thing, however, was clear. Charleston's leaders were adamantly opposed to any change in the status quo at Fort Moultrie. When Colonel Gardner visited Charleston on November 16, he was told that the city would not permit him to receive reinforcements.[15]

At Moultrie, after November 8, the pace of the garrison picked up. In light of what he had encountered, Seymour drew up specific suggestions. The fort should, he urged, immediately close its gates, and civilians should enter only if accompanied by an officer of the garrison. There should be no more casual visits by the curious, the nosy, or the hostile. All enlisted men ought to be ordered to remain inside the fort's walls from retreat to Reveille. (This would have included those married men whose wives lived just outside the gate.) During hours of darkness, Seymour further proposed, the garrison ought to maintain a "running guard"— walking sentries — on all walls but the front, where a guard was already stationed. Doubleday could take command of the west wall, Talbot the south, and Seymour the east. The fort should also keep its flanking artillery pieces loaded. Everyone should practice what their duties would be if it came to an assault. Gardner approved all the proposals. He, like most of them, had finally grown unnerved by the feverish mood in Charleston.

The garrison piled hand grenades in strategic spots for easy access. For the first time the guards at the gate were ordered to keep their muskets loaded. Moultrie's artillery teams began practicing during nighttime hours, the explosions echoing and the flash of canister candling the November darkness. Even Foster was uneasy. He now worked his men day and night, because, as he wrote his superiors in Washington, "of the peculiar state of the public feeling here and the wishes of several officers of the garrison." In one day his men erected two temporary platforms that could serve as the bases for four pieces field artillery.[16] By November 18, ten days after the incident at the arsenal, as Doubleday later recalled, "we considered ourselves reasonably secure against a *coup-de-main*."[17] Everyone waited for whatever would come next.

By early November army headquarters in Washington had finally reacted to the specter of secession and some of its implications. The situation in Charleston seemed especially combustible, so Secretary of War Floyd assigned Fitz-John Porter, an officer with the Adjutant General's Office, to travel to South Carolina, analyze the situation, and report back. (Amazingly, Floyd gave this order on Election Day. One cannot help but be struck by the remarkable casualness, an absurd attitude of muddling through, held by so many officials during these few days.) Porter left Washington immediately, actually arriving in Charleston the very day that Seymour had unsuccessfully tried to extract the ammunition from the arsenal. Porter inspected the installations throughout the harbor, spoke to some officers, and reviewed Moultrie's records. He did all this quickly and efficiently, then departed. On November 11 he handed the army his report. It was scathing.

He began by saying he found the officers sober and energetic, capable of performing their duties, "with some exceptions, punctually and promptly." He did not specify what "exceptions" he meant, but the observation was hardly complimentary. The enlisted men, he said, were "intelligent and obedient, but do not move with the alacrity and spirit indicating the existence of a strict discipline." It should be noted that military verbiage was given to ornate politeness and euphemisms, so these were strong words, and his report then grew even more concrete and biting. He said that the fort held its stores in shacks outside the gate and kept no watch on them. In fact, he considered Fort Moultrie virtually unguarded, that precautions should have been initiated weeks earlier. He considered the garrison too small, and — like Gardner had a few weeks earlier — he urged the army to send reinforcements. As to Fort Sumter and Castle Pinckney, he did not think it necessary or advisable to place troops in them, at least at the moment. Finally, as to Lieutenant Colonel Gardner, Porter did not make a specific recommendation, but he did state that "much discretion and prudence are required on the part of the commander to restore the proper security without exciting a community prompt to misconstrue actions of authority. I think this can be effected by a proper commander."[18] The implications of Porter's report were clear: Gardner was not the "proper commander."

The day after he handed in his report, Porter visited Major Anderson, toiling desultorily on Jefferson Davis's West Point commission, and told him that Floyd wanted Anderson to take over Fort Moultrie, that he should go immediately to Washington. Anderson and Porter went to see General Scott. Scott, who had a habit of bickering with the War Department, had been given no inkling of either Porter's mission to Moultrie or of Anderson's approaching appointment. The general was miffed, but advised Anderson that Fort Moultrie ought to be reinforced by Washington. If not, he should transfer his command to Fort Sumter.

Anderson also spoke to George W. Cullum, an officer who had recently reconnoitered the harbor and its forts and considered himself something of an expert on the military complexities there, as well as on the mood of its population. Cullum told Anderson that the army ought to immediately place a company of men in Castle Pinckney, station four additional companies at Fort Sumter, and fill out Moultrie's depleted complement. This show of strength, he felt, might calm down the volatility in Charleston. If Washington failed to do this, his advice was the same as Scott's: move the garrison to Sumter.[19]

The next day the major took the train to Washington, where he conferred with Secretary of War Floyd, who reminded him how explosive Charleston was at this moment, that *no action should be taken that might light a spark*. With Floyd's orders in his head — they were not written on paper — Anderson returned to New York to say good-bye to Eba and his two-year-old son, Robert, Jr. Eba's delicate health, which made any travel difficult, would seem to preclude her making the trip. She would wait for him, as she had for years, at the Brevoort House.

Anderson felt he had one more duty to perform. He wrote a note to his old friend, Senator Jefferson Davis, saying that his assignment to Fort Moultrie would prevent him from continuing work on the West Point commission. Years after the war, Davis would maintain that Anderson's letter revealed his sympathies to be entirely with the cause of the South, that secession was a reasonable response to the situation. Davis, however, could never substantiate these claims.[20]

At Fort Moultrie Talbot wrote his sister: "Yesterday morning it was announced in the city papers, among the telegraphic intelligence, that Col. Gardner was to be relieved in command of Fort Moultrie, by Major Anderson of the 1st Artillery. . . . I do not know Major Anderson who is coming here, but he is said to be an excellent officer, able and discreet. Such a one is needed at this time."[21]

Anderson arrived at Fort Moultrie on November 19. He did not need Secretary of War Floyd or General Scott to advise him how to act. A garrison like Moultrie, dragged down by a superannuated ninny like Gardner, desperately needed discipline. The U.S. Army manual stated that the best form of military discipline came when a soldier saw the national interest as in his own best interests, but until that unusual fusion occurred, it added, discipline came when the commander offered calm impartiality, prompt firmness, and character.[22] These were qualities Robert Anderson had in full—especially character.

Anderson would never allow his command to realize that his health was at all precarious, nor for that matter that he was supposed to strengthen the posture of the garrison without riling the civilian population—an impossible contradiction. He hated to reveal weakness or uncertainty, and military tradition demanded that he seem in complete command, almost serene. For the next five months he maintained this facade.

So many things isolated him. The army demanded a certain aloofness of any commanding officer, and his natural shyness and bookish tendencies, his advanced years and strong religious feelings, all set him apart from his fellow officers. The only man he knew when he arrived was Seymour, and him hardly at all.[23] Over the next five months, he would chat on occasion with one or another of his officers, especially Wylie Crawford, perhaps because of the doctor's natural intelligence and curiosity, and perhaps because Crawford was a bit removed from the chain of command. Most of the time, however, Anderson stayed slightly apart, isolated from the others.

Talbot's first reactions to his new commander were quite positive. He admired Anderson's "grave and polite demeanor." "He is a quiet & apparently decided man," Talbot wrote his mother a week after the major arrived. Talbot suspected that Anderson intended "gradually to tighten the reins of discipline without attracting the special attention of the garrison or of outsiders, until the post should be placed in an efficient condition." Talbot was glad. "For my part I feel a sense of relief after the previous state of things, when everybody and nobody was in command, orders given one day countermanded next, valiant, or rather, absurd defiance the tone of one day, pusillanimity, that of the following." Talbot's description of the garrison's chaos before Anderson's arrival was more damning than even Porter's report to Washington, for it reflects almost as badly on Gardner's immediate subordinates — Doubleday and Seymour — as it does on Gardner.[24]

Major Anderson's initial impressions of the garrison and its situation were hardly favorable. Two of the officers, Seymour and Talbot, he reported to Washington, were in "delicate" health and would not "be able to undergo much fatigue." Two of his privates were ill and seven others were in confinement for some infraction or other, an enormous percentage of his forty-eight privates.[25] Nor was he pleased by his supplies of victuals, a problem he never entirely solved — and one that would finally lead to war. He had less than two months' supply of basics like bacon and flour, and these were being stored in an unguarded shack outside the main gate. He discovered that the garrison had to purchase its beef and fresh vegetables from uncertain suppliers in Charleston, and to pay for these provisions, when they could get them, with cash deposited in the city by the U.S. Treasury.[26] If all went well, this should not be a problem, but he suspected that all might not go well.

Charleston's tensions were approaching hysteria. Men in the city were quite openly making threatening comments about Moultrie. It seemed to Anderson that the fort's vulnerability was an invitation to disaster; "The storm," he wrote Washington, "may break upon us at any moment." Despite Floyd's verbal instructions, he worried that *inactivity,* under the circumstances, would be the most dangerous tack. He was still unclear in his mind, he said, whether the administration intended to make every effort to hold the various forts in the harbor, but if they wished to do so he had several strong recommendations. Foster was working hard on preparing Moultrie's outer defenses, and he might be finished in a couple of weeks — if nothing untoward happened before that — but improving the walls of the fort would not be enough. Two high sand dunes several hundred yards east of the fort would allow sharpshooters to fire down upon the garrison. Anderson planned, he said, to level them soon. His most serious problem, he stated, was that the fort did not have enough men. If they were besieged, his entire complement would have to stand at the walls virtually twenty-four hours a day, and this activity would exhaust them in a few days. "The garrison now in it," he emphasized, "is so weak as to invite an attack."

He was also concerned, he added, about his other responsibilities: Fort Sumter and Castle Pinckney, both essentially unguarded. Sumter was especially important since it was both "the key to the entrance of this harbor" and was situated so that an enemy there could destroy Fort Moultrie. Lieutenant Snyder's workmen were making progress on Sumter, he said, but they needed more time to get it ready to defend itself. As to Castle Pinckney, it was virtually set, and Anderson advocated placing a small unit of soldiers there. A force from the city would hesitate to besiege Fort Moultrie since Castle Pinckney could bombard Charleston with ease. In fact, he considered Castle Pinckney so critical to Moultrie's defense that he made the following request: If the government was not going to send reinforcements to the harbor's forts immediately, would the administration permit him to send an officer and about thirty of Foster's *workmen* to Castle Pinckney? They might be able to arrive there without raising suspicions; then, after making the necessary repairs, the officer could train the workers on how to use the fortification's artillery pieces.

His advice was essentially the same as Gardner's and Porter's; he needed more men at Moultrie right away, and he begged the government, if it was serious about maintaining a presence in Charleston Harbor, to garrison both Fort Sumter and Castle Pinckney *immediately.* To fail to do this, Anderson warned, might very well cause the bloodshed that the administration wished to avoid. But, he cautioned, any attempts at reinforcement had to be done secretly, for Charleston would attack all the forts if they suspected any change in the status quo.

Anderson closed this first report with a final plea: "I will thank the Department [of War] to give me special instructions, as my position here is rather a politico-military than a military one."[27]

This note, like all the garrison's mail, went in a sealed bag by boat to Charleston, to the post office there, then wended its way, in fits and starts, by slow-moving trains and city wagons and other trains and small boats, until it arrived at headquarters. In the very best of circumstances the process took two days, often much longer.

Amazingly, despite the tone of disquiet in Anderson's message, the administration did not respond. Four days later he wrote again.[28] He warned Washington, "There appears to be a romantic desire urging South Carolinians to have possession of this work," and that some "intelligent and efficient men in this community" had, "by intimate intercourse with our army officers," discovered Moultrie's "weak points, and the best means of attack." He did not specify who these men were, nor which army officers might have been their sources of information, but it is intriguing that on the very day he arrived at Moultrie, Henry Gourdin, one of Charleston's secessionist leaders, and brother to Robert Gourdin, wrote him a warm, welcome-to-the-community note.[29] During the next several months Gourdin and the major would visit a number of times and correspond often, becoming quite friendly in the process. It seems probable that Gourdin was at this stage one of Anderson's sources about the mood in Charleston.

Another likely source was Colonel Benjamin Huger. Huger and Anderson had been friends for years. Huger was a native of Charleston and a member of one of its most prestigious families. Of the high-ranking officers in the army, he was the one with the most intimate connections there, and Secretary of War Floyd had sent him to take Captain Humphreys's place at the arsenal the same time he'd sent Anderson to Fort Moultrie.

On November 28, the day Anderson wrote his second report, Huger came to visit him. Frantic Charlestonians had been clamoring about rumors they had heard that Washington was sending reinforcements, which would arrive shortly by steamer. Huger therefore had come to find out if the major knew anything about this. Anderson said no, and Huger returned to the city and, according to Doubleday, persuaded some Charlestonians not to attack Fort Moultrie, saying that if they did so he himself would join his old friend Anderson in fighting them.[30]

On December 7 Huger was ordered back to Washington, leaving Captain Humphreys behind at the arsenal. In the capital Huger spoke to both Floyd and President Buchanan, urging them to send Anderson explicit instructions about what he was authorized to do in an emergency. At any moment, Huger warned, Major Anderson might face a confrontation with Charleston's militia or even a mob. Huger also contacted General Scott, who had just arrived in Washington, and pressed him to send reinforcements. This was a remarkable suggestion for Huger to make, since he knew that such an action would likely lead to war, but his lifetime of service to his country, combined with his almost forty years of friendship with Anderson made him choose, for this moment, the American flag over the Palmetto.[31]

In Anderson's second official report, on November 28, in light of his concerns about an attack on the fort, he reemphasized that the best way to keep Moultrie secure was to place garrisons in both Sumter and Castle Pinckney. He added that if no reinforcements were sent, the best place for his command would be Fort Sumter. He also asked Floyd specifically what he ought to do about a new problem that had just arisen. A South Carolina officer had demanded that Foster hand over the names of his workmen, so the state could enroll appropriate men into their militia units. Foster had said no, but Anderson was convinced the South Carolinians would grow more insistent.

He did receive a reply on this matter. He was ordered to turn any workmen over to the state authorities if he was satisfied they were properly enrolled. He was also told, incidentally, not to lower the height of the two sand dunes — the ones that would have allowed sharpshooters access to Moultrie's interior. Washington mistakenly believed that the dunes were private property and had houses on them, and, besides, they said, if Anderson leveled the dunes, he could thereby "betray distrust, and prematurely bring on a collision." Washington reminded Anderson, as if he were too dense to have noticed, the "present excited state" in Charleston "demands the coolest and wisest judgment."[32]

The administration's reaction to rising tensions was to *avoid* action. Anderson, desperate to prevent a collision, and far more privy to the mood in Charleston than was Washington, considered such inactivity the most dangerous stance. On December 1 he sent a third note. He said that "things look more gloomy" than they had three days earlier. Captain Seymour had just come back from Charleston and told him that the excitement there was explosive.[33] Apparently, the city was still stirred up by those rumors that supplies and reinforcements were being sent, despite the efforts of Huger and the *Courier* to calm things. Some men had told Seymour that "anything that indicates a determination on the part of the General Government to act with an unusual degree of vigor in putting these works in a better state of defense will be regarded as an act of aggression." If Charleston sensed any change, the militia would instantly attack Fort Moultrie.

Anderson himself had just had a visit with two Charlestonians — presumably one of whom was Henry Gourdin — and they told him that as soon as South Carolina seceded (when their Convention met on December 17), the state would demand the forts in their harbor, and would assault them if they were not handed over. As an aside, the major said in this report that some female friends of his officers' wives had been urging them to leave Sullivan's Island; he considered this another portentous sign. Crawford reported to him that a friend had told him that the garrison should expect an attack within two weeks.

The government did finally accept one of Anderson's suggestions: his notion about sending workmen to Castle Pinckney. Anderson was so anxious to put this plan into action that he sent one of his own meager handful of officers, Lieutenant Jeff Davis, to supervise the operations. By December 3 Davis had thirty laborers and four mechanics there, along with Pinckney's regular ordnance sergeant. This small force might be enough, especially if trained and armed.

Davis's departure strapped them at Moultrie, where all the officers were already performing extended duties. On one occasion Captain Seymour's wife, Louisa, and Mary Doubleday stood watch so that their husbands could get some rest.[34] Foster pleaded with his superiors to provide him another engineer right away so that Davis could return to Moultrie to share the burden. On December 10 Lieutenant Richard Kidder Meade arrived. Meade was twenty-five years old, strikingly handsome, and intelligent. Unlike the other federal officers under Anderson's and Foster's commands, Meade was a *true* Southerner, a product of an old family of Petersburg, Virginia. At that moment, his father, a prominent Democrat, was serving as James Buchanan's minister to Brazil, but Lincoln's recent election would cause the senior Meade to resign his post. During the coming crisis poor Lieutenant Meade would find himself whipped to and fro by conflicting pressures.[35]

Meade immediately went to Castle Pinckney, relieved Davis, and pushed his workers to finish repairing the fort. He discovered that he had insufficient lumber on hand to complete all the tasks, and that the merchant in town who had been selling lumber to them now refused to send him any more, but at least he was able to fix the main gate.[36] There was less he could do about training the workmen. At the very least, they would need to be armed with muskets, and none were available there. He told this to Foster, and the captain began thinking more seriously of acquiring some guns for them. He'd heard growing whispers of a coming attack.

A potentially frightening part of Anderson's December 1 report was a note that Captain Seymour had recently been warned that South Carolina was about to place an artillery battery on Sullivan's Island, somewhere beyond Fort Moultrie. The purpose of these guns would be to prevent Anderson from receiving additional supplies or men, but the guns might also be turned to fire upon Moultrie. Anderson personally did not take very seriously the rumors about these unseen guns. Others were less sanguine.

On December 11 the redoubtable Mary Doubleday wrote her sister. "A crisis is very near," she reported. "Within a few days, we hear — and from so many sources we cannot doubt it — that the Charlestonians are erecting two batteries." One, she said, would be at Mount Pleasant, a tiny village along the harbor's edge, just west of Sullivan's Island; the other beyond Fort Moultrie, somewhere past the Moultrie House. Her husband, Captain Abner Doubleday, also became convinced that South Carolina was preparing to threaten them with artillery. "In the first week of December," he would later recall, "we learned that cannon had been secretly sent to the northern extremity of the island." He added that "two thousand of the best riflemen in the State were engaged" to assault Fort Moultrie, "to shoot us down the moment we attempted to man our guns."[37] A remarkable scenario, if true. Unfortunately for high drama, no one else on either side of the crisis confirms the Doubledays' feverish imaginings. Nor was the rumor even plausible. South Carolina's authorities did not have such artillery readily available, except for a few guns at The Citadel in Charleston, and the guns were still at that military school a month later. Nor did Charleston at that moment contain a hundred well-armed sharpshooters, to say nothing of two thousand. Those it did have were far from well-disciplined. Captain Doubleday was correct about one thing: An assault could be expected, and fairly soon, but South Carolina was not prepared. As yet.

By early December, Anderson was not quite as panicky as the Doubledays, but he was uneasy. He pressed his superiors in Washington more firmly for a decision about what course they were going to take. If they decided to surrender the forts, they should tell him right away. If they wanted to keep the forts, he again begged them to send reinforcements, or at least a fleet of some kind—to prevent any movement of Carolina militiamen about the harbor, with the resulting loss of Castle Pinckney and Fort Sumter. But he did offer Washington a warning, in an uncharacteristic expression of his own analysis of broader political matters. If they took either course he suggested, their actions might "cause some of the doubting States to join South Carolina." As for himself, he said, "I shall go steadily on, preparing for the worst, trusting hopefully in the God of Battles to guard and guide me in my course."[38]

The matter now lay in uncertain and wary hands in the nation's capital.

CHAPTER FIVE

Twilight of the Old Union

Washington was in disarray. Laborers worked unenergetically on several building projects. The Washington Monument was only partly erected, its truncated form ugly against the skyline. Up the hill, the Capitol symbolized the tectonic pressures within the nation's politics. Its dome had been removed, but a new one had not yet been put in place. Scaffolding leaned against the structure. Around it, strewn upon the grass, lay a clutter of building materials and workmen's sheds. The statue of Armed Freedom, intended to top the new dome, stood, slightly askew, near piles of wood and coal, as unimposing as the United States Army.

The political mood in the city had come to stink as badly as the noxious open canal that cut through the heart of town. When James Buchanan had entered the White House in 1857 social events seemed quite jovial, but the city's social fabric had frayed beyond repair. Politics, often mean-spirited, sank to appalling nastiness as the two main political parties held their conventions. In the summer of 1860, after the Democrats split into two sectional wings — one backing Stephen Douglas, the other, John C. Breckinridge — the rhetoric grew rancid.

America had never been homogeneous. Its racial and religious and class divisions were palpable, and often held an undertone of violence. Distinctions had always existed between immigrants and those who felt superior because of their nativity. The nation's regional conflicts were far more complex than a simple rivalry between an abstract North and South. Flatlanders felt alienated from those who dwelled in the hills, New Englanders from Midwesterners, Easterners from Far Westerners, city residents from country folk.

The politics of 1860 tended to hide, if not obliterate, all these rivalries, resentments, and hostilities. It was easier to shriek about "North" and "South" than discuss more ambiguous issues. Politicians might be vapid individuals uncomfortable with subtleties, but most were clever fellows who simplified their rhetoric to persuade the credulous. A few of them, of course, were true believers. By the winter of 1860 the nation's capital had become a gumbo of all of these types. Debates were rancorous, posturing was the norm. Reasonable discussion leading to solutions became, at best, unlikely.

At the center of all this nastiness was the unfortunate president, the courteous and diplomatic James Buchanan, whose destiny was to preside over the last moments of an America that was about to disappear.

In 1860, when most people spoke of the "Union," they meant a relatively loose confederation of sovereign states. The Civil War was about to alter that concept. Another notion it would make passé was the idea that the presidency had virtually no real power. Up to this moment, a president like Andrew Jackson might veto legislation and strike dramatic poses, or one might rattle sabers like Monroe, or even drag the country into war like Polk, but the traditional interpretation of the Constitution—particularly among Democrats like Buchanan—was that Congress, not the presidency, was responsible for setting domestic policy. Only it could initiate and pass economic legislation, and since governmental actions tended to cost money, logic dictated that power lay up on The Hill, not in the White House. But at this moment this Congress contained too much flammable emotion, combined with far too many gasbags, to produce reasoned discussion—especially when an answer had to be arrived at quickly before secessionists had had a chance to solidify their position. Here, in essence, was Buchanan's dilemma. His philosophy of government could not stand erect in the cyclone winds of 1860. He also had another problem, not one simply a matter of constitutional interpretation; it involved his personality, the very man he was.

"Old Buck," as some affectionately called him, was a kind man, firmly religious, decent, and extraordinarily courteous. Out of respect for republican values, he maintained a relatively simple lifestyle. He liked to stroll most days for an hour or so along Pennsylvania Avenue, chatting with friends and nodding to acquaintances along the way. On Saturdays, when the Marine Band offered free performances on the lawn around the Executive Mansion, he would wander out and amiably shake hands and brush shoulders with the audience. He listened politely to almost everyone, his high white collar pressed rigidly against his jaw, his head cocked a bit to the side. A tall, ruddy-faced, silver-haired, distinguished-looking old gentleman, he tended to nod occasional encouragement to those who spoke to him, as they rattled on about some pet idea. Those who did not know him well often assumed that the nodding meant agreement, while Old Buck was merely being a good fellow who would consider it rude to confront a guest with open opposition. He had been in government all his adult life, and had found geniality a successful approach. His manner had usually held him in good stead during the diplomatic phases of his career, including a tour as minister to Russia, then, later, to Great Britain. He was the first important American to suggest that the United States might acquire Alaska from Russia, and he was able to wheedle concessions from China at a time when France and Great Britain considered military force the only way to deal with the Manchus. In fact, Buchanan was better suited temperamentally for international diplomacy, a profession wherein people understood that amiability did not mean friendship, where ambiguity, not decisiveness, is expected. Being president, particularly at this time, unfortunately, required a rougher nature than his.

Buchanan was not quite as irresolute as he seemed, as most of his contemporary critics imagined. It is true that during this crisis he changed his basic stance several times, but he had no clear precedents to draw from. Some advisers pointed to 1832, when South Carolina had rejected a tariff and refused to allow inside the state the collection of Federal duties. President Jackson had sent a small military force to Charleston Harbor and threatened to lead a larger force himself. But the cases were really quite dissimilar. In 1832 South Carolina had been objecting to a specific law, not the very structure of the Union, and she had been acting alone. In 1860 South Carolina might conceivably acquire no less than fourteen allies — the other slave states — especially if the president or Congress played the game clumsily.

Buchanan may have been unsure about the best way to proceed, but his uncertainty was not inane. Some situations require audacity or firmness, others demand delicacy and tact, a willingness to overlook insult and braggadocio. A wise leader keeps his eyes focused on the ultimate goal. In Old Buck's case his personality and training led him to avoid doing anything that might lead to war, and in this situation, he believed, any military action would only make things worse. The Border States would likely throw their lot with their Deep South brethren. And if Maryland and Virginia went out, Washington City, caught between them, would be lost. If Kentucky and Missouri joined the Deep South, commerce along the Ohio and Mississippi Rivers would be threatened. Also, banking institutions in New York and Philadelphia, which were closely tied to the Southern economies, might teeter and fail. Disasters would pile upon disasters.

War, Buchanan was also convinced, would accomplish no positive result. If everyone would remain calm, the crisis should pass — perhaps soon, if Congress could discover some legislative mechanism to appease Southerners anxious about Lincoln's election. The important thing was to maintain lines of communication and to search for the best means of reconciliation with the South. He considered the concept of secession absurd — and, more important, unconstitutional. Yet, simultaneously, from a constitutional point of view South Carolina's politicians seemed only to be expressing their opinions, and the Constitution guaranteed them the rights of free assembly and free speech. Besides, Congress had never passed a statute defining state insurrection, nor was there now a law on the books permitting a president to coerce a state.

Buchanan promised, in his annual Message to Congress in December, that he intended to maintain all the "property" owned by the federal government—and this would have included the forts in Charleston Harbor—and he said that he would continue to enforce the laws. How he would do these things remained murky. The difference between, say, collecting federal revenues in Charleston Harbor and the "coercion" of South Carolina was a distinction he never defined. He told Congress that this problem was really theirs, that they should pursue whatever legislation they considered necessary.

Buchanan, moreover, staggered into the crisis leading a system divided in new and more ominous ways. Of the fifteen hundred clerks working for the government, many felt a stronger allegiance to their home states than to Washington. Some began to wear blue cockades on their coats, the same symbol of secession young men were wearing in Charleston. Most of the government's departments, therefore, contained men, dealing each day with confidential materials, whose loyalty was at best dubious. Both the army and navy were riddled with those who would be traitorous if it came to war. For example, every message Major Anderson wrote to Washington was directed first to Adjutant General Samuel Cooper. In March 1861 Cooper would resign and join the Confederacy. The army's quartermaster general, Joseph E. Johnston, would soon become one of the Confederacy's best generals. The acting head of the Surgeon General's office had been a brother-in-law of Senator Jefferson Davis. The chief of the Washington Navy Yard and most of his subordinates were openly disloyal. The matter of allegiance even infected Buchanan's cabinet, a group of men whose advice he often sought.

The cabinet's most prominent member was Secretary of State Lewis Cass. He was born during the Revolution, and had been something of a war hero during the War of 1812. He was secretary of war under Jackson, where he supervised both the Black Hawk and Seminole Wars, as well as Jackson's venture against South Carolina in 1832–33. He had been a senator, and in 1848 the Democratic nominee for the White House. He possessed, therefore, a remarkably distinguished record. But age had worn him down. During most of that autumn he was quite ill, and not in

Washington. Buchanan did not much miss him. Cass was a pleasant enough fellow, but Old Buck tended to find him annoyingly windy and pontifical. During Cass's absences, the State Department was run by his assistant, William Henry Trescot, a charming South Carolina planter, whose family by coincidence also owned a cottage about a hundred yards or so from Fort Moultrie.

Trescot had had little experience in either diplomacy or government when Buchanan chose him as assistant secretary of state in June 1860, apparently because Trescot had once authored a book on diplomatic history.[1] Trescot's main role in the drama of 1860 derived from the fact that he was the highest-ranking South Carolinian in Buchanan's government. As the crisis developed Trescot found himself called upon by both sides to act as intermediary—particularly during the month between Lincoln's election and early December when Congress came back into session. Although he scurried about the city, trying desperately to act as peacemaker, he was inevitably drawn into the orbit of the three Southerners in Buchanan's cabinet: Howell Cobb, Jacob Thompson, and John Floyd.

Cobb, secretary of the treasury, was the best known of the three. He was an intelligent, jolly fat man, given to fine jokes and high spirits. Buchanan liked him very much; almost everyone did. An influential Georgian, Cobb had served as Speaker of the House, and had at one point hoped he might be the 1860 Democratic nominee. He was easily one of the most influential men in the South. He owned a thousand slaves but had never been a devout secessionist. After Lincoln's election he held out for a month, but the pressure on him from other Southerners grew too great and he became the first to resign from the cabinet.

Jacob Thompson, of Mississippi, Buchanan's secretary of the interior, was not an easy person to decipher. He was quiet, studious, and hard-bitten. He kept his opinions to himself. Buchanan leaned on him for advice. (During the Civil War, as an agent of the Confederacy, he would work in Canada, developing plots to swoop across the border and free Southern prisoners or to burn Northern cities like New York, activities requiring a man chary about revealing himself.) Trescot would admit that Thompson's "general views I never did understand clearly."[2]

John Floyd, secretary of war, was in a critical position as the crisis developed. He had been governor of Virginia and had a typical Border State mentality — he sympathized with the South but opposed secession. Both sides found him untrustworthy, and both were correct. Floyd's War Department in 1860 was a tiny and somnolent institution, divided into eight bureaus, including the Adjutant General's Office, the quartermaster, the paymaster, and so on. Seven of its eight bureau chiefs had been in the army since the War of 1812, and even prior to that. These eight men never met as a general staff; each merely ran his own bailiwick. General Joseph G. Totten, head of the engineers, was still on top of his game, though others were less so. In Washington the *entire* War Department, all eight bureaus, had only ninety-three employees. They arrived each morning about eight-thirty, shuffled a few papers, then left by midafternoon.[3] Floyd's job was to administer this tiny kingdom. By tradition Congress determined the size of the army and regulated its rules. The president, as commander-in-chief, could use it — more or less as he saw fit — within certain policy guidelines laid down by Congress. As to the secretary of war, army regulations gave him no power over military discipline or promotions. He was responsible only for "providing for" the army — that is, supervising its finances and accounts, seeing that it was properly supplied. His tasks were solely administrative. Properly done, they required a methodical personality, a person with clear, crisp methods — qualities that Floyd wholly lacked.

During his gubernatorial years in Virginia Floyd had been involved in some complicated state banking scandals where he possibly took kickbacks, though it seems more likely that he simply was combining his several troublesome qualities. He was always frivolous about details and casual about public monies. He considered himself a vigorous man of action, bold in both private and public ventures, and he frequently refused to listen to advice. He was, essentially, a ninny. Under his hand the nation's War Department drifted, wafting a spreading odor of corruption and inefficiency. Senator Jefferson Davis, himself recently an outstanding secretary of war, grew restive at the rumors. As chairman of the Senate's military committee, Davis felt it was his responsibility to keep an eye on the department. Although a House committee was unable to find anything precisely dishonest, it did conclude that Floyd had been doing a shoddy job, and it spanked him with a censure vote of no confidence. He might have resigned, but he stayed in his position, and brooded. He blamed Jefferson Davis for his humiliation. Worse was to come.

In 1858 Floyd had begun an arrangement with a businessman named William Russell, whose business included carrying supplies to the army's western forts. Russell played the stock market — and overextended himself. In 1857 his bubble burst and he came to Floyd and asked for succor. The scatterbrained secretary, concerned that if Russell went under the army would have trouble supplying its isolated garrisons, agreed to a scheme to keep Russell afloat. Floyd would sign drafts paying for Russell's transport work in advance. Floyd's drafts were backed by the credit of the United States, so were virtually equivalent to money. Russell could take them to a bank as collateral to borrow cash. With these loans, William Russell had enough money to pay off his most immediate debts. But the ease of all this induced him to recklessness. He spent the money quickly, then went to Floyd for more. The process continued. Floyd was such a poor administrator that he kept no accurate and systematic records of these transactions. Senator Judah P. Benjamin of Louisiana, a canny individual, somehow got wind of what was happening and went to Floyd to press him to cease his silliness. Even Buchanan heard something about it and ordered him to stop. Floyd promised both men the same: yes, absolutely, he would do it no more. Then he'd sign another draft. All of this unraveled late in 1860, just as the crisis in Charleston Harbor was coming to a head.

On December 22 Buchanan learned of the entire affair. He was stunned. Floyd's time in the administration was dwindling to a close. Buchanan asked his vice president, John Breckinridge, one of Floyd's many relatives, to persuade the secretary of war to resign. Floyd whined and grumbled, and spoke about his "honor," but Breckinridge privately pressed him, and Floyd finally said yes. Breckinridge told this to Buchanan, and the president felt much relief. He expected to receive Floyd's resignation at any moment. The Virginian, however, had his own definitions of such things as speed, and honor. Days passed, critical days. He continued to come to crucial cabinet meetings, where everyone in the room knew the truth and was impatient to see him depart. He did not — and diplomatic Old Buck did not know how to fire him.[4]

Floyd's various problems during the fall of 1860 distracted him and kept him from focusing on the nation's most immediate military problem, the garrison at Fort Moultrie. Throughout November he waffled, while politics in Washington and tensions in Charleston bumped back and forth into each other.

On November 9, three days after Lincoln's election, Buchanan held a cabinet meeting. He had just received word about the incident at the arsenal in Charleston. The president was no fool. He was relatively confident that war was not in the offing, but he was concerned that hot-blooded Carolinians might do something that could throw them all into a stew. How about the garrison at Moultrie? he asked his cabinet. Should it be ordered to move to safer quarters at Fort Sumter? They discussed it. In the end Buchanan decided that moving the garrison now might be seen as a provocative act, and therefore must be avoided. But Lieutenant Colonel Gardner must be replaced; Major Anderson should take over down there.[5]

During the next few weeks both Floyd and Buchanan danced to and fro as stresses mounted. Trescot and Cobb persuaded Floyd that sending reinforcements would be unwise — that to do so would be considered improper behavior in a Southern gentleman. From the time of this conversation Floyd's tone became strident concerning Southern rights. Up to then he had been opposed to secession; he now gradually became a fire-eater. Perhaps, with the prospect of national humiliation staring him in the face over the Russell scandal, he was retreating to his regional base.

Buchanan was also facing new pressures. Secretary of State Cass was back in town, though suffering moments of dizziness. Although physically weak, Cass, an old soldier, considered it important to reinforce Anderson. He was joined in this belief by Buchanan's dour attorney general, Jeremiah Sullivan Black. The two went to see the president to try and change his mind. They warned him that a Charleston mob might attack Moultrie at any moment, slaughtering everyone inside. Buchanan grew rattled at that thought. He decided they were right, and that reinforcements must be sent immediately. He sent a messenger to get Floyd. A few minutes later the secretary of war arrived, and Buchanan advised him of this latest change of plans. Floyd was flabbergasted. He and Buchanan then had, as Trescot later described it, "a very animated discussion." Floyd tried various arguments to talk the president out of this move, but Buchanan was determined. Finally, Floyd said the president should at least wait until General Scott arrived in town from New York. On the surface this ploy was absurd—neither Floyd nor Buchanan liked Scott or respected him—but it worked. Buchanan said he would await the old general. Floyd rushed out into the night and tracked down Trescot. The secretary was "much excited," Trescot would recall. He swore to Trescot that he would chop off his hand before he would sign an order to reinforce Anderson. The South Carolinian offered a possible solution. Suppose, he said, he himself wired Governor Gist and asked him to write a letter promising that the forts would be safe—so long as Washington sent no reinforcements? Floyd agreed it sounded like a good idea. And so it came to pass.

When Buchanan read Governor Gist's message, it satisfied him that the worries of Cass and Black were misplaced. He also received a letter from South Carolina's most famous secessionist, Robert Barnwell Rhett, probably reacting to a request from Trescot, warning the president that sending reinforcements would cause the very thing he was scrambling to avoid. "If you send any more troops into Charleston Bay," the Carolinian radical warned, "it will be bloody."[6]

As November ended, Washington was trapped in stasis. The administration was becoming as divided as the nation. The days were getting shorter, the night air colder. At the capital city's train station you could hear the shouts of coachmen promising cheaper fares, the cracks of their whips, the clatter of wheels and the clomping of horses's hooves plodding down the dirt avenues. And everywhere the moist splat of tobacco juice being spat. Congress would open its session on December 3, and as that date approached representatives straggled into town, carrying in their luggage an inordinate amount of anger and determination.

Congress opened its session, listened to a minister pray for peace and guidance, and heard the reading of Buchanan's Message. Congress seemed little affected by either admonition. The president's studied prose about the "property rights" of the federal government put the conflict between secessionists and the federal forts into the world of lawyer's jargon. This was hardly an accident. Buchanan had wanted to squeeze all the emotional juice from the issue, to reduce it to a dry abstraction. The lawyers and politicians of Congress, he hoped, could then arrive at some solution.

In fact, some of them did try. During the next few weeks the House formed a "Committee of 33" and the Senate a "Committee of 13" to see if they could work something out. Both groups considered a variety of proposals. Discussions droned on into the next year. During the first days of March, literally hours before Lincoln's inauguration, they unenthusiastically voted on a few possible compromises. It was far too late. Emotions by then had made the sides too unmovable. It is not clear that any form of compromise was ever possible, or that if something had been passed by Congress it would have prevented the coming war. The most talked-of solution involved a package of laws and constitutional amendments called the Crittenden Compromise, after Senator John J. Crittenden of Kentucky, its most respected supporter, which would have constitutionally guaranteed the safety of slavery where it already existed, and would have broadened its potential domain by extending the Missouri Compromise Line, so that any territories below it could become slave states. To some, this compromise package might seem reasonable, assuming one was willing to accept the possibility that American slavery might get bigger — especially in the likely event that the United States would expand southward. Had the compromise been speedily passed, however — and rapidity was certainly unlikely — it yet would have been too late to prevent the secession of several states, and any attempt to deal firmly with these wayward sisters would have led to the secession of others.

All of this, however, was a moot question, because Abraham Lincoln helped to squelch any compromise. As far as slavery was concerned, Lincoln's position was clear — he detested it. But he accepted the principle that each state had a constitutional right to decide whether it wanted the institution or not, and that the federal government had no right to dictate to a state what it must do about it. In December he wrote an old friend from Georgia: "Do the people of the South," he asked, "really entertain fears that a Republican administration would, *directly* or *indirectly*, interfere with their slaves? If they do, I wish to assure you, as once a friend, and still, I hope, not an enemy, that there is no cause for such fears. . . . You think slavery is *right* and ought to be extended; while we think it is *wrong* and ought to be restricted. That is the rub. It certainly is the only substantial difference between us."[7] Lincoln and his party, in other words, merely wanted to restrict the *growth* of slavery, but did not consider it their right to challenge slavery where it *existed*. He was, however, determined to prevent its expansion. That same month he wrote letters to two different congressmen about it. In one note Lincoln stated, "Entertain no proposition for a compromise in regard to the *extension* of slavery." In the other he wrote, "There is no possible compromise upon it. . . . On that point hold firm, as with a chain of steel." He used a fateful phrase. "The tug," he said, "has to come & better now than later." The tug was indeed coming, and it was coming in Charleston Harbor.[8]

As Congress tried in committee rooms to structure a compromise, many of its members, especially Southerners, preferred making bombastic speeches. The galleries often filled with admiring women. "We spend so much time in the Senate," one woman recalled, "that many of the ladies take their sewing or crocheting, and all of us who are not absolutely spiritual provide ourselves with a lunch." "If we must secede," she added with a flourish, "let us do so becomingly."[9] Congressmen were hardly unaware of the presence of so many appreciative ladies, and may have played a bit to the audience. On the last day of December the rotund Senator Judah P. Benjamin of Louisiana provided the observers with such a stirring secessionist peroration that they broke into loud applause. On a motion from the floor the galleries were cleared — "a circumstance," *Frank Leslie's Illustrated Newspaper* noted, "that had not occurred for years."[10]

Down at President's Park James Buchanan was not feeling so ebullient. The drumbeat of secession battered at him. Years after the war, Wylie Crawford was chatting with Jeremiah Black, Buchanan's attorney general, about those days. The subject of Judge Andrew Gordon Magrath came up, of how Magrath had risen in court the day after Lincoln's election and flung his robes aside. Black told Crawford that when Buchanan heard about it he was quite shaken, that it disturbed him more than almost any other event.[11]

The old president wished to seem calm and in control, but his tensions and exhaustion peeped through at times. He grew even more tentative than usual, and showed uncharacteristic waspishness. Stories were bruited about that he was cracking under the strain, exaggerated tales his enemies loved to hear. After the war the wife of a Southern congressman wrote a venomous little book about those days, in which she claimed dubiously that Lewis Cass, secretary of state, said that "the President is pale with fear. He divides his time between praying and crying."[12]

Old Buck was not quite that strung out, but he was certainly anxious about the trend of events. During the first half of December he lost two cabinet members, Howell Cobb and Lewis Cass. Cobb departed amicably when it became obvious Georgia would soon secede, and Cass left in a huff when Buchanan refused to send reinforcements to Charleston Harbor. Old Buck missed Cobb's pleasant company, but considered Cass no loss.

Buchanan stewed about Anderson's situation at Fort Moultrie. The rumors floating up from Charleston about the prospect of violence worried him. Even Eba Anderson got involved. Early in December she arose from her sickbed in New York and journeyed to Washington where she confronted the president. He would later describe their meeting as "painful." She was, she told him, quite nervous about her husband's situation at Fort Moultrie; she feared he might be attacked at any moment by a wild mob.

What Buchanan said to Eba is unknown, but he brought up the encounter during a discussion he had on December 8 with a delegation of South Carolina congressmen, in town that week for the opening of Congress. Buchanan told them he was concerned about some sort of mob action against Fort Moultrie and mentioned his meeting with Eba. The Carolinians, knowing that their days in Washington were drawing to a close, wanted to make sure that the status of the three federal forts in the Charleston Harbor remained unchanged. Within days, South Carolina would leave the Union, they informed Buchanan, and when she did, she would send commissioners to Washington to arrange the transfer of the forts to the state. The president need not worry about Charleston mobs, they said, but he better understand that sending reinforcements would rouse South Carolina to action. They did not mention, however, the flurry of excitement in Charleston on November 28, when a mere rumor of reinforcements had almost led to an explosion. This incident had occurred just before these five congressmen departed for Washington. Memories of that event must have still lingered, but it would have been impolitic to mention it.

Nor was Buchanan entirely candid with them. He did not tell them that he had no intention of turning over the forts. As far as he was concerned, he was not constitutionally empowered to do so; only Congress could so act. He did not emphasize this point just now. In Buchanan's mind, familiar with diplomatic double-talk, he was being quite clever. He had forced the representatives to guarantee that there would be no popular violence against Anderson's garrison. And he had only promised not to send reinforcements *immediately*, leaving himself open, he believed, to sending them in the future, if he considered it necessary.

The next day, when Buchanan met again with them, they handed him their written understanding of what had been said. Buck read it carefully and made only one objection. They had written that there would be no assault on the forts "provided" that there were no changes in the forts' status. The president told them he did not approve of that word since it seemed to bind his hands. They, less sophisticated than he in diplomatic parlance, struck the word out. They tried hard to get some clear promise from him about the forts; then, unable to get one, they rose to leave. As they made their good-byes, Buchanan said amiably that this arrangement was essentially "a matter of honor between gentlemen," that written documents were unnecessary. "We understand each other," he said.[13] Perhaps they did; perhaps not.

Remarkably, Buchanan was unaware, while speaking to the delegation of Carolinians, that his government had just sent a man named Major Don Carlos Buell to Charleston on a mission that would alter forever any "agreement" the president may have made.

At Fort Moultrie Robert Anderson, writing edgy letters to headquarters, pleading for assistance — and advice — remained uncertain about his role. He continued to receive no assistance from Washington, and the little advice he received consisted of cautionary warnings against stirring up hornets. Around the major's head the buzz of secession grew louder.

CHAPTER SIX

Commanders and Chiefs

O n December 7, Don Carlos Buell, one of a handful of officers connected to the Adjutant General's Office, visited Secretary Floyd and was ordered to undertake a delicate assignment. He was to review the situation at Charleston's forts, and to give Major Anderson a message. The content of this message was so delicate that the secretary did not wish to put it in writing. Buell was to memorize it, then verbally pass it on to Anderson. (Presumably, Floyd recognized the porous condition of the government's private correspondence during recent weeks.) Buell was to remind Anderson to avoid confrontations. If one occurred, however, Anderson was ordered to hold the federal position in the harbor. Buell later recalled that he was supposed to tell Anderson that "The duty of maintaining defensively the authority of the Government was distinctly affirmed."[1] This sentence is awkward, but it seemed to imply that Buchanan's administration expected Anderson to do *whatever was necessary* to maintain the federal presence there.

Buell arrived in Charleston two days later, and had to spend the night at a hotel. During his few hours in the city he heard much talk about grabbing the federal forts, words that persuaded him that South Carolina's authorities would soon find themselves unable to prevent mob action.[2] The next day he made a quick tour of all three forts and came away convinced of the obvious: Moultrie by itself was much too vulnerable to count on, but Fort Sumter was potentially almost invulnerable. Having made his tour about the harbor's installations, Buell relayed Floyd's message to Anderson. No doubt the two majors chatted about Anderson's precarious status.

The following morning, as Buell prepared to leave, he admitted to Anderson, "You ought to have written evidence of these instructions."[3] A very precise and cautious man, Buell understood how tenuous Anderson's situation was, and also how verbal instructions had a habit of being misconstrued — or, worse, later denied by Washington. He therefore put Secretary Floyd's orders, for the first time, into writing, and he made a copy of them to take back to Washington. He opened this written "memorandum" with a reminder of how much the secretary wished to avoid a "collision" in Charleston. Floyd wanted Anderson to know that the government had purposely not sent reinforcements or "taken any measures which might add to the present excited state of the public mind." Floyd was confident — unlike Buell — that South Carolina's authorities could restrain acts of popular violence, but if not, if any of the forts was attacked, or if Anderson had "*tangible evidence of a design to proceed to a hostile act,*" then — and only then — he could move the garrison to any one of the three forts he chose. And if he *were* actually attacked, the secretary expected him "to defend yourself to the last extremity."[4] Buell said one more thing to Anderson as he handed him the memorandum: "This is all I am authorized to say to you, but my personal advice is, that you do not allow the opportunity [of moving to Fort Sumter] to escape you."[5]

Buell departed for Washington. There, he verbally reported to Floyd on his trip, and handed over his copy of the memorandum. At some point during the next few days Floyd actually glanced at it, then scrawled across it, "This is in conformity to my instructions to Major Buell," and signed his name. Did Floyd recognize that he had, in essence, just authorized Anderson to move to Fort Sumter? There is no way of knowing, but Floyd was notoriously casual about details, so it seems plausible that, after speaking with Buell with half an ear, he merely signed the document. He probably never read it, certainly not with any care.

Floyd did show Buchanan the memorandum. The president read it, but he certainly did not fully understand its implications, the possibility that Anderson might move. The only part of the note Buchanan commented on was that, if it came to battle, Major Anderson was being ordered to fight "to the last extremity." Old Buck's cautious instincts made him urge Floyd to moderate the meaning. The secretary therefore wrote Anderson that, if his garrison was "invested or attacked by a force so superior that resistance would, in your judgment, be a useless waste of life, it will be your duty to yield to necessity, and make the best terms in your power." To surrender under those circumstances would "be the conduct of an honorable, brave, and humane officer, and you will be fully justified in such action." Floyd also told the major that he was not to share this message with anyone, even his own officers, unless absolutely necessary. Anderson received this message on December 23, two days before Christmas.[6]

At Fort Moultrie, during the days after Buell's visit, the effects of the crisis began to wear the tiny garrison to a nub. Given the cranky mood in Charleston, Anderson assumed a mob might arrive on any night. Even if no mob appeared, it seemed likely that the state's militia would assault them, and soon. The small size of the garrison meant that it was stretched far too thin. With only the few men he did have, he had to scramble simply to man the walls of Fort Moultrie.

He grew desperate. Foster, he thought, was wasting time. The engineer was designing projects for Moultrie that would have been admirable had the situation been different, but were too time-consuming for Major Anderson's patience. He also was not pleased when Foster actually broke down the fort's walls in two places to build what Anderson considered overly ambitious brick bump-outs when temporary wooden structures might have been sufficient. Unfortunately for the major, according to U.S. Army regulations he had no direct power over Foster, and he found this, at best, difficult. He wrote Washington in obvious frustration. Although Captain Foster was "generally disposed to accede to the suggestions I have ventured to make," and while he felt no "unkind spirit" toward the engineer, "I must confess that I think where an officer is placed in as delicate a position as the one I occupy that he should have the entire control over all persons connected in any way with the work entrusted to him. Responsibility and power to control ought to go together."[7] This issue was never entirely resolved. It would remain a pebble in both officers' shoes throughout the crisis.

Anderson went to Charleston in early December and had a conference with Mayor Macbeth and other notables. They tried to assure him they would be able to prevent mob violence, but they also said blatantly that all three forts "*must be theirs* after secession." He highlighted this phrase in a letter to Washington to show his superiors the determined, and therefore dangerous, mood in Charleston.[8] Despite the confident assurances of the city fathers, he was convinced the South Carolinians were about to attempt some sort of foray. If it came to that, he knew, he must fight, and when he did, it would trigger a civil war.

He was ready to try anything honorable to avoid that outcome if he could. "I think an appeal to arms and to brute force," he wrote his friend Robert Gourdin, "is unbecoming the age in which we live. Would to God that the time had come when there should be no war, and that religion and peace should reign throughout the world."[9] Unlike Floyd and Buchanan, Anderson had concluded that the arrival of more troops, if done immediately—and, more important, quietly—would be more likely to maintain peace than doing nothing. So long as federal soldiers were at Moultrie, they would seem a symbol of "coercion" to secessionists, and therefore unacceptable. He was convinced that Washington could not have it both ways: maintaining a presence in the harbor and keeping it small.

One day in December, two laborers at Fort Sumter were killed when a cannon they were mounting plunged down upon them. Dr. Crawford, responsible for tending to Foster's workers, went out the next day. While there he encountered several South Carolina militia officers checking on the fort. They were so audacious they then crossed over to Moultrie and tried unsuccessfully to inspect it as well.[10] A few days later the *Mercury* published a detailed article on Fort Sumter, along with a large drawing of it, and in the middle of its description the newspaper noted in passing that the fort was so strong, whoever held it could "defy any attack by a fleet of vessels." Furthermore, the *Mercury* implied that taking Sumter would be relatively easy, because "an entrance may, at the present state of construction, be easily made." An assault force, it was stated, could put scaling ladders against the walls and slip into the wide-open embrasures on the second floor.[11]

Anderson informed Washington about all this interest. "I hear," he wrote his superiors, "that the attention of the South Carolinians appears to be turned more toward Fort Sumter than it was, and it is deemed probable that their first act will be to take possession of that work." The problem, he said, was that Fort Sumter was simply too easy a target—"a tempting prize," he called it—and he considered that fact dangerous to his garrison, and potentially disastrous to America. He respectfully suggested that the government destroy all the ammunition at nearby fortifications, like Fort Pulaski in Georgia, to keep it out of the hands of impatient Carolinians. "Anything that can be done," he wrote, "which will cause delay in their attack will give time for deliberation and negotiation, and may, by God's blessing, save the shedding of blood."[12] Anderson, who had seen too much of war, was now trying to save the nation from a holocaust.

Despite their differences over the pace of engineering work, Captain Foster, like Anderson, was haunted by his own growing concern for Fort Sumter and Castle Pinckney, which he, like Anderson, considered part of his responsibility. Foster had one advantage—he could arm his "loyal" workers, assuming he could pick any out. Foster, apparently acting independently of Anderson but keeping him informed, wrote Washington on December 2, asking that he be permitted to withdraw a hundred muskets and ammunition from the arsenal in Charleston. He intended to arm loyal workers at both Sumter and Castle Pinckney, fifty at each, he said. The next day the foreman of the workers at Sumter spoke to his men to find out if some would be willing to fight to protect the fort. Most said no. They might be willing, they said, to stand up against a mob, but they were afraid of trying to hold off well-armed Carolina militiamen. Foster had purposely sent his most reliable men to Castle Pinckney, but he was not even sure of them. After he learned of the foreman's failure to find enough stalwart fighters at Sumter, he thought better of his notion and wrote Washington that he considered it unwise — at this time — to arm his workers.[13]

Another week went by. Foster began to feel renewed confidence in the situations at Castle Pinckney and Sumter. Both Meade and Snyder were now keeping their fort gates closed to outsiders. The mood of the laboring crews, his two officers told him, had improved. The officers pressed him to give them guns, and he agreed to try.[14] The result was a flurry of flying feathers in Charleston and Washington.

At some point on December 17 Foster arrived at the arsenal, presumably passing through the gaze of the twenty militiamen assigned to keep an eye on the building. Foster asked Captain Humphreys, who had replaced Colonel Huger, for two muskets to arm the ordnance sergeants at Castle Pinckney and Fort Sumter. Humphreys, ever the bureaucrat, said he was not authorized to give him the two guns — but added, as an aside, that Foster could have *forty* of them.

Humphreys's rationale was simple, and deliciously wrapped in government red tape. Colonel Huger had not left behind a written document allowing the two ordnance sergeants to have muskets, so they could not have them, Humphreys was clear on that. But the October request for forty guns, he reminded Foster, *had* been officially approved in Washington, and that approval had never been rescinded. Everyone had forgotten about this but Humphreys, who now told Foster that the forty muskets Floyd had approved were still sitting here, neatly boxed, waiting to be picked up.

Foster, used to the labyrinthine nature of the army, took these forty muskets with him. No one attempted to stop him. He gave one to each of the ordnance sergeants, and stored the rest in the magazines at Castle Pinckney and Fort Sumter, half at each, intending that Meade and Snyder might use them to arm loyal

workmen, if such could be found.[15] The next day excited messages
rattled about.

In the morning the leader of South Carolina's militia, Major
General John Schnierle, arrived at the arsenal, all atwitter. He
told poor Humphreys that the removal of the muskets had caused
an uproar in the city, and that, according to the ordnance captain,
"some violent demonstration is certain unless the excitement can
be allayed." Besides, Schnierle said, Colonel Huger, before he left,
had promised Governor Gist that the arsenal would not turn over
any of its weaponry to the federal troops.

Humphreys was in a bind. He was clearly the sort of person
who liked things neat and orderly, who would hardly feel comfortable with the idea of mobs, to say nothing of the prospect that
he might have gotten his tail caught between conflicting orders.
Humphreys felt he had no choice. He looked right at Schnierle
and guaranteed that he would get the muskets back, by the following night at the latest. He immediately scribbled off a note to
Foster, telling the engineer of his predicament, and of the promise
he'd made Schnierle, then added, "I beg that you will return them
to me."[16]

That evening Foster went to talk to the major about all this.
Anderson, who had been constantly reminded by Washington to
avoid trouble, calmly suggested that Foster return the guns.

By now Foster had grown angry. He wrote a note to his superiors that night, one whose tone tumbled about with anger and
anxiety, defiance and caution. He said that he had no personal
knowledge of a violent mob reaction in Charleston, and, even if
there was, "I am not disposed to surrender these arms under a
threat of this kind." As he saw it, if the city hotheads would use this
as an excuse, some sort of confrontation was inevitable. He was
tired of knuckling under. On the other hand, he did not want the
responsibility for initiating a war, so, having gotten his grumpiness
off his chest, he said that he had agreed to meet the next day with
Humphreys and Schnierle; also, by the way, that he was bumping
the decision up to Washington. He closed this message with a sigh,
stating that if Congress did not act soon, a conflict here was "not
improbable." (It is interesting that Foster did not expect Buchanan
to do anything.)

The following morning, December 19, Foster conferred with Major General Schnierle and some other prominent Charlestonians. After the meeting he felt calmer. Foster saw virtually no evidence in the city of unruliness. The men at this meeting, furthermore, convinced him that their only motive was to prevent the possibility of mob action, not to threaten. He promised them that he would wire the Ordnance Office in Washington for a decision on the matter.

What the Ordnance Office would have done about the muskets became moot, because Secretary Floyd stepped in. The same day Foster had his meeting with Schnierle, someone in Charleston wired William Henry Trescot. Although the diminutive planter had resigned from the Department of State by this time, he had agreed to stay in the capital a while longer to expedite things because of his contacts with both sides. The evening air in Washington was crisp as Trescot rushed to Floyd's residence to find out what this rumor about forty muskets meant. The secretary was ill in bed, but when Trescot showed him the telegram Floyd grew agitated. He had not, he said, ordered any muskets moved from the arsenal. This was outrageous. They must be returned at once. Unfortunately he was too sick to rise from his confinement, so he asked Trescot to find Floyd's assistant at the War Department and get him to wire Captain Foster immediately, using Floyd's name. Trescot saw to it.

It was well after midnight in Charleston when two urgent wires from the War Department clacked into the telegraph office, one to Foster, the other to Anderson. Their tone was so strong that they were rushed to a revenue cutter, which sliced through the darkness to Sullivan's Island. Anderson and Foster were roused from their beds and handed the messages. The one to Foster told him that if he had taken any arms from the arsenal he was to "return them instantly." The one to Anderson simply informed him about the order to Foster. The officer of the revenue cutter waited for a reply. Foster wired Floyd, "I shall return them in obedience to your order." First thing the next day he did so. He also sent Floyd a longer message of explanation, adding that he took the secretary's telegram to mean that he was not expected to fight for either Fort Sumter or Castle Pinckney, that he was merely to keep the gates and shutters closed, and if these were knocked down by the South Carolinians, Foster's men inside should do nothing. If this conclusion was incorrect, he said, he hoped the government would provide him with clear instructions about what to do in an emergency.

As it turned out, General Scott and President Buchanan recently had been wrestling with that very question.

For weeks Winfield Scott, America's highest-ranking soldier, had been worrying about the situation in the South, but he was powerless to do anything unless he could get the ear of the president, and this was a problem. Scott and James Buchanan had long had cool relations, going back at least to the Mexican War. But as the election of 1860 approached, the general deigned to provide the president with some written advice. Lincoln's election seemed assured, Scott began in a long memorandum, and it would be followed up, he was sure, with the secession of one or more states. He was personally not opposed to the concept of secession, and said that perhaps the United States might easily divide into four separate confederacies, at least until this crisis had passed. But under the present circumstances, he went on, secession might be accompanied by attempts to take over certain Southern forts. He mentioned nine by name, scattered here and there. Six of them had no garrisons at all. The other three — including Fort Moultrie — were profoundly undermanned. Scott urged Buchanan to strengthen all nine forts. He did not specify how. The next day — probably after an inquiry from Washington — Scott sent a "Supplement," offering a few more specifics. He wrote that the army had five available companies it might use, a total of about 250 men.

The president, rightly, considered Scott's urgings absurd. Buchanan could certainly not realistically fortify six empty forts and three partially empty ones with such a small number of soldiers. Besides, even making the attempt, he thought, would be seen by many Southerners as a form of "coercion." Buchanan sniffed at Scott's clumsiness, and ignored it. The only apparent effect of Scott's "views" was that they may have encouraged Buchanan's natural cautiousness, making the president think that the government's military power was even weaker than it was. In fact, the administration had many more available fighting men than Buchanan now believed. The old general had been rather far off in his estimate, for he did not include several hundred recruits and assorted other soldiers readily available for garrison duty. But this fact probably was unimportant. A show of strength might have caused Southern hotheads to think twice about their actions, but, more likely, as Buchanan thought, it could have triggered an immediate war, with who could know what results.[17]

During the next few weeks Scott, cut off in New York, remained isolated from the critical decision-making process. His pride and ill-health prevented him from rushing to Washington as the crisis evolved, even when Secretary Floyd ordered all mail from Charleston to come solely to Washington, bypassing the old general entirely. By December Scott—spending much of each day overeating and suffering from acute diarrhea, keeping his aching feet and legs propped up, sitting in a wheelchair or lying back on a chaise—decided that the nation's desperate situation demanded his presence. He dragged his dropsical body to the capital.

When he arrived in Washington on December 12 he met with Secretary Floyd, proffering his advice about garrisoning the nine forts. Floyd remained unconvinced, but he did agree to set up a meeting with Buchanan. Three days later the two went together to visit the president. That morning snow was falling on the city, hiding its ugliness beneath lovely white mounds. Inside the Executive Mansion, Scott pressed for a more forceful policy, but Buchanan rejected the notion out of hand. He said he thought it likely that only South Carolina would secede, and that she would then send commissioners to Washington. If that occurred, he would turn over any document they brought with them to Congress, which might be able to arrive at some sort of adjustment without the crisis coming to blows. Scott pointed out that Congress would take too long, and that the situation in Charleston was approaching a critical stage. Fort Sumter was unoccupied and a handful of Carolinians could slip over any night and take it, leaving Fort Moultrie even more defenseless. If the government waited for an actual attack on Moultrie, Scott said, it would not have time to send reinforcements.

Floyd interrupted, disagreeing with Scott on this latter point. Not far from Washington, he said, at Fort Monroe, were hundreds of well-trained troops. Across the James River from them, at Norfolk, was the powerful naval steamer *Brooklyn*. At the first sign of trouble in Charleston, he added, the administration could send the *Brooklyn* and a complement of Fort Monroe's soldiers to the rescue. (It would have taken at least two full days, perhaps more.)

The septuagenarian general tried to talk sense to the two civilians, who were totally ignoring matters of logistics and the likelihood that in war things had a habit of going wrong. He also reminded Buchanan about what Andrew Jackson and he, Scott, had done in 1832 about Fort Moultrie and Charleston. Buchanan simply shrugged. He did not consider the two cases comparable.

The general departed, but he did not give up. Several hours later he wrote a long note to the president, following up on his earlier remarks regarding the events of 1832. It was no use. Buchanan had already decided on what his course should be: waiting for others to act.[18]

It appeared to be up to the South Carolinians.

On December 17 South Carolina's convention met in Columbia. It chose General David F. Jamison, a calm and well-respected leader, to preside. In his opening remarks Jamison said he trusted that their connection to the United States was over. He noted that the North, jealous of the South, had grown aggressive, that almost every Northern state had passed ordinances nullifying the federal fugitive slave laws. To remain in the Union, therefore, would be "fatal." What he meant was clear: Slavery was not simply a *part* of the South, it defined it. White Southerners must now secede to ensure their very way of life.[19]

A few minutes later the convention passed a resolution that transferred its meetings to Charleston because of recent reports of a local small pox outbreak. On their arrival by train in Charleston the next day, the delegates, along with the governor and his staff, were greeted by cheering mobs and a fifteen-gun salute — the number of shots, of course, equaling the number of slave states. (It was during the next twenty-four hours that the flap about the forty muskets occurred.)

On December 20, shortly after one o'clock, the convention, without debate, voted for secession. Anna Brackett, a school-teacher from New England, noted that "the negroes, who, on hearing any unusual noise, always made their appearance at all the gates, stood in groups at every passageway."[20] St. Michael's tolled her bells in glee, and a frenzied celebration splashed across the city. Taverns were crowded with happy, shouting roisterers and the streets with reeling drunks. Citizens lit barrels of rosin on street corners, shot off firecrackers, and blasted rockets into the sky. Somebody stretched a huge sign across the outside of a house: THE WORLD WANTS IT. The partying went on till after midnight. The air was redolent with gunpowder, excitement, and alcoholic vomit.

That evening, as the streets still blazed with bonfires and the hot flames of optimism, the convention's delegates met again. They had decided to sign their secession document in public, before a large audience. They convened at six-thirty, and in solemn procession trooped over to Institute Hall. This huge building, completed only the previous year, had an auditorium that could hold 2,500 people. A Lutheran minister, Dr. John Bachman, opened the ceremony with an invocation. He asked the Lord for wisdom, and also prayed that God would "enable us to protect and bless the humble race that has been entrusted to our care."[21] (Even at this moment slavery was never far from their thoughts.) About seven o'clock the 169 delegates rose, a few at a time, and stepped slowly to the front to sign their names, while the massed gallery of men and women watched from above, yelling and clapping. Sitting among the delegates, by special permission, was the old Virginia secessionist Edmund Ruffin, intently staring, his dream becoming reality. Finally, after two hours, John Laurence Manning, ex-governor, was the last to sign. He picked up the document, grinned widely, and held it aloft, as the throng cheered mightily. General Jamison arose and announced in a clear voice, "I proclaim the State of South Carolina an Independent Commonwealth."

A loud huzzah exploded from the audience. Men threw their hats in the air, women fluttered handkerchiefs. Someone opened the doors and shouted out to the waiting crowds that the deed had been done. A great animal roar erupted. The bells of St. Michael's and other churches rang out once more. Celebrants at The Citadel fired cannon. It was nine-thirty, December 20, 1860, an historic moment.[22]

The December air that night was unseasonably warm. The wind was still. At Fort Moultrie the garrison could hear the sounds of celebration — the rockets and firecrackers and pistol shots. They could make out the flames of the still-flickering bonfires in the streets and the rocket trails against the sky.

The two sides — Charleston and the federal garrison — were separated by no more than four miles of brine; they were divided by a schism over "allegiance." White Charlestonians were displaying their ardent loyalty to South Carolina — or perhaps their relief that slavery was now safe, their "way of life" secure. They had shrugged off the uncomfortable mantle of federal connections and wrapped themselves in the Palmetto flag. To most, it was not a *change* of allegiance. South Carolinians had been moving toward this moment for thirty years. Most had been raised in a world that had taught them they were very special.

The men of Fort Moultrie, unlike the joyful Charlestonians across the way, had not been handed their allegiance at birth. They had *chosen* the object of their loyalty. Each soldier, for his own reasons, as an adult, had pledged an oath to the United States. The majority of Moultrie's men were immigrants who had purposely left their native lands. Most of the rest had been born in either the Border States or the North. All of them had stood each morning at Fort Moultrie as the American flag was raised to the top of its staff with its many stars symbolizing a great Union.

As the garrison listened to the revelry across the water, they could sense danger. A crisis had been approaching for weeks. The distant sounds of merrymaking meant that secession was about to crash against them.

CHAPTER SEVEN

Slim Pickens, Stout Fort

"I believe it is my destiny to be disliked by all who know me well."
— FRANCIS W. PICKENS

F rancis Pickens was a child of privilege, born into vast wealth, a member of one of South Carolina's most prominent families. His grandfather had been a successful general in the Revolution, then a congressman, then Commissioner of Indian Affairs. His father, Andrew Pickens, was a Phi Beta Kappa graduate of Brown, had married rich, had become richer in successful planting, then had become the first man from upstate to be elected governor. The Pickenses were cousins of John C. Calhoun, who was so taken with Andrew that he named his first son after him.

Francis, unlike his father, attended South Carolina College, but he withdrew in his senior year over some difficulty involving mess hall regulations; already his temperament and manner seemed a bit unsettled. When young Francis first entered politics, Calhoun termed him "the most promising man in the state." During the nullification crisis of 1832–33 Francis made a remark that would be remembered in South Carolina for many years. Someone asked him whether he was not afraid of the consequences of such a direct confrontation with Washington. "Fear!" he replied. "Mr. President, I was born insensible to fear!" He was twenty-seven years old.

In 1860, now fifty-five, he had not matured all that much. He had become a portly man with receding hair, a lumpish face, and watery, deep-set eyes. Some people considered him a fine speaker, others found him pompous and tiresome. He was, indeed, quite full of himself. He could be haughty and was frequently overbearing. He was opinionated and often dogmatic, and he was far too given to nasty pettiness, especially with those whom he saw as threats — which turned out to be most of South Carolina's political and social leaders. He also had prolonged bouts of moodiness, at times filled with self-doubt, hesitant and cautious, at other times impulsive. He could be overly confident in his judgments and made little attempt to control his tendency toward rashness, which he preferred to consider boldness.

Had Francis Pickens been governor of South Carolina at any other time, his unfortunate personality would have gone unnoticed to history. The position — limited to a single, two-year term — was traditionally but a figurehead, a pleasant little honor given to state leaders at some point late in their careers. South Carolina had no political parties, and virtually all political power remained with the legislature. Ironically, the governor's official responsibility over the militia, a little-noticed and empty right, became Pickens's main source of power during the crisis over Fort Sumter. After South Carolina actually seceded, the governor was handed the duties performed by American presidents — including the right to oversee "foreign" diplomacy, which in this case was interpreted to mean relations with Washington. Eventually, most crucial decisions would be made by others — Buchanan, Lincoln, Davis. Yet, for a few weeks between December and February, it seemed as though Francis Pickens would be able to bring about war all by himself.

In the antebellum era, South Carolina's state legislature chose the governor. In 1860 rival candidates spent weeks attacking each other. Pickens, who had recently ended a term as minister to Russia, arrived in the state at the very last minute and presented himself as a moderate, compromise candidate. The legislature took four days and seven ballots to decide, but on December 16 it agreed on him. His official inauguration took place the next day. When the secessionist convention decided to move to Charleston, the new governor rented a suite at the Charleston Hotel for himself and his lovely young wife, and set up his office three blocks away on the second floor of the City Hall. He put a simple, hand-lettered sign on the door, and was ready for business. He was also ready for action.

On December 19, even before the South Carolina Convention voted on secession, it agreed to send a delegation to Washington to negotiate the transfer of all the federal properties in the state, especially the three forts. The delegation's assignment was to inform Buchanan officially about South Carolina's secession, then to open negotiations. Most of the convention was optimistic that a conflict could be avoided, but if Washington refused to give up the forts South Carolina would have to take them — with all that that implied. The convention, however, as its *Journal* noted, hoped for "the continuance of peace and amity between this Commonwealth and the Government at Washington."[1]

Francis Pickens was not so patient. After his election on December 16, and even before his official inaugural the next day, he wrote a remarkable letter to his friend President James Buchanan. This note was an accurate mirror of the new South Carolina governor — bombastic and ill-informed.

Robert Barnwell Rhett had told Pickens that the guns of the federal forts were no longer pointing seaward, that they had been turned and were now trained directly on Charleston. Perhaps he believed it. Rhett was quite unsophisticated in things military, so he may have misinterpreted the goings-on at the three forts, where workmen were indeed muscling a few cannon into position. Or maybe Rhett was simply hoping to stir things up, to initiate some incident.

Pickens opened his letter to the president: "I am authentically informed that the forts in Charleston harbor are now being thoroughly prepared to turn, with effect, their guns upon the interior and the city."[2] He was, he added, particularly concerned about Fort Sumter, that federal soldiers might try to man it. "I would most respectfully, and from a sincere devotion to the public peace, request that you allow me to send a small force, not exceeding twenty-five men and an officer, to take possession of Fort Sumter immediately, in order to give a feeling of safety to the community." Pickens told Buchanan that putting Carolina militiamen in Fort Sumter should be no problem. "There are no United States troops in that fort whatever, or perhaps only four or five." (He was being typically casual and vague, but had he wanted to be sure of his facts, any reasonably knowledgeable citizen of Charleston would have informed him there were exactly two, Lieutenant Snyder and an ordnance sergeant.) "If Fort Sumter could be given to me as Governor, . . . then I think the public mind would be quieted, under a feeling of safety." Pickens closed his note snippily, "If something of the kind be not done, I cannot answer for the consequences." Pickens, reputedly smart enough, had written a letter that had as much charm as a colicky baby. He was often socially inept, but he had just proved himself to be asinine.

On the morning of December 17 he handed this message to Daniel Heyward Hamilton, who had been, until his resignation the day after Lincoln's election, the United States Marshal in Charleston. Pickens ordered Hamilton to go to Washington and contact Trescot, to make arrangements to hand the note to Buchanan. Trescot no longer held any official position with the government, but had yet to leave Washington. When Hamilton arrived at his door and explained his mission, Trescot said he would try to arrange an appointment with the president.

On December 20, the day South Carolina seceded, Hamilton and Trescot arrived at the Executive Mansion, where Hamilton handed Pickens's unopened message to Buchanan. The president stood quietly reading it while Hamilton waited. Old Buck, the professional diplomat, showed little reaction. He told Hamilton he needed time to formulate a proper response, perhaps the next day. Buchanan signaled Trescot to remain.

When Hamilton departed, the president handed Trescot the note. The Carolinian was stunned at its tone, both pugnacious and obtuse. Trescot also recognized that Buchanan was quite annoyed — which could have serious consequences. Two weeks earlier the president had virtually committed himself to South

Carolina's congressional delegation, saying that he would take no action against their state. Now, with Pickens's message as a goad, Buchanan might feel justified altering that position. Trescot felt he better do something, and quickly. He either made a copy of the letter or borrowed the original, then rushed across town and showed it to Jefferson Davis and John Slidell, two of the Deep South's most respected senators. They were aghast at Pickens's clumsiness. Trescot then contacted South Carolina's two remaining congressmen in town, Milledge Luke Bonham and John McQueen. Both had been at the earlier meeting when Buchanan had seemed to indicate a do-nothing policy. They, too, shook their heads in disbelief. The three composed and sent a telegram, urging Pickens to withdraw his letter before Buchanan was forced to respond to it. Pickens wired back immediately, agreeing.

The following day Trescot wrote Pickens a long follow-up message, outlining Buchanan's reaction in greater detail. Trescot's words obviously echoed things Buchanan had said to him. The president, Trescot explained, was deeply resentful at the pressure implied in the message, feeling he had for weeks been acting graciously toward South Carolina's concerns. He had, for instance, fired Lieutenant Colonel Gardner for trying to move arms from the arsenal. (This was a simplification; Gardner had been relieved at least partly due to his incompetence.) Buchanan had also refused to reinforce the garrison at Fort Moultrie, and he had accepted Cass's resignation over this issue, even though the secretary of state was "the oldest, most eminent and highest member of his Cabinet" (another self-serving recollection, since Old Buck had been happy to see him go). The president had been hammered by the Northern press for these actions, and Congress had even started talking about investigating his administration. He had accepted all this, and more, because of his "determination to avoid all risk of collision."

As an aside, Trescot himself added that he had just spoken to Floyd that morning. The secretary of war had promised him "that nothing will be done which will either do you injury or properly create alarm." Trescot apologized that his wording here was rather vague and said he could not be more precise because of questions of confidentiality, but Governor Pickens ought to relax. "No order has been issued that will at all disturb the present condition of the garrisons." Trescot concluded his note saying that, if the state's commissioners were unable to pry the forts away from Washington, "the whole issue is fairly before you, to be met as courage, honor and wisdom may direct."[3]

Two days later Pickens wired Trescot again. He had heard, he said, that thirteen men had just arrived in Charleston by train, on their way to Fort Moultrie, that they were part of a hundred and fifty reinforcements that Washington was sending. He demanded to know whether Buchanan had any intention of reinforcing the garrison, "or to transfer any force from Fort Moultrie to Fort Sumter," and concluded peremptorily, "I want a clear answer on this immediately. Until the Commissioners shall negotiate at Washington, there can be no change here." Trescot may have been annoyed by the governor's haughty tone but he tramped over to Floyd's again, unaware that the secretary had just been asked to resign over the Russell fiasco. When Trescot asked Floyd about any reinforcements, the secretary whined that "his position ought to be appreciated." He said he was being constantly watched, that his actions were misrepresented. It was all the fault, he said, of the Republicans, who hated him more than other Southerner. Then he drew himself back from this self-pity enough to tell Trescot to advise Pickens once more that no reinforcements were being sent. As to moving Moultrie's garrison to Sumter, he did not think that likely. And since South Carolina's commissioners would be arriving soon to negotiate the takeover of all Federal properties in that state, it seemed to Floyd unnecessary to be unduly jumpy about something as implausible as Anderson's moving to Sumter.[4]

Francis Pickens remained jittery. He kept hearing all these rumors: reinforcements, no reinforcements; a move to take over Sumter, no such movement. He had been granted the power to deal with some of this, but was uncertain how best to proceed. During the past few weeks the state legislature had been contemplating South Carolina's military situation. It had called for the organization of ten regiments of soldiers, and had stipulated that Governor Pickens was authorized to use them to resist any attempt by "the General Government of the United States, or any officer thereof" to try to coerce the state. Coercion, they said, would include not only any overt act, but even an "intention" to commit such an act — for instance, if Washington simply gathered some troops together that *might* threaten South Carolina.[5]

The legislature also started the process of purchasing new weapons, though this would take time. On December 20 Pickens received a report that the state's arsenal in Columbia had only several thousand old muskets, 34 cavalry pistols, 3 swords, and 1,580 sabers.[6] Contemplating military action with such arms would have been foolhardy.

As far as Washington sending reinforcements, Pickens could do little about it other than bluster, something he was inclined to do anyway. But he could try to separate rumors from fact — hence his agitated notes to Trescot. He tried other ways, as well. On the day of his inauguration, December 17, he sent an envoy, Lieutenant Colonel John Green, to Virginia to snoop around, particularly to find out if anything was stirring at Fort Monroe. Once there, Green traveled to nearby Norfolk and contacted a man named Charles Norris, the leader of the local Minute Men. He asked Norris to keep a watchful eye on Fort Monroe and report any doings to South Carolina. While at Norfolk, Green also hired a workman at the naval yard. Under this arrangement, the man would let them know if any ships there seemed to be preparing for action. Pickens later admitted that he received frequent spy reports from Norfolk.[7]

As to whether Major Anderson's garrison might move to Sumter, Pickens could nose about himself. On December 20, the day South Carolina officially seceded, he spoke to Captain Humphreys of the arsenal and quizzed him about a rumor he had come across that very morning — that twenty men were being transferred from Fort Moultrie to Sumter. Was this true? Humphreys said he doubted it, but promised to ask Captain Foster. The same day, Foster received Humphreys's query and wrote back immediately, saying he would not send Pickens any such official denial — especially on this particular day. Let Pickens check with Washington.[8]

On the evening of December 20 a civilian watchman at Fort Sumter came to Lieutenant Snyder and reported something fishy going on near the fort's wharf. Snyder went to look. What he saw he later passed on to Captain Foster. A small boat, coming from the city, had appeared out of the darkness without lights. She was moving slowly near the wharf, apparently sounding the waters thereabouts. After a bit she moved away, apparently toward Moultrie. Snyder could see her settle herself in about six hundred yards away, probably anchoring.

That same evening a boat had also approached Castle Pinckney, circling it for a bit. The watchman there shouted at her, asking what she wanted. A voice called back through the chill night air, "You will know in a week."[9]

Whether the vessel near Castle Pinckney and the one near Sumter were one and the same, Foster was not sure, though he did know that the *Nina* was at least one such. She was back the next night, along with another small steamboat, the *General Clinch* (named, ironically, to honor Eba's father). About nine o'clock or so they stationed themselves between Moultrie and Sumter. Foster was angry at the presence of the boats but was uncertain what to do about them.

Anderson also reported to Washington about the vessels. He was positive they were there "to prevent, if possible, any troops from being placed" in Fort Sumter. He was still rather sure, however, he could slip past them and get to Sumter if Washington authorized it, though he would have to leave behind most of his stores.[10]

Actually, Anderson was more concerned than his report indicated. These boats were something new, and to him quite ominous. He knew that both carried armed men. What was the purpose of these vessels? To spy on him, or to descend suddenly on Fort Sumter? Or, perhaps, to carry an attack force against Moultrie itself? He did not like their presence. Not at all.

The boats, in fact, were Pickens's idea. Robert Barnwell Rhett, Jr., owner of the *Mercury*, and son of the famous fire-eater, had suggested to the new governor that the state could place 500 armed men on a steamer and anchor it between Moultrie and Sumter, preventing any attempt to garrison Sumter, either by men from Fort Moultrie or reinforcements from outside.[11] Pickens had rejected that specific proposal, but had decided to refine it. He would later supply different versions of how he implemented the plan. One version had him simply ordering a military aide, Colonel James Johnston Pettigrew, to organize some sort of patrol system between Moultrie and Sumter. A second version had the governor taking a much more forceful role. In this one he personally spoke to Captain Charles H. Simonton, the man in command of the Washington Light Cavalry. Its members, many from the city's most prominent families, were at present guarding the entrance to the arsenal. Pickens later claimed he'd told Simonton to take some troops and sail back and forth between the two forts. If they saw Anderson's men attempting to cross, they were to stop them, "at all hazards," sinking them if necessary. They were also, then, to take Fort Sumter. How to accomplish all this would be up to Simonton.[12]

Which of these versions was accurate, if either, is not important, for Pickens did initiate some sort of orders. The two steamboats, *Nina* and *Clinch*, carrying between forty and a hundred and twenty men, did arrive each evening between Fort Moultrie and Fort Sumter, and steam back and forth.

Other people were also checking up on the forts. About December 19 Major Walter Gwynn, another of the governor's aides, rode out to Sumter to look around. His report, apparently, caused a ripple of anxiety in Charleston, though why is unclear. A few days later, on December 23, Edmund Ruffin agreed to join members of the legislature on a military tour of the harbor. Ruffin was unimpressed with Castle Pinckney, but Fort Sumter awed him. He wrote in his diary that if a sizable garrison were placed inside, "it would be extremely difficult to be taken."[13]

All this talk of Sumter had increased noticeably once Pickens and the state convention arrived in town. What was there about it that drew the fascinated attention of so many people?

On any December evening in 1860, just as darkness enveloped Charleston Harbor, casual strollers on the Battery or over at Fort Moultrie could have just made out its form, squatting lumpishly near the harbor's mouth, like an ancient pyramid rising from the sea, an ugly mound of brick and stone. Nothing around it would have softened its stark lines or given it a human scale. It was a dark, desolate, lonely thing. A cousin of Château d'If.

In the decades before the Civil War, America's defense system, based as it was on congressional parsimony, consisted of a tiny professional army that, in theory, could be moved rapidly and plugged into any exploding crisis. The government maintained scores of forts, some sprinkled along America's international borders with Canada and Mexico, others along its shorelines. Most of these forts remained unoccupied. The purpose of each was merely to remain in readiness, so that it could, if necessary, protect a key region from outside attack. Fort Sumter was one of these.

The army had several hundred men who specialized in "ordnance," an arcane science involving, primarily, artillery and ammunition. If heavy guns and cannonballs are left outside, uncared for, they suffer from the elements. Iron rusts, the guns get plugged up with windblown sand, their bores can even twist a mite in extreme temperatures. From time to time, therefore, the army would cull through its list of experienced sergeants, choose a few, and designate them "ordnance sergeants." Their duties involved caring for a post's arms, ammunition, and other military stores. This assignment often involved isolated posts where they served as the only military presence. Each morning, in solitude and quiet, they would raise the American flag; each evening they'd lower it again. In between these two rituals they would take care of the government's ordnance. They cleaned and polished the artillery, they coated the piled cannonballs with protective grease. In seacoast forts like Sumter, they also maintained the harbor light, which shone above the walls each night. The life of these sergeants — lonely, tethered to mundane routine — was comparable to that of lighthouse keepers. The army took this factor into account, paying these men a monthly bonus of five dollars, almost half the base salary of a U.S. Army private. The army also tried to choose only married men, who could then have some company at their windswept posts.[14]

In 1858, according to Abner Doubleday, the only regular occupants of Fort Sumter were one of these sergeants, his wife, and two children. Their only method of contacting the outside world was a small rowboat. "One wild and stormy day," Doubleday writes, "when the wind was blowing a gale, the sergeant was suddenly struck down with yellow fever." His poor wife tried to signal the garrison of Fort Moultrie, a mile across the harbor, or anyone else on Sullivan's Island. She stood at Sumter's parapet and waved a sheet back and forth. No one noticed. She felt she could not leave her feverish husband, and she grew desperate. She placed her two small children in the rowboat, faced it toward Sullivan's Island, and pushed it off. Despite the shrieking winds and high, churning waves, she prayed they might make it. The tide was surging westward past Sumter, and she felt it might carry them safely to land. Before the children left, she handed them a letter that pleaded for medical assistance, and told them to give it to the first person they encountered. In good weather it normally took six men, pressing hard on their oars, fifteen minutes or so to get from Sumter to Moultrie; how long the two children were in that rowboat is impossible to guess. Somehow their vulnerable, tiny craft made the journey safely to Sullivan's Island. A doctor eventually was able to cross back, but, according to Doubleday, it was "too late to be of any service."[15] This story highlights the isolation of Fort Sumter.

Early in the nineteenth century South Carolina had itself owned several military bases—Fort Moultrie, Castle Pinckney, and Fort Johnson—but all of them were of dubious military value and expensive to maintain, and, when asked to do so, the state gladly ceded them to the United States, along with other unspecified sites along its exposed coastline that the army might choose to fortify in its defense system for the region.[16] The army's Board of Engineers was also satisfied with the arrangement. The forts—at least Castle Pinckney and Fort Moultrie—provided a solid basis for a regional defense system. The army, however, wished to add another fort.

Soldiers appreciate the value of crossfire. Two men with guns, separated by a few dozen yards, shooting at the same target, are far more dangerous than the same men firing side by side. If the U.S. Army built another fort somewhere opposite Moultrie, every enemy ship running between them would come under crossfire.

Ships' gun crews would be split, half of them on the port side, half on the starboard, reducing their potential firepower. The effect on attacking vessels would be murderous. And any ship staggering through would then have to face Castle Pinckney.

The Board of Engineers found, however, that the harbor offered no convenient spot on its south side upon which to site a new fort. If they put it on Morris Island (the harbor's southern lip), the guns of the new fort would be too far from Moultrie's guns to provide the desired crossfire. There was, however, a large sandbar stretching northward from Morris Island. In 1827 the engineers performed careful soundings along this shoal and concluded that with a proper foundation a fort could be erected there. Two years later they began. They referred to their future fortification as "Fort Sumter," named after a famous Revolutionary War general from South Carolina, Thomas Sumter, the original "Game Cock." But in five years all they had accomplished was to lay an untrustworthy timber-based foundation that sat several feet under water whenever the tide was up. They were in no hurry; no enemies immediately threatened the nation. Then, in 1834, the engineers suspended operations due to some nagging legal and political problems. These were resolved in 1836 and work was again begun.

Meanwhile the army had changed its mind about the fort; it had decided to make Fort Sumter one of the world's greatest fortifications, using all the latest military ideas. Cannon could now shoot farther and hit harder. Sumter's walls would be thicker and higher than specified in the original plans. The fort's guns, 140 of them, would require an especially strong base. The engineers decided to build the foundation entirely of rock, lots of it—much of it, ironically, from quarries in New York and New England.

All this took years. The engineers were only able to lay granite blocks down when the weather permitted and when the tide was just right. Heat and disease also complicated the schedule, along with the usual difficulties involved in getting materials.[17] The citizens of Charleston watched the structure of the fort as it gradually rose above the harbor's surface. Vacationers at Sullivan's Island could hear the crack of tools against stone and brick.

The development of Fort Sumter became a normal part of the city's scenery, of its life, for two decades. A woman later recalled, "What a grand frolic it was to the young people, and sometimes, too, for a party of children, to be taken across the water to visit Fort Sumter, to climb even to the top of the parapet."[18]

Between 1854 and 1856, as the project neared its end, a war was being waged on the far-off Crimean Peninsula of Russia. Some of the world's Great Powers, as they termed themselves, fought there: Great Britain, France, Russia. The United States took the opportunity to send observers, their primary assignment being to check on the latest military hardware. In 1856 Secretary of War Jefferson Davis handed in his official annual report. He noted that the Crimean War had demonstrated the excellence of the kind of fortifications being built by the United States. Russian coastal forts, using similar plans and materials, had performed admirably when facing Britain's best naval firepower. General Joseph Totten, of the Corps of Engineers, came to the same conclusion. His forts, he thought, would do just fine.[19]

What, then, was this new fort like?

Her basic structure had a footprint of two and a half acres. The fort was intended to accommodate almost a thousand men to man its 140 cannon, placed in three tiers. A gun on the top tier, out in the open, was said to be *en barbette*. There, it was easier to load, and you could elevate it as much as you wished. Guns designed for horizontal firing were often placed inside thick-walled rooms with arched, bomb-proof ceilings. Such rooms were termed *casemates*. Guns inside casemates fired through narrow *embrasures*. Thus, the cannon on Fort Sumter's top tier were en barbette; those slated for the bottom two tiers would be casemated.

The fort contained two large barracks and, standing between them, a three-story building with offices and living quarters. Each structure had its own water supply in catch basins and cisterns, designed to capture and hold the area's frequent downpours. Around the fort's exterior (*scarp*) walls on all sides, stretching out for a dozen feet or more, depending on the tide, wrapped a girdle of crushed rocks. One could rather easily walk entirely around the fort for a leisurely look up at its walls, stretching overhead about fifty feet (at low tide). These walls appeared to be formed of solid brick, but in fact were constructed mostly of slabs of concrete, then coated with bricks. At the top of the walls was the parapet, coped with massive bricks, each a foot and a half thick. The parapet jutted out more than a foot from the rest of the wall, and was held in place by fine *corbels*—small buttresses—the only real decorative touch to the fort's exterior.

Casual observers had a sense that the fort was a basic pentagon because it had five main sides. In fact, there were ten sides, including short, but important, sections creating flat angles where the five main walls would have otherwise butted awkwardly against each other. Each wall had a specific designation, and the names were revealing. To the engineers, Sumter had a "left" side and a "right" side. The terminology revealed that the fort was designed to look *out* toward the harbor's mouth, to face out to sea, to be ready to fight invading fleets out on the water. Its weakest side was its back—the "Gorge," they called it—321 feet from side to side, facing south by southwest, toward Morris Island. The engineers had assumed that, during a battle, the fort would get supplies and reinforcements from Charleston, so they had built a 171-foot stone wharf on the Gorge side, directly opposite the main gate. The water around Fort Sumter was quite shallow. Deep-sea vessels could not approach the fort or its wharf, but smaller boats from Charleston could get there in fifty minutes. As long as the fort's garrison could count on support from the city, it could hold out almost indefinitely.

Outside, stretching left and right alongside the Gorge's outer wall, was the Esplanade, a wide, granite-flagged walkway, which formed the top of a T with the wharf. During construction, the engineers piled materials and equipment here, just beyond the gate, then brought them in as needed.

Sumter, like most forts, also had several minor sally ports, but most people entered through the gate. Just within the outer gate, on the right side, were two rooms next to each other. The first was for the guard, the second for the officer of the day. In theory all who arrived at Sumter would be stopped here.

Entering through the gate, past the two guardrooms, one walked through a long, dark, stone-and-brick passageway. Beyond it, at the core of the fort, was a one-acre, open parade ground, a gloomy place, with the ambience of a grim prison yard. The walls, towering above it, blocked out most of the sunlight even on sunny days, casting shadows across everyone within. The outside world seemed very far away.

CHAPTER EIGHT

Eventide

Christmas, 1860. Some New England Yankees still considered Yuletide folderol, popular silliness, but most of the nation had been somewhat won over to images from the works of Charles Dickens and Washington Irving and from Clement Clarke Moore's "A Visit from St. Nicholas."

In Charleston Edwin Christy's Minstrels were in town for the season, performing at Institute Hall—which would change its name to Secession Hall during their engagement. The Minstrels, who originated in New England, had already riled some citizens a week before their first performance when they asked the City Council to permit "colored persons" to attend their shows, a prospect previously against the rules of the hall. A few citizens, to make their own position clear, had placed a sign near the stage door promising DEATH TO YANKEES. The Minstrels, no fools, were in the entertainment business, and the high point of their Christmas Eve performance came when two dancers in blackface whirled about the stage, waving Palmetto flags. The thrilled audience whooped its delight.[1]

Elsewhere in town the Christmas season proceeded normally. Slaves were given their traditional vacation days. Stores were festooned with decorations, and Santa Claus came to Von Schaak & Grierson's. Most holiday emphasis, however, was on food, not gifts. One young man wrote his sister about that year's Christmas party, where children, he said, were "well supplied by Santa Claus," their presents being "a Crying Baby, box of toys, and some sugar plums."[2] The *Mercury* described the city on Christmas eve: "King-street was thronged by indulgent mammas and sanguine youngsters, all intent upon the morrow. The markets were crowded, and a brisk business was driven in turkeys, and all the multifarious good things which go to make up the Christmas dinner. The firing of squibs was general and uninterrupted, and everybody — young and old — seemed to be affected with a kind of preliminary jollity. We believe the night wore away without any serious disturbance of the public order." Wylie Crawford, who had come over from Fort Moultrie on Christmas Eve to buy presents, thought Charleston seemed calm enough, though he sensed a subtle volatility in the city.

At Fort Moultrie tensions fluttered like windblown tinsel. A distinguished old lawyer from the city, James Louis Petigru, had recently visited. South Carolina's best-known opponent of secession, Petigru was a gentleman of such reputation that Lincoln was considering him for a high judicial appointment. Petigru made no secret of his disgust over the recent proceedings in Charleston, and he got away with his contrary position only because the city's leaders liked and respected him — and perhaps because they viewed him simply as a crank with little influence. He told Fort Moultrie's officers he deeply sympathized with their plight. He warned them they would be attacked soon if Washington did not soon surrender this place, and he literally wept that South Carolina had reached this level of insanity.[3]

Just before Christmas one of the garrison's officers told Anderson that militia units from outside Charleston had recently begun arriving in town, and scaling ladders were being prepared. Crawford, after his return from town on December 24, wrote his concerns into his diary: "Council of War in the city. Troops to make the attack selected." South Carolina's engineering officers came to Sullivan's Island and quite openly surveyed a site at which to place a battery of artillery.[4]

Events were clearly moving toward a crisis. A Carolinian, Charles S. Bull, wrote a friend on December 19: "Everybody seems to be talking about taking *Fort Moultrie* and nothing else." At West Point, a young cadet from South Carolina asked permission to withdraw from the Military Academy. He was an only son, he said, and he felt he had better go home "to protect my mother in time of danger."[5]

The rambunctious Robert Barnwell Rhett, Jr., went to see Pickens about this time. He had, he told the governor, just received a letter from a friend in Washington, a person who was in a position to know what was going on there. Major Anderson was on the verge of seizing Fort Sumter; Pickens ought to act immediately and grab Fort Sumter now and not wait for the commissioners' negotiations.

Major Anderson spent Christmas evening attending a party the Fosters were giving, but he stayed only a short while, departing when the children left, returning to his quarters at the fort.[6] He had things on his mind. The day before, he had jotted a note to a friend in Boston. Moultrie was far too vulnerable, he wrote, and "there is scarce a possibility of our being able to hold out long enough to enable our friends to come to our succor." He tried to be optimistic, he wrote, "Trusting that God will not desert us in our hour of trial." On Christmas he wrote another acquaintance, "My plan has always been to try to do my duty honestly and fully; and to trust that, in the good sense of justice of the people, they would give me credit for good intentions, even if my judgment should turn out not to have been good. . . . I do not deserve the least credit for what I am doing—nothing more than anyone else would do in my position—and, perhaps, not half as well as many others would do."[7] In neither letter did he mention that he had just decided on a bold stroke, one that could easily turn into disaster.

Anderson planned to spirit the garrison across to Fort Sumter in small boats. If discovered rowing across by Pickens's armed steamboats, they would be pathetically vulnerable. Even if they somehow made it, it was almost inconceivable that they would have enough stores to hold out at Sumter for very long. In any case Buchanan's government might well repudiate the major's action, then court-martial him.

But Anderson had been doing some math. Charleston's newspapers were readily available at Fort Moultrie. He knew that the convention's commissioners had departed on Christmas Eve, and he calculated that they would schedule their conference with the president for the day after Christmas. Since, as Anderson knew, Buchanan was unlikely to accede to their wishes, the commissioners might — that very day, December 26 — wire Pickens of the failure of their mission. Depending on the time of day, it was not impossible, though unlikely, that an assault on Fort Moultrie could come before nightfall; more realistically, the next day, December 27. If he was going to make a move, therefore, he would be wise to do it on Christmas night. It was probable that the various spies, including the two patrol boats, would be less vigorous on that day. He also noted that the moon would be almost full, giving him enough light to make the journey across, using several small boats.

Although Anderson did not tell anyone why, he strongly urged his officers to go to church on Christmas.[8]

He had been turning the whole thing over in his mind for days, trying to sniff out any conceivable facet of the plan that might go wrong. He was quite concerned about the two dozen wives of enlisted men, plus their many children, half of them mere infants. He felt he could not leave them behind, but his genteel nature would hardly permit him to place them in great danger. Also, he could not expect them to move instantly, at his orders. Important items — diapers, perhaps — might get left behind. Nor could he expect the children to be able to remain silent in the well of a boat, even if their lives depended on it.

He devised a ruse. He already had announced that, since Moultrie might be attacked soon, he wanted to put the women and children, plus their belongings, out of harm's way, to house them temporarily in the empty structures at Fort Johnson, across the harbor. The enlisted men's families, he said, should pack their belongings, and he would ship them there, along with a large amount of commissary stores, perhaps on Christmas Day. He justified putting the food supplies at Fort Johnson by saying that the garrison, if attacked, could not hold out more than a few weeks, and he did not want their opponents to get the federal foodstuffs. Anderson

ordered young Lieutenant Hall, the garrison's quartermaster officer, to make plans for this transfer, using the three fairly good-sized
schooners hired by the Engineering Corps. The vessels should be
enough to carry the families and all their goods, as well as enough
food to last them for some time. Anderson also casually suggested
to his officers that they might wish to forward most of their personal effects there, too. The garrison thought the major's proposal
sounded sensible, and suspected nothing.

Local spies, of course, learned about the coming transfer of the
families and the goods, but remained unconcerned. Women and
children over at Fort Johnson represented no danger. Performing
like a magician with a pack of cards, Anderson had military hardware taken from Fort Sumter and sent to Moultrie, then returned,
hoping to befuddle the spies further with this hocus-pocus.[9]

Anderson was particularly concerned that his garrison would
be helpless while rowing across the harbor. During these moments, lasting perhaps several hours, a force of local militiamen
could take over the abandoned Moultrie and use its guns against
the fragile crafts. Even after his men arrived at Fort Sumter they
would remain vulnerable for hours while they unloaded the boats
in darkness and carried the stuff inside, an operation that could
easily take all night. He stewed about what might be done to nul-
lify the danger. The simplest option would be to spike Moultrie's
guns pointing toward Sumter. If you drove a large nail or rod into
a gun's vent hole, then broke it off, this could temporarily prevent
an enemy from using it on you. But spikes were notoriously inef-
ficient deterrents if the enemy had sufficient time to remove them.
Anderson casually asked Abner Doubleday what might be the
best way to make their artillery unusable. Doubleday suggested
that they could burn the wooden gun carriages. This would take
longer than spiking the guns but was much more guaranteed of
success. Doubleday did not think the question odd; they had been
considering what to do if assaulted and forced to surrender. Two
weeks earlier Crawford had told his brother, "We are mining the
work and will leave it a heap of ruins before it is taken."[10]

By Christmas Anderson had worked out all the details in his
own mind. Unfortunately the weather that day turned nasty. He

postponed his plan for twenty-four hours — still informing no one. He would await tomorrow and hope that the weather broke.

December 26. It was forty degrees. A cold fog slithered across the beach. A misty rain fell, and one could hardly make out Fort Sumter in the distance. But Anderson sensed, for some reason, that the sky would soon clear; he decided that today was the day for his coup. His career was on the line. Their lives were about to be in hazard — and perhaps the nation's as well. But he had decided to take the step, as he later wrote Washington, "to prevent the effusion of blood."[11]

Early in the day he told Foster and Hall he wanted to move the families and provisions to Fort Johnson on this day. He quietly confided to Foster his real mission, but he did not yet tell Hall. He felt forced to tell Foster because, following the army's rigid divisions, he could only use the engineer's rented schooners and barges if he first received Foster's official permission.

Throughout the morning of December 26 and into the afternoon men packed provisions onto Foster's boats, tied up at Moultrie's wharf, just north of the main gate. Two Carolinians stood by, watching everything. They followed Hall almost everywhere he went, making no attempt to hide their curiosity. Whenever he left the wharf and entered the fort they stood just outside the gate. Finally one of them, overcome by suspicion, confronted the lieutenant. That was a lot of food being loaded into one of the lighters, too much, he said, for these women and children. Why was that? Hall replied noncommittally, but whatever he said satisfied the man. At one point, a box marked "1000 ball cartridges" was loaded by mistake, but it was whipped off before the spies became more suspicious.

In early afternoon the women and children were gathered up and placed on board. About three o'clock, as Hall prepared to leave, Anderson told him his secret plan. The lieutenant, he whispered, was to go to Fort Johnson, as they had already discussed, but when Hall got there he was to keep everyone and everything on the boats on the excuse that he had to determine the best place at the site to deposit them. He should stroll slowly around and take his time. When he heard two signal guns go off at Fort Moultrie, he would know to head directly to Fort Sumter. He should tell the Charlestonian who skippered the vessels that he had been unable to find acceptable accommodations at Fort Johnson, and then to go on to Fort Sumter.[12] Hall understood, and departed with his small armada.

The brittle December sun would set just before five. According to Anderson's calculations, he would have four hours to transfer his entire command before the first armed steamboat left Charleston and placed itself between the two forts. Commercial vessels coming to Charleston that day—great ships arriving from afar, small craft bringing bales of cotton from the barrier islands, fishing boats—all should reach the city by sunset, but it would be unwise for him to be too confident. The moon, only two days shy of full, would rise at 5:42, just after the last moments of twilight. The rain clouds had drifted off, and if the night sky remained clear the harbor would gleam bright beneath the moon. Fine for lovers, convenient for transporting goods—not so inviting to men who would have to skulk quickly out of sight before possibly being blown out of the water by angry South Carolinians.

The Engineering Corps owned three six-oared barges and two four-oared boats, in addition to the lighters they had rented in town, which Hall was now using. Anderson intended to use the three larger barges to transfer the garrison. If all worked satisfactorily, he might send the boats back to pick up some more supplies—gunpowder, cartridges, the kinds of things he had not wanted to send with Hall because of the spies. After he had spoken that morning to Captain Foster, the engineer had sent messages to his two subordinates—Meade at Castle Pinckney and Snyder at Sumter—to come over that afternoon with their boats.

After Hall and his three lighters had departed, Anderson checked on the status of the barges. Just before five o'clock he found Meade and Snyder safely moored in a small cove, a quarter mile down the shoreline from Fort Moultrie. The two officers were crouched behind the rocks, along with their rowers, so that no one from Moultrieville could accidentally spot them. Their two barges lay in the water nearby. They had also brought along a third barge and it bobbed in the water, empty, awaiting the venture. Anderson hurried back to Moultrie to implement the rest of his plan.

The sun began to set beyond St. Michael's steeple.

Abner Doubleday was in his quarters, thinking about tea. He decided to search out Anderson, to see if the major would care to join him and Mary. He crossed the parade ground and climbed the stairs to the parapet, where he saw Anderson standing amid a cluster of officers, and approached them with his invitation forming on his lips. He noticed they all seemed especially solemn. The major saw him, left the others, and walked over. The garrison, he said, was leaving Moultrie immediately and going to Fort Sumter. Doubleday would have twenty minutes—and only twenty minutes—to have Company E ready to march out the gate with muskets in their hands and knapsacks on their backs. This was not an absurd order. All the men were within the fort at that moment, and Anderson had had the foresight that morning to order everyone, officers included, to have their knapsacks packed each morning from that day on, on the excuse that the fort might be attacked momentarily.

Doubleday raced down the stairs and ordered his company to form on the parade. As his men grabbed their muskets and toted their equipment, most assumed that an assault force had just landed on Sullivan's Island and was coming for them.

Doubleday did not wait for them to get ready. He rushed to his quarters. He now had, he estimated, less than ten minutes to tell Mary. He was anxious about what might happen to her. Unlike the wives of the enlisted men, officers' wives were not expected to cross to Sumter, and they might soon be confronted by outraged Carolina goons. Traditional Southern "gentility" would dissuade a mob from committing ugly acts on women, but in the past few months Northern men aplenty had been hanged by Southerners. Who could be confident that something nasty might not happen to Mary—or, for that matter, to Marl Foster and Louisa Seymour?

When Doubleday burst into their suite, Mary was preparing tea. He told her she had to leave instantly, to get out of the fort before too late; the enemy might arrive in minutes and she must find a place to hide. They threw her belongings into some trunks and he found two men to carry them to one of the sally ports and thrust them outside the walls. She followed. He said good-bye emotionally and left her standing there as he returned to his company, which had gathered with their guns and knapsacks on the parade. Mary hurried to the home of the post sutler, who lived nearby; then, later that evening, to the cottage of the chaplain, Matthias Harris, and his wife. As to their belongings, the Doubledays were fortunate in that they had already crated most of them up and sent them to New York. Some of the other officers were less lucky. Most of them, especially the Fosters, lost some personal items — "music, bird-cages, and other fancy items," according to a later report, with a total valuation of $15,000.[13]

Anderson's plan was for the garrison to cross in two waves. He, Doubleday, and Company E would go in the first one. If nothing untoward happened to the first wave, the boats would return for Company H. Anderson chose Lieutenant Jeff Davis, Doubleday's second-in-command, the tough soldier who had risen from the ranks due to his Mexican War exploits, to remain back at Moultrie, to load and man the guns that pointed toward Sumter. Davis was to open fire on any vessel attempting to interfere with their passage. During the next few hours — perhaps minutes — the fate of the nation would depend on whether one of Pickens's ships lurched out of the night at them.

It would take at least fifteen minutes for the first wave to row across, more likely twenty or more. It would take an additional few minutes to disembark at Sumter; then there was the return trip. Probably an hour total. Then Seymour's Company H would make its crossing, at least another half hour, adding the time it would take Seymour to move his men from the rocky beach into the boats. The second wave would also carry the eight regimental band members, minus most of their instruments. Foster would be in charge of rear guard after Davis left. His job would be to protect the second wave's passage, then to spike the guns, to burn the gun carriages of those cannon facing Sumter, and to cut down the flagpole. If his men had time, and the second wave's boats came back again, they all should grab as much ammunition as they could, plus all important artillery paraphernalia they could lay their hands on. This was Major Anderson's plan.[14]

When Doubleday left Mary and arrived with his company at Moultrie's main gate, Anderson was waiting for him, an American flag folded under his arm. The major led the way down the narrow island road toward Moultrieville, then partway through it till he reached the cove where the boats were hidden. It was dusk now. The soldiers tried to be quiet but their equipment clanked a bit as they walked. Most of the island's population had long since departed, but a few hardy souls still resided in Moultrieville. No one, however, seems to have noticed the men marching by.

Snyder and Meade stood up from their crouch when they saw Anderson approaching, Snyder nervously clutching a sword. Company E clambered into the boats, moving as quickly as their equipment and heavy winter coats would allow. Snyder's boat, carrying Anderson, the flag, and a portion of the men, pushed off first. Snyder, the engineer, of course, knew Sumter and the workmen there better than anyone else, so it would be prudent for him to arrive first, and the major felt it was his responsibility to be the first of the garrison's officers to step into Fort Sumter, in case it came to court-martial. Meade's boat would come next with more of the company, and Doubleday would bring up the rear. Since Doubleday's boat, rowed only by his soldiers rather than the far more proficient laborers that Snyder and Meade were using, it was likely to take him and his craft quite a bit longer to get to Sumter. But an odd thing happened.

The sea was calm, and the moon was just silvering the sky and the water. Snyder and Meade saw a vessel coming toward them and quickly turned their barges back toward the shoreline of Sullivan's Island, where they waited for the unknown boat to pass. It turned out to be one of the two guard boats, the *General Clinch*, tugging a disabled ship. Snyder's and Meade's barges stayed put unnoticed against the murky block of the island, but Doubleday's boat, plowing clumsily through the water, got trapped in the middle of the channel, the steamboat bearing down on it.

For once in his life Doubleday moved quickly. While the

paddleboat was still fairly far off, Doubleday whipped off his hat
and told his men to take off their military coats and lay them over
their guns, which were lying at their sides just below the gunwales. He yanked his own lapels back to hide the polished but-
tons. He hoped that in the darkness the men on his boat would
seem just a bunch of workmen returning to Fort Sumter. He saw
the steamer pause about a hundred yards off; then, apparently satisfied, it moved slowly away. Doubleday and his men breathed
easier, and started rowing again toward Sumter, which glowered
silently beneath the moon.

A few minutes later they bumped against the wharf. They instantly encountered laborers. A few of the workmen realized what
was happening and began to shout hurrahs for the Union; others
were feverishly hostile. Doubleday formed his men on the wharf,
their bayonets at the ready, and ordered them forward. The
laborers, facing cold steel, staggered back. He was still herding
them inside the fort, and taking over the guardroom at the gate,
when Anderson and the others arrived. Minutes later, the three
barges were sent back to bring over Seymour and his company.

It was about seven o'clock. Charleston's patrol boats would be
prowling soon. At Moultrie, meanwhile, as the second wave got
ready, the rear guard prepared themselves: Lieutenant Davis; Fort
Moultrie's ordnance sergeant, Thomas Williams; the two pugnacious buddies from Company E, Privates Digdam and McDonald,
who had until recently been in confinement for fighting; Captain
Foster and his brother-in-law, Edward Moale; several nameless
others; and Wylie Crawford, who had volunteered to stay behind
with them, and who was making a subtle emotional transition
from surgeon to soldier.

Davis and the enlisted men loaded and aimed the five guns
that pointed toward Sumter. After the first wave got safely across
and the second was moving toward Sumter, he and most of the
remaining enlisted men also departed. It was now Foster's responsibility to protect the last boats. He was watching their passage
with a spyglass when he suddenly realized that another boat was
approaching them. Foster and Crawford ran to one of the loaded
32-pounders. Foster stood next to the gun, ready to open fire,

while Crawford peered out as the scene developed in the moon-light. These two men, neither one officially a fighting man, were on the brink of launching a war. Crawford, using Foster's spy-glass, stared out at the steam vessel. But it passed by, oblivious.

As the second wave disappeared within the deep shadow of Sumter, Crawford and Ordnance Sergeant Williams shot the sig-nal guns that told Hall the coast was clear. The skipper of the rented schooners sensed what the signal meant and tried to pre-vent Hall from taking the boats to Sumter, but Hall and a sergeant shoved the captain into the hold and took off, arriving shortly after Seymour.[15] It was not yet eight o'clock.

Much at Sumter still needed to be done. A place for the fami-lies had to be found; the situation of the laborers had to be solved; Fort Sumter had to be readied for a likely attack; the last of the soldiers at Moultrie, plus as much of its supplies as possible, had to be brought over.

One barracks at Fort Sumter was designated for the women and children, but it had no furniture or bedding. During the night bunks were set up for them, and bedding was made by using some wood shavings the laborers had left in a pile.[16]

The laborers were divided into two groups, those who could be trusted and asked to stay — fifty-five of them — and the others, about a hundred. Anderson promised all of them that Foster would pay them shortly, thus mollifying the dissidents some-what, whom he put on one of the schooners that Hall had used for the women and children. They departed with their baggage, ex-pecting to be taken immediately to Charleston. They were sailed around the harbor all night, then deposited temporarily back at Sumter in the morning, from which they were removed late in the afternoon.

The worst seemed over. Anderson was terribly relieved. God, it seemed, was on their side — and on the side of America, which had probably been spared a war. Perhaps now, with enough time, wise counsel in Washington could somehow solve the issue without bloodshed. Lieutenant Davis brought out a small bottle of brandy he had received at the Fosters the night before. Someone pro-posed a drink to celebrate their success, and they sipped from the

flask. Robert left with a candle and started to write. He first jotted a note to Eba, reassuring her that he was all right.[17] Then he
carefully worded a short official report to Washington.

On Sullivan's Island Mary Doubleday, accompanied by Reverend
Harris and his wife, paced the sands of the beach much of the
night, staring nervously out toward Sumter.[18]

At Moultrie Foster was completing the last acts of his assignment. He, his brother-in-law Edward Moale, and Ordnance
Sergeant Williams, who knew how to do these things, hammered
musket ramrods into the vents of all the cannon.[19]

A dinner party in Charleston heard the shots signaling Hall to
move. The host of the gathering, Williams Middleton, told his
guests that he thought he knew what the two shots meant. He and
Rhett, Jr., had called upon Governor Pickens that morning and
had suggested to him that he order his militia to take Fort Sumter.
Middleton now believed, he said, that that was just what Pickens
had done, that the signal meant Sumter was now safely theirs.[20]

The militiamen on one of Pickens's two guard boats also heard
the signal gun and mildly wondered what it was.[21] Sometime well
after the garrison was ensconced at Sumter, the *Nina* took its position between the two forts, completely unaware that her mission
was now irrelevant.

Edmund Ruffin was perhaps the most perceptive of the lot.
Now that South Carolina's secession seemed complete, he was
on his way to Florida, to urge that state to take the plunge. He
boarded a steamer at one of the Charleston's wharves at 7:10. In
the darkness the ship moved through the harbor between Sumter
and Moultrie. Nothing seemed amiss. He was standing on the
upper deck, catching some breeze and looking out to sea. The
steamer was approaching the harbor's mouth when the old man
heard quite clearly two loud explosions from behind him, coming
from Moultrie. He returned to his quarters and sat down to write
in his diary. He remarked, "I supposed this firing, at so unusual an
hour must have been a signal for something."[22] (It seems likely that
it was Ruffin's steamer that so spooked Foster and Crawford.)

Late that night one of Anderson's officers wrote a note to a
relative in Troy, New York. The garrison, he said, had just estab-

lished itself at Sumter, "This impregnable fortress," he called it. He felt exhilarated. "Tomorrow morning, the stars and stripes will be hoisted over our new position, although the sight will sting South Carolina to the quick.

"Hurrah for Major Anderson!"[23]

Under normal circumstances, the fate of Robert Anderson's garrison would have been unimportant. In 1860 the world's population was about 1.2 billion, few of whom would ever hear about him or Fort Sumter.

The khedive of Egypt was feeling cranky about the slow progress of the Suez Canal, and Édouard Manet was completing his *Spanish Guitar Player*, the first painting he would exhibit at next year's Salon. The Tsar's government was putting together the greatest edict in Russian history, the emancipation of the serfs, to be released in a few weeks, and Charles Darwin's *Origin of Species* was starting to cause a minor stir. Karl Marx was spending his days reading and taking notes at the British Museum, Joseph Lister in Glasgow was contemplating antisepsis, and Ignaz Philipp Semmelweis was practicing it in Hungary with extraordinary results. Southwest Africa had a boom in ostrich feathers, Dr. Livingstone was tramping about East Africa, and the first laborers from India had just arrived in southern Africa to work Natal sugar plantations. In Boston the captain of a slaver was on trial. The British had captured his fast ship with its six hundred unfortunates and had turned him over to an American court, which would convict him.

In New York, at Phineas T. Barnum's establishment, queues of the mordant were noticeably long. Optimistic entrepreneurs in northwest Pennsylvania were pumping oil, and in Colorado energetic young men were scrabbling for silver and lead. In October a Pony Express rider from California clattered into St. Joseph, Missouri, then telegraphed eastward; words from the West Coast thereby took only twenty-two days to reach the East.

There was conflict around the globe. British and French troops had just occupied Peking and purposely burned the Summer Palace. Not far away, the terrible bloodbath of the Taiping Rebellion continued. Garibaldi and his Thousand Redshirts besieged

Gaeta. Nasty events burbled in Ecuador and Syria and Brazil. In New Zealand British soldiers attempted, with little success, to track down Maoris—who had an annoying habit of skittering away to their *pa* fortifications.

Births and deaths, anguish and joy, starvation and discovery. The day-to-day lot of most people was spent like squirrels and barn owls and squid, gathering sustenance, ingesting it, defecating, then falling asleep—to rise again the next morn to perform the same routine. Unaware of events in Charleston Harbor.

Robert Anderson's actions in December 1860 modified the course of history—in ways he never could have imagined. He had hoped by moving to Sumter to maintain America's status quo, to hold back the prospect of war. But he stirred up far different fates . . .

CHAPTER NINE

Dueling Flags

On December 27, just after dawn, someone in Charleston noticed smoke above Sullivan's Island. Mayor Charles Macbeth, contacted at his home, immediately ordered two city fire companies to assist Moultrie's garrison. The firemen were boarding a steamer when John Kenny, a resident of Sullivan's Island, approached them in a rowboat. Kenny had been one of Foster's masons, working on Moultrie. He was also one of Charleston's militiamen, and he had been secretly tipping off his unit, the Meagher Guards, about events at the fort.[1] He shouted to the firemen the astonishing news about Moultrie: Anderson had skipped over to Fort Sumter during the night. Kenny said he did not know what the smoke was; perhaps the garrison's rear guard was burning down the whole fort.

When Governor Pickens was informed, perhaps recognizing his unfortunate tendency to overreact, this time he chose prudence. He sent investigators to Fort Sumter to check the validity of the story. If Anderson had indeed moved the garrison, Pickens considered the action outrageous. South Carolina's representatives had seemingly received a firm promise from President Buchanan just a few days earlier. Had Buchanan broken his promise?

During the next few hours, and in the week to come, the leaders of South Carolina were apoplectic at Anderson's coup. They believed that all the forts in their harbor belonged to South

Carolina, and had simply been on loan to Washington; only Buchanan's "promise" had prevented their immediate takeover by the state. If Anderson *had* actually moved, the governor would look like a fool, and Francis Pickens was not the sort to accept slights gracefully. As far as he and the other leaders of South Carolina were concerned, it was one thing for their state to secede from the United States, but it was completely unacceptable for Major Anderson and Fort Sumter to consider seceding from South Carolina. In mid-morning the governor's spokesmen boarded a steamer and headed to Fort Sumter. They carried what they themselves termed a "peremptory" message.

At Sumter the men could see their breaths in the chill December air as they inspected their new home. They were not comforted by what they examined. Fort Sumter, despite its imposing facade, screamed out its weaknesses. Although it had fifteen guns mounted, these would have offered the garrison scant protection against a determined assault. All but one aimed toward the Atlantic, and none could adequately defend the Esplanade or the wharf. Not only were the cannon pointed in the wrong direction, they were mounted for long-range fire and few could have been depressed sufficiently to hit an assault party at the base of the walls. An attack force could land at one of the undefended sides and spread out to search for weak spots. And there were many of these. The embrasures (the windowlike openings for cannon) on the first tier were only chest high above the rocks surrounding the fort. Most were covered with simple wooden shutters or a layer of bricks, but anyone with a hammer could knock his way inside in no time. The embrasures on the second tier were even more accessible to those with ladders, consisting of yawning openings, each eight feet by eight feet.

The fort also had several other weaknesses. The large building just inside the Gorge wall had been designed, among other things, to house officers' apartments, and the ground level of each three-storied apartment had a door that opened on to the wharf side. In theory each apartment would eventually have its own "patio" on the Esplanade, separated from the rest by wooden fences. When

Anderson's command arrived, the workmen had not yet gotten around to erecting the privacy fences for the patios, and the loop-holed backdoors of each apartment were invitations for attackers, who could bash them in with simple battering rams.

The main gateway had two four-inch-thick wooden doors, held in place by wooden crossbars, but a single barrel of gun-powder would blow them open. As Lieutenant Davis said on looking at this doorway: "Trust in Providence—and the main gate, after it is bricked up."

Even more than with Moultrie, Anderson's tiny garrison would have to stretch itself thin simply to stand atop the walls, to say nothing of blocking every access route to the fort's interior. They could hardly expect it to hold back an assault party for long—especially if Governor Pickens sent one in the next few hours. When Dr. Crawford returned from Moultrie that day he readied his bandages and set up an amputating table.[2]

The garrison was preparing for an attack that morning when Pickens's two representatives arrived: Colonel Johnston Petti-grew and Major Ellison Capers, both dressed in formal uniform. The two were escorted to a small room on the second floor of the Gorge, where Anderson and several of his officers awaited them. The major invited them to sit but they refused. Pettigrew was rel-atively under control, but Capers was edgy and agitated, hardly able to control his outrage. Anderson on the other hand, ap-peared calm.

Pettigrew said that Governor Pickens was astonished that the major had chosen to *reinforce* Fort Sumter. On the contrary, Anderson responded, he had simply moved his command here, something he had a perfect right to do.

Pettigrew said that when Pickens had been chosen governor a few days earlier, he had been told that Buchanan had promised South Carolina there would be no changes in the harbor, espe-cially to the status of Fort Sumter. The governor had hoped to ef-fect a transfer of all federal properties in the state without any resort to arms, but Anderson's transfer had made bloodshed likely. (There it was, an open threat, a virtual guarantee that South Carolina was about to attack. And, presumably, shortly.)

Anderson said he knew of no such agreement between the president and ex-Governor Gist. So far as he had been able to observe, he said, South Carolina's soldiers had been preparing to attack Fort Moultrie, and that was why he had moved.

Young Capers could no longer hold himself back. How, he said, could Anderson have thought himself threatened? The major replied that he had been worried about the armed steamers that passed Moultrie every day. He had become concerned, he said, that they were about to drop off an assault force north of Moultrie, which would then take over the high sand hills within easy range of its walls. This, he said, was why he had made the move, to *avoid* bloodshed. He had done this entirely on his own responsibility.

Capers expostulated. Those steamers were simply maintaining a patrol, that one of their main duties had been to prevent some sort of mob action against Moultrie by Carolina hotheads. Anderson said he had no way to know that. He reiterated that all he had wanted was to avoid bloodshed. He was not hostile to the South, he said, far from it. As far as he was concerned, "my sympathies are entirely with the South," and he pointed to his officers: "These gentlemen know it perfectly well." As far as he was concerned, the differences between the two sections "were brought on by the faithlessness of the North." Pettigrew and Capers stiffly nodded their complete agreement. But several of Anderson's officers were not pleased by his open expression of sympathy for the South's concerns. Despite his fond feelings for the South, Anderson said, his primary duty here in the harbor was to represent the government of the United States.

"Well, sir," Pettigrew said, "however that may be, the Governor of the State directs me to say to you, courteously but peremptorily, to return to Fort Moultrie."

The major's reply was quite clear. "Make my compliments to the Governor, and say to him that I decline to accede to his request; I cannot and will not go back."

"Then, sir," Pettigrew said, " my business is done." He and Capers turned and haughtily departed.[3]

As soon as Pettigrew and Capers left the room, Anderson told his officers to order everyone to gather on the parade ground. He had something in mind, something involving the flag.

People have been using emblems for thousands of years to announce something about themselves. They have displayed their clan's tartans, their school mascot, symbols of their gods or messiahs or corporations. They have honored their mothers, their military units, their nations, and the Easter bunny. Their armies have entered battle carting the personal insignia of an individual leader or representations of their town's chief guild. They have carried banners, ensigns, pennants, and even the head of some poor sot, a recently vanquished foe. Flags are convenient standards because they are light. Unlike a totem pole or a dismembered body, it is easily movable, and if of proper size can be seen at great distances. If you wish to indicate from afar — at sea, for example — who you are, a large flag is efficient.

When America was first inventing herself during her Revolution, each ex-colony, as it declared statehood, adopted its own flag. Massachusetts used a pine tree emblem, New York sported a white field with a black beaver on it, South Carolina's bore a rattlesnake. Few Americans in 1860 were flag fetishists. The piece of cloth was merely one more symbol of their country, along with the eagle. The army's artillery branch became the first part of the service to use a flag officially, adopting the practice in 1834, mostly because they manned seaport fortifications. The infantry began carrying it in 1841, a few years before the Mexican War pumped up the flag's importance a bit. The cavalry, however, did not officially begin to carry the country's flag until 1895 — despite stirring images in countless western movies.

Until Robert Anderson altered history on December 27, 1860, the symbol used most regularly by the U.S. Army was a coat of arms: the eagle, with its shield, some arrows, and an olive branch. The events at Fort Sumter focused the attentions of the nation on the flag (though even then it did not take on the full mantel of almost religious sanctity until late in the century, when masses of foreigners arrived and caused some Americans to use the flag as a sort of weapon, a cloth club with which to emphasize their superiority). There can never be any "true" meaning for any flag, because it is an organic symbol, changing and evolving with circumstances. Today, the American flag signifies, among many things, freedom, baseball, McDonald's hamburgers, the Ku Klux

Klan, Abraham Lincoln, and Charles Manson. Its meaning represents a thousand images and constructs, not all of them savory. As Shelby Foote once ruefully said about the Confederate flag, one cannot prevent yahoos from grabbing one's symbol and waving it about, giving it their own perspective.

As Anderson admitted to Pickens's two representatives, he felt sympathy for the South, but he failed to add that to him the South was simply a part of the United States, and not an independent, sovereign unit. During the past few weeks, in his lonely responsibility at Fort Moultrie, he had read the hot-blooded speeches of South Carolina's politicians. He felt desperately isolated. Unlike the rage that consumed Doubleday, Anderson's primary emotion was sadness. He felt spasms of annoyance at South Carolina's leaders, but his loathing for war, along with his orders from Washington, made him suppress his private angers. Yet he held tight to certitudes. Robert Anderson had served his entire adult life under the flag, and understood that the army emphasized that the flag's honor, like a man's reputation, had to be defended.[4]

According to army regulations, each coastal fort was to have two American flags, stored in a special box when not in use. Each morning the sergeant of the guard would remove one or the other and raise it over the ramparts. A "garrison" flag was huge — thirty-six feet from side to side and twenty from top to bottom — and meant to be seen from great distances. Its massiveness required that it be of fine, relatively light material, but, unfortunately, this meant it could tear rather easily in high winds. So each fort also had its smaller "storm" flag, twenty feet by ten feet, that it would fly in foul weather.[5] In the coming events both of Fort Sumter's flags would play their part.

It was about noon when Robert Anderson raised the American flag over Fort Sumter. Today, it is a mostly forgotten event, certainly less riveting than the photographed huddled forms atop Mount Suribachi, and less venerated than Francis Scott Key penning "The Star-Spangled Banner." That the Fort Sumter scene has faded from memory is ironic, because it was far more important and had much greater immediate and long-range impact than any

similar event in American history, far more than any words spoken by Lincoln until his 1863 Gettysburg Address. Anderson's
simple — and really quite normal — act of raising that totem of the
United States deeply stirred the national porridge of patriotism.
From that moment — or at least the time a couple of weeks later
when *Harper's Weekly* and *Frank Leslie's Illustrated Newspaper* simultaneously included emotional depictions of the ceremony — the
fate of Fort Sumter became a symbol of the nation.[6] Fort Sumter
stopped being merely one of dozens of federal forts inside seceded
states. Sumter had been "important" for weeks; now it became an
emotional magnet. Anderson's transfer to Sumter, then his raising
of the flag above it, tied the hands of, first, Buchanan, then, later,
Lincoln. Why? What was there about the event itself that caught
the attention of so many?

Just before noon those at the fort gathered. Wylie Crawford
was at Moultrie at the time, but he interviewed some who were
there and wrote a note in his diary about the ceremony at Sumter.
The band, he said, stood on the ramparts, far above the parade.
Anderson's soldiers remained below. The workmen squeezed together in clumps toward the sides, while a small armed guard of
soldiers eyed them carefully. Women and children solemnly
milled about the detritus of the fortress building materials. Anderson stood by the flagstaff with the halyard in his hand, as a sergeant positioned himself nearby holding the flag across his hands.
In the middle of the group was Reverend Matthias Harris, who
had just arrived. When everyone was in place, Major Anderson
took off his hat, knelt on the ground, and, while still holding the
rope, bowed his head. Others on the parade kneeled as well. Harris raised his voice. He thanked the Lord that the garrison had
made it safely across. He prayed with great feeling that the flag
they were about to raise would soon float again over a united nation, one that would remain prosperous and at peace. He asked
God that this flag never be dishonored.

When Harris finished, Anderson rose to his feet. The soldiers
presented arms, and, as the major began to pull on the halyard with
the help of the sergeant, the huge garrison flag rose in the air while
the band on the ramparts played "The Star-Spangled Banner." The

men of Anderson's command shouted great huzzahs. Then, Crawford's diary states without comment, the garrison — the majority of
whom had been born in Ireland — decided to give three very loud
cheers for the Old Sod, and did so with gusto.[7]

Over at Fort Moultrie, Foster, Crawford, and the enlisted men
saw the flag rising above Sumter, and they, too, lustily cheered.
Colonel Pettigrew and Major Capers were still aboard their boat,
returning to the city from Fort Sumter, when they also noticed it,
rising above Sumter's high walls, catching the December breeze,
fluttering its stars and its stripes against the sky, and over Charleston Harbor.[8]

By the time Pettigrew and Capers's boat bumped against the
wharf, the city was aswarm with rumor and rage. Citizens clustered on street corners and in the major hotels to discuss their options. Crowds gathered around bulletin boards at the two main
newspapers, impatiently awaiting clerks to pin up the latest news.
Uniformed young men bustled to and fro. Here and there one
could hear the beat of drums calling soldiers to action. One citizen
wrote his father, "The occupation of Fort Sumter by the Federal
troops, from its commanding & almost impregnable position, has
been regarded by our people, with great apprehension. . . . We are
in a state of anxious suspense as to the next act in the drama. . . .
It would seem that we have been treacherously dealt with; the die
has been cast, and we may now look for civil war." Another man
jotted quickly into his diary that evening, "Excitement today was
immense. . . . Various rumors afloat."[9]

All this frothing seems absurdly melodramatic. One wonders
how concerned with Anderson's transfer were Charleston's less
well-to-do: the German saloonkeepers, the Irish seamstresses, the
grizzled tars at the wharves, the prostitutes, the schoolteachers —
to say nothing of the half of the population that was black. In a famous passage, Mary Chesnut mused uncomfortably as to what
the city's slaves might be thinking of all this. During the bombardment in April 1861 she wrote, "Not by one word or look can
we detect any change in the demeanor of these negro servants.
Laurence sits at our door, as sleepy and as respectful and as profoundly indifferent. So are they all. They carry it too far. You

could not tell that they hear even the awful row that is going on in the bay, though it is dinning into their ears night and day. And people talk before them as if they were chairs and tables. And they make no sign. Are they stolidly stupid or wiser than we are, silent and strong, biding their time?"[10]

We do not know what most Charlestonians thought about Anderson's move to Sumter, but we can safely suspect that many adult whites did feel some reaction. We can assume that white male clerks at the downtown stores and warehouses were aroused, since many were enrolled in military units, which instantly became more active, and their families and friends certainly felt tugs of emotion. Most of the state's politicians were in town at this moment, since the South Carolina Convention was still officially in session, and their presence inevitably roiled the pot. No doubt plenty of folks simply looked forward to observing some action, strictly as entertainment.

It is not certain who initiated that afternoon's dramatics. South Carolina's governors were not expected or permitted to act decisively. On this day, December 27, 1860, Governor Francis Pickens did write out several dramatic orders, but it is possible he was acting simply as a functionary of the convention. Early that afternoon, the convention met to discuss the apparent changes in the harbor. Robert Gourdin, one of its members, rose and read a note he had just received from Major Anderson, perhaps brought to him by either Pettigrew or Capers. In it, Anderson said that the move had not been ordered by Buchanan, that he had done it on his own initiative. A resolution was proposed that Pickens was "authorized and requested to take immediate possession of Fort Moultrie and Castle Pinckney." The resolution also proposed that the governor try to "recapture" Fort Sumter (the word indicating that they had assumed Sumter was already theirs), and if he could not do this, to destroy it. Another resolution urged Pickens to place batteries of guns near the harbor's mouth to prevent Anderson from receiving reinforcements.[11]

Anderson's move to Fort Sumter embarrassed Pickens. He had been assuring the citizenry that he'd removed that possibility; now, in office only a few days, grumblings about him were already heard. Mary Chesnut wrote in her diary her reaction to all this: "One of the first things which depressed me was the kind of men put in office at this crisis. Invariably some sleeping dead head long forgotten or passed over."[12]

When Pettigrew and Capers returned to Charleston from Fort Sumter, they hurried to the governor and his council. The mood in the room was grim. Pickens ordered Pettigrew to gather a force and take over Castle Pinckney. They all assumed this action would result in bloodshed. Their information about the status of Castle Pinckney was sketchy; they were not sure whether Anderson had also sent men there during the night. Although Pinckney was not as large as either Moultrie or Sumter, it did have a high and thick wall and two tiers of cannon. Charleston had no artillery to use in an assault. All Pettigrew would have was a few half-trained companies of local citizens — full of enthusiasm for wearing sporty duds and marching past young, fetching ladies. Civilians who knew nothing of battle beyond what they read in the *Mercury*, some novels, and a few sanitized histories might speak confidently about "taking" Castle Pinckney, "brushing aside" all its defenders, but an actual move against it could become quite ugly. Even assuming it fell, there might be weeping in Charleston this very evening. Moreover, by moving against Castle Pinckney, Pickens was committing an act of military aggression against the United States, thus making any prospect of peace unlikely. He and others would argue, rather childishly, that, after all, Anderson had started it, and that, furthermore, Castle Pinckney *belonged* to South Carolina, that this fortification was simply on loan to the United States. Besides, there was that "devastation" Anderson had perpetrated upon Fort Moultrie. As the *Mercury* bellowed, "Spiking the guns and burning the carriages was as much an act of war as loading and firing the guns."[13]

Pettigrew and Capers departed on their mission. They called up three of Charleston's military companies. Messengers raced from place to place, contacting those called into immediate service, finding them often at home or at work. All over town, young men scurried about in great excitement. Each had to change into his uniform, perhaps say a few brave words to anxious families, then hurtle to The Citadel's Green, where they were to gather.

Charleston's population was alerted within minutes. Excited citizens and weeping loved ones drifted through the streets. Some moved off to the dock where the soldiers at some point were to board the steamship *Nina*. Others headed down to the Battery. From there, one could stare out at Castle Pinckney a mile away. With opera glasses you could expect to see events there clearly.

Luckily, Charleston was physically a small metropolis, and the soldiers were able to assemble at The Citadel by about two o'clock. Together they marched, carrying their weapons, the several blocks to a wharf on the Cooper River. As they arrived, with that tumult of emotions any group of men feels on their way to battle, they encountered a crowd awaiting them. The young soldiers had to press their way through the throng to make it to the boat. The whole scene was a stew of camaraderie, jollity, lubricity, and idiocy, along with much waving of delicate handkerchiefs and calling out of names, of open sobbing, of parental pride, of manly hearts a-beating, of cheering, of good-byes.[14]

In the midst of all this a remarkable scene occurred. Lieutenant Meade, still at Castle Pinckney, sent Sergeant Skillen, the fort's ordnance sergeant, to Charleston, probably to reconnoiter the situation there. Skillen arrived by boat about two o'clock. A large percentage of the town's white population was already in an uproar, cursing that blackguard Anderson and vowing to hang him, or some other violent retribution. Skillen now wandered about the city while Pettigrew's men were assembling to attack his fort. The sergeant hastened back to Castle Pinckney to tell Meade what he had seen, though it is possible he had not learned precisely where Charleston's militia was headed.

Pettigrew's attack force boarded the *Nina* and shoved off about four o'clock. Less than thirty minutes later the boat bumped against Castle Pinckney's wharf. Daylight was almost gone, the wintry sky had grown charcoal gray. The crowds at the Battery could just make out their arrival, the dropping of the *Nina*'s gangplank, and the city's young soldiers tumbling down onto the island, with determined expressions and fixed bayonets.

A sentry at Fort Sumter spotted the *Nina* and its occupants, and told Anderson. The major and Doubleday used their spyglasses to try and discern the events at Castle Pinckney in the evening's deepening murk. Anderson muttered angrily that he was considering using his artillery to knock out the harbor lights, but, perhaps remembering the restrictions of his orders, he maintained self-control.[15]

Lieutenant Meade was in his room at the fort, writing, when a sentry came and told him a boat with armed men was on its way. Meade ordered the main gate closed and barred. Most of his thirty workmen raced up to the parapet to see the approaching *Nina*, but Meade ordered them to their quarters. Wisdom overcame their curiosity and they retreated out of harm's way just as the boat landed, some of them reportedly to hide under beds and in closets. Except for Skillen, the ordnance sergeant, and his family, young Meade was quite alone. He stood at the parapet watching, as Pettigrew and his men ran around the side of the fort and pounded on the gate, huffing and puffing and halloing, demanding entrance. When this brought no response, they dug out their two ladders and prepared to scale the walls. Pettigrew told most of his attackers to aim their muskets on the parapet, to shoot anyone trying to man the big guns pointing out of the embrasures. Pettigrew and a dozen of his men climbed up. There they were, standing inside Castle Pinckney. Meade stood, waiting for them.

As Pettigrew's men rushed to open the gate, he strode to Meade and began to read aloud from Pickens's orders. Meade interrupted him. He refused, he said, to recognize any authority the governor of South Carolina might claim to have within this fort. The two then walked downstairs to the parade ground. Sergeant Skillen, who had been living here for quite some time, with only his wife and his daughter, Katie, for company, was furious. He paced back and forth, muttering. "Damn it! This is a pretty thing to happen to a U. S. fort."

Pettigrew had the American flag pulled down and replaced by the only available alternative, a red flag with a single white star recently flying above the *Nina*. South Carolina's legislature had called for a new flag several days earlier, just after secession, but decision-making processes moved slowly, and it would be another month before South Carolinians could agree on an official symbol. Why the *Nina* used a red flag with a single star is not clear, but it did, and thus it was this piece of cloth that was used in the first official military action that one day soon would be called the Civil War.

As this ceremony was going on, Skillen's daughter Katie stood by and watched. She was sixteen, perhaps seventeen, and strikingly pretty. The young South Carolinians could not help but be aware of her presence, and the fact that she was weeping. "Don't be afraid," one of their officers said to her, "nobody shall hurt you."

"I'm not at all afraid," she replied. "I'm *mad*, to see our flag go down and that dirty thing take its place." And she added that it certainly took a lot of very brave fellows to capture a fort occupied by only two soldiers and a girl. (A few days later the Skillens were sent north. After the war Sergeant Skillen was actually returned to his position at Castle Pinckney, and Katie came back to Charleston, where she married a local citizen.)

Lieutenant Meade refused to watch the flag-raising ceremony. He went to his room to compose a report. When Pettigrew came to him, Meade asked whether he was to be a prisoner. No, Pettigrew replied, but if Meade left this fort, he would not be permitted to return, unless he gave his "parole." The young lieutenant, quite properly, refused this, since to offer a parole to Pettigrew would be to recognize South Carolina as a foreign government with which the United States was at war. Then, in a remarkably incongruous moment, Pettigrew diffidently asked Meade if the South Carolina militiamen could have permission to use the fort's cooking stove. (During the next few months those on both sides felt uncomfortable with genuine hostility and often found it impossible to behave like thugs. This phase of the war, predictably, eventually passed, leaving behind pleasant myths about a chivalric conflict.) Lieutenant Meade told Pettigrew that he could hardly give any such permission to what, legally, were a band of pirates.

Colonel Pettigrew was aware that, at this very moment, another force of South Carolinians was about to move on Fort Moultrie. He asked Meade if Moultrie was actually mined, as rumor had it. The lieutenant answered with a shrug. A few minutes later Meade departed Castle Pinckney for Sumter, crossing the harbor in the darkness.[16]

―――――――

Back in Charleston, Francis Pickens had sent two companies to surround the arsenal, while other soldiers seized the federal Custom House in town. He also ordered a large force to advance on Fort Moultrie.

By late afternoon, just as the last of Pettigrew's infantrymen were departing on the *Nina*, four additional companies of soldiers met at Citadel Square, a bit over 200 of them, purportedly artillery specialists, led by Lieutenant Colonel William G. DeSaussure. Their assignment was to steam over to Sullivan's Island and take Fort Moultrie. They were to be very cautious in all this since workmen from there thought the fort might be mined, and the smoke rising above its walls indicated that Fort Moultrie had already been sabotaged. Pickens's orders to DeSaussure stipulated that the purpose of the expedition was to "prevent further destruction of public property, and as a measure of safety also."[17]

It was eight o'clock or so when they arrived outside Moultrie's walls. The gate was closed and everything inside seemed still. Colonel Charles Allston, one of Pickens's aides, stepped forward. "Surrender," he shouted inside, "in the name of the governor of South Carolina." Finally DeSaussure ordered that a ladder be placed against the wall, and he and two enlisted men climbed into the fort and unlocked the gate. Ordnance Sergeant Williams was the only soldier left. He indicated he would not attempt to repel these hundreds of men. Allston, DeSaussure, and some enlisted men stepped gingerly about the interior of Fort Moultrie, still queasy at the prospect of exploding mines.

They had brought with them the *Clinch*'s own flag, white with a Palmetto on it, and looked around for a place to raise it. They finally decided to place it in one of the guns overlooking the harbor. With that accomplished, they fired off three rockets, the signal that Fort Moultrie was theirs, then settled down for the night. Because of the reputed mines, most of the expedition remained outside the fort's walls.[18]

The weather the next day was fair, but the day after that it started to sprinkle, and then on December 30 it turned mean, the sort of wintry blow that sailors loathe. It rained on and off for almost a week. This may have saved Anderson's little garrison at Fort Sumter—for the nonce.

CHAPTER TEN

The Wolf at the Door

"We have so often cried wolf, that now, when the wolf is
at the door, it is difficult to make the people believe it."
— JAMES BUCHANAN, 1856

Senator Wigfall rushed through the streets of Washington, his ears awash with rumors he had just heard that
Major Anderson's garrison had slipped across to Fort
Sumter. Wigfall wanted to know for sure and figured that, if anyone in this city should know, it would be the commissioners who
had arrived only yesterday from South Carolina and were staying
in an elegant residence in Franklin Row. He was not by nature a
patient man.

Louis Trezevant Wigfall is easily the most colorful character
in the story of Fort Sumter. He was tall and muscular, with broad
shoulders and a sturdy neck. His thick black hair, beginning to
streak a bit with gray, tumbled about his face in disarray. His
black eyebrows jutted over his piercing eyes and gave him a distinctly roguish appearance. One observer said he had the eyes of
a beast, another said he had the look of a pirate. Reckless with
money and almost always in debt, he was widely said to drink to
excess — this in a bibulous era, exceedingly tolerant of planter
drunkenness. He was a man of uncertain habits and, betimes, un-
steady step with a reputation for violence that went back many
years when he had participated in two duels, plus one additional

shooting. Although those incidents had occurred a generation earlier, there lingered something vaguely sinister and deliciously romantic about him. One woman described a few hotbloods in Washington, who, she said, "out-wigfall Wigfall." He had become a verb. Two weeks earlier he had addressed the Senate. "I do not believe," he said, "that I owe allegiance to the United States," and he hooted at "the clap-trap of 4th of July froth and the idea that there is anything of sacredness in a compact between nations."[1]

He had married a striking young woman whose Rhode Island parents were quite wealthy, but this match failed to cover his debts. Bankrupt, hounded by creditors, Wigfall decided to try his hand in Texas, raising cotton. It did not take him long to fall into debt again, but this did not dissuade him from speaking out publicly, calling stridently for secession. He ran for the Senate just as John Brown led his band into Harpers Ferry. The uproar helped to get him elected, and he strutted into Washington three weeks after John Brown's hanging in December 1859. He immediately attacked his party's moderates, for, among other things, being soft on women's rights and the racial question. Men like Stephen Douglas, he said, "think a woman a man with a petticoat on, and a negro a black white man." They had, he said, the ridiculous view "that everyone is created free and equal." By December 1860, after less than one year in the Senate, he had become one of the nation's best-known spokesmen for secession and a Southern Confederacy. Now, on December 27, in Washington, he was on a mission.

When he arrived at where the commissioners were staying, they were preparing for their one o'clock conference with President Buchanan. William Henry Trescot was also there, offering them advice about what they might expect. Wigfall burst in and announced his news. His words landed like a bombshell.

The five men were still excitedly discussing it when Secretary Floyd arrived, apparently just to say hello. What, the South Carolinians demanded of him, were the facts? Had Anderson actually gone to Fort Sumter? Impossible, Floyd insisted; Anderson had been under direct orders not to do anything, certainly not to move to Sumter.

Floyd immediately rattled off to his War Department to see what news he might find there, and Trescot rushed to the Senate, where he encountered some Southern stalwarts, including Jefferson Davis. They all agreed to confront Buchanan immediately. At the Executive Mansion, Senator Davis told Buchanan he had just heard reports of "a great calamity," and that the president was "surrounded with blood and dishonour on all sides." Buchanan collapsed into a chair and moaned that calamities never seemed to come alone. He assured them that Anderson's move, if such turned out to be the case, would have been done completely against his policy. Other Southern senators arrived, and joined the testy chorus. They pressed the president to wire Anderson immediately, and order him, if he had gone to Fort Sumter, to return to Moultrie right away.[2]

It was a critical moment. The exact timing of all these events is unclear, but this conversation at the White House probably took place about noon. If so, and if Buchanan had sent such a telegram *immediately*, along with an explanation to Governor Pickens, it is possible that South Carolina's expeditions against Castle Pinckney and Fort Moultrie might have been forestalled. The end result, however, would likely have been about the same, only the timing would have been different. James Buchanan had long since made his mind up. He was *not* going to negotiate with the commissioners; that was a congressional matter.

Buchanan refused to act precipitously. He wanted, he said, to discuss the matter first with his cabinet. Besides, he wanted more information directly from Major Anderson. He told his disgruntled Southern visitors he must put off meeting the commissioners until the next day.

During the following weeks Buchanan's government, like something molten, was remolded by pressures. Cabinet meetings followed cabinet meetings. Various cabals formed and reformed, as key individuals looked to influence the president, and control events.

Floyd's position during the next twenty-four hours was bizarre. Buchanan had in essence fired him several days earlier, but had given him a bit of time for dignity's sake. Floyd, irksome as always, had not yet resigned, and at this moment, since he was still officially secretary of war, he was called upon for his presumed expertise. At the first of the two cabinet meetings that day Floyd blustered. He read aloud a formal statement that Buchanan should order Anderson to get out of Fort Sumter; in fact, preferably, to leave South Carolina entirely. Secretary of State Jeremiah Black reminded the group that they had been shown Major Buell's message to Anderson on December 21, less than a week ago. Black recalled that it had given Anderson the right to move if he considered himself in any danger. Nonsense, Floyd sputtered. Black then proposed that they look at the document. A messenger brought it, and the cabinet read Buell's words, slowly and with care. But even then, the cabinet members, like the nation, remained divided. Three of them concluded that Buell's words did give Anderson the leeway to transfer; three — all from the South — said they did not. Their differences — of temperament and connections and nativity — began to metamorphose into hostility.

On the afternoon of December 28 Buchanan had a grueling two-hour session with the commissioners. They expressed their outrage about Anderson's move. They reminded the president that he had guaranteed — on his honor as a gentleman, the commissioners insisted — that there would be no changes in the federal forts in Charleston Harbor. They pressed him. Buchanan finally snapped back at them: You push me too hard, he said. You don't even give me time to say my prayers, and I always ask God's advice before I make any important State decisions.

The commissioners were not satisfied with this religious defense. They demanded formally that he surrender all federal properties in South Carolina, then left in ill-humor. James H. Adams, one of the commissioners, and the least stable of the three, wired Charleston a rather hysterical description of the conversation with the president, urging the state "to prepare for war immediately." According to Doubleday's later account, this telegram triggered a panic in Charleston, a fear that the American fleet was about to come and bombard the city. Local banks, Doubleday claimed, immediately "suspended specie payments." Civilians on Sullivan's Island were told to evacuate.[3]

The next morning Buchanan held another of his many cabinet meetings, this time without Floyd, whose resignation had at last appeared. After much discussion, Buchanan said he would write something and present it to them that evening. A few hours later, at their next session, he read his statement to them. Apparently there was little comment from anyone, but half privately thought he had yielded too much, the other half considered his reply too firm.

Twenty years later Jeremiah Black vividly recalled that after he left that meeting he could scarcely sleep. The more he considered Buchanan's reply to the commissioners, the more agitated he became. He concluded his only recourse would be to resign, though perhaps threatening to do so might have an effect on the president. It did. The president became highly disturbed at the prospect of losing his secretary of state on top of everything else, and sent for him. Black told Buchanan he found the proposed message to the commissioners intolerable. Buchanan was miffed; he just wanted to be shed of this hairshirt that was chafing his last weeks in office. He said to Black: If you can do better, fine, but have the message back to me by this evening. The secretary of state raced across the lawn to the office of the attorney general. He and Edwin Stanton knocked out a relatively firm response to South Carolina, and had it done by dinnertime. Its key phrase would be the president's reply to South Carolina's demand that he order Anderson's garrison out of South Carolina: "This I cannot do; this I will not do."

So there it was. The following day, after reviewing the document one more time, Buchanan sent it to the three representatives. It was December 31.[4]

That evening, as the year 1860 wound down, Winfield Scott was feeling better than he had in days, chipper even. He had been worrying about whether South Carolina might take over Fort Sumter; to make matters worse, the soldier's ailment had grabbed his bowels, and for several days he did not stray too far from a chamber pot. But Anderson's actions in Charleston Harbor had lightened his mood considerably. Early on December 28 Scott had sent an urgent message to Floyd, apparently unaware that the secretary of war's tenure was essentially over. When he received no reply, two days later he sent a note directly to the president. He said he was still quite unwell, "But matters of the highest national importance seem to forbid a moment's delay," and he hoped Buchanan would forgive the urgency of this letter. He wanted permission, he said, to send 250 soldiers to Anderson.[5]

Meanwhile, Floyd's position at the War Department had been taken by Joseph Holt. Holt had a good, clear lawyer's mind and wrote in crisp prose. A Kentuckian, he had far more backbone and sense than Floyd, and, unlike the Virginian, really *was* a man of honor. (Perhaps Wigfall sensed this about him, because as soon as Wigfall heard about the appointment he wired Charleston: "Holt succeeds Floyd. It means war. Cut off supplies from Anderson and take Sumter soon as possible."[6])

On December 30, even before his appointment became official, Holt began actively working with Black and Stanton to brace up the administration. While the secretary of state and the attorney general were whipping out their pages of prose about South Carolina's demands, Holt was meeting with Isaac Toucey, secretary of the navy. At some point on that day they put specifics together, using Floyd's original notion about sending soldiers from Fort Monroe down to Anderson on the *Brooklyn*. They did this without consulting Scott, though they did of course speak to Buchanan about it.

All in all, Scott began to feel much more upbeat. The government might not be following his plan—at least not yet—but it had decided on action. Poor Anderson, down in Charleston Harbor, would not be left out like some goat tied to a tree. Besides, Scott's stomach ailment had passed and he was able to return to his usual habit of eating gluttonously. Following a fine New Year's Eve repast he met with the president. Later on, the recollections of Scott and Buchanan about that night's discussion did not jibe. Buchanan remembered that he said that the troops should be ready to board the *Brooklyn* at a moment's notice, but that he, the president, wanted to await the response of the commissioners to a note he had sent them that day. Scott, who did not want to use the soldiers from Fort Monroe anyway, agreed that this sounded prudent. He thought it would be unwise to strip soldiers away from Fort Monroe in Virginia and preferred using recruits stationed in New York. Sometime during the next forty-eight hours, Scott convinced Buchanan to accept his ideas.[7] One thing that had been bothering him was the lack of secrecy of Holt's plan. The general correctly assumed that, if the government used the *Brooklyn*, Charleston would immediately be notified by spies in Virginia. (Scott might not have had to look far to find spies. His own adjutant general, Samuel Cooper, who read all military correspondence, and Scott's secretary, Lieutenant Colonel George W. Lay, who penned most of the general's "confidential" orders, both resigned from the army a few weeks later and joined the Confederacy.)

New Year's Day was usually an occasion for sociability, especially in governmental circles. Men of note held open houses, and friends and acquaintances would drop by for brief visits. The day held much forced gaiety and pretentious hospitality, enlivened a bit as the day wore on by large bowls of eggnog and hot punch at each reception. But this year's festivities were different. The mood in the capital had the ambience of a dark alleyway.

At the White House James Buchanan, already rattled by events and worn by tension and not enough sleep, received intentional snubs and humiliations from Southerners who considered it a splendid idea to be publicly rude to the president. Some in Buchanan's reception line wore blue cockades to show their support of South Carolina and secession. A few stalked past him, scowling, refusing to shake his hand. To an old man of his temperament, after a lifetime embracing the proper ceremonies of diplomacy and genteel politics, these snubs must have galled painfully. Worse was to come.

The following day Buchanan met with his cabinet. The discussion was rolling back and forth, leading nowhere, when the commissioners' reply arrived. It was as though an unpleasant odor had entered the room. The reply was pompous and insulting. Even as feckless as Buchanan had been lately, he was affronted by its tone. The document reviewed how conciliatory the president had been heretofore about the garrison, returning the muskets to the arsenal, for example. Yet now, with the garrison moved to Sumter, when "Major Anderson waged war," Buchanan had refused to disavow the action and order him out of that fort, even though the move was "a hostile act in the highest sense." By doing nothing about this, "you have probably rendered civil war inevitable." The commissioners added: "Be it so. If you choose to force this issue upon us, the State of South Carolina will accept it."[8]

Rather than reply to the message, James Buchanan chose a useful diplomatic tool; he simply returned it with an attached note that he declined to receive it. His response arrived at the commissioners' rented residence too late. They had already departed in a huff, leaving behind wisps of magnolia pride and palmetto hauteur.

The president and his cabinet discussed what the government might do, though they left with different impressions of what was said. Jacob Thompson, the secretary of interior, a Southerner quite meticulous in matters involving his honor, was clear in his mind that they had made no concrete decision. Three days later he wrote an acquaintance in Charleston that it was unlikely the administration would send reinforcements to Charleston unless something changed down there. (The vessel carrying more soldiers and supplies had already departed for Charleston as Thompson was wiring this message South.) What Thompson did not realize is that some sort of decision had in fact been made at the January 2 meeting, that several members of the cabinet heard the president say—or at least indicate—he was ready to send reinforcements. The secretaries of war and of the navy left the meeting and began to implement the decision.

General Scott had been conferring with a naval expert who convinced him that the waters of Charleston Harbor were far too shallow and too tricky to permit the *Brooklyn* to run into Fort Sumter.[9] Far better, this expert said, was to use a lighter craft. The navy did have a few such ships available, but unfortunately none had the capacity to carry the large quantity of supplies involved. Logic suggested they use one of the large *civilian* steamships that regularly made the Charleston route. Scott began to seek one out.

———

Governor Pickens was convinced that Washington would be sending troops of some sort to Charleston Harbor at any moment, either an attack force or reinforcements for Anderson. In either case he wanted to be prepared. When most of his military advisers warned him that the state was hurtling toward military disaster, he refused to back down, saying he would not listen to a council of war that proposed moderation. When they advised him that Fort Sumter could dominate the harbor, and even destroy Fort Moultrie, Francis Pickens sneered and shrugged. He said, "If we are to occupy no place, because our troops are raw and inexperienced, then we will have to abandon the State." Logic told him that Buchanan's position was also weak, that political squabbling would tie the president's hands.[10] Pickens admitted his own military ignorance, but he was making a discovery about military experts, one that Lincoln, too, would soon find: Those who understand war, who know about discipline and logistics, about hygiene and training, about bad weather and poor communications and accidents, these men are often chary at the idea of aggressive action. They recognize that heroism is fine for books, but that disaster lurks everywhere.

Late on the afternoon of December 28, just after receiving Adams's disturbing message, Pickens took a boat to Sullivan's Island to check on things for himself. He discovered there were no mines in Moultrie after all, but the situation there was not good. The gun carriages burned by Anderson's men — and how that "destruction of public property" outraged him! — would take two weeks or so to replace. Moreover, if Anderson opened up on Fort Moultrie, its walls were not strong enough to hold back heavy fire for long. Probably not one of his militiamen had ever fired a cannon; few had ever even seen it done. Practice would devour precious gunpowder. Luckily, Castle Pinckney had a fair supply, and it was quickly divvied out to Moultrie, but if it came to a fight in the next few days Moultrie would use all its available powder in an hour or two. Moreover, the soldiers at Fort Moultrie could not practice soldiering and build up the fort's walls at the same time. Pickens listened to all these problems, gave orders, and left.

Things at Moultrie did not immediately improve. You cannot train civilians easily to be soldiers; that takes skill, and time. As to the walls of the fort, Pickens received a note on December 30 from Walter Gwynn, whom he'd put in charge of that job. Gwynn admitted he was discouraged. "I have not accomplished much," he wrote Pickens. He said he could round up only thirty-seven of Foster's workmen. "They worked very well for four and a half hours, when they informed me that they had not dined. I could not do else than permit them to get something to eat. We called the roll — twenty-two men promised to return at the expiration of three-quarters ($\frac{3}{4}$) of an hour. At that lapse of time but three reported for duty." Gwynn took a boat to the city to see if he could find workers, but most of his efforts there were fruitless.

Inevitably, the heavy labor was given to slaves. Within a few days forty slaves owned by the South Carolina Railroad were sweating at Fort Moultrie. Others were soon sent. The *Courier* was pleased to report that the Reverend Mr. Prentiss forwarded "twenty hearty, strong negros" to help the cause. The *Mercury* claimed, "We learn that 150 able-bodied free colored men of Charleston yesterday offered their services gratuitously to the Governor, to hasten forward the important work of throwing up redoubts wherever needed along our coast."[11]

Pickens, meanwhile, broadened his scope. He ordered the complete takeover of the arsenal. Captain Humphreys, the paper-shuffling storekeeper, was assured that South Carolina would not exactly *take* the arsenal but, henceforth, neither he nor any of his fourteen enlisted men would be permitted to come and go without first receiving permission. Humphreys thought about it and decided the restriction on his movements was unacceptable. He wired Washington that he would demand that the state's soldiers leave; if they refused, he would consider the arsenal "occupied," pull down his flag, and surrender. That same day, even before Humphreys's superiors could respond, Pickens ordered the arsenal occupied. When the militiamen arrived, Humphreys surrendered. He asked that he be allowed to salute his flag before he took it down, and was permitted to do so, but only with a thirty-two-gun salute — that is, one for each state *except* South Carolina, which no longer considered itself part of the Union.[12] Pickens had just made his state militarily much stronger. If it came to a fight, he no longer had to arm his soldiers with the ancient flintlocks in South Carolina's arsenals. The state was hardly ready for a real war yet, since its gunpowder was still insufficient and its artillery weak, but things were improving.

The governor and his advisers, concerned about reinforcements to Sumter, discussed what to do about the mouth of the harbor, which contained four separate channels. Sealing them all could severely damage the city's commercial lifeline, so Pickens and his council compromised. They concluded that several channels could be blocked by dropping hulks; they also yanked up buoys and extinguished all the harbor's beacons and lighthouses. Since the channels were tricky and constantly changing in a swirl of silt, only expert local pilots could guide ships between the shoals. At night it would be almost impossible for a sizable vessel to enter. But just in case, Pickens ordered patrol boats to watch the waters between the harbor entrance and Sumter. Twenty soldiers from one of the city's volunteer companies patrolled each night, starting at seven o'clock. Guns at Moultrie could fire at intruders along the northern side of the harbor's entrance, but Charleston had nothing across the way, nothing on Morris Island. Pickens decided to put an artillery battery there.

A cold, dank wind blew across the dunes on the afternoon of December 31 as steamers chuffed back and forth between Charleston and Morris Island, bringing soldiers, slaves, and supplies. The arrivals began setting themselves up in an abandoned hospital, just about out of range of Fort Sumter's guns. More men arrived the next day, and more supplies—barrels of food, timber, hundreds and hundreds of bags to fill with sand, wheelbarrows to move stuff. The weather was raw as they got to work. During daylight hours the slaves, about two hundred of them, shivered in the cold, and at night they slept outside on the sands, because, it was said, there was not enough room for everyone in the tiny building. The soldiers, soon numbering almost three hundred, also worked hard and uncomfortably. Most were infantrymen.

The most important soldiers on Morris Island were a handful of terribly young cadets from The Citadel in Charleston.

The Citadel had been created by the state legislature in the 1840s to train worthy young boys from South Carolina in the arcane skills of soldiering. Now half its students, recalled from Christmas vacations, went to work on Morris Island. They had been trained somewhat in artillery usage, and their school did own some artillery pieces, which they had practiced on. Within a week, with the aid of the slaves and their infantry colleagues, the cadets had built a quite adequate battery of 24-pounders. Their cannon faced east, toward the Atlantic, hidden from view behind some high dunes and further protected by sandbags. The guns sat, well-braced, on a flat timber floor. The deepest channel access into the harbor ran right in front of them. If Buchanan sent reinforcements to the garrison, it was likely they would pass directly in front of the guns and the forty or fifty cadets.

All of Pickens's feverish activities during these days—especially moving troops out to Fort Moultrie and placing cadets across the harbor—were dependent upon the forbearance of Robert Anderson. The governor assumed that Anderson would not attack first. But if reinforcements came, and were fired on, it was highly likely Anderson would react. As things stood, Sumter could probably destroy Fort Moultrie in a few hours; it could also prevent the free movement of all ships about the harbor. Then, federal reinforcements could land at Fort Sumter at their leisure, and without effective opposition. Washington could send more ships down and land men on the outer islands, then bombard the city. No other state had yet joined South Carolina in secession. This might all get very ugly, and very quickly. Much would depend on Major Anderson.

At Fort Sumter the garrison's work had been moving vigorously. As the rain poured down, Foster's remaining workers and the soldiers tried to seal up the gaping embrasures. The laborers pressed masonry into all the musket loopholes and sally ports, and placed iron bars to hold the shutters firmly closed. They also mounted a few guns each day, pushing and pulling them carefully into positions where they might serve to hold off an attack from the city. The fort could not withstand a genuine assault by a large force, but its situation was gradually improving.

The physical comfort of the occupants was something else altogether.[13] During the last hours before transferring to Sumter, Anderson had emphasized to Hall to get as much coal as he could from Fort Johnson. But, as often happens, haste and confusion intervened, and Hall failed to pick up any coal. Sumter had had a trifling amount, but it could not last. Once the garrison was in place at Sumter, Hall went over to Moultrie, now occupied by South Carolina volunteers, to see if he might be allowed to bring back with him some fuel, as well as the winter coats many of the enlisted men had left behind. He discovered that the militiamen had already expropriated a whole box of greatcoats for themselves. Colonel DeSaussure was civil to him, but said that the status of the "public property" at Moultrie, fuel for example, had not yet been decided. Two days later Lieutenant Snyder and four enlisted men took two boats to Charleston. As his men purchased some fresh meat and other stores, Snyder went to see Pickens at the Mills House. The governor quizzed Snyder carefully about whether the artillery at Moultrie had been booby-trapped. In turn the lieutenant asked the governor whether, as a matter of civilized behavior, Major Anderson would be informed if South Carolina was about to attack them, so that the women and children could be transported from danger. Pickens agreed that the families would be permitted to go to Sullivan's Island if they chose, cautiously not stipulating whether or not he might order an attack. As to supplies and mail, Pickens said the garrison could come each day with a boat and get their mail but no food or other goods.

Pickens changed the subject. Would Major Anderson, he asked, go back to Moultrie if ordered to do so by President Buchanan? Certainly, Snyder answered. The governor then asked a remarkable question: Would Captain Doubleday lead the garrison back to Fort Moultrie if Pickens himself ordered it? Absolutely not, said Snyder, nor would any of the other officers. Presumably, Pickens just wanted to find out if there was any mutinous feeling among the officers. Their conversation ended, Snyder returned to his boats. He discovered that the city policemen had expropriated those supplies his men had just purchased.

Louisa Seymour was still on Sullivan's Island and she asked the authorities at Fort Moultrie if she could have permission to cross to Sumter but this was refused. The two sons of Moultrie's sutler, however, offered to sneak her over, and on a dark night they did so. Mary Doubleday, also turned down, had grown impatient and wanted to be with her husband. Rather than await permission, she merely strode up to one of the boats carrying laborers across, stepped in, sat down at the stern, and told them to start off. A nearby sentry eyeballed her, but made no attempt to interfere. A few minutes later she was standing on Sumter's wharf, and she and her husband retreated to his quarters. Abner Doubleday broke up a mahogany table they owned to supply them with a bit of extra warmth.

These additional women at Sumter made Anderson nervous. Unlike the "camp women," these officers' wives were "ladies," and in that era and that bleak environment they would be a genuine distraction. Anderson told his officers it would be best if the women left. Mary Doubleday and Louisa Seymour crossed immediately to Sullivan's Island, rowed over late at night by the same two boys who had brought Louisa across.

In early January Anderson's younger brother Larz arrived at Sumter, accompanied by Robert Gourdin and one of the Hugers. The governor had okayed a visit to the fort, so long as the two brothers did not speak privately — hence the presence of Gourdin and Huger. Larz was an energetic, forceful person, a successful businessman from Cincinnati with political connections. In late December he spoke to some prominent Democratic leaders in Washington, as well as to General Scott. Although he had no certain idea that the administration was moving toward a military solution, it could not have escaped him that the mood of the town was sour. He wanted to share his reactions with Robert, and he left for Charleston on January 2. Although this was the day Joseph Holt officially took over at the War Department, and before the decision was made to send reinforcements to Sumter, Scott may have implied something to Larz. Whatever Larz said to his brother, Robert was depressed after Larz left. He believed war now inevitable. His goal in coming to Fort Sumter had been to allow time for compromise and thus avoid bloodshed. He had apparently failed.

Two days later, unexpectedly, Larz reappeared at Sumter, bringing with him reports of a national groundswell of support for Robert's transfer to Sumter. On New Year's Eve the people of Reading, Pennsylvania, had given Robert Anderson a thirty-three-gun salute. During this week he was being celebrated by similar salutes in Seneca Falls and Schenectady, New York, as well as in New York City, in Burlington, Vermont, in Philadelphia, and in Boston. More impressive to Robert, who had yet to receive a word from Washington about his movement from Fort Moultrie, was Larz's report that the House of Representatives had just voted 125 to 56 in favor of a resolution to "fully approve the bold and patriotic act of Major Anderson in withdrawing from Fort Moultrie to Fort Sumter." The same resolution supported Buchanan in anything he might do "to enforce the laws and preserve the Union."

An even more remarkable appearance at Sumter that day was Eba Anderson's. She had decided to make her presence felt in Charleston Harbor, and obviously had known that Larz would be in Charleston. By some legerdemain she had been able to track down a man named Peter Hart, who had served as her husband's orderly during the Mexican War, and was now a member of New York City's police force. Hart, in his late thirties and married, for some reason agreed to accompany her, to assist Major Anderson in a time of need. They arrived in Charleston and checked into the Mills House where Larz was still registered and waiting for them. Eba asked Pickens if she might visit her husband, and the governor would not be so ungracious as to deny her, though again he did insist that Gourdin go along. Pickens also said that Peter Hart could go to Sumter to act as a personal servant for Major Anderson, as long as he swore he would not be a combatant if the situation arose. And so the little party boarded a steamer for the fort: Eba, Larz, Hart, and Gourdin. When Robert saw Eba land at the wharf, he hurried out to her. She was exhausted and unwell, but he greeted her warmly. A few minutes later she was carried up to his quarters where they visited for a few brief minutes. She was satisfied. She had shown Robert she loved him, and she would leave Peter Hart behind to care for her weary and increasingly gray husband. The group left at four o'clock, and she and Larz were on the evening train out of town. Also traveling north on that train were the other officers' wives, who had found Charleston's atmosphere inhospitable.[14]

In his pocket Larz carried a message to the administration from Major Anderson. A week earlier Anderson had written his superiors that the work on Sumter was progressing, that he thought he could control the entire harbor from his position, "as long [within reason, of course] as our Government wishes to keep it." Anderson had received no response to that note, so he sent this message with Larz. He told Washington his men were in excellent spirits, and that each day they were mounting more guns, closing more embrasures. If none of the laborers proved treacherous, he was confident the garrison could hold out against any force South Carolina could bring to bear on him. He added, however, a portentous note. His previous message, sent December 31, had mentioned that South Carolina had landed some soldiers on Morris Island who were, he presumed, working on a battery. "At present," Anderson now wrote in a cautionary way, "it would be dangerous and difficult for a vessel from without to enter the harbor, in consequence of the batteries which are already erected and being erected. . . . We are now, or soon will be, cut off from all communication, unless by means of a powerful fleet, which shall have the ability to carry the batteries at the mouth of this harbor." He also said, "I shall not ask for any increase of my command, because I do not know what the ulterior [undisclosed] motives of the Government are."[15]

Two days after Eba and Larz left, some laborers arriving at Fort Sumter for the day's work carried one of the local newspapers containing an article that claimed the *Star of the West* was on its way with reinforcements. Crawford jotted into his diary: "We do not credit it entirely." Anderson was sure Scott would never send troops on a merchant ship.[16] As they all were discounting the story, the *Star* was only a few hours away.

In early January General Scott had sent Lieutenant Colonel Lorenzo Thomas up to New York to investigate the possibility of leasing a civilian vessel that might be used to reinforce Anderson.[17] Thomas discovered that the army could lease the *Star of the West* for $1,250 a day. Its present captain, John McGowan, would remain in command.

Cornelius Vanderbilt had built the *Star* in 1852, and it had recently been improved. It was a good-sized, two-deck, sturdy steamer, built mostly of oak and copper, 228 feet long. Important for this operation, she had only a twelve-foot draft, and therefore could make it comfortably across the bar, except at low tide if she were fully loaded. Ship's captain McGowan had never actually steamed into Charleston Harbor, but Thomas was able to hire an experienced New York pilot who claimed that, although he, too, had never been to Charleston, his basic knowledge should be all they would need. Perhaps most important, the *Star* was at this moment docked in New York at Pier 29, empty of goods and ready to depart. According to the agreement, its civilian owner would personally buy certain supplies — some vegetables and fresh beef — and load them on his ship, then McGowan would leave, as if for New Orleans. Perhaps this way, none of the many Southern sympathizers in New York would get wind of what was afoot.

Thomas moved quickly. He crossed over to Governor's Island, just off the tip of Manhattan, where the army maintained a base, and made arrangements for 200 recruits there, along with plenty of small arms, to be readied for departure the next afternoon, to transfer clandestinely to the *Star.* Oddly, for ventures like this, everything went according to plan. The *Star,* soldiers aboard, crossed out of New York's harbor at nine o'clock that evening, January 5. Scott's goal of secrecy seemed to be holding up. Thus far.

Rumors ricocheted about Charleston. Some came from friends in Washington and New York, some from the normal desire to embellish a story for dramatic effect, some from a variety of liquids being imbibed in Charleston's saloons. The newspapers' bulletin boards were a constant source for gossip. Buchanan, it was said by some, would be completely accommodating to secession. No, he was adamantly opposed. The Virginian Winfield Scott was about to overthrow Buchanan and turn the government over to the South. No, Scott was about to lead a vast army down to destroy Charleston. One rumor suggested that many states agreed with South Carolina about secession, so many that only New England, except for maybe Rhode Island, would stay aloof. No, a great fleet was on its way to attack. No, it was only the *Harriet Lane*. And on and on.

On January 6 began a flurry, then a blizzard of reports about the *Star*. The *Mercury* that day received some information and reported, "Despatches from New York say that the steamer Star of the West, of the Panama Line, coaled up yesterday with unusual celerity. The rumor is that she is to carry troops to Charleston, but this is ridiculed at the Steamship Company's Office."

This article, appearing first on the *Mercury*'s bulletin boards, created a spasm of growing anxiety in the city. Telegrams of inquiry sped outward, other telegrams tap-tapped back in response. The *New York Times* printed an article that day stating that the *Star*'s destination was Charleston, as did the New York *Evening Post*. Someone in New York wired Charleston immediately with that story.

Tuesday, January 8, more reports flooded in. Secretary of the Interior Thompson had finally learned the truth and wired down at five that afternoon. The indefatigable Louis T. Wigfall telegraphed Pickens that the *Star* was likely coming, and that she should be expected at any hour. Both of the city's major papers announced in their early editions that the *Star* was definitely steaming toward Charleston. The *Mercury* story began: UNITED STATES TROOPS HASTENING FROM ALL POINTS SOUTHWARD. THE STAR OF THE WEST, WITH REINFORCEMENT FOR ANDERSON, DUE HERE TODAY. The city grew feverish. By midafternoon people were peering out to sea. Some had spyglasses or opera glasses, others simply stared with goosebumped anticipation.

Governor Pickens's ships, scouting the harbor's entry, watched for hostile vessels. According to their orders, if *Clinch* saw a vessel approaching in the darkness, it would show one blue light and two reds; this signal requested that the unknown ship identify itself. If the answer was unsatisfactory, the *Clinch* would shoot off rockets indicating: "ENEMY! ENEMY!" South Carolina's artillerists at Moultrie and on Morris Island were to open fire. As Pickens wrote the commander of Fort Moultrie: "There must be all proper exertions made to prevent the reinforcements — *let the consequences be what they may.*" The governor of South Carolina had ordered his soldiers to open fire on American troops.

All was peaceful aboard the *Star of the West,* a virtual vacation cruise. The sky was clear, the air almost balmy. The soldiers spent most of their days on deck, enjoying the mild sea breezes. Whenever another vessel hove into sight, their officers hustled them below to keep them out of sight, hoping to arrive at Charleston Harbor incognito. It was stunning to discover, two days at sea, that their hoped-for secrecy was likely futile. During a quiet moment one of the officers decided to glance through a New York newspaper he had brought with him, published the afternoon they had boarded the steamer. He came across an item reporting that the *Star of the West* might be leaving New York that day carrying reinforcements to Fort Sumter. The officer immediately read the article aloud to his compatriots. They all agreed they might be steaming toward a battle. None had been in one, and they asked Captain McGowan what to expect. He was hardly reassuring. It was "a very unpleasant business," he said. He recalled how a ship he was on had been fired at by a Mexican battery for half an hour before being able to fire back. It had been exceedingly nasty, he said. Anxiety on the *Star* grew palpable. The soldiers preferred getting to Fort Sumter unscathed, not ending up on the bottom of Charleston Harbor.

The steamer made good time. By Tuesday morning, January 8, it was already only about ten hours or so from Charleston. This created a problem for McGowan. He was under orders to enter the harbor in early morning and to steam directly to Fort Sumter before he was noticed, but at their present speed he might arrive at the harbor's mouth before nightfall, where inevitably he would be noticed. He slowed down, then decided to stop his ship entirely. For three hours they remained motionless, not far south of Myrtle Beach. Some of the soldiers fished over the side.

At dusk McGowan started southward again. If the *Star* was attacked, men were prepared to fill in any holes below the waterline with mattresses. When they arrived at Fort Sumter, McGowan might have only a few moments to remove men and cargo, so the provisions they had brought were put on deck. The enlisted men spent the night huddled in the ship's coal bunkers. Almost all the lights aboard were extinguished. Waves softly rocked the steamer. The engines harrumphed methodically and the ship's great paddle splashed them toward their goal.

The *Star* arrived off the harbor about one-thirty in the morning. Everything was dark. The sky was clear, but the moon had not yet risen. McGowan, his first mate, the pilot, and several others peered uneasily toward the harbor. Something was not right. None of the harbor's beacons were where they were supposed to be. No buoys were visible to lead them through the tricky channels. The only light from Charleston Harbor was a faint one, probably at Fort Sumter. Off to their right side they detected a tiny light and assumed it was another vessel. They would have to wait until daybreak, when they could see their way. But of course by then they, too, could be observed.

January's weather in Charleston is moody. There are days so springlike one feels a desire to wear light clothing and contemplate pleasurable pastimes. Then, in a trice, Atlantic winds and storms can remind one who is in charge. This day—January 9, 1861—was one of the glorious ones. A marvelously blue sky. The temperature rising into the upper sixties. A slight breeze. The morning began with a narrow haze laying atop the harbor, but the sun baked it away in minutes. It was a fine day to be alive.

Or to begin a war.

A few minutes past six. Dawn grayed the air. Seabirds woke and started to swoop, searching for prey for breakfast, cawing at each other impatiently. The soldiers aboard South Carolina's patrol boat stared toward a large vessel out to sea off their port side. They could tell from her silhouetted outline against the morning sky that she was a merchant vessel, but was she a friendly one, or an enemy? (Ten boats would arrive and dock at the city's wharves during that day, and seven others departed for ports in the West Indies, Europe, New York, and others. War is all very exciting, but business is business. The Bank of Charleston would maintain

its usual relationships with northern banks until well into 1862.[18])
The *Clinch* lit three signals: one blue light, two red: "WHO ARE
YOU?" The other ship made no reply. The *Clinch* turned abruptly
and headed up the main channel into the harbor, firing signal
rockets. The *Star of the West* slumped in behind, with an American
flag floating from its aft flagstaff. Aboard the *Star* some men noticed, a little over a thousand yards off their port side, sticking out
of the featureless sands of Morris Island, a flagpole, which seemed
peculiar, and flapping from it was an odd, bright-red flag. Those
who looked closely may have detected the outline of a palmetto on
it. The *Star*'s paddles splashed her slowly across the bar.

It was just after Reveille at the Citadel cadets' camp. A sentry
paced the beach. Through the morning's haze he made out the
Clinch moving quickly, not far off. He saw it fire its signal rockets.
Then he noticed the approaching *Star.* He shouted the news to the
sergeant of the guard, and the drums beat out the long roll: "PRE-
PARE FOR ACTION!" The infantry companies, there to protect the
artillery battery, grabbed their rifles; the cadets hurried to their
guns, each young man moving to his assigned position. Major
Peter F. Stevens sighted his guns as best he could. He had only a
single, rather primitive instrument with which to make his calculations. Hitting a target with an artillery piece was difficult in the
best of circumstances; hitting one moving was even more prob-
lematic. To do so successfully, with dubious gunpowder and virtually no prior practice, was hardly to be expected, but Stevens,
the cadets' commander, intended to do the best he could. He
aimed his first shot well in front of the *Star,* as a warning shot. He
climbed to the top of the sand wall hiding his battery, peered out
at the passing merchant vessel, then softly said to the cadets behind him, "Commence firing."

At number-one gun the cadet captain said, "Number one,
fire." A young man named George Edward Haynesworth, nick-
named "Tuck," pulled the lanyard. By most definitions, Tuck
Haynesworth had just fired the first gun of the Civil War. (Of the
nine cadets manning that one cannon, four would be dead by
1865.) Major Stevens saw the shot skip well in front of the *Star*'s
bow. If she were friendly she would stop her engines immediately.

On board the *Star* there was consternation. Lieutenant Charles R. Woods, the officer in command of the 200 reinforcements, was outraged. He and Captain McGowan had been given a huge garrison flag before they'd left New York and been told to raise it if fired on. Major Anderson certainly would recognize that as a signal, and join in to protect the unarmed merchant ship. The huge American flag was flung up the flagstaff at the bow, dipped as a sign of distress, then raised again, where it fluttered in the morning breeze. At Morris Island they considered this an act of defiance, and Stevens called for his second gun to fire, this time directly at the ship. It hit the water near the *Star* and skipped past. They fired number three, and missed. The *Star* moved more quickly now. Again the battery fired, each cannon in turn. One cannonball struck her near the bow. The cadets at Morris Island could hear the dull thunk. (So could the recruits hiding in the coal bunkers.) Then each gun fired one more round. Soon the *Star* was too far off. In all, two rounds hit her and another went through her rigging. None did real damage, though they certainly frightened McGowan, who recalled, perhaps, his discomfort in Mexico.

The *Star*'s paddles were working harder now because the tide was racing out. She had to remain in the center of the main ship channel, and this took her straight toward Moultrie. The commander of Fort Moultrie, Roswell Sabine Ripley, was an excellent artillery officer. A West Pointer from Ohio, years earlier he had met and married a Charleston widow while serving at Fort Moultrie. He had resigned his commission and settled down in the city. When Pickens had sent him to Moultrie, he immediately began whipping his troops into some semblance of discipline, though he was unsatisfied with the results for weeks. On this occasion he knew his soldiers would be clumsy with the cannon, and he was aware he did not have much gunpowder on hand. He also strongly suspected that Anderson would open fire on him, and Ripley's walls were very vulnerable to fire from Sumter. He could see that Anderson had just run his guns out, those facing away, toward Morris Island. The patrol boat *Clinch* had sent a messenger to Ripley that this was indeed the ship they had all been fearing. As Ripley looked through his spyglass he saw that the approaching merchant steamer was well out of range, but he signaled one of his gun crews anyway. "Gunner number thirteen," Ripley said, "prepare to fire. Fire!" Its ten-inch ball sailed harmlessly off in the relative direction of the coming vessel. (The *Mercury*'s melodramatic account has Ripley jumping atop the parapet, and, thinking that Sumter was about to open fire on them, shouting, "Well, fire away, boys, but you'll all be in Hell in five minutes.") Moultrie was able to get off a few more ineffective shots, then it was over.

On board the *Star of the West* Captain McGowan and Lieutenant Woods conferred. Woods had never seen a battle, and McGowan was frightened of participating in another one. They also spied a small, swift steam vessel slicing through the harbor toward them and were apprehensive, believing it might block their exit. They hurriedly agreed to turn the *Star* to starboard. With the ebb tide pushing them along, they should be out of this infernal harbor in minutes. As it was, in his haste, McGowan's ship scraped its bottom three times against the sandy floor before escaping. A day or so later she was back in New York.

At Fort Sumter these past forty-five minutes had been a time of decision — and of indecision, whose effects would linger for months.

Abner Doubleday, on duty early that morning, was on the parapet as dawn glimmered in the east. He noticed the incoming merchant steamer and thought it might be the *Star*, which was reportedly on its way. He was focusing his spyglass on her when he heard the report of a cannon firing from the hidden battery on Morris Island. He did not see the splash of the warning shot, but in a few minutes he saw the steamer raise a huge American flag, followed almost immediately by a second shot. He raced down the steps of the nearest tower to Anderson's quarters, burst in, and announced the news. Should he, he asked the major, beat the long roll? Anderson assented, and Doubleday whirled from the room to search out a drummer. A few minutes later most of the garrison was on the parapet in various stages of dress. One corner of the fort had four guns facing Morris Island, but since the garrison had spent the past two weeks preparing for an infantry assault from

Charleston, the guns were loaded with grapeshot to repel waves of attackers. It took more time to change their loads to solid shot.

Anderson stood with a clump of officers, staring out at the drama. Wylie Crawford, nearby, watched the scene through a spyglass, keeping up a commentary on what he could observe. He reported that the ship was raising and lowering her flag, a signal of distress. Anderson ordered that Sumter's flag be dipped in response, but when someone ran to do it, it was found that the halyards were too tangled to move. Anderson was angry and excited. He had spent almost two months trying everything he could to avoid a confrontation. Now here was the American flag being fired upon. Although he could now see that the ship was indeed the *Star of the West*, and he was aware that yesterday's newspapers had speculated it would be coming here carrying reinforcements, there were no soldiers in sight. And he still considered it unlikely that his friend General Scott would send troops on a civilian ship, or do so without informing him they were coming. Was the firing simply the action of a gun crew on Morris Island out of control?

He was under very clear orders, repeated several times, to avoid anything that might initiate a conflict. If he ordered his own guns to fire, a national civil war would almost certainly ensue. The Morris Island guns were doing no damage to the merchant ship, and in fact he had absolutely no realistic hope of his own guns reaching them. When Fort Moultrie fired a couple of ineffective rounds at the ship, Lieutenant Jeff Davis asked if he could run out two guns they had pointing toward Moultrie. Anderson assented, but told Davis to await orders before opening fire. He was still cogitating his move when told that Davis's cannon were ready to fire. Corporal Francis E. Oakes of Boston, twenty-three years old, a clerk by trade when he'd joined the army, held the lanyard and awaited orders. Everyone looked to Anderson for some decision. The *Star* was turning now and moving rapidly out toward sea.[19]

It was all over quickly. South Carolina's guns ceased firing. The *Star* slipped toward the horizon. The moment for action was past. Anderson said, "Hold on; do not fire. I will wait." The major told his men they could stand down, leaving two men at each gun for the moment, just in case. He called his officers to come with him to his quarters for a council of war.

In Washington Senator Wigfall would hear of the events that day and crow with hot delight, "Your flag has been insulted; redress it, if you dare."[20]

CHAPTER ELEVEN

Hostages

"Sumter is impressed upon my life. I have lived
years in the events that have transpired here."
— SAMUEL WYLIE CRAWFORD, MARCH 14, 1861[1]

"[I feel like] a sheep tied watching the butcher
sharpening a knife to cut his throat."
— ROBERT ANDERSON, DESCRIBING
HIS WEEKS AT FORT SUMTER[2]

The *Star of the West* was hardly out of sight when the officers gathered in Anderson's quarters to discuss their options. Anderson was seething. He explained to them some (though not all) of Washington's restrictions, then laid out what actions he proposed to take. He would, he said, starting immediately, use Sumter's guns to close the harbor to incoming ships of any kind. He polled his officers for their reactions, beginning with young Norman Hall, who said he concurred. The others then spoke, one at a time. Foster said he agreed with Anderson and Hall. (One member of the garrison later recalled that Foster was so enraged by the inaction of Sumter's guns that when he left this meeting he ran back up to the parapet, where he crushed his hat in anger and muttered about insults to the flag.) Doubleday, of course, was also for a tough stand. Snyder was not only for firing at *incoming* ships, but at local vessels carrying reinforcements or supplies between Charleston and outer forts like Fort Moultrie. Meade, the Virginian, however, said he preferred a more moderate approach, one that would not lead to an immediate civil war. Crawford and Davis proposed that they contact Governor Pickens first; perhaps he would disavow the actions of his two forts. If he refused, they could then close Charleston Harbor, as Major Anderson proposed.[3]

Anderson was beginning to calm down, and the suggestion of Crawford and Davis made some sense. He scrawled a note to the governor, diplomatically saying he assumed Pickens did not sanction this morning's hostilities, which had no "parallel in the history of our country or of any other civilized government," and added that this assumption had been the only reason he had not fired back instantly. He warned Pickens, however, that if the action of the batteries was not disclaimed, "I must regard it as an act of war, and I shall not permit any vessel to pass within range of the guns of my fort." He handed the message to his adjutant, Hall, and sent him to the city. It was mid-morning.

Charlestonians were frenetic. Rumors were caroming from street corner to street corner. When the *boom* of the first shot had echoed throughout the city, people had tumbled from their homes and run to vantage points where they could observe the harbor. Women in swirling skirts and men on horseback had vied for space. The morning air was crisp and clear, but the action was taking place almost six miles away, making it impossible to see exactly what was happening, even with the spyglasses or opera glasses a few had brought with them. Just as suddenly the incident was over. There was silence in the harbor. The *Star of the West* was seen to be moving out to sea. Was she sinking? Would she turn about and drop off reinforcements on either Morris Island or Sullivan's Island? Would a bloody encounter then begin out there, sometime in the next few minutes? One thing seemed clear: War had begun.

The *Mercury* squirmed with pleasure. Firing on the *Star,* it gloated, "has wiped out a half century of scorn and outrage." Old Buchanan would have to send more troops now, and powerful naval vessels like the *Brooklyn*. Major Anderson would certainly use his guns to close Charleston Harbor.

It was all quite romantic, and deliciously exciting. Young men, buttoning their uniforms, could be seen rushing determinedly about. Before the day was out Pickens ordered several more units to guard Morris Island against a probable attack. Families proudly watched their heroic young men depart for the front. Crowds gathered at the bulletin boards to get the latest news and to share gossip. Rumors, rage, fear, excitement — all fluttered about like confetti.

Then a small boat moved out from Fort Sumter, heading to-ward Charleston; above it floated a white flag. It carried a young officer in full uniform. More rumors: The officer had come to sur-render the fort. No, a bulletin board announced, the officer's mis-sion was to say that Anderson would bombard the city unless *it* surrendered.

As soon as Lieutenant Hall's boat arrived at the wharves, a crowd gathered. He said he had come to see the governor with a message from Major Anderson. He was escorted to City Hall, moving with some difficulty through the press of citizens. The governor met Hall politely, read the note, and said he would show it immediately to his cabinet, then return with an answer.

It was two in the afternoon when Pickens sent his reply, puffed up with self-righteous bombast. He declared that obvi-ously Anderson was unaware of "the precise relations" between South Carolina and Washington. The state had seceded, and that matter "does not admit of discussion." Anderson's move to Sumter was "the first act of positive hostility," and President Buchanan had been warned that any attempt to send reinforcements would be seen as another "act of hostility." To prevent bloodshed, Pick-ens added, he had personally placed ships at the harbor's mouth to warn off any ship carrying reinforcements. The batteries firing on the *Star* had been following Pickens's orders to do so if an enter-ing ship did not stop after a warning shot. "This act is perfectly justified by me. . . . In regard to your threat in regard to vessels in the harbor, it is only necessary to say that you must judge of your own responsibilities."

Lieutenant Hall departed. In light of the mood in Charleston, Pickens was wise enough to order two of his aides to accompany him back to his boat.

Anderson and his officers read the governor's reply. They had no way of knowing that no patrol had stopped the *Star* and warned it off. Since their arrival at Sumter they had received no message from Washington. Though logic would suggest that sending the *Star* meant the government wanted to reinforce them, they had seen no soldiers aboard her. Pickens's murky prose had seemed to imply that Buchanan had some sort of understanding with South Carolina. Perhaps he did.

It was about three o'clock. Anderson had had time to think about the ramifications of carrying out his original threat to open fire on any ship entering the harbor. Sumter would almost certainly be assaulted immediately and the fort was not ready. He wanted to put a few more guns in place; this would take at least two days. He also was gravely aware that this whole thing was about to explode into real war, and with it would come, he believed, a complete shattering of the Union. He certainly did not want to be the person responsible. Anderson wrote a brief dispatch to army headquarters, and sent it immediately, along with his original note to Pickens and the governor's reply. They would be hand-carried to Washington by Talbot whose weak lungs were betraying him in the wintry cold of Fort Sumter. Anderson also wrote a letter asking Pickens to allow Talbot to carry his package of messages North. The major said he had decided to "refer the whole matter to my Government." He would not close the harbor "until the arrival from Washington of the instructions I may receive"; he assumed it would be soon, a week perhaps. When Talbot handed Pickens Anderson's latest message, the governor read it, and admitted he was pleased. The lieutenant took the evening train north.

A few blocks away South Carolina's legislature was meeting. The state's House passed resolutions supporting everything surrounding the *Star* incident: Pickens's actions and words; the firing on the ship by the cadets and by Fort Moultrie. At the Senate, however, a small incident revealed some deeper emotions. William Izzard Bull, a wealthy planter, hot-tempered in the best

of circumstances, was beside himself. The Senate had opened
with a reading of Anderson's message to Pickens and the governor's reply. Bull called Anderson's note "the greatest indignity
that has ever been cast upon this State. For a mere commandant
of a fort to send so insulting a message to a sovereign people . . ."
He sputtered to a stop as he tried to find the right words. "It fills
me with all the indignity possible to result from the greatest insult
that could be put upon a people." This did not make much sense,
but he continued. "And then, Sir, for the Executive of this commonwealth to take no notice of the insult, but to send in return a
message which would only have befitted the President of the
remnant of the United States . . ." Again he paused. Around him
the other legislators began to stir. He had just attacked Pickens,
and might say worse. He continued, "I do not know what motion
I can make!" He then responded to Anderson's dispatch with a
phrase employed by men actively seeking a duel: "The first message I treat with contumely, contempt, and scorn!" The noise in
the Senate grew. "And, Sir, if the House will hear me out, in regard to the second, I would simply offer a resolution — That the
Governor be requested to do his duty!"[4] A moment later the Senate went into executive session and visitors were told to leave.
The inflammable words of Senator Bull had revealed a growing
sentiment among some of the citizenry: Pickens was too soft on
this whole issue. Some had been suggesting he should have taken
Sumter when it was empty. Others, that he should have ordered
an attack on the fort as soon as Anderson had made his move.
Now there was all this dillydallying, all these . . . words.

In truth, Pickens had contemplated such actions, but the governor had had to consider the means he had at his disposal. At
some point that very day he wrote Senator Jefferson Davis for
help; that evening he ordered the state's most respected engineers
to give him a concrete plan to take Sumter.

The engineers produced a report the following day. In it they
urged the governor to forget a surprise assault by ill-trained volunteers. They proposed a bombardment from shore batteries to
weaken the garrison, to be followed eventually by an attack by infantry landing from boats. The engineers carefully specified that

their plan would take many weeks to prepare, and would require more artillery and much more gunpowder, all of which would have to be purchased out of state.

Pickens read the report and recognized its implications. Unless Anderson was persuaded to surrender Fort Sumter immediately, Pickens would have to take the long view. This would demand two things: patience and much more money. South Carolina was not noted for either. The day after he received the report, therefore, Pickens decided to try an interesting gambit. He sent two members of his council to Sumter to insist that Major Anderson give Pickens the fort right away. They were to imply that Sumter would be attacked immediately if it was not handed over. Anderson met the two at the wharf and walked with them just inside, where the South Carolinians pontificated at great length while Anderson listened.

As he understood it, they were presenting him an "ultimatum." In military practice an ultimatum precedes a battle by only a short period. For the past two days, since the *Star of the West* had been fired on, Anderson had watched Carolinians scurry about the harbor in feverish activity. More troops had been rushed out to the islands. Five hulks had been dragged out to the mouth of the harbor. Four of them, filled with granite, were sunk, and the fifth was anchored in the one remaining channel, ready to be sunk at a moment's notice if a Union fleet appeared. These five worn-out brigs had, in fact, been presented to South Carolina by generous citizens from Savannah. The hulks actually accomplished little; tidal waters pushed them aside. Yet rumors that the port was now blocked caused many merchants to take their trade to Savannah, a hundred miles away.

When Pickens's two emissaries finished speaking, Anderson asked them to wait while he discussed their message with his officers. Meade, the Southerner and the least bellicose of the officers, suggested this matter ought to be decided by their superiors in Washington, that one of them ought to go there and present it to the administration. Curiously, for some reason the others agreed, even though Talbot's mission involved the same question — what to do about Fort Sumter? Perhaps, being professional soldiers, they all simply wanted to pass the proverbial buck up the chain of command. Besides, it would give them more time to prepare Sumter for an assault.

They met together with Pickens's messengers. More orating. The Carolinians said that the old United States was falling apart. Mississippi had seceded two days earlier, Florida and Alabama were leaving the Union that very day, and others would follow; Virginia was bound to join them. In South Carolina, they said, emotions were running high. Twenty thousand volunteers were merely awaiting orders to fall upon Fort Sumter, which they would tear down brick by brick, with their bare hands if necessary. The harbor waters would redden with blood. Major Anderson said he wanted to do all he could to settle the matter peaceably and suggested that all diplomatic means ought to be exhausted before stepping into war. Suppose, he said, Pickens sent a man to Washington to hand-carry South Carolina's ultimatum, along with one of the garrison's officers. They could all then await the administration's response. In a sense he was proposing a truce, although no one used that word.

That afternoon, when his messengers told the governor Anderson's offer, Pickens quickly agreed. It gave him the time his engineers had asked for. He wrote a note to Buchanan, demanding Fort Sumter, and chose Isaac W. Hayne, the state's attorney general, to carry it North. The following day Hayne, accompanied by Lieutenant Hall, Anderson's adjutant, left for Washington.[5]

The mood in the national capital had not improved since that joyless New Year's Day. If anything, the atmosphere had curdled. As the British minister wrote home, "The expedition of the 'Star of the West' to Charleston, and her return without landing reinforcements, tend to make the Government and the army the objects of ridicule." At a dinner party in Washington a few hours after the *Star* slunk out of Charleston Harbor, Senator Robert Toombs of Georgia, highly respected but recognized as a bit of a tippler, was heard to say that the ship had been sunk, and that he only wished those who sent her had been on her at the time. General Scott was at this dinner and quite rightly took offense, since it was obvious to everyone in the room that Toombs was referring to him, and perhaps the president. Scott responded sharply. Toombs sassed him back. The elderly, corpulent general rose to his swollen feet and waddled toward the equally heavyset Toombs. The two were forcefully separated.[6]

In this highly charged atmosphere the president wrung his hands and searched desperately for some solution. When Talbot arrived in the capital he was taken to the White House to give his report. A week later the lieutenant told a friend he was shocked at Buchanan's demeanor, his quavering voice, his uncertainty. "The president," he said, "seemed like an old man in his dotage." At least that is what Talbot allegedly said, though the recollection was dredged up five years later by someone else, long after Talbot's death. According to this same report, when Buchanan met the lieutenant, the president laid his hand on the young man's shoulder and asked, "Lieutenant, what shall we do?"[7] It seems on the surface pathetic: the lost, elderly politician asking this young officer to help solve the nation's riddle. But Buchanan's question — assuming he did ask it — would have been quite reasonable. Talbot was the first person to give the president an eyewitness account of all these events, of the transfer to Fort Sumter, the leadership qualities of Major Anderson, the *Star* incident, the mood in Charleston. Asking his opinion about their options was no more peculiar than Anderson's asking his officers the same question several days earlier. A wise leader looks broadly for advice.

The central problem was that the president was trying to juggle a score of flaming torches while spinning valuable platters on each elbow and each kneecap. For a man who preferred tranquillity, these were not restful times. Anderson's garrison at Fort Sumter was clearly important, symbolically if nothing else. Buchanan's mail was filled with advice about what to do, some quite rude. Newspapers screamed raucously, but not with one voice. His meal and nap times were constantly being interrupted by visits from agitated politicians. Worried businessmen wired him hysterical notes about a recent downturn in the economy. The mayor of New York City had announced that his city should secede from the United States. There were rumbles that the Pacific states might separate from the rest of the nation, rumors that a band of Virginians might attack Washington to prevent Lincoln's inaugural. Assassins reportedly lurked in the capital. What about Richmond? New Orleans? Baltimore? What might the British government do? Was that scamp Napoleon III planning some venture in Mexico?

Four states — South Carolina, Mississippi, Florida, and Alabama — had now declared themselves out of the Union, and each contained Sumter-like problems. On the day Mississippi had voted to secede (the same day the *Star* was fired on by the Citadel cadets) some artillerist in Vicksburg, seven hundred miles from Charleston, opened up on a ship steaming down the Mississippi River. During that very week, in half a dozen states, still in the Union, militia units impatient for secession were grabbing federal properties: arsenals, forts, ships, hospitals — in all, twenty-three separate properties. Most had been empty or untended, but not all. No one was killed in these incidents — yet.

In the North there had been a wide, angry reaction to Charleston's attack on the *Star of the West.* "Secession" was just a dull legal abstraction to most Northerners, but firing on the flag stirred deep juices of unconscious patriotism. Hotels and public buildings in New York City suddenly began hanging American flags outside their entries. One woman in Washington saw an immediate change of attitude among her acquaintances. "It is strange how our sympathies change in a minute," she mused. "I see who this morning said — and I believe in all sincerity — that nothing could induce them to fight against the South, ready now to take up arms."[8]

To make matters far worse, Buchanan had just been informed about a bothersome incident in Florida.

In April 1860 Lieutenant Adam Slemmer, slender and bespectacled, quiet and solemn, earnest and unpretentious, was assigned to take command of the First Artillery Regiment's Company G, stationed at Pensacola. He arrived there just as secessionism agitated the meager population of Florida.[9]

Florida had been acquired by the United States in 1819 and had not become a state until 1845. Most of its whites lived in a narrow line just south of Georgia and Alabama and felt a strong connection to those states, welded to them by family and economic ties. Pensacola, out at the far western corner of the panhandle, was isolated, but its bay was deep and protected by a series of low-lying outer islands. The navy had built a large base there, and to protect it the army had sprinkled four forts about the harbor.

Fort Pickens, the largest of them, was begun in 1829, the same year as Fort Sumter. Fort Pickens was in fact the larger of the two, for it contained 210 guns and could house over 1,200 artillerists, almost double Sumter's capacity. But in January 1861 it lay empty, sitting gloomily at the far western tip of Santa Rosa Island, a forty-mile-long, featureless landmass that served as the harbor's main windbreak. Closer to the naval yard was Fort Barrancas, the only installation manned by soldiers. Housed in barracks were Lieutenant Slemmer's forty-seven enlisted men. Not far away was the shabby town of Warrington with its shacks lined up shoulder to shoulder along a boardwalk, attended by blowing white sand and clouds of mosquitoes.

Lieutenant Slemmer had heard about secessionist takeovers both in Mobile, Alabama, and in Apalachicola, Florida, and considered transferring his command to Fort Pickens, across the bay. At midnight on January 8 a gang of about twenty men was slinking toward Slemmer's company barracks when a sentry heard them and shouted a challenge. The men kept coming and he fired a shot. Their footsteps were heard racing away. (This incident occurred seven hours before the cadets fired on the *Star of the West*, so it could actually be considered the first shot fired in the Civil War.)

A few hours later Slemmer received a dispatch sent by Scott on January 3. The lieutenant was ordered to do his "utmost" to prevent his forts from being seized. The next day he and his men crossed to Fort Pickens. Two days later a ragtag Southern force arrived at the naval yard, took it, and hauled down its American flag.

By his dash, by fate, Lieutenant Adam Slemmer had taken the same path as had Robert Anderson. He had withdrawn his command from a vulnerable position to a much more defensible spot on an island. From this moment on, the federal government—first

Buchanan, then Lincoln—would have two key forts to deal with, both in almost the exact same predicament. This complicated things.

Under instructions from Buchanan's administration, the army and navy sent a fleet and hundreds of soldiers to beef up Slemmer's little band. Unlike Sumter, Fort Pickens was at the harbor's outer mouth, in a position to be reinforced without interference.

Before the fleet dropped off the reinforcements, an order arrived from Washington to do nothing, unless attacked. Secession leaders wanted a truce because they were about to open their first meeting in Montgomery; they did not wish to initiate an incident at this delicate moment. Ex-president John Tyler had been pressing Buchanan not to take any bellicose actions since a group calling itself the Peace Convention would be opening in Washington in a week. Why roil up bad feelings right now? Buchanan had concurred, for the moment. But the fate of Slemmer's little company of soldiers in Pensacola Bay was intertwined with that of Anderson and his garrison.

Even though Buchanan had agreed to a Pensacola truce, he told his three military advisers to design a way to send Anderson reinforcements. The president did not want them sent as yet, but he did want an expedition planned, just in case. Had reinforcements been sent, however, the effort probably would have succeeded. What this would have accomplished, of course, is debatable. Anderson would simply have had more food and men— that is to say, South Carolina would have had more hostages. If Washington truly wanted to relieve the situation in Charleston Harbor, the only way was to eliminate the military force growing each day on the islands around Fort Sumter. Attempting that, even if the U.S. Army were suddenly and miraculously quadrupled in size, might cause the secession of every other slave state, and perhaps even those of the Far West.

At the end of January Isaac Hayne, who had been in Washington for three weeks, handed Buchanan South Carolina's ultimatum, somewhat watered down by Pickens's expressed willingness to pay cash for the fort. Buchanan dawdled another week, then sent

Hayne an official rejection. Hayne, like the commissioners before him, packed up his belongings and his Carolina pride and left town in a dithering rage, firing a departing rude salvo at the White House. It seemed likely that Francis Pickens would now order his guns to open fire on Fort Sumter. At least the garrison thought as much.

The prospect of an assault had always been there, intensifying during certain periods — just after their arrival, following the *Star of the West* incident, when the envoy Hayne stomped out of Washington, and so on. But on most days the garrison's life felt almost typical, moving to its own rhythms. Theodore Talbot, having returned to Sumter from Washington, reassured his mother. "It is true," he said, "that of necessity we are very vigilant, but we manage notwithstanding, to eat, talk, have our jokes, and take our natural rest, very much after the fashion of other folks."[10] They were prisoners or hostages, depending on how one viewed it, but even so, their hours rolled on fairly normally. Around them always was the constant smell of the salt waters, the melancholy braying of seabirds, the fretful whimper of waves flap-flapping against their rocks. They watched boats pass by them every day, heading either into the city or toward the world at large. They could hear the laughter of passengers on large ships steaming by and, when the wind was right, the distant sounds of music from Sullivan's Island. On one memorable day in early March young Lieutenant Davis's sister, Annie, whom he had brought to Charleston for schooling, gave him a wonderful present. Charleston's spring flowers were blossoming, and she sent some jasmine to the fort. Its aroma wafted about them, reminding them of the outside world, and was oddly refreshing. Crawford told his diary how much the scent evoked "the woods and freedom."[11]

They were all physically laboring very hard, of course, and this was taxing, and they lacked some things that had brightened their prior existence: tobacco, for example; the feel of grass beneath their feet. But they took their pleasures in odd moments. Some played "ball" for fun. (It would be curious to know, given Abner Doubleday's presence, whether this game they played was baseball, but the source used only the word "ball.") Some found amusement in the game of leapfrog. Others, for something different to do, rowed Sumter's rowboat around and around the fort. Some men went fishing and actually caught a few blackfish and eels. On a more serious note, four enlisted men went to Charleston as witnesses in a murder trial involving an incident they had observed the previous summer on Sullivan's Island.[12]

On Sundays they were permitted some rest, but received only sporadic formal spiritual guidance. Their official chaplain, Matthias Harris, had been ordered out of state for his antisecessionist utterances. Apparently, the day of the December flag raising had been the only occasion he'd appeared at Fort Sumter. On January 10 the Catholic bishop of Charleston wrote Anderson that he was sending a priest, Patrick Ryan, to perform those religious duties that some at the fort would "feel consolation at fulfilling." The bishop promised Anderson that the priest would act only in "his ministerial capacity," and therefore would not try to foment rebellion among the fort's Catholics, who constituted the majority of both the workmen and enlisted men. Father Ryan did perform mass at Fort Sumter occasionally; how often is uncertain.[13]

Spirituality may be comforting and leapfrog and ball might be pleasant diversions, but most of life revolves around the mundane: the weather, physical comfort, health, and sustenance.

In early January it grew dark at Fort Sumter before five-thirty. The night temperatures were in the mid-thirties, and fierce Atlantic winds made it seem colder. During the garrison's first weeks there it rained most days, sometimes in torrential downpours. On February 2 six inches of windy rain poured down; in March a vicious storm sank a ship in the harbor. Even when the skies were clear the fort retained a constant, dispiriting dampness. On March 19 the air grew unseasonably chilly and to everyone's surprise it began to snow, heavily. Large, wet flakes fluttered down and landed like tiny feathers on the battlements, softening the lines of the guns. Over two inches fell atop Fort Sumter's parapet. A few miles away, in South Carolina's interior, the snowfall measured over half a foot. This was an aberration. Usually the temperature at the fort seldom dropped below freezing, but the sea air still retained a bone-chilling power. It did not help that the garrison, while practicing firing, blew out most of the windowpanes in their quarters. They covered the holes temporarily but still an invidious chill slithered inside.

On January 5 Crawford jotted into his diary, "Fuel short. Yesterday I placed a sentry over the coal which was fast going. Our fuel is restricted now. The officers had but general fire. None in the bedrooms. Camp women restricted. Hospital [allowed] one fire." Other items they lacked were soap and candles.

The families made due somehow, the workmen too, but these mostly nameless men, women, and children remained in the background, a chorus in a Greek play, gray, formless things with hardly a murmur as evidence of their presence. One can imagine their discomfort and their fear. Lying upon damp mats on stone floors, huddled within their rank clothing in the darkness without enough blankets, eating miserable food, often half cooked, unbathed for weeks, fearfully listening for the shouting, which might come at any moment, that the South Carolinians had begun their assault on the fort. Sumter would have been a gloomy residence during the summer. In mid-winter its inhabitants' existence was little better than most of Charleston's slaves, perhaps worse. The meager supply of food and fuel sped the departure of some of the laborers, and all the women and children.

After several weeks at Fort Sumter, Anderson decided to send the families out of harm's way. As he wrote Washington on January 21, "They will be in the way here if we should, unfortunately, be engaged in hostilities." He did not say so, but he was probably becoming concerned about their drain on the provender. In fact, how they lasted so long is an enigma. Crawford, who had been going through Sumter's food supplies a few days earlier, jotted down that the fort had eighty-six "enlisted men and [eight] laundresses entitled to rations," meaning there were nine women and eighteen children who were not. A few children were subsisting by breast-feeding, but most had been weaned. What did the nine women and a dozen or so children eat? One can assume that the others shared whatever they had with those hapless souls, but the image of half-frozen families with insufficient food is hard to dislodge.

Anderson contacted Henry Missroon, an agent for the main shipping line between Charleston and New York, about taking away the families. One of its steamers, *Marion,* was already docked at Charleston, and loading up to leave. Missroon, after checking with Pickens, who chivalrously agreed, gave his price for passage: $12 for each woman, $6 per child, not including breast-feeding infants who traveled free. Two wives who had been staying on Sullivan's Island came to the fort with their children.

On February 1 the women and children shuffled from Sumter's wharf onto a small lighter, which took them back to the *Marion,* still docked at the city wharf. When the *Marion* finally steamed out of the city and passed Sumter, men stood silently at the ramparts, watching it. The women and children leaned against the ship's railing and stared across at that windswept mound of brick and stone that rose like a mesa from the sea. They fluttered their hands in farewell, a few waved handkerchiefs. As the ship moved by, the men gave out three great cheers that could be heard by the passengers. Anderson, standing among those on the parapet, gave a small signal and a cannon belched a single salute. The men erupted in one final cheer, then their voices tailed off as the *Marion* moved away.

These families would be quartered on an army base in New York's harbor, but they did not fare especially well. The army failed to provide them with enough food or fuel, and they suffered mightily. Most of them, already desolate and lonely, with clothes designed only for southern climates, felt bone-chilled in the frigid, far-below-zero temperatures. A few days after their arrival Eba, as the major's wife, visited them. She was appalled by their spartan facilities, their inadequate provisions, and immediately wrote in outrage to the authorities. Anderson found out about the families' miserly rations, and he also complained. The Reverend Henry Ward Beecher's congregation in Brooklyn heard about their plight and raised money for them. By March their situation had somewhat improved.[14]

The garrison's health itself showed signs of decay. The whipping winter winds took their toll. Men caught colds. Talbot's tubercular cough grew worse. In January Crawford treated thirteen men for various ailments. Four suffered some sort of "wounds" or "injuries." Most of the other nine had colds or fevers or digestive problems (the great killers of the coming war). By March, although the weather had naturally gotten warmer, the effects of hard labor and poor food and little sleep began to take its toll. More were injured. Crawford's notes began indicating many cases of dysentery, and a great many more men suffered from respiratory problems. He wrote his brother, "The men are beginning to show signs of their long confinement." Doubleday, also concerned, wrote his wife about the problem. Dr. Crawford, he told Mary, "is afraid it will spread."[15]

The U.S. Army handbook, designed for general guidance, was clear about matters of health. It urged that one should avoid dampness. "Next to perfect cleansing of the premises, dryness ought to be carefully promoted, by keeping up in damp and unhealthy districts sufficient fires, and this agent will promote ventilation as well as warmth and dryness." Good advice. Unfortunately, the garrison at Fort Sumter had little fuel to use for heat. To maintain a modicum of light at their guns in case of a night assault and in the night-duty officer's room, they took small quantities of oil from the fort's tiny lighthouse and used it in jerry-built lanterns. They were cautious not to overuse this oil since their lighthouse now would provide the only beacon to guide any reinforcements that might be sent to them by night. Having no lights for one's quarters could become dreary on long winter nights, but staying warm was more crucial. Since few had brought their winter greatcoats, standing guard, especially after sundown, could be brutal. The problem of fuel was not just an issue of physical discomfort, either; there was the matter of food. The always helpful military handbook advised that breads should be baked well. But how?

In fact Sumter had plenty of wood that might have been readily used. The unused barracks offered a great deal of timber as part of its floors and walls. There was also all the wooden framework employed in those unusable gun carriages—which the garrison lacked the manpower to fire. Anderson seems never to have seriously contemplated dismantling the barracks. To an old soldier, such a "destruction of government property" would have been almost unthinkable. Nor is there evidence that any of his officers proposed it or criticized Anderson for not ordering it done. Instead, the men of the garrison, their families, and the laborers routinely suffered in the harbor's damp chill. Most of the available fuel material came from temporary shacks, half a dozen of them, which workmen had built on the parade ground before their arrival. One by one these shacks disappeared. The last to go was a sturdy blacksmith shop, which they had kept for last. It came down in late March. How they heated their food after that is a mystery.[16]

In all this the officers were especially affected. More than the enlisted men, the "line" officers had to stand guard at night. Talbot was usually too ill to perform this duty, and the punctilious Foster refused to permit his engineers, Snyder and Meade, to serve in this capacity during the first few critical weeks, even though they had volunteered. Eventually he permitted them to take their turns, but Meade was gone for a week, returning home to Virginia when his sister grew deathly ill. Lieutenant Hall was not even at the fort, taking his month-long sojourn in Washington. By military tradition Major Anderson did not serve this duty, though he was often awakened to deal with some unexpected event near the fort, an important message or messenger from Charleston or Washington, an unknown ship coming too close to the wharf. On one fairly typical evening, for instance, the officer of the guard noticed that patrol boats were whizzing about the harbor most of the night, that signal rockets were being shot in the air, and that some guns could be heard going off on Morris Island. "We have no idea what was the cause of the excitement," Talbot wrote his mother, "but they get up these stampedes so frequently that we do not pay much attention to them." Such might have been true, but the duty officer would have had to check on the situation.

Such vigilance was exhausting but necessary. The garrison had to be ever watchful in case South Carolina sprang a sneak attack. There was even an unlikely prospect that some hotheaded Carolinians might attempt an assault on their own. There was also the possibility that Washington might try again to reinforce them.

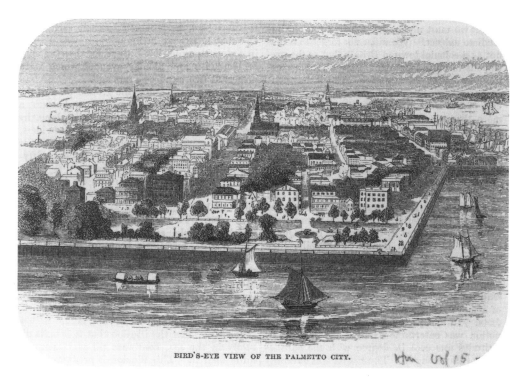

BIRD'S-EYE VIEW OF THE PALMETTO CITY.

Charleston in 1857. *Courtesy Library of Congress*

South Carolina became the first state to secede after this meeting in
Charleston on November 12, 1860. *Courtesy Library of Congress*

View of Charleston Harbor, showing Castle Pinckney (behind ship's
masts), Fort Sumter, and Morris Island (far right).
Courtesy Library of Congress

Top, Fort Sumter, as it stood in the middle of Charleston Harbor.
Bottom, Castle Pinckney, another of the forts surrounding the harbor, "in
possession of the South Carolina troops." *Courtesy Library of Congress*

Eba, Robert Jr.,
and Major Robert
Anderson.
*Courtesy Library of
Congress*

The officers at Fort Sumter: (back row) Capt. Truman Seymour,
Lt. George W. Snyder, Lt. Jefferson Davis, Lt. Richard Kidder Meade;
(front row) Capt. Abner Doubleday, Maj. Robert Anderson,
Asst. Surgeon Samuel Crawford, Capt. John Foster.
Courtesy MOLLUS, Massachusetts

Edmund Ruffin, one of the South's most outspoken secessionists. *Courtesy National Archives*

Charleston's Floating Battery, a kind of armored warship, was the most unusual innovation of the battle. *Courtesy Library of Congress*

The families of the soldiers at Sumter were evacuated two months before the battle began, only to suffer hunger and cold at an army base in New York Harbor. *Courtesy Library of Congress*

The bombardment of Fort Sumter, depicted by Currier & Ives. *Courtesy Library of Congress*

A scene from the battle on the Floating Battery, showing the teamwork necessary for artillery battle. *Courtesy Library of Congress*

Another view of the battle, this one from Cumming's Point, with Charleston in the background at left, Sumter in the center, and Fort Moultrie at right. *Courtesy Library of Congress*

The Confederate flag was raised over the defeated Sumter. At left is the original flagstaff, broken by the bombardment. *Courtesy Library of Congress*

Charleston was besieged throughout the war, ending as a city in ruins. *Courtesy Library of Congress*

Necessary or not, this vigilance took a toll. During Hall's extended absence, only three officers — Doubleday, Seymour, and Davis — were available to serve as officer of the guard all night, following a full day of hard physical labor. Luckily for the three men, Wylie Crawford had volunteered to join them in their turns. Despite Crawford's good health, the resulting drain of energy began to affect even him. He wrote his brother about one night's duty, "I should not have gone on guard, for my throat has been sore for three weeks and will not get well in this salt air." A month later his throat still felt sore; he had lost a good deal of weight. Lieutenant Hall's return in February was helpful and Talbot did stand duty off and on when he was strong enough. But even in those circumstances, it meant that the duty officers had to remain awake every few nights.[17]

Some of their exhaustion might have been more bearable if their food supply had been different. They had brought with them the army's usual grim menu — salt pork, hardtack, moldy flour, some peas, a few other things. Foster's workmen had had a fairly large supply of food on hand, and when the majority of them departed this might have been divvied up, but except for a few vegetables this was not done because of the bureaucratic wall separating fighting soldiers from engineers. Foster had purchased these provisions from his separate account, therefore this food could not, according to tradition and regulations, be eaten by the garrison.

The number of workers at Fort Sumter was not fixed. The majority were semiskilled day laborers and no one considered them important enough to keep a precise roster. Each time an assault seemed in the offing, a few more departed. Those who remained did much of the muscle work during the first weeks, using thick ropes and pulleys to drag the heavy cannon into position on the parapet or shoving the guns into the first tier's embrasures. During the early days after Anderson's arrival at Sumter, the laborers, with the aid of some soldiers, worked frantically to prepare the fort to repel an assault. It took them about three weeks. They had finished the first, critical phase a week after the *Star of the West* episode, and then Foster sent some away, a few at a time, retaining the most skilled. By late March, with about half of them remaining, Foster finally ran out of most of his own stock of provisions, and the workers began eating the garrison's commissary stores. Anderson attempted to send these last laborers away, but the authorities in Charleston shrewdly said no. In the end, therefore, the matter of food was no longer neatly divided into two separate accounts.

The military had long recognized the ill effects of the wrong sort of diet and urged commanders to provide their men with fresh provisions, with "well-baked" bread, oatmeal, and "good potatoes."[18] When the garrison was lodged at Fort Moultrie it had been able to purchase fresh produce and fish either in Charleston or from dealers who hawked wares on Sullivan's Island. Now those heady days were long past. Tobacco-yearning enlisted men began chewing cotton. Even writing paper was short. In January Anderson asked Washington to send him some thin, lined paper to write his reports on; a month later Foster was apologizing to his superiors for using only half-sheets of paper.[19]

After the garrison's transfer to Fort Sumter, Governor Pickens had clamped down on casual attempts to send supplies to the fort. Pickens himself offered them provisions from town, but Anderson had turned it down because he had not liked its tone, which smacked of a favor. Anderson pointed out that the army had traditionally bought and paid for its supplies in the city, and it should retain that right. There must be no condescending favors involved.

After Lieutenant Hall's departure on January 11, Anderson put Dr. Crawford in charge of the commissary. The physician, a much more careful and methodical man than the young lieutenant, made a precise inventory of their food supply. The results were not encouraging. They had four months' supply of their basic ration of pork and flour — even less, of course, since the women and children had to be fed. They had only half a small barrel of salt, no candles, no soap, a little vinegar. The enlisted men were immediately placed on half-rations of coffee and sugar, and the officers voluntarily went without both. Awareness of nutrition at that time was paltry, but even in their rudimentary knowledge they knew that without ascorbic acid — found in lemons, limes, and vinegar, among other things — they would soon contract scurvy, the ancient sailor's complaint, leading inevitably to bleeding gums, weakness, and death. (Federal soldiers in Pensacola during these weeks did contract this ailment.)

On January 20 Pickens suddenly sent a boat to Sumter with a supply of fresh food. Two hundred pounds of beef. Fresh potatoes and turnips. Other things. The men happily unloaded it and rushed it to the mess hall. A feast was planned. Then Anderson heard about its arrival. He sent word immediately to pack up those provisions and send them back. He would not permit Francis Pickens to act Lord Bountiful, the plantation master deigning to be generous to his "people." The garrison returned to its sorry diet of dubious pork and iffy hardtack. Crawford's diary made increasing note of their lack of fresh provisions.

Eventually, Anderson's friend Robert Gourdin interceded. How he assuaged everyone's feelings is unclear, but on January 31 he arrived at Sumter's wharf with some fresh beef and vegetables. He went in and spoke with his friend Anderson for a long time. Two days later some more fresh provisions arrived, this time even including the precious commodity sugar. After that, more food. Most of these provisions had a short shelf life and were merely designed to supplement the garrison's diet with some reasonable nutrition. The men would continue to depend mostly on their regular ration to carry them through each day. However, they were beginning to run noticeably low on even this.[20]

In the middle of March a wealthy gentleman in New York, hearing of the garrison's hunger pangs, sent its officers, through Dr. Crawford, several boxes of fine foods. Rumors were abounding that Washington was about to surrender the fort so Governor Pickens allowed the shipment to be delivered. Talbot wrote his mother about these mouthwatering "epicurean delicacies." "We cannot," he said, "make up our minds whether to eat them as rapidly as possible, so as to dispose of them before leaving, or whether it is not better to hoard them up in view of a long, protracted siege. In the meantime the patés etc. are so tempting that the grave question is being resolved in a most natural way." As Doubleday later more laconically recalled, these delicacies "were fully appreciated."[21]

Like the tidal waters surrounding it, Fort Sumter's garrison lived by its own rhythms. They watched, as best they could, the South Carolinians expand their batteries. The men of the garrison could not see everything, since much work was hidden from view, but they made educated guesses — generally, but not always, correct — about what was going on out there. They worked on their own defenses. The finished filling in the second-tier embrasures and most of those on the first tier. They moved cannon from here to there, to match what they observed on the islands. They bricked up the main gate, one of the fort's weakest spots, leaving room for only one man to walk through, and placed a howitzer a few feet back, pointing its muzzle directly at that passage. If an assault force was able to break through the outer wooden gate, they would have to stumble, one by one, through the brick opening, and face grapeshot.

The soldiers also designed a variety of nasty devices to hold back an assault. They stuck barrels of gunpowder into two piles of rocks out beyond the Gorge wall, and trailed the lanyards inside the fort. If triggered, rock splinters would hurtle in all directions with deadly effect. Nearby, on the Esplanade, they placed two cannon, facing each other about a hundred feet apart, ready to sweep the area. Anderson also had the wharf meticulously mined. They stacked piles of hand grenades in key spots along the parapet and in the stairwells. When flung from the walls, each grenade was calibrated to explode a few feet above the ground. They built seven wooden, open-topped boxes called *machicoulis,* lined their bottoms with thick iron plates, and laid them on the parapets, where they jutted beyond the edge, then bolted them firmly down. The boxes had small holes in their bases, permitting soldiers to sit inside and fire down on attackers.

Seymour also designed three large explosive devices, made from barrels stuffed with stones and gunpowder. One day, when testing one over the side, it exploded in a huge *bang,* throwing missiles in all directions. Passengers aboard a nearby ship reported this contraption, and the local papers spoke ominously of "infernal machines."

One of Foster's German carpenters, a man named Witzmann, built a *cheval-de-frise* outside the walls. These wooden thingamajigs, like logs with long, pointy sticks through them, had been used in Europe to slow down cavalry attacks. Witzmann stared at a rough sketch, then went off and hammered together a peculiar structure like nothing else in the world, and placed it outside the walls. Baffled South Carolinians drifted past on boats to examine it with their spyglasses, trying to decipher what it might be.[22]

In general the mood in Fort Sumter was surprisingly calm, even upbeat, though a few frictions surfaced now and then. What things were like in the enlisted men's quarters is unknown, but some of the officers had spats, mostly over bureaucratic distinctions between the roles of engineers and line officers. Anderson and Foster continued to feud about the engineer's overly meticulous building standards.[23] But in general such difficulties were muted. As Crawford wrote his brother, "How trifling party differences appear in view of the great danger to our country now. We, here, have forgotten them all as we stand around our flag, unfurled every morning over our guns, dearer than ever to us now that we know and feel that it is in danger." The surgeon was amazed that enlisted men who had recently been in the guardhouse, some shackled in balls and chains (like Privates Digdam and McDonald), were now performing their duties cheerfully. A Northern newspaper published a letter from one of the enlisted men: "We have enough to eat and drink," it said. "Our fuel is scarce, but that is nothing. . . . Major Anderson is a true soldier, and so are the other officers, and the men would die for him. I only wish we had a chance to give the rascals hell." In February the enlistments of two of the men expired, but they agreed to stay on, though they were no longer officially in the army and would not receive pay. As they said, they wanted to "see it out."[24]

Anderson's mood, and probably the entire garrison's, had improved mightily as the mail started up again after he and Pickens worked out an arrangement where the mail would be picked up each day at Fort Johnson.

To Anderson, the most important messages came from Washington. For weeks, after his transfer from Moultrie, he had heard nothing official from his superiors. Lonely and isolated and not terribly healthy, he stewed about how the administration was reacting to the things he had done — even what his father-figure

Winfield Scott thought of his actions. On January 19 Talbot returned from the capital. He had been gone only a week, had spent
only three days there, but it had seemed longer to those waiting
anxiously at Fort Sumter. Talbot wrote his mother about the reaction to his arrival at the fort: "My return has been a cause of great
rejoicing to the command on account of the pleasant tidings that I
brought with me. . . . Major Anderson cried like a child when I
gave him all the affectionate greetings sent him by his companions
in arms." On that evening's parade, when the entire garrison gathered as usual by the flag, the major read aloud to them the com-
mendation he and they had received from General Scott. The men
gave out a great cheer. The next day Robert wrote Eba a long letter. He still felt deeply moved. He quoted at length from some of
the kind remarks he had received, then closed, typically, saying he
had done nothing special. He was, he said, simply attempting to
do God's work.[25]

The most important note he received from Washington came
from Secretary of War Holt, dated January 10. It reflected an
awareness that the *Star* had been fired on and had turned around,
but made no comment since the story had not yet been confirmed.
The message's main gist was that Holt wished to "express the
great satisfaction of the Government at the forbearance, discretion, and firmness with which you have acted, amid the perplex-
ing and difficult circumstances in which you have been placed."
Holt called the garrison's transfer to Sumter "brilliant," that it was
"in every way admirable, alike for its humanity and patriotism, as
for its soldiership." As to how Anderson should proceed: "You will
continue," the message continued, "to act strictly on the defensive;
to avoid, by all means compatible with the safety of your command, a collision with the hostile forces by which you are surrounded." In a follow-up letter written a few days later, after the
dust of the *Star* had settled, and after speaking to both Talbot and
Hall, Holt wrote, in reference to that incident, "your forbearance
to return the fire is fully approved by the President." Holt even
apologized that Anderson had not known about the coming of the
reinforcements, and promised him that, since the garrison at the
moment seemed safe, it was not the administration's "purpose at

present to re-enforce you," since to do so would likely lead to war. The major should keep them informed of any change in his situation so they could be prepared to act.

Holt concluded this note with a remarkable statement that the decision to reinforce or send supplies was now going to be Anderson's. Having stated this, the administration had just cleverly turned the responsibility over to an army major. If anything went wrong, they could claim it was his fault. And they knew, from speaking closely to Talbot, that Anderson was loyal to the Union but would do nothing provocative because he was so intent on avoiding civil war.[26]

"Major Anderson of Fort Sumter" came to symbolize "the Union" during the early months of 1861. For a bit he was the idol of many Americans. His mail was filled with gushing letters of love and support. Elderly veterans of the War of 1812 wrote him, children scrawled out their devotion. The legislatures of at least five states passed resolutions to honor him personally. Babies were named after him, a play was produced about the "Hero of Fort Sumter," and a song—the "Fort Sumter Quickstep"—was published in Boston. The citizens of Taunton, Massachusetts, raised money to buy him an engraved sword. In Beverly, New Jersey, where two of his daughters were attending school, the town gave him a thirty-three-gun salute, then followed that up with a three-gun salute for Maria and another for Sophie. He received dozens of offers to send him military aid or supplies. Some notes came from Democrats, some from Republicans. Even the *Mercury* admitted that "The people of South Carolina have been measurably disarmed by their sympathy for Major Anderson." Two of his nephews wrote him from Kentucky saying that the secessionist movement in that state was muted because he had personally stood up against it. Senator Crittenden of Kentucky wrote him the same thing.

On many afternoons Anderson sat at a table in his spare quarters replying, as best he could, to this outpouring. To everyone he was clear: he loved the Union, and he loathed war. To an old friend in Pennsylvania he wrote, "I shall do all that I can, with honor, to prevent the occurrence of so sad an event."

Anderson even jotted a note to Governor Pickens with this sentiment. Newspapers in New York had carried an item that he was ill, and Eba, all aflutter, had telegraphed Pickens asking about it. The governor had immediately wired her that the report was false. Anderson wrote him a thank-you note, closing with this sentiment:

> I hope in God that the time may soon come when a change in circumstances, and the pleasure of an acquaintance will justify my subscribing myself —
> Your friend,
> Robert Anderson

On occasion his letters reflected anxiety, but most echoed his trust in the Lord's wisdom. God, he believed, had permitted him to slip across to Fort Sumter unseen. He reasoned that this proved God wanted peace in America. In some ways he considered himself merely a tool of the Divinity, but he was not a religious fatalist. Anderson recognized his own role in putting off military action as long as possible.[27]

What he did not sense was that much of the outpouring of affection for him came because he was "standing up to secession," not because he was maintaining peace. The adulation for Robert Anderson would end soon when it became clear he was a man of peace, not war. Pedestals are precarious.

Watchfulness was normal at Fort Sumter, but real tension came in spasms. In late January the state legislature held its final session in Charleston and adjourned. One of its last actions was to pass an ultimatum demanding the *immediate* surrender of Fort Sumter. They were tired of delay. A reporter for a Northern journal sent his superiors a message on February 4: "The war spirit runs very high here, just now." Young people, he said, clamored for war, egged on by the *Mercury*, among others.[28] The seceded states were opening their convention in Montgomery on February 4. These shouts for action probably stemmed partly from a fear that some "foreign" agency, even a Southern Confederacy, might try to control South Carolina's destiny.

At Sumter the garrison heard of the growing tensions in the city. They knew rafts were being constructed there to carry an assault party. In February they heard something that triggered great concern. The *Baltimore Sun* published a letter sent on February 7 from someone at the fort. "We expect to be attacked every day," the person wrote, "before my letter reaches you." Crawford told his brother, "You have cause for all your concern for us, for we daily, I may say hourly, anticipate an attack." The garrison, he said, was moving out of its quarters into more protected areas, "bombproofs," within the walls. He was making the final arrangements to have his hospital ready the next day. Talbot wrote his mother, "Rumors constantly reach us from the City of their intention to attack us in a few days." Anderson wrote his four-year-old son a little note that made Eba sob when she recognized it as a father's good-bye. Several days went by. Hayne's mission in Washington had just ended. An assault would likely come now.[29]

Both sides in the national dispute used Washington's birthday to pay homage to the great man. They celebrated in Montgomery and Savannah, Philadelphia and Richmond, Boston and New Haven. In Charleston the cadets at The Citadel fired a salute of thirteen guns for the original thirteen states, followed by seven more for the seven states of the Confederacy. The cannon's roars could be heard out at Fort Sumter. There, following Anderson's orders, the garrison fired a salute of precisely thirty-four. The shots came thirty seconds apart, giving interested South Carolinians a chance to listen, and count. According to Anderson's mathematics, there were thirty-four states — including South Carolina and the new state of Kansas. At least one Carolinian was not amused, calling Anderson's actions "impudence."[30]

In late February and early March there occurred a few small dramas that no one thought much about, but put a human face to abstractions like "secession" and "states' rights." A young black man, Thomas Moore Lynch, but called "Jim," had been performing duties for Crawford, Snyder, and Meade. He was paid for these services, but he did not tell the officers that he was a slave and that he turned over some or all of his earnings to his owner. Lynch was a bright fellow, literate (despite South Carolina's laws against slaves knowing how to read), and would from time to time correspond with his mother in the city, who was probably also literate, and who may or may not have been a slave. Toward the end of February, he wished to visit Charleston. The officers made a formal request that he be permitted to go to the city and return unmolested, and Lynch received a written permission from the state's secretary of war. As soon as he arrived in Charleston, his owner stepped forward and claimed he had some correspondence between the mother and her son. These letters, he said, were highly provocative, for they claimed that, if a fight with Fort Sumter began, the slaves of Charleston would rise up and aid the Union troops. The owner's statement was absurd on several levels. By what alchemy could Jim have claimed to know the sentiment of the city's slaves since he had not talked with them for months? Later, Charleston's authorities claimed that his mother had been sending him secret military information about South Carolina's army, information useful to the enemy. This claim was even more bizarre than the first, for how could his mother know more than was being published each day in the city's papers?

Anderson at first ignored the issue. Crawford came to him and complained as soon as he had heard that the young man was being detained, but Anderson simply shrugged. As an ex-slaveholder himself, he knew the rules. If an owner hired out his slave, he had a perfect right to change his mind. Especially if he thought the status or attitude of the slave was being tampered with. Eventually this became the crux of the matter, which began to revolve around the question of whether federal soldiers were "tampering" with the peculiar institution of slavery, encouraging Lynch to be less obedient, to be disrespectful, to be less humble, to be . . . *uppity.* Here lay the essence of the South's fears.

When Anderson finally got involved and wrote the authorities in Charleston, his complaint did not involve Thomas Lynch, the human being; he merely noted that his officers were being inconvenienced in not having a servant. He also expressed mild indignation that his garrison was being accused of tampering with a slave's psyche. But, as Anderson said, "His Excellency [the secretary of war] mentions in his letter to me, received yesterday, that the boy is a slave, and, of course, that ends the matter." Anderson's response resulted, no doubt, from his background, the attitudes of his class toward "inferiors," and his desire to maintain the tenuous peace in the harbor. He was a decent man, noticeably kind to his enlisted men, concerned about the feelings and lives of others — consider, for example, his earlier actions and words when dealing with Indians or Mexicans. But he never expressed any opposition to the institution of slavery. On the other hand, it ought to be noted that, among Anderson's writings, there exists no record of any disparaging comments about blacks, as are often found among the words of Stephen Douglas, Wylie Crawford, and even Abraham Lincoln, among too many others. In the case of Lynch, Anderson's position was to speak up for his officers — and, perhaps more, under the circumstances, to indicate clearly that he and his garrison were in no way agitating the slavery issue.

Another incident took place in mid-March. One evening a slave paddled a canoe to the wharf and told the officer of the guard that his master had beaten him nearly to death. He asked for sanctuary. The officer sent him on his way. The law of the United States was clear — it was illegal to aid a runaway slave.[31]

On the other hand, Charlestonians on occasion attempted to suborn the fidelity of those in Fort Sumter. Anderson himself received a dozen letters reminding him of his Southern roots, and others in his command were lured to betray their cause. At Fort Johnson, a plan was concocted to offer several thousand dollars to one of the mail-boat soldiers if he would betray the garrison. The man they gave that offer to — a grizzled Irishman — whispered back he would see what he could do, and would report to them on his next trip over. He said that, although he and his comrades had no interest in fighting, they were being watched very carefully by the officers. When he never responded, the South Carolinians concluded that Sumter's officers had figured out something was afoot and quashed it. The entire story sounds fanciful, but not impossible. An enlisted man, paid eleven dollars a month, might well consider such a vast sum attractive, but there is no other record on either side of such an incident.[32]

About this time the garrison was shocked to hear of the actions of Brigadier General David Emanuel Twiggs, the commander of one of America's seven military districts, the Department of Texas. Twiggs was in his early seventies, a tired old man, strongly sympathetic to secession. His command, designed to guard the border with Mexico and control the nonwhite and non-Anglo population of the state, was — for the American army of that era — quite muscular, made up of 2,328 men, including Robert E. Lee and Charles Anderson, a brother of Robert. It had become obvious by December that Texas might secede, and Twiggs had repeatedly written Washington for advice. No specific orders came back. In mid-February Twiggs told one of his officers, "If an old woman with a broomstick should come with full authority from the State of Texas to demand the public property, I would give it up to her." Two days later, a large mob, with no real authority, appeared in San Antonio, where Twiggs kept his headquarters, and demanded he surrender his entire command. He considered it for a few hours, then verbally agreed. He sent out orders to all nineteen posts to turn over "everything" to the Texans. A few minutes later he left for New Orleans, where he was greeted with open arms by the Confederacy, which designated him one of its highest-ranking generals. (A year later he died in his sleep.) His actions were stunning. This was no single arsenal or even a fort like Sumter. Twiggs's vast command consisted of a large percentage of the nation's fighting force and its equipment. The fact that Twiggs abandoned the soldiers of his command and their families was especially despicable. They were forced to straggle, unarmed, out of the state. A force of Texas militia actually captured a third of them before they could leave, doing so, amazingly, one day before the guns went off in Charleston Harbor, beginning the war.

At Fort Sumter the reaction to Twiggs's actions was disgust. "Twiggs's treason," Talbot wrote his sister, "is the most outrageous thing that has occurred yet." Robert Anderson's brother Charles, still in Texas, wrote him a month later, calling the surrender "treason, pure and simple," and blaming it partly on Twiggs's "senility-dotage." Many Americans elsewhere also recognized the contrast between Twiggs's dishonorable surrender and Anderson's remarkable courage. Buchanan's new secretary of the treasury, John Adams Dix, who had sent a message to his revenue cutters in January that they should shoot anyone attempting to haul down the flag, now wrote Anderson saying how ashamed he was of Twiggs and how much he admired the major. (Privately, Dix admitted he intended this letter to stiffen Anderson's backbone, in case the major might be having his own doubts about the Union.[33])

Perhaps Anderson's most interesting letter on the subject came from Eba. For some weeks this ex-Georgia belle had been growing increasingly furious. In early February she wrote her husband, "I would never be found in the same confederacy with South Carolina." She also snorted that if Buchanan turned over Fort Sumter to South Carolina, Robert should ask the government "to let you blow it up, sky high, on leaving." Three weeks later she heard about Twiggs. "I felt my cheek burn with indignation," she wrote Robert. "I swear, my dear husband, though your life is more precious to me than my own, I would rather know that you were dead — yes, *dead!* — than have to see you and call you husband, after you — having proved yourself such a traitor — such a villain!!" She then gushed sweetly how proud she was of him. She told him she had gotten mail from General Scott referring to him as his "son" and from a prominent politician in Kentucky saying that his stand at Fort Sumter had saved that state for the Union. Robert was not alone, she reminded him. What he was doing was winning him imperishable glory.

This was very heady, powerful stuff, all very nice, but Anderson and the garrison still had to deal each day with the prospect of battle, surrounded more and more by guns and thousands of enemies.[34]

CHAPTER TWELVE

The Boys on the Beach

"We are on the verge of civil war."
— JEFFERSON DAVIS, JANUARY 10, 1861

S ince the autumn of 1860, emotional eruptions had been dressing South Carolinians in uniforms: first the election of Lincoln, then secession, Anderson's transfer to Sumter, and so on. In Charleston soldiers had been tramping about the streets for months, and volunteer companies had been arriving in the city by train each week and were being sent out to the islands. By early March the state had more than a hundred companies, 8,835 men. Most were not actually stationed in Charleston Harbor, but they were prepared, even anxious, to come if called to protect their motherland. Their motives were as varied and tumbled as could be expected from thousands of hearts: male companionship, a need to feel heroic, a desire to seem adult, to get away from the restrictions of home life with parents or wives. Others were simply angry or ornery. A British observer described the men he saw at the camps in mid-April: "Some with the air of gentlemen; others coarse, long-haired fellows, without any semblance of military bearing, but full of fight and burning with enthusiasm, not unaided, in some instances, by coarser stimulus."[1]

For many, there was something else: a determination to defend their hearths from outsiders' hands. Ironically, in this quintessential slave state with its elitist politics, many devoutly believed they were serving to protect freedom and democracy. They used terms like "coercion" to define any attempts by Washington, by the "North," by the Black Republicans, to tell them what to do. Most were generally not very articulate about it, but they were prepared to fight for their ideals.

As it turned out, before they fought their enemies they first had to be turned into soldiers, and many of them were ambivalent about army life. Sometimes they hated it, sometimes they were positively entranced by its odd pleasures. A well-to-do young man wrote his brother from his encampment on the tip of Morris Island, "This life suits me exactly, but I'm getting a little tired waiting for an engagement."[2]

Most volunteers discovered over time that military life offered few opportunities for manly heroism; it was mostly drudgery and boredom. "There is such monotony in camp life," one wrote home, "that it would puzzle the mind of the most ingenious intellect to interest you." Often they simply sat around, buffeted by cold winds and rain, waiting for something to happen. Not surprisingly, they also discovered that the uniforms of their peacetime militia jamborees were inadequate. Comfort and sturdiness, they now realized, were far more important than snazzy accoutrements. A good blanket was more serviceable than a red sash.[3]

So was palatable food. Military meals are often little better than swill. In fact, many were indeed "swill," which originally meant a foodstuff made from cornmeal mixed with water. In the countryside such thin porridge sometimes formed a family's main meal, at other times it was slopped to hogs. A letter from one of the island camps described their diet as mostly coffee and "liquid hominy." Another wrote home that "the coarse fare we get here does not agree with me."

Some of the new soldiers caught crabs, some fished, some discovered a bed of oysters and gobbled them raw. Most early volunteers were from Charleston; they found that city's civilians quite generous. Wives tried to be supportive, though some were concerned about the prospect of real fighting. Sally Hampton, a mother of three small children and the lovely young wife of a plantation nabob, wrote a sweet and sardonic letter to a friend in New York. Her husband had volunteered for service and was presently away from home as a captain of a cavalry company. "When men," she said, "are called upon to part — they think forever — from wives & children & friends near & dear, they live perforce a somewhat ideal life & believe themselves already famous as patriots or fallen in a soldier's duty." Mary Chesnut jotted down a story about a woman she had chatted with. The woman had just returned from visiting her husband out on one of the islands. He had been gone for months and she had decided to take him some clothes. He was, she found to her dismay, now far too thin to wear them. Perhaps most disturbing to her was how jolly he was, how much he seemed to like this military life. He did, however, persuade her to stay an extra day or so, perhaps for connubial dalliance. She had not come prepared to spend the night, but, she delicately told Mrs. Chesnut, "She tied her petticoat around her neck for a nightgown."[4]

The men at most encampments, however, saw few women, and missed them. Reporters, passing through, noted that the soldiers had put signs on their tents, a few wry: BLEAK HOUSE, DRUNKARD'S DEN, DICK'S HOTEL, RATTLESNAKE'S HOLE. Some signs were feisty: YANKEE SMASHERS, THE LIVE TIGERS. Others sighed for absent femininity: LADY EMILY, CLARA, DIVINE EMMA, GENTLE DOVE.

When the crisis began, the city's women made bandages, they sewed uniforms and even cartridges, they cooked and sent baskets of cold chicken and cakes over to the camps. A number of soldiers were well-to-do young men who had happily signed on as privates. As a result, a few units dined sumptuously on fine foods prepared by their own slaves, body servants who served them in camp. One man recalled that his company feasted on "Champagne, madeira, and sherry, paté de fois gras, and French green peas, sardines and Spanish olives, Spanish cigars, and other luxuries." He ruefully added that later on, when their commissary was much tighter, they would have considered a single sweet potato a fine repast.[5]

One result of the proximity of Charleston was the easy availability of intoxicants. Enterprising businessmen would travel to the islands and sell demijohns of various spirits. By January a legislative committee reported its concerns about the slapdash discipline at the arsenal, especially the ease, it said, of getting liquor from nearby suppliers. The legislature gave Pickens the power to declare martial law over any region he thought needed it, and on January 31 he issued an order establishing martial law on Sullivan's Island. Colonel Ripley at Fort Moultrie, a teetotaler himself, had no patience for indiscipline. He convened courts-martial for drunkenness and meted out harsh penalties. He seems to have had some success, but the problem was not confined to his area alone. In March Pickens declared martial law over the other side of the harbor.[6]

Southerners in general, and South Carolinians in particular, were a prickly bunch, proud of their independence. Amateurishness was not simply a pose, it was proudly practiced. The notion of taking orders was hard for some to swallow. An interesting report, probably accurate, described a flare-up on Morris Island. A company of volunteers from upstate grew disgruntled after going three months without their promised $11-a-month payment. Several had wives at home who were in distress. The men were also cranky because their supplies of food had been insufficient. A hungry private finally snapped and yelled at the unit's commissary. He wanted bread, he said, then stepped forward and slapped the commissary across the face. The other pulled a knife and the two fought until they were held apart. The private was arrested and placed in the guardhouse. With the monotony and the pitiless cold winds, it was hardly surprising when similar tussles occurred at other camps. After all, many of these young men were the equivalent of college freshmen away from home for the first time.[7]

Green soldiers make mistakes, most trifling, some fatal. One morning at Castle Pinckney a young member of the Carolina Light Infantry was shot and killed by an overzealous sentry. A volunteer stationed at the arsenal, no doubt horsing around or inebriated, fell from a window to his death. One unlucky volunteer fell from a railroad car as it was arriving in the city and was crushed. Another died of gastroenteritis. (He would be the first of well over a hundred thousand such deaths during the coming war, when more soldiers would perish from sickness and diarrhea than from cannon fire.) A young volunteer at Moultrie, who had just had his eighteenth birthday, was playing with his pistol, yanked it out of his belt, and shot himself in the thigh. According to his obituary, as he was carried away he told his comrades that his only regret was that he would not be there when they took Fort Sumter. A few days later a nineteen-year-old from upstate named James Clark Allen was killed in a terrible accident. His unit was quartered on the second floor of the Moultrie House. He and his comrades had just finished a dress parade, and he tore back to his room, dropped off his gun and knapsack and other appurtenances, then sped out the door. One of his messmates, slower than he, staggering up the steps with his musket, bayonet fixed, had just reached the top of the stairs when Allen charged out of his quarters. The bayonet entered Allen's right eye, and killed him.[8]

Another amateurish incident occurred during the early morning of March 8. Batteries on both sides of the harbor were practicing loading and firing their artillery. At Fort Sumter Anderson and a few of his officers watched through spyglasses, scouting the location and caliber of South Carolina's hidden guns. About eight o'clock that morning the officers noticed that a battery on Morris Island was about to fire. They were particularly curious about this one, since its three large cannon were uncomfortably close to Sumter's weakest spot, her main gate. The first piece opened with a loud report, then the second. Finally the third. This one, however, was different. Instead of being loaded merely with gunpowder, it contained a cannonball. At Sumter they watched it soar upward toward them, straight at their gate, then fall a bit short, ricochet off the water twice, and smash into the stone wharf before caroming into the water. The wharf at that spot was made of rubble, and they could see splinters of stones explode into the air when the ball hit. Could this be the beginning of an assault? The gate, which had been open, was slammed shut. A drummer beat the long roll. The shutters over several of the guns were opened. The officers on the parapet stared at the island camps, searching for any sign that a general attack had started. They noticed that men along the beaches looked up in shock, uncomfortably aware that Sumter might choose to retaliate. Soldiers on the sand scattered and flung themselves behind the dunes. Slaves who had been digging trenches and filling sandbags moved equally quickly. Within moments the island sands appeared empty of human life. Only a few tethered horses remained in sight. Anderson chortled, perhaps his only laugh in months. The other officers and enlisted men joined him, shaking their heads at the inanity of amateur militiamen. It was time for breakfast and they wandered away to eat.[9]

After breakfast, however, Anderson grew impatient at the lack of any explanation. He jotted a message to Morris Island, asking for clarification, and an apology for what had been an error. Seymour and Snyder were to carry the note. They were preparing to depart when a boat arrived with Major Stevens, the same man who had commanded the cadet battery during the *Star of the West* incident. He admitted sheepishly that it had been his gun and apologized for the accident. Anderson used the opportunity to emphasize that the incident might have led to real hostilities, and that his own forbearance indicated how much he wanted peace. It absolutely did, agreed Stevens, who complimented Anderson on his patience. Stevens remarked as he was leaving that, unfortunately, real war might not be far off, now that Lincoln was in the White House.[10]

Mildly amusing moments like this resulted from an inherent problem for South Carolina: Her soldiers were far from ready for war, but some of them, and many civilians, wanted immediate action. Francis Pickens knew how unprepared his state was. He sent agents scurrying off to purchase gunpowder and guns, called on his state to send him more recruits, and asked slaveholders to supply him with as many hands as they could spare. The soldiers arrived sporadically in clumps. It is impossible to guess how many slaves were used in building the island fortifications. Thousands, certainly, perhaps as many as twenty thousand, males mostly, but some females. Few slaves stayed long, most about a week; their owners needed their services to prepare the fields for spring planting. (During these months slave brokers of Charleston held several large and successful auctions.) Slaves built gun emplacements, put up barriers of sandbags and cotton bales in front of Moultrie's walls, dug trench lines in the sand from one battery to another. They also helped to build two military innovations devised by South Carolinians, the Iron Battery and the Floating Battery.[11]

———

In early spring the *Courier* printed a small item: Courtenay's, a bookstore on Broad Street, had been selling a large number of copies of two technical works, one called *Notes on Seacoast Defence,* the other, *Instruction for Heavy Artillery.* Building and using artillery is complicated, and South Carolinians wanted to be ready. The state had only a few military engineers and but a few professional artillerists like Roswell Ripley out at Fort Moultrie. Instead of becoming frozen by insecurity, determination made South Carolina willing to improvise. A famous local novelist, William Gilmore Simms, and a cashier at one of the banks, Clement H. Stevens, suggested that South Carolina build a battery of heavy guns on Cummings Point, a peninsula poking up from Morris Island directly toward Fort Sumter. The tip of Cummings Point was close to the fort and aimed at her fragile Gorge. Their idea was to lay three large columbiads (heavy cannon) on the island's sand, then cover them with a roof angled severely backward like a wedge and made of layers of the iron used in railroad tracks. Although the guns of Fort Sumter, of course, would be able to pound the island battery just as easily, Sumter's walls were perpendicular and therefore vulnerable, especially its wooden main gate. Also, according to their design, the Iron Battery's gun teams would be protected between each shot by lowering heavy shutters to close the embrasures in front of the columbiads. The notion was not unique, but it was unusual. Anderson's and Foster's reports to Washington about its erection were wary and concerned. Nor were they likely to feel much relief on March 8, the day of the "accidental" shooting, since the shot from this battery landed uncomfortably close to the gate.[12]

Everyone agreed, however, that South Carolina's most interesting military innovation was the Floating Battery. For weeks, Charleston's citizens could stroll over to the Cooper River wharves and watch workmen hammer together a remarkably ugly, ungainly craft, like nothing anyone in the city had ever seen. The officers at Fort Sumter could also observe it from their parapets, and could wonder about it. What they were seeing would quite soon change warfare. It was, essentially, an armored warship. The central notion behind it had been bruited about Europe for the

past few years. Several nations, especially the French, had exper-
imented with such a vessel. By mid-1862, after the *Monitor* had
slugged it out with the *Virginia* (usually mistakenly called the *Mer-
rimack*), such ships became famous, but in 1861 it was still only an
untried idea, with three main problems. Its weight would be huge,
so how could it move? Its builders considered a makeshift steam
engine, then decided instead to have other ships push or drag it
around, making it more of a barge than a warship. Another issue
was the effect of the recoil of its own guns. This might break it
apart. Then there was this question: When it came under the
pounding of Sumter's guns, wouldn't it founder? The designers
and builders claimed confidence, but neither the public nor the
soldiers who would have to serve aboard her were so sure. Two
ladies from the city went to look at it and came away disturbed.
They decided it looked unwieldy and might become "a slaughter
pen" for the men aboard. Lieutenant Davis, out at Sumter, got a
letter from his sister Annie, still at school in Charleston. She had
heard, she said, that men were disinclined to serve on the ship.

The vessel was about a hundred feet long and twenty-five feet
wide, made mostly of huge pine timbers, twelve inches square. At
the front was an odd structure that nowadays would remind one
of something that then did not exist, the snout of a tank. Its forward wall was almost four feet thick, with four windows to act as
embrasures for heavy artillery. To protect the gunners from shots
from above, the builders placed a foreshortened gable roof,
sweeping back from the front. The vessel's front was covered with
six layers of iron, bolted together. Gunpowder would be kept toward the back, well protected by thousands of sandbags, which
also acted to counterbalance the weight of the front. Cannonballs
were stored in bins beneath the floorboards just behind the guns.
To keep the vessel from becoming far too heavy, the builders left
the entire middle of it completely open to the air. At its rear was a
hospital for the wounded with a dozen cots, which would be
staffed by a regular surgeon, a gentleman who had served in the
Crimean War. The original notion had been to maneuver her up to
within a few hundred yards of Sumter's walls, from where it could
whale away at the weak main gate, but a lack of enthusiasm for

serving aboard her and a general derision at her prospects changed the minds of those in charge. She was far too unwieldy to move beyond the harbor, and what they eventually did was drag her away from her mooring and hide her in a protected cove behind one corner of Sullivan's Island. They then nailed her down with four great wedges to keep her from swaying in the tide. They did this secretly, at night, and neither Anderson nor Foster could figure out for some time where she had gone, though they would find out — eventually.[13]

By early February Pickens's overbearing manner was causing several top people to resign in disgust. A member of the influential Ravenel family wrote in his diary on January 31, "Pickens ought never to have been elected Governor." In fact, "were it not for the critical state of affairs now existing, he would be called to account & perhaps impeached." Such political tensions may have led Pickens to consider cathartic action. Some of his advisers told him everything was set, except for some fuses that would arrive soon from Richmond. The state's soldiers were fairly well trained, and were anxious to do something. A visitor to the city overheard a conversation between a young lieutenant and a friend. The friend opposed an assault out of squeamishness about the amount of bloodshed likely to result. The exasperated lieutenant disagreed. "Why, good heavens, Jim!" he said. "Do you want that place to go peaceably into the hands of Lincoln?"[14]

A young soldier on Morris Island and his buddies were outraged that Pickens had not yet flung them against Sumter in an all-out assault. He recognized that many of them would lose their lives, but he was confident they could take the fort in three days and plant their new flag on its ramparts. He abruptly broke off his letter . . . then started it again the next day. He and his comrades were now all excited, he said. An officer had arrived the previous evening, just as he had been penning his letter, and had told them that Isaac Hayne up in Washington had presented Buchanan an ultimatum, and it had been refused. The officer thought the president would now send reinforcements, and these would certainly land right here. The young writer said that they all had given up their plan to shuck off to Pensacola, Florida; they were now ready for combat here, "cool and determined to fight to the last and show no quarter."[15]

On February 6 Pickens wrote an order to have all the batteries set for a forty-eight-hour bombardment of Fort Sumter. Colonel Ripley, at Fort Moultrie, a quick-tempered professional soldier, was distinctly unhappy. His guns were not ready, he said. Among other things, they lacked enough ammunition to do but slight damage to Sumter's walls. He reminded his superiors that "I have made frequent efforts, orally, written, officially, & unofficially, to obtain the necessary articles," but his pleas had been ignored. More important, he emphasized, "No forty-eight hours' firing will bring down Fort Sumpter, unless the Comdg. officer chooses to surrender to avoid civil war. Physically, it is merely an impossibility, and as for the moral effect [the exhaustion of Sumter's defenders], I leave it to the consideration of candid minds whether brave men, or desperate men, are to be turned from their purpose by forty-eight hours' turmoil and confusion." He sniffed that "political" motives might initiate a bombardment, but he wanted those who ordered it — Francis Pickens — to understand that it would fail, at the cost of using up valuable ammunition. (A month later Ripley was still testy. He complained he had no one at Moultrie who could fix gun carriages, his artillerymen were "indifferent" soldiers, and his infantry troops, who were ill-equipped with proper weapons, were "entirely unfit to meet the enemy."[16])

Pickens seemed unmoved by such arguments. In fact, he seemed prepared to order an immediate assault — except that it was Race Week in Charleston, traditionally the merriest time of the year. It would not only have been unseemly to begin a battle now, it would have been exceedingly unpopular with the city's most prominent party givers. Mrs. A. M. Vanderhorst, for example, one of Charleston's wealthiest ladies, told her diary about her gala. "The music was fine, the gentlemen & ladies in high spirits, and the supper under the shining silver with the sparkling champagne most enlivening." The dancing went on till morning. She smirked to her diary that someone had announced to her that "it was indeed the party of the Season." Out in the countryside the wealthy were beginning to engage in fox hunts, to play cards and blindman's bluff, to dance. One rich planter's wife wrote her brother in mid-February that "If there is no war & I don't have another lung trouble, we mean to have a very gay Spring."[17]

The governor, however, had other plans. On January 20 Senator Jefferson Davis had written him, urging him to let the problem of Fort Sumter be taken over by the new Southern Confederacy that would be created in a few weeks. Davis reminded Pickens that the "little garrison in its present position presses on nothing but a point of pride. Stand still." Pickens wrote back immediately. He admitted that South Carolina was not ready to open an immediate attack. But, he added, "In two weeks I hope to be ready to speak with authority. I think 48 hours hot fire will do the work, and when ready I shall move certainly." If the Confederacy was able to get Sumter without bloodshed, "I will rejoice, but if not, blood will flow." In this same letter Pickens, who had a tendency to flip-flop on issues, admitted that military matters were confusingly "scientific," with their arcane language about *sabots* and *merlons* and *quoins* and hundreds of other terms. He also said he thought Davis himself would make an excellent president for the coming Confederacy. The context of the compliment reveals his recognition that Jefferson Davis, the West Point graduate and ex–secretary of war, would be far better suited to handling the "scientific" issues surrounding Fort Sumter.[18]

In a long, rambling letter to Howell Cobb, one of the South's most respected men, Pickens put his finger on the precise issue at hand. The ownership of Fort Sumter, he said, was critical to the very concept of secession. To deny the right of South Carolina to possess it was "a denial of its independence." He was determined, he told Cobb, to get Sumter *before* March 4, in other words, before Lincoln became president. Right now, Buchanan was weak; if Sumter was taken over before Lincoln's inauguration, Old Abe may not take the matter personally, and might let it pass. Pickens also wrote Robert Toombs, another prominent Southern leader, that he expected his army "to be ready by Friday night [February 15]" to "take the fort or to silence it." Governor Pickens was getting itchy. If other Southern leaders did not act quickly and decisively, he was likely to plunge them all over the edge.[19] The issue was now up to several dozen men in Montgomery, Alabama.

Montgomery, a town of 9,000 people, about half of them slaves, wobbled uncertainly along several hills overlooking the Alabama River. Incorporated only in 1837, it was still quite raw. Sophisticated South Carolinians like Mary Chesnut sniffed at the city's vulgarity, its higgledy-piggledy unpaved streets, which turned to viscous mud after every rainstorm, its swarms of merciless mosquitoes. They noted some nice mansions, owned by wealthy planters who used the town as a depot from which they could steam cotton south to Mobile, but were unimpressed with the city's two main hotels, whose carpets were soggy with tobacco juice and whose meals were far below the standards of Charleston. The *Mercury* suggested seriously that, when the Confederacy chose a permanent capital, Huntsville, Alabama, or Macon, Georgia, would be far better choices. Montgomery's only advantages lay in its central location in the Deep South, its decent transportation, the fact that it was the home of the prominent fire-eater, William Lowndes Yancey, and that it had a state capital building that could house meetings of a new government. On February 4 fewer than forty delegates from six states held their first session, opening their meeting beneath the watchful gaze of three different portraits of George Washington.[20]

They orated a few days, then on February 9 they adopted, for convenience' sake, the entire eight volumes of United States statutes and agreed on Jefferson Davis to act as their first president. Few of them had originally had him in mind as their favorite candidate, but he seemed a good second choice. Also, as reporters from the *Mercury* and the *Courier* wrote home, the looming prospect of war over Charleston Harbor highlighted his military background. Three days later, well before Davis himself arrived in town, the delegates took another important step, passing a resolution claiming sovereignty over all questions involving Fort Sumter, among other issues, previously falling to the six separate Confederate states. Francis Pickens was immediately wired about this decision, but apparently did not entirely concur. Work on the batteries around Sumter suddenly slackened, but then, a few days later, the pace quickened once more.[21]

On the evening of February 17 Jefferson Davis arrived in Montgomery to much fanfare and salutes from numerous guns. He spoke a few words to the large throng outside his hotel suite, then went to bed. He was tired, and not terribly pleased by his new role. Unlike many optimists, he thought a civil war really was approaching. It had been his ambition to lead men in battle, not to be a politician. Davis was in some ways much like his friend Robert Anderson. Both were born in Kentucky, just a few years apart, and had graduated from West Point. Both had married the daughters of wealthy planters, and both were quiet, rather reticent, bookish individuals. Both were men of medium height with delicate health and noticeably erect posture. Though neither was a true aristocrat, each was invariably courteous. Davis, when in the mood, could be more charming and was a better conversationalist, but Anderson had a finer sense of humor and seemed much less stern to those around him. Another key difference lay in their politics. Anderson disdained the political world, while his friend obviously embraced it, however reluctantly. And their views on secession were far apart. Davis was unenthusiastic at the prospect but accepted its legitimacy; Anderson was opposed to the concept, to say nothing of its practice. Their similarities had made them firm friends. Their differences would, in a few weeks, make them enemies.

President Davis chose his cabinet with an overly delicate desire to placate each Confederate state by choosing a single representative from each, leading him to his first serious error. When it came time to pick his secretary of war he had William L. Yancey of Alabama in mind. But Yancey declined the position and put forward the name of Leroy Pope Walker, who had been angling for the job. Walker was an intelligent lawyer of good character, but he was utterly unqualified for this position. He had never been an administrator and knew nothing of the military. Yet he was now expected to supervise, among a thousand other details, contracts regarding the caliber of cannon and the quality of gunpowder. He was a powerfully good chewer and spitter of tobacco, but in military matters he was in way over his head. At least he had the good sense to admit it to himself. He wired a Southern artillery expert, Pierre Gustave Toutant Beauregard, and asked him to come to Montgomery and give him advice.

On February 18 Pickens wrote to those in Montgomery that he was prepared to open fire on Sumter within five days. Since he seemed to be pawing the turf in preparation for this attack, the ever-vigilant Senator Louis Wigfall wired him from Washington on February 20 that the administration had decided to send an entire armada to Charleston. This rumor was close to accurate, since Buchanan was considering a plan to send relief ships to Sumter. Exactly how Wigfall found out about it — on that day General Scott wrote the first orders organizing the expedition — is unclear, but others in the capital were also wiring Pickens to be on the lookout for Union ships. On February 22 the *Mercury* contained two articles on the specifics of an expedition. That day the men on the island batteries worked furiously until late at night. The next afternoon Pickens, apparently rather drunk, made a speech at The Citadel, promising that Fort Sumter was about to be theirs. As it turned out, all of Charleston's concerns were premature. Buchanan learned that the Confederacy was sending some of its own commissioners to Washington to discuss the various issues, and once again he ordered Scott to hold the expedition in abeyance.[22]

This whole ruckus made those in Montgomery nervous about the situation in Charleston. On February 22 the Confederate Congress, to take the game away from Pickens, passed a resolution that the Confederacy must have possession of Fort Sumter "as soon as practicable." The next morning, Davis sent a military engineer, William Henry Chase Whiting, to Charleston, to observe South Carolina's military readiness. It was a delicate mission, since he was to be the first official representative of the new Confederacy to arrive in Charleston. A few days later Whiting, a brittle military intellect with no patience for fools, sent back a scathing report, criticizing much of what he had seen. Most of the batteries, he noticed, faced Sumter, not the equally critical mouth of Charleston Harbor. If Washington sent an armada, it would probably land soldiers on the outer fringes of the islands and attack the batteries there. South Carolina was unprepared for this eventuality. Whiting even considered the guns facing Fort Sumter inadequate. When Davis received this report, he recognized he had better do something concrete about Charleston, and do it immediately. If a battle began in the harbor, the Confederacy must win it. Any loss would inevitably weaken morale inside the Confederacy and hurt its image with potential friends in places like Virginia and Great Britain.[23]

On February 26 P. G. T. Beauregard arrived in Montgomery. The befuddled Secretary of War Walker, glad to see him, grasped his hand in greeting. Beauregard, said Walker, was "just in time to assist me out of a great dilemma" and asked him specific technical questions about ordnance. Walker and Beauregard later met with Davis, and the men spoke, among other matters, of the defenses of Charleston.

The next day Beauregard was strolling along the streets of Montgomery when people rushed up to him and shook his hand. President Davis, they told him, had just appointed him the first brigadier general in the Confederate Army, and was ordering him to Charleston. This news apparently came as some surprise. To a man with Beauregard's ego, being named the highest-ranking officer in the new army would have felt gratifying. He had written Davis two weeks earlier asking for a military position, but he had wanted something near his home in New Orleans, perhaps to command the growing Confederate force in Pensacola. He was wholly unfamiliar with Charleston and its people. In fact, Davis's choice of Beauregard was curious. At about that same time he named Braxton Bragg to take over at Pensacola. Unlike Beauregard, Bragg had served at Fort Moultrie and knew Charleston's harbor well. But Beauregard had a reputation as an excellent artillery man and Bragg was recognized as a good trainer of recruits. Presumably Davis, with Whiting's report in hand, felt that Beauregard's skills were better suited to Charleston and Bragg's to Pensacola. If so, he had proved himself an excellent judge of men, a reputation he was not always able to maintain.[24]

Pierre Gustave Toutant Beauregard stood 5'7", with a muscular 150-pound body. Born in a parish twenty miles south of New

Orleans, his parents were prominent, well-respected sugar planters, not terribly rich but part of Louisiana's Creole aristocracy. The boy did not speak English till he was twelve, and even during the Civil War he retained a perceptible Creole accent. On first meeting, most people were struck by his "foreign" appearance. He skin was smooth and olive-complexioned. His eyes, half-lidded, were dark, with a trace of Gallic melancholy about them. His hair was black (though by 1860 he maintained this hue with dye). He was strikingly handsome and enjoyed the attentions of women, but probably not excessively or illicitly. He sported a dark mustache and goatee, and he rather resembled Napoleon III, now ruling France — though he often saw himself in the mold of the more celebrated Napoleon Bonaparte. In fact it had been romantic, exciting tales of that Corsican's victories that had long ago sparked the young boy's imagination and made him decide to become a soldier.

Beauregard arrived at West Point just after his sixteenth birthday. His favorite teacher was his professor of artillery, Robert Anderson. They grew close and some evenings Pierre ate dinner with the Kentuckian. Anderson became so fond of him that after Beauregard graduated, the young Creole stayed at West Point to serve as Anderson's assistant artillery instructor. When the Mexican War exploded, both served with Scott's army; both won admiration for their courage and their ability to use artillery.

After the Mexican War Beauregard had spent most of the next dozen years in and around New Orleans. On one occasion he even ran, unsuccessfully, for mayor, which was quixotic given his personality. He was extremely reserved, even stern, seldom smiling. A deeply proud man, he could be inordinately touchy. In a city as determinedly gay as New Orleans, he did not like to dance or socialize, and remained almost friendless in all his years there. He preferred working or remaining home with his wife and children. Ironically, when he arrived in Charleston, he became the city's social lion. Perhaps his distant reserve was seen as quiet strength, his Catholic, Creole air as aristocratic mannerism. It was well this was so, because Charleston did not usually take much to outsiders. Beauregard saw the delicate nature of his position, and energetically greased the hinges connecting politics and military and the social affairs in the city.

As a military leader his strengths were valuable and his weaknesses unimportant. Later, during the Civil War, his determination to follow the "rules of warfare," written down by men like Antoine Henri de Jomini, made it hard for him to adapt quickly to liquid battlefield conditions. At Shiloh his strength of will saved the Confederate army; on other battlefields he did less well. In a confined space like Charleston Harbor, where geometry was more important than imagination, he was at his best.

As soon as he arrived in town he paid a call on Governor Pickens. During the next few days he carefully inspected the military situation in the harbor, traveling from one battery to the next, talking to officers, observing gunners in practice. He concluded that Major Whiting had been absolutely correct, that many of the guns were in the wrong position. He ordered a bunch of them moved. He made the harbor's mouth more dangerous to enter, and he focused some guns on the places where reinforcements for Fort Sumter might likely stop, at the wharf's landings, for example. He had four huge Drummond lights, purchased in New York, placed in strategic spots, to highlight anyone attempting to enter at night. He asked for more cannon from elsewhere, and the guns began to arrive. He screwed down the discipline even more on the camps skirting the harbor.

Within two days of Beauregard's arrival Anderson wrote Washington that his presence would guarantee South Carolina's "skill and sound judgment in all operations." Then he added, unconsciously aware of how much he was revealing his own affection for the Creole, "God grant that our country may be saved from the horrors of a fratricidal war!" Beauregard, writing to Montgomery, referred to Anderson as "a most gallant officer." In a gesture of affection he sent several cases of fine brandy and whiskey, along with some boxes of cigars, to his friend Robert and the other officers; Anderson, either out of pride, pugnacity, or punctiliousness, returned them, saying they had undoubtedly been mistakenly sent against Beauregard's orders.[25]

At the end of March all the South Carolina Convention's delegates and some guests were given a show. They climbed aboard two ships, which took them on a tour. Guns boomed welcomes for them. They also listened to band music, especially the ever-present "Marseillaise," South Carolina's chief patriotic air since secession, and "Dixie," which the *Mercury* had been suggesting as the Confederacy's national anthem. This excursion provided a sumptuous meal aboard. As a warm spring sun beat on them and cool winds blew a pleasant sea breeze about their shoulders, they sipped champagne served by quiet slaves, ogled the grim, high walls of Fort Sumter, and even espied a pacing Major Anderson. They looked at the Iron Battery, they reviewed troops, they returned home late in the day, their eardrums echoing the barrage of artillery explosions, which had greeted them everywhere. It had all been delightful. "Nothing occurred," said the *Courier*, "to mar the pleasures of the day, and the occasion will long be remembered by all participants."[26]

CHAPTER THIRTEEN

Takes Two to Tango, But One Can Do the Twist All Alone

"I die for food."
— SHAKESPEARE, *AS YOU LIKE IT*

At Fort Sumter it was apparent by mid-February that neither South Carolina nor the new Confederacy was likely to spring a sudden assault. Both would apparently wait to see what Lincoln would say and do; perhaps he might agree that Fort Sumter had been Buchanan's problem, not his; maybe he would be willing to give it up. Unlikely, Fort Sumter's officers thought, but possible.

Had they read Lincoln's letters, they would have known better. For months, the president-elect had stayed in Springfield, Illinois, publicly remaining mum about the evolving crisis. Privately, he had written letters indicating his absolute determination, among other things, to keep Fort Sumter. He said that if the fort was grabbed by Southerners or given up by Buchanan, he would retake it — and he told friends to relay these attitudes to General Scott. Many urged him to accept some sort of compromise on the questions lacerating the nation. He refused. He considered secession political blackmail, and rejected compromise, or what a later generation would call *appeasement*. "The tug," he had said, "has to come."[1]

Major Anderson and his officers pondered the incoming president's attitudes, but none of them had any solid news — until mid-February when Lincoln left Springfield and began meandering toward Washington, stopping along the way to give a few speeches. What he reportedly said did not make those at Sumter feel confident about the prospects for peace. Some of his remarks were inane. In Cleveland he described the present crisis as "artificial." "Let it alone," he said, "and it will go down by itself." At Philadelphia he said there was "no need of bloodshed and war," but he offered no solutions. Some of his comments were pugnacious. In Indianapolis Lincoln declared that holding or retaking federal forts ought not to be considered "coercion." At Fort Sumter, of course, the officers knew better. Crawford wrote his brother, "If Mr. Lincoln fancies he can carry out the policy indicated by his speech at Indianapolis he will find himself very much mistaken." In New York Lincoln shouted — to long and loud cheering — "It may be necessary to put the foot down firmly," and he made some sort of stomping gesture to indicate his own determination. His words offered no hint of a peaceful solution.[2]

As word of these speeches was first reported, the garrison's officers became angry or despondent. Talbot wrote his sister, "The coercion policy he talks of will inevitably plunge the country into civil war." Crawford told his diary he was "Depressed by news in the papers. No encouragement from Lincoln speeches." Anderson felt less pessimistic, perhaps because he trusted more in God's kind hand, but he was hardly Pollyannaish. "Dark clouds," he wrote during Lincoln's trek to Washington, "still hang over our beloved land." He felt quite anxious about the new president's cabinet. "We have had enough," he said, "of third class men, broken down politicians, as Heads of Depts. at Washington." Then he added, "The inner wheels of our political clock must be of the finest metal, and they must be true, or it will run down."[3]

On February 23 Lincoln arrived in Washington early in the morning. He dropped off his bags at Willard's Hotel, Washington's most famous establishment, ate breakfast in his suite, then strolled over to the White House for a courtesy call on Old Buck. Buchanan was meeting with his cabinet, but when a messenger handed him Lincoln's card he leaped from his chair and said giddily, "Uncle Abe is downstairs," rushing off to greet him.

After his visit with Buchanan, Lincoln went to see Winfield Scott. What the two men said that day is unknown, but the fact that Lincoln sought him out right away is fascinating. Military matters were apparently much on his mind. [4]

That evening Lincoln met informally with members of the Peace Convention, still in town and winding up their sessions. One of its members told Lincoln it would be the new president's decision "whether grass shall grow in the streets of our commercial cities." Lincoln mildly replied that, if it were up to him, the only grass growing in America would be in its fields and meadows. Someone asked if this meant he would go to war over slavery. He stiffened. In a few days, he said, he would be taking a Constitutional oath. When he did so, he said, he would be swearing to make sure the Constitution was "respected, obeyed, enforced, and defended, let the grass grow where it may."

Three days later Lincoln met privately with a delegation from Virginia. That state was perhaps the most important in the country at this moment. Less than half the South had seceded; the rest looked to Virginia for leadership. During the previous few weeks secession had actually failed in votes in five Southern states, including Virginia. A majority of Virginians had voted against secession, but most also felt a kinship with their brethren farther South and would not condone any attempt to coerce the Confederacy. Lincoln did not want to rile Virginia's leaders if he could avoid it, and spoke to their representatives with care and concern. Their leader that evening was the elderly, dignified William C. Rives. His voice a-tremble, Rives told Lincoln that if force was used against any Southern state, Virginia would secede, and he, himself, would fight. Lincoln stood up and rushed across the room to the old man. "Mr. Rives, Mr. Rives!" he reportedly said. "If Virginia will stay in, I will withdraw the troops from Fort Sumter!" A few days later a German diplomat asked Lincoln if the reports of his alleged encounter with Rives were true. Yes, Lincoln replied, "A state for a fort is no bad business."[5]

On March 4 hundreds of armed soldiers lined the pathway between Willard's and the Capitol. Snipers stood atop buildings alert for assassins. Lincoln himself seemed calm as he entered his carriage and a parade band struck up "Dixie." A few minutes later he was standing next to the Capitol, addressing the curious crowd. Some of his words were what today may be called Lincoln-esque in their beauty, though they lacked the remarkable poetry and power of his later prose. He tried to assuage the concerns, the angers, of his fellow citizens. He appealed to "the better angels of our nature." From Charleston's point of view, his key points were these: (1) no state could lawfully secede; and (2) "The power confided in me will be used to hold, occupy and possess the property and places belonging to the government." Lincoln had actually wanted to use sharper terms here but had been persuaded to soften them a bit.

Standing toward the rear of the audience stood a glowering Senator Wigfall, his arms angrily folded across his deep chest. "Inaugural means war," he wired Charleston. "There is strong ground for belief that re-enforcements will be speedily sent. Be vigilant."[6] During the next day or so, a frisson of rage and anxiety rippled across the Confederacy. "Old Abe Lincoln was inaugurated today," Emma Holmes wrote in her diary. "His speech was just what was expected of him, stupid, ambiguous, vulgar and insolent." The *Mercury* was almost insensible with outrage. They called him a "vain, ignorant, low fellow," "a blatant old ass," and "a most preposterous buffoon." Four commercial steamers, waiting at Charleston's wharves till the inauguration to see if Lincoln's words would be conciliatory, steamed off on March 5 to avoid a possible blockade.

At Fort Sumter Wylie Crawford confided to his diary that he and the other officers could not decipher the implications of the speech. "Does it mean peace or war?" he wrote. In New York Eba was equally confused. She wrote her husband that she had at first assumed Lincoln's words meant only one thing: "war, war, war." But she admitted a few days later that she felt less certain.[7]

One day after his inauguration Lincoln received what he considered a bombshell, its fuse lit by Major Anderson. For months Anderson had done all he could to maintain peace in America. He understood war better than most Americans, and hated it so much he would rather accept the existence of the Confederacy than fight. He had hoped that, given time, the Deep South might rejoin the Union, but if not, so be it. He was not alone in this dream. Prominent leaders of both parties, men like Stephen Douglas and William Seward, held similar views. But as March 4 approached, the garrison was running out of provisions and Anderson believed he would have to surrender the fort within a few weeks. He was politically savvy enough to know that such a critical decision ought to be worked out by politicians, not an army major, and he worried the new administration might not have sufficient information about the situation in Charleston Harbor to make the correct — in his mind, peaceful — decision.

Thus as February came toward its close he ordered his officers to estimate what size military force it would take to relieve the garrison. This was a hard assignment. None of them knew the exact nature of the army facing them, how many soldiers there were, or where all the guns had been placed, but each officer was quite convinced that the only way to relieve Sumter successfully would be to land a large army on Morris Island and sweep away its batteries. That island would become a battlefield; results there would be uncertain. They were not yet aware of General Beauregard's recent appointment but they did know that Jefferson Davis's government had taken command of the harbor, and they could assume changes would be made, and soon. Any military estimates the officers made would of necessity be vague and unreliable. Anderson knew this but he wanted something concrete to offer the new administration, something that would encourage it to be cautious. Within a few hours he had each officer's best guess. Snyder thought 2,000 soldiers and a strong naval fleet might be enough at this moment; Doubleday and Foster were sure at least 10,000 regulars would be necessary. Anderson figured 20,000. He put their estimates into a message to Secretary Holt, and included a statement about the fort's dwindling provisions. He wanted his note to arrive in Washington before March 4, Inauguration Day, so that Holt could turn it over to the new president just as soon as Lincoln took the oath.[8]

On March 3, following tradition, James Buchanan moved out of the Executive Mansion and spent the night at a friend's house.

The next morning he was up early, signing a few congressional bills and chatting with some members of his cabinet who had dropped by to say good-bye. At noon his administration would end, and he was quite jovial. Holt entered the room carrying Anderson's recent message. Buchanan glanced at it, showed it to the others, and indicated, doubtless with a sigh of satisfaction, that in a few minutes Major Anderson's report would be Lincoln's problem, not his.[9]

Lincoln had chosen Simon Cameron to be his secretary of war, but Cameron had yet to be confirmed by the Senate. Given this precarious moment in American history, Holt had agreed to stay in his position for the nonce. On the afternoon after Lincoln's inauguration, Acting Secretary of War Holt sent Anderson's report and an accompanying statement of his own across the lawn to the new president. Lincoln read it, recognized its meaning and its importance, and summoned Holt. The president wanted to know one thing right away: Since Anderson's report was startlingly bleak, was the major to be trusted? Holt, a cautious man, mildly said he had no reason to distrust Anderson's loyalty.

Lincoln said nothing more about that subject, but he seems to have noted Holt's possible reservations. A few days later Lincoln surprised Mary Doubleday, who was in the capital, by calling on her. He asked if she would permit him to read any letters her husband might have sent her. This visit had actually been simmering for two months. In mid-January, after the *Star of the West* debacle, and Anderson's agreement with Pickens to allow Washington to decide what to do next, Doubleday had not liked watching the South Carolinians erecting their batteries on both sides of the harbor, seeing the ships passing the fort night and day, hearing the sounds of Southern artillery men practicing their aim. Fort Sumter might have used its own guns to stem all this, but Anderson had refused to do so. Doubleday, in his frustration, had written Mary a letter expressing his annoyance. She in turn had sent it to Abner's brother, Ulysses. He, a Republican, made a copy of it and sent it along to Lincoln in Springfield, adding a personal note to the president-elect, "Depend upon it, Maj. A's heart is not in his duty."

Lincoln now had Anderson's ominous, and perhaps exaggerated, report in his possession. This was why he went to Mary to discover if her husband's other letters revealed sinister motives in Anderson's behavior. He also wanted to discover if the letters spoke about Sumter's provisions. After reading them, then speaking to others like Scott, who knew Anderson well, Lincoln was, apparently, satisfied with the major's loyalty.

Part of the problem was Holt. In January Holt had been told by Lieutenant Hall what the status was of their provisions. The secretary also had a memorandum from Hall, which, according to the army's own records of February 21, clearly showed "what articles are required at Fort Sumter," how many rations they had. Holt knew what a military "ration" was, what a soldier was fed each day. Simple mathematics would have told him how long the fort's provisions could last. If he chose not to do the arithmetic, or if he had done so and now covered up his knowledge to preserve his own image — and Buchanan's — casting a subtle shadow across Anderson's reputation, it was a contemptible act of cowardice.[10]

Lincoln's first weeks in office were not easy. He was assembling his government, and anxious office seekers were beseeching him, plucking at his elbows at every turn. He discovered that his treasury was virtually empty, his army was demoralized, his civil service rotten with treason and uncertainty. Seven states had flown away, seven others watched his every move. He had personal acquaintance with only a few members of his government — at least two of whom were confident they would have made a better president than he. His political party was brand-new and riven with divisions. The Supreme Court was dominated by opponents. Lincoln had served only a single term in Congress, and that, a dozen years earlier, as a member of a different party, the Whigs. He had practically no experience as an administrator. In some ways he seemed less confident and in less control than had Buchanan.

To those who did not know him well, Lincoln appeared an affable sort, but something of a rube. His pronunciation of certain words sounded painfully rustic to sophisticated ears. His tendency to tell humorous, country tales to entertain or emphasize his points smacked of the cheap theatrics of barnyard politics. He did have several qualities that were immediately important. He sometimes had a way with words; he could make a sentence ring. And, unlike men such as Jefferson Davis, he was perfectly content to learn from outside sources. Later, during the war, he spent days poring over military textbooks, culling from them certain shards of wisdom his generals often lacked. His greatest strength was his complete confidence in a few principles. The most important of these was that secession was illegal. In his lawyer's mind, what the Confederate states had done was null and void. He did not have to *re-create* the Union since it had never truly been altered. He had only to erase the notion of secession from the minds of certain misguided Southerners, and he would do whatever was necessary to accomplish this task. He would overlook insulting behavior (from men like General George McClellan) and listen with patience to the self-righteous preening of scores of political hacks. He would try whatever he thought might work, and avoid whatever might encourage the theory of secession.

Yet here, on Lincoln's first full day in office, March 5, he was faced with that remarkably slippery topic that had befuddled so many others: Fort Sumter.

The immediate issue was timing. Anderson's report, handed over by Holt, indicated that the garrison's days were numbered. Lincoln asked Winfield Scott to read the report. The general did so and saw nothing startling in it. He returned it the same day, with a notation, "I now see no alternative but a surrender." Lincoln trusted the old man's judgment on military matters and was dismayed. The new president had assumed he would have an extended period to make some decision on Sumter; now it appeared he had only a few weeks, and, apparently, would have no option but to surrender the fort. Giving it up would be a painful humiliation for himself, as well as for the Republican party, which had never before held the White House.

As he attempted to arrive at some solution to the puzzle of Fort Sumter, Lincoln recognized that the status of that one fortification was only part of the picture. He had to make sure his administration felt no blows from anywhere else, so he sent a message to Scott to "exercise all possible vigilance" about the status of all other federal installations. He was especially concerned about Pensacola and was well aware that a large Confederate army there was besieging Fort Pickens. He dreaded the possibility he might lose it as well as Fort Sumter, but knew that their situations were different. Unlike Sumter, Fort Pickens still had military assistance nearby. The fleet and troops that Buchanan had sent down in January, before the "truce," still waited outside the mouth of the bay. Lieutenant Slemmer's little force could be defended by the fleet or reinforced at any time. Lincoln told Scott to see to it that the soldiers aboard the fleet reinforced the fort immediately.[11]

Amazingly, the commander of the fleet refused. When Captain Henry A. Adams received Scott's dispatch, he assumed the new administration in Washington was so dense it was unaware of the truce, and he used a bureaucratic ploy to justify his inaction. He wrote a note to the Navy Department that the orders had come from General Scott, not the navy, and that any change of the balance at Pensacola was so weighty that orders would have to come to him through proper channels. Adams gave this message to one of his young officers and told him to wend his way, as best he could, through the Confederacy to Washington. This adventure took quite some time. As a result, Adams's remarkable decision did not reach the capital for many crucial days. Lincoln, trying to determine what to do about Fort Sumter, naturally assumed his position at Pensacola was solid. Since he felt confident about Pensacola, he could contemplate surrendering Fort Sumter, thinking that the reputation of his administration for forcefulness would remain sound.[12]

On March 9 Lincoln met with his cabinet for its first session. He explained, to the shock of several, Anderson's predicament. Edward Bates, the new attorney general, wrote in his diary, "I was astonished to be informed that Fort Sumter, in Charleston Harbor, *must* be evacuated"—indicating Lincoln had told them there was no other way out. That same day, and probably a result of the cabinet meeting, the president wrote Scott, asking him three specific questions. How long could the garrison's provisions last? Could the government send them supplies in time? If not immediately, could it be done with a beefed-up military? General Scott replied that it would be impossible to estimate precisely how long the food would last, but certainly less than seven weeks. The army, he added, did not have on hand enough force to break through to reinforce Fort Sumter. It might do so with 25,000 soldiers and a large fleet, but this would require acts of Congress (which was not even in session) and six to eight months of training for the troops. It was, quite simply, impossible. General Joseph Totten, the army's most respected expert on military engineering and a designer of Fort Sumter, concurred.[13]

The administration's initial thoughts about Fort Sumter reached Charleston immediately, sent south by various messengers. The first report arrived in Charleston the day after that first cabinet meeting. The *Courier*'s correspondent in Washington wired south that a top "Republican senator" (Seward, probably) had said "there is no earthly doubt" that the garrison would be withdrawn within two weeks. On the next day, March 11, came more reports. Senator Wigfall announced that the evacuation would come in five days; a friend of Seward's wired the same. The *Courier* pinned a notice to its bulletin board and published a longer report the following day. The *Mercury* contained a similar story.

The weather was glorious in Charleston. The sky was clear and blue, the winds almost balmy. Perhaps it was an omen. Joy percolated through the city and out to the camps. They had won! Colonel Ripley permitted his artillerymen to fire a hundred blank cartridges in celebration. Other batteries here and there fired into the air with enthusiasm. At Fort Sumter the officers had heard nothing directly, but they did examine the city's newspapers every day for news, and there seemed no reason to disbelieve the stories. They also noticed that work on the island batteries slowed and almost ceased. They, too, became excited. As Crawford noted in his diary, the report "raised all our feelings to the highest pitch." Anderson, a cautious soldier, reminded them all to continue actively improving their fort, but he told them to start making an inventory of what they had on hand, a clear sign that he thought they would be going home soon. Crawford looked around and felt a quiet pride. There was their flag, a bit weatherworn by now, still flying, "yet undishonored." "Weeks of excitement and toil," he told his diary, "have made it dear to us, and this old glorious fortress, yet untouched by the invader."[14]

On March 15 General Scott, speaking to a Senate executive session, said he thought Anderson ought to be withdrawn. He even mentioned to a Charlestonian that the garrison *would* shortly leave. The *Courier* reported both these stories, and added, "So that point is settled." Edmund Ruffin, in Charleston to participate in any military action, decided to leave. "I will wait no longer to witness it," he wrote on March 18. "I have not the least expectation of the occurrence of any fighting here." But still no official word. Crawford became testy by this prolonging of the inevitable. They were running out of food and their health was deteriorating. He had no patience with Lincoln's inaugural talk of firmness. He wrote his brother, "All this talk of 'occupying, holding, and possessing' the forts is nonsense." At the island camps Confederate soldiers grew uneasy. One young man said he had heard all the rumors that Anderson was leaving "tomorrow," but that "many tomorrows have come and gone and the stars and stripes still float from the flagstaff at Sumter."[15]

The problem was simple. Lincoln had not been entirely convinced of the need to evacuate. On March 15 he decided to put a single question to each member of his cabinet: "Assuming it is possible to now provision Fort Sumter, under all the circumstances is it wise to attempt it? Give me your opinion in writing on this question." Each of them responded, some briefly, some at length. Most thought it *might* be possible to get supplies to the fort, but imprudent since it would likely result in civil war. Simon Cameron, finally in place as secretary of war, an elderly, tall, and slender man, astute and shrewd, had listened carefully to his military advisers and come away firmly opposed. An attempt was likely to fail, and, if nothing else, make the new administration look foolish. Even if it succeeded, he said, any additional provisions could only last so long, and then they would have to try it again. Others of the cabinet held similar views. Only two supported any attempt. Salmon Chase, secretary of the treasury, thought sending food not *likely* to lead to war. Lincoln's postmaster general, Montgomery Blair, the youngest of them, a combative, hatchet-faced graduate of West Point and an emotionally charged hater of secessionists, insisted that *not* sending provisions would convince the rebels the administration had no backbone, and this by itself would lead to war.[16] To Lincoln, the central point raised by Chase and Blair seemed worth considering before making a final decision. Lincoln decided he wanted more information, and sent several emissaries down to Charleston to scout out the ground.

Stephen Augustus Hurlbut, born in Charleston, had lived in that city thirty years then moved to Illinois to practice law. There he made the acquaintance of Abraham Lincoln. In early March 1861 Hurlbut was visiting Washington when he received a note from the president asking him a favor. Would he be willing to travel to Charleston immediately to check on the atmosphere there, and see how the city might react to a ship carrying supplies to Anderson's garrison? Hurlbut departed right away, arriving early on the morning of March 24, a Sunday. He went to his family's church and attended service, after which he stood outside, chatting with old friends. Lincoln had wanted him to test the mood of the city's population, and it was here, near the entrance of this church, that Hurlbut spent probably no more than a single hour talking to individuals matching his own well-to-do background, forming his impression. That afternoon he visited an old friend, Judge Petigru, then went to the home of his sister and her husband, where he spent the night. Whether he had a chance to speak to anyone else is unknown. The following evening he boarded a northbound train. He had spent thirty-six hours in Charleston, but it seemed quite enough to form a clear opinion. He had a good lawyer's crisp mind, and on his trip back north he wrote a cogent report for the president. He pointed out that he had observed military equipment and supplies moving inexorably toward Charleston. The people he spoke to in the city, he said, held a "unanimity of sentiment": they were opposed to the Union. Most, he added, wanted a peaceful separation, but a loud minority thirsted for battle. He was convinced that a ship coming to Fort Sumter, even if it carried only provisions, would be stopped.[17]

Hurlbut's trip had been quiet, prudent, and uneventful, much like the man himself. The second person Lincoln asked to go to Charleston cast off sparks in all directions. The exact mission of Ward Hill Lamon, one of Lincoln's law partners, has never been clear. His autobiography provides his own version of those several days, but his account is hardly trustworthy. He was a large, muscular man with a taste for alcohol and a greater concern for a good tale than for accuracy. Like Louis Wigfall, he prided himself on his machismo, generally carrying both a large knife and a gun, and also like the senator he was a bit of a fool, with an uncontrollable need to swagger and bring attention to himself. Lincoln could and did use him as a bodyguard on many occasions, but why the president chose to send him to Charleston on a delicate diplomatic errand is, at best, curious. It is possible Lincoln — or perhaps William Seward, as some have suggested — was utilizing Lamon to confuse those in Charleston with his antics. If so, the trick worked.

Lamon traveled to the city and arranged a meeting with Pickens. The two men got along famously. Pickens warned Lamon that any attempt to provision Sumter would result in war, then permitted him to visit Fort Sumter. When Lamon arrived at the fort everyone knew he was from Washington. He spoke privately to Anderson for over an hour and indicated to the major quite clearly that the garrison would shortly be evacuated from the fort.

Anderson could now be sure they would be leaving soon. After all, Lamon was a direct messenger from the White House — the *first* one Major Anderson had spoken to during all his months in the harbor.

To nail down matters further, when Lamon returned to Charleston he asked Pickens if the governor would permit a naval vessel to come and pick up the garrison. No, said Pickens, but he would allow them to use a civilian steamship. Fine, replied Lamon. He was returning now to Washington, but would be back in a few days to make the final arrangements. In fact, Lamon had absolutely no authority to give such a promise. Even more remarkable, as soon as Lamon returned to Washington he wrote Pickens a letter *confirming* their conversation. His trip made such an impression on Charleston's atmosphere that someone wired the good news to Savannah and arrangements were made to bring an excursion train from that city, carrying gleeful Georgians on a sightseeing boat trip out to Fort Sumter where they could walk around the empty fortification.

One footnote to Lamon's visit: As Major Anderson and he were walking about the parapets, Anderson mentioned that he had mined the wharf, as well as set up some booby traps outside the walls. Lamon misunderstood him and told Pickens, just before he left town, that Major Anderson intended to blow up the fort. This led to a dust storm. Rumors had been circulating in Montgomery that Anderson was contemplating such an act, and Confederate Secretary of War Walker had previously asked Beauregard about the stories. Now Lamon had confirmed them, and the major felt forced to write calming notes to Beauregard. Anderson even heard from Scott about it. The general sent him a firm message about blowing up the fort: "I forbid it as your commander, it being against your duty as soldier & Christian." The major wearily replied to the general that he was "deeply mortified at the want of confidence in me." He was pained, he said, by Scott's questioning his "Christian" nature. He did not remind his old mentor how weak and unwell he had been when first assigned here, or how tiring and draining the four months had been on him, with so much of the responsibility for the fort—and the nation—on his shoulders. He did not tell Scott how gaunt he had become, how gray his hair had turned, how deep-set and smudged his eyes had grown from exhaustion. But he did sigh, "I must say that I think the Govt. has left me too much to myself, has not given me instructions, even when I have asked for them, and that responsibilities of a higher and more delicate character have been devolved upon me than was proper." And he told Scott that it had been only his reliance on God that had gotten him through these times.[18]

For a while after Lamon's visit the garrison felt confident about their approaching withdrawal. They calculated that he would arrive back in the Capital on the 27th, and they expected to hear something official immediately thereafter. But no such message ensued. "No order yet for our withdrawal," Crawford jotted in his diary on March 29. "We cannot understand why we are neglected."

The next day he wrote with discouragement, "No special news. Time drags heavily for us."[19]

What they did not know is that Lincoln had arrived at a new conclusion. He had changed his mind and was now contemplating action. Why? Had his conversion come as a result of pressure from several Republican governors who were in town? Or a conversation he had with old Francis Blair, the feisty father of his postmaster, Montgomery Blair? Francis Blair had stomped in when rumors of withdrawal had swirled about the city and had angrily told Lincoln not to do it. The aged Blair had once served Andrew Jackson and was, himself, a grim old patriot. Lincoln was apparently impressed, maybe swayed, by the man's fervor. Also, there was the fact that up to March 28 Lincoln had been accepting General Scott's opposition to action, but on that day the general sent one memo too many. He wrote Lincoln, suggesting that the administration should withdraw even Slemmer from Pensacola, because, Scott said, doing so would encourage Unionism in the Border States. Lincoln had been assuming general Scott's cautionary advice had been motivated solely by *military* necessities. Lincoln now expressed outrage that the general was offering suggestions based on *political* factors, which threw a shadow across all of his prior opinions, especially those on the subject of Fort Sumter.

The day after Lincoln received Scott's latest note, he called a cabinet meeting and, in light of the doubt that now lingered about the general's views, again polled his advisers on whether they supported more assertive action. As it turned out, this time they tilted slightly in that direction. It probably made no difference. The president, it seems, was willy-nilly edging toward a more decisive approach. He wanted to present an image of a dynamic administration. He asked his cabinet members about the legality and feasibility of using ships to collect revenues stationed just outside Charleston Harbor. He also began to plan, not simply contemplate, an expedition to relieve Major Anderson. Lincoln did not immediately commit himself, but he gave orders to start the process. He was still assuming (mistakenly) that he was about to learn that Lieutenant Slemmer at Fort Pickens had been reinforced, per presidential orders. In Lincoln's mind, apparently, that news *might* be sufficient. The administration could then present itself as being strongly activist, and Lincoln could contemplate withdrawing Anderson without seeming weak. Meanwhile, as he awaited positive news from Pensacola, he decided to pursue the creation of a new relief expedition for Fort Sumter. Time was getting short for a decision about Anderson's garrison. The president wanted to keep his options open. If he had a relief expedition ready at hand, he would have the freedom to use it — or not, depending on circumstances. If something unexpectedly happy turned up in the next few days, he could cancel the expedition at the last minute, but otherwise . . . let the chips fall.

Though he never admitted it, Lincoln may even have concluded that a war was inevitable, and it would be far better for the Confederacy to fire the first shot, that he was looking for some clever way to maneuver Jefferson Davis into that position. Davis himself was thinking along the same lines, trying to come up with some gimmick that would goad Lincoln into premature action. Davis wired Braxton Bragg about the Confederate troops at Pensacola: "There would be to us an advantage in so placing them that an attack by them [the Union force] would be a necessity."[20]

The specific plan about *how* to aid Fort Sumter evolved rather rapidly. The idea of sending assistance to Sumter's garrison, of course, was hardly new. The *Star of the West* had tried it, New York businessmen had offered to sponsor an independent attempt, and Buchanan had actually begun preparing another such venture during his last weeks in office. The central problem came from the ominous batteries South Carolina was building on both sides of the harbor's entrance. On February 5 Major Anderson had written Washington that he considered it almost impossible for any rescue fleet to get to him, unless it was either extremely large or "a small party slipping in." A few weeks later Confederate Secretary of War Walker wrote Beauregard from Montgomery that it was likely Lincoln would try to slip reinforcements in on whaleboats during the night.[21] The idea of utilizing small boats, rather than large steamers like the *Star of the West*, had been discussed in

Washington for weeks, but Lincoln was especially drawn to the specific plan of Gustavus Vasa Fox. Maybe it was the complete confidence of the chunky ex-navy man that appealed to the president. Or perhaps the timing was right; it may be that Lincoln had decided — for any of a number of possible reasons — to plunge ahead and provision Fort Sumter, and he found Gus Fox hovering nearby, anxious as a schoolboy.

Fox was born in Massachusetts, the son of a physician. He graduated from the Naval Academy in 1841 and spent fifteen years at sea. In 1856 he married a wealthy young woman from Massachusetts, daughter of a prominent politician, and he left the navy to become a salesman in the textile business. When he heard about the disaster of the *Star of the West,* he concluded the failure had derived from trying to squeeze a large vessel through one of the harbor's narrow channels. His solution was twofold. First, use steamtugs with light draughts, sturdy and quick, that could bypass the channels entirely and slip directly over the bar. Second, have them enter the harbor at night. The provisions — and reinforcements, if the government wished to send them — could initially be placed aboard a large steamer, then transferred, outside Charleston Harbor, to the tugs. Protected by a powerful naval fleet lying outside the bar, and by Fort Sumter's cannon inside, the tugs should easily slip up to Sumter. Fox had studied recent military conflicts, especially the Crimean War, and was not impressed with the capacity of land-based guns — like South Carolina's — to do much damage to fast-moving ships. Speed and aggressiveness — these were the necessary qualities. The only other problem, as Fox saw it, was that there were then only three such tugs available, all civilian ships in New York, but if the government acted quickly and hired them, everything else could work smoothly.

In January, shortly after the *Star* debacle, Fox wrote a letter about his ideas to his brother-in-law, Montgomery Blair, and Blair in turn showed the note to Winfield Scott, who spoke to Fox on February 5. The general was impressed enough with Fox's plan that he took him to see Secretary of War Holt. Later, Fox and Lieutenant Hall spoke on several occasions about the things Sumter needed and the problems in getting them there. Fox told

Hall what he had in mind, and was confident Hall, in turn, would describe the plan to Major Anderson.

In March, with the new president contemplating action, Blair told Fox to come forward and again explain his project. Fox pounced on the opportunity. He wrote his wife that Blair had assured him he would be famous if he succeeded, a greater star even than Robert Anderson. On March 13 Fox was in Washington. Two days later, during the crucial cabinet meeting when each member was told to explain his stand about provisioning Sumter, Fox was in the room. On March 19 he gleefully wrote his wife from Washington: "Our Uncle Abe Lincoln has taken a high esteem for me." Lincoln, he said, "wishes me to take dispatches to Major Anderson at Fort Sumpter with regard to its final evacuation and to obtain a clear statement of his condition which his letters, probably guarded, do not fully exhibit."[22]

On the evening of March 21 Fox arrived at Fort Sumter, escorted there by an old navy friend, Henry Julius Hartstene, forty-eight years old, weather-beaten from years at sea, recently resigned from the United States Navy and in command of South Carolina's fleet. Fox had stopped in Charleston on the way and received permission from Pickens. The governor had asked whether the visit was "pacific" and Fox assured him it was. At the fort Fox first handed Major Anderson three official messages from Washington. One involved Fox's orders from Secretary of War Cameron, another was from Governor Pickens giving Fox permission to cross over. The third came from Scott, praising Anderson and suggesting he ought to be promoted for his actions. Fox spoke to Anderson for an hour or so. The major gave him an up-to-date report on the meager status of their provisions, then walked him about the parapet. Lieutenant Hall had indeed told Anderson weeks earlier that Fox had spoken to him several times in Washington about sending an expedition to Sumter, so Anderson was now careful to explain how absurd such a venture would be. Although it was late at night, the moon offered enough light for him to point down at the places where boats carrying provisions might try to land and how each spot would come under brutal bombardment from batteries on one side of the harbor or the other.

While they were standing there, they suddenly heard the splash of oars from somewhere out of sight in the darkness, which seemed to confirm Fox's theory that small boats could maneuver at night, unseen, to the fort. At this, Anderson emphasized how South Carolina's patrols would intercept any approach, but Fox replied that Fort Sumter's guns could prevent that. The major was adamant that any attempt was bound to fail, to say nothing of the fact that it would initiate war.

As a result of this conversation, Anderson believed that if Fox had previously held any wild ideas about trying a relief expedition, he now had seen enough to understand its absurdity. Anderson considered the subject closed, but the following day, just in case, he wrote Washington about a matter Fox had mentioned the night before. The harbor was so shallow around the fort, he said, that vessels with ten-foot draughts would have to stop at least forty feet back and carry goods to the fort in rowboats, a cumbersome operation, and highly dangerous since thirteen of Fort Moultrie's guns could pour deadly fire on the landing site.

After Fox's departure from Charleston Beauregard spoke to Hartstene about what had happened at Sumter. "Were you," the general asked, "with Captain Fox all the time of his visit?" "All but a short period," Hartstene replied, "when he was with Major Anderson." Beauregard sighed, "I fear that we shall have occasion to regret that short period."[23]

Astonishingly, Fox had actually just convinced himself that he had been correct, that his scheme was feasible—though he decided *not* to relay this opinion to Anderson since the major was so frankly opposed to any such attempt, and maybe even had "Southern sympathies." (It is interesting that Captain Hartstene of the South Carolina navy did think a venture such as Fox's might actually get into the harbor. Hartstene believed that low-draft barges could slip by him on a dark night. He was aware that ships could pass each other in the dark—as thousands of Southern ships would prove during the war, passing the Northern blockade of the Carolina coastline.[24]) Since Fox decided to be cagey with the major, he also failed to suggest that the garrison ought to go on half-rations to lengthen their potential stay at

Sumter. Nor did Fox later admit to the president that he had failed to mention this. Lincoln therefore acted during the next few days on the assumption that he had many weeks to make up his mind about what to do. In fact, the window of his opportunity was closing fast. When he finally did discover the truth, Lincoln would act so hastily and clumsily that he made several critical mistakes.[25]

From the point of view of Anderson and his officers, Fox's visit had been an investigative one, a reasonable attempt to acquire information about their status. They had indicated to him that their food would last only a few more days, and that they were increasingly hemmed in by Beauregard's batteries. The only rational conclusion one could come to, they had to assume, was their withdrawal from the fort. This is why they found Lamon's visit quite understandable. Unlike Fox, who was at best a low-ranking representative of the War Department, Lamon seemed very close to the president. When Lamon indicated that they would be evacuated shortly, they had no reason not to believe him. By the last days of March, therefore, they were looking forward to the end of their long, tiring nightmare. Foster wrote a friend in the city that he would like to see him again socially, but could not spare the time since he would be too busy doing inventories, "till the moment of our departure."[26]

The garrison did not realize, as they inventoried the federal property at the fort, that the president was, even then, deciding on a decisive act. At the end of March Lincoln asked Fox what he would need to accomplish his plan, and within a few hours Fox wrote down his specifications. Lincoln took this list and ordered Simon Cameron and Secretary of the Navy Gideon Welles to begin preparations. They should have everything ready to go by April 6, eight days away — just in case he decided to go ahead with Fox's plan.

Between March 30 and April 6 Washington was the scene of much scurrying, both physical and mental. Beneath the surface slithered the machinations of the secretary of state. William Seward's activities during these days were almost certainly not treacherous in the normal sense, though his motives have remained

elusive. One of his assumptions had been that, in the face of secession, patience was the best policy. Another had been that *he* was
the best-qualified man in the country to control events, and he had
assumed he was going to do so, that he would act like a British
prime minister, consulting Lincoln as Disraeli might consult
Queen Victoria, but little more. (Had someone as incompetent as,
say, Franklin Pierce been president, or as brainless as Warren G.
Harding, Seward's attempt to alter traditional roles might have
permanently changed the government, for good or ill.) The Fox
expedition brought his scheming to the surface, and abruptly ended
it. The bureaucratic maneuvers and in-fighting during that week
are convoluted, but the essential story is this: Seward decided to
reinforce Fort Pickens in Pensacola, and did so without consulting
his cabinet colleagues at either the Navy Department or the War
Department. Other than the embarrassments and angers that
arose when his game was revealed, the main result was that the
navy's most powerful vessel in the Atlantic, the *Powhatan*, was sent
to Florida, and did not accompany Fox's fleet as Fox had hoped.
Later on, Fox would blame the failure of his expedition on this
omission, but this claim was absurd. His plan had been doomed
since early March, if not before, and the changes Beauregard had
recently made in the harbor batteries only intensified that truth.
Secretary Seward's efforts, therefore, merely muddied things up;
they did not change the ultimate results.

The critical fact in all this was Lincoln's April 4 order to Captain Fox to deliver "subsistence" to Fort Sumter, and if he met any
opposition the naval force with him would use its guns; Fox was
also to deposit 200 reinforcements at Sumter. When Lincoln informed Fox to make all his final preparations and leave immediately for Fort Sumter, Fox expostulated that he needed more time.
His plan, he reminded Lincoln, required three special tugs, and,
although he had spoken to their New York owners, he had not yet
actually leased them. He also had to gather the provisions and assemble the soldiers, then travel with everything south 632 miles,
and . . .

The president stopped him. The difficulties were understood.
The attempt must be made. Lincoln reportedly then added, "You

will best fulfill your duty to your country by making the attempt."[27] Assuming that this sentence was accurately recalled, it might have merely meant, "I understand but it's the best hope we have," or it might indicate that the president was sending Fox to Charleston Harbor to jostle Jefferson Davis into striking first. The question is interesting, but insoluble.

Fox rushed to New York. He pieced together a little flotilla, and departed. A large civilian steamer, the *Baltic*, carried the barrels and boxes of supplies, as well as the two hundred seasick, raw recruits, who knew far less about artillery than the South Carolina militiamen at Fort Moultrie who had been annoying Ripley by their incompetence. Ordered to protect the *Baltic* were three naval vessels, the *Harriet Lane*, the *Pocahontas*, and the *Pawnee*. None was especially imposing, but all were well enough armed that they could have prevented Captain Hartstene's pitiful little fleet from coming out past the bar to attack the *Baltic*. All four vessels, however, were too large to pass into the harbor. Fox's scheme depended on the three tugs, each bearing a deliciously paradoxical name: *Freeborn*, *Yankee*, and *Uncle Ben*. As fate would have it, none of these tugs arrived in time. The owners of the *Freeborn* actually decided before it even left port that the entire venture seemed absurd, and they kept it home. A vicious Atlantic storm scattered the rest of Fox's ships. The *Baltic* and the three naval vessels would eventually arrive off the bar piecemeal, but the gale winds blew the *Yankee* well past Charleston, all the way to Savannah, and pushed *Uncle Ben* into harbor at Wilmington, North Carolina.

Fox's expedition was to be a total failure—that is, in terms of any success in relieving the garrison. But its mere attempt had far-reaching effects.

CHAPTER FOURTEEN

The Yellow Brick Road

"April is the cruelest month."
— T. S. ELIOT, FROM *THE WASTE LAND*

A
s for Fort Sumter's officers, Washington's military bu-
reaucracy ground along as if nothing special was happening. Anderson received word he was being assigned
to take over as superintendent of the army's Western Recruiting
Service in Kentucky, beginning the end of June. The timing of the
decision was simply following standard practices for this time of
year, as if Major Anderson were sitting at a desk in New York and
not atop several hundred kegs of gunpowder. Lieutenant Talbot
was informed he had been promoted to brevet captain, was being
reassigned from the artillery to the Adjutant General's Office,
and was being posted to Oregon Territory. He was to report in
early April. Under the circumstances at Fort Sumter, Anderson
asked Washington if Talbot might be permitted to stay a few days
longer — until the situation changed. This request was granted
without comment. Meanwhile, the army's paymaster came to the
fort and handed the men their quarterly wages with no concern
about where they could spend the money.

The spirit of the garrison began to flag. They were pawns in a
test of wills, powerless, isolated, waiting. Ward Lamon had indicated that they would be leaving, that their long imprisonment

232

would be over soon . . . but no other word from Washington. Their routines ticked off slowly, like the minutes on an invisible clock. Reveille. Breakfast. Artillery practice. Lunch. On and on.

The same dark walls still pinched out most sunlight. The same Atlantic winds whined through the embrasures. The same faces, day after day. Dr. Crawford wrote his brother that he was worried. "The men are beginning to show signs of their long confinement. My sick report is increasing." He jotted into his diary that they were "Looking anxiously for the messenger." Abner Doubleday wrote Mary, "Everyone is weary of the confinement here. It is nothing but walking around the parapet, eating and sleeping." Talbot wrote his mother that he was especially concerned about the enlisted men. "The strain," he said, "on both mind and body has been too long continued and many are giving way in health and spirits."[1]

They were also running out of food. On March 21 they had six barrels of flour, but a week later they had only one. They still had some moldy hardtack, pork, and rice, but little else, a few carrots and some cabbage. Foster's supplies for his workmen had been reduced to cornmeal and grits, plus a few codfish, and the garrison had been turning over part of its own subsistence to the laborers. Anderson decided it was time to send away the last of the workmen, except for half a dozen or so who could be used to row a boat. He had only kept them around this long because, after Lamon's visit, he was sure the garrison would be abandoning this post shortly and he wished to leave it neat and properly tended. Foster paid the laborers off on March 31; they awaited formal agreement from Charleston. There was no reply.

On April 1 Anderson wrote Washington about the parlous state of their provisions. He said he had not previously said much about their food since the army had been "fully informed from time to time." He had told Fox, he said, that the garrison *could* have held out till sometime after April 10, *if* he had put them all on reduced rations, but since he had heard nothing he had not done so. As it was now, they could hold out "about one week longer," and this was only if Governor Pickens permitted the workmen to leave. Otherwise, obviously, they might be eating their last food by about April 5. Two days later, having *still* heard nothing from Washington, Anderson wrote again, this time a bit more frantically. They were almost out of food, and it now appeared as if Pickens was about to prevent them from purchasing any more even meager amounts from the city. "I must, therefore, most respectfully and urgently, ask for instructions what I am to do as soon as my provisions are exhausted. Our bread will last four or five days." He closed edgily, "Hoping that definite and full instructions will be sent to me immediately."[2] He sent this despairing plea northward, feeling a bit like he was flinging these messages over the parapet, into the winds. All he received back was — silence. He still had no intimation that Lincoln's government had begun to stagger into action, although Fox was already in New York, making arrangements that would change everything.

As Anderson and the rest waited, alone and isolated, rasped by tension, an incident occurred that nearly crushed the major's will.

It is difficult to determine a person's intelligence, but there is no question that Captain Joseph Marts, skipper of the *Rhoda A. Shannon,* a schooner out of Boston, was astonishingly ignorant. He would later admit he had heard something of trouble in Charleston, and that some sort of Confederacy had been established somewhere down South, but beyond that he was really not much of a reader and did not follow the news. His employers in Boston were unconcerned with Captain Marts's vacuity. A wise businessman understands valuable markets, and the owners of the *Shannon* had contracted to send a large load of ice to Georgia, which would be feeling the first hints of sweltering summer days. Unfortunately, Captain Marts did not know the region well, and gale storms off Cape Hatteras confused him further. Late in the morning of April 3 he espied through a dense fog what seemed a landmark for the entrance to Savannah's harbor, and he headed toward it. Since these waters were unfamiliar, he ordered one of his crew up into the rigging to hold an American flag and wave it about to attract attention. This, Captain Marts thought, should cause a pilot to come out and guide him through the channels to port. When it had no result, he told the crewman to climb down.

They would, he decided, just go in willy-nilly. It seemed a splendid plan.[3]

The fog was lifting as he crossed the bar. Off his starboard side, though he did not know it, was Sullivan's Island, with Fort Moultrie and several new batteries designed to blow entering ships out of the water. Standing on the steps of the Moultrie House, unaware of the coming drama, were Francis Pickens and General P. G. T. Beauregard, here to inspect things, doubtless startled by what they were about to witness.

At Fort Sumter the officers, eating a late lunch, were expecting nothing extraordinary. Most of their guns were locked behind heavy closed shutters. They rather hoped to hear today, or perhaps tomorrow, that they were being evacuated. Their only recent annoyance was that a South Carolina revenue cutter, a war vessel, had anchored a mere 200 yards off Fort Sumter's walls. They did not know what this meant, but it seemed intentionally provocative. Anderson intended to ask and find out.

About two-thirty Fort Sumter's sergeant of the guard ran into their mess hall. Batteries on Morris Island, he said, had just opened fire on a schooner entering the harbor, clearly bearing the Stars and Stripes. The long roll was beaten. The garrison rushed to action. They could now clearly hear explosions from the Southern batteries. Anderson ordered several guns readied. The situation was very like the *Star of the West* incident, but three months of further tension had squeezed their nerves. South Carolina had many more guns in place, of course, and so did Fort Sumter. While Morris Island's batteries were firing, Lieutenant Davis was able to ready a gun to fire, and he rushed over to the major and told him he was set. Lieutenant Hall also signaled his gun was ready. Everyone looked at Anderson. They had spent too many weeks suppressing their rage, watching their foes, unhindered, build gun positions aiming directly at their heart. Opening fire now, to defend their flag, not only seemed right and honorable, it would have been cathartic, an orgasmic release. Only Robert Anderson stood between them and vast satisfaction. A simple word from him, a nod, would have been sufficient. Instead of giving the order, he called for an immediate conference of his officers. As

they stood there he polled them. Should they fire or not? Five —
Doubleday, Foster, Hall, Crawford, and Davis — said, very firmly,
yes! Four said they were against it: Talbot (who would change
his mind a few hours later, after thinking about it), Seymour, and
the two young engineers, Snyder and Meade. Since Lieutenant
Meade came from Virginia, his caution was understandable.

Those opposed argued that it was too late to prevent the batteries from firing on the ship, which, in fact, had now backed away
and was clearly anchored out of range near the bar. It was best to
get more information. They could always open fire later, perhaps
within the hour, if they did not receive satisfactory replies. Anderson was stuck in the middle. To his more bellicose officers, he
again seemed weak, perhaps even craven. Unlike them, who knew
little about the nature of his orders, Anderson felt handcuffed by
his restrictions. Although his orders had come from John Floyd
and Joseph Holt, neither any longer secretary of war, Lincoln's
government had never bothered to inform him of any policy
changes. He also knew, and his officers had only surmised, that
Lamon had privately assured him only a week earlier that they
would all be leaving shortly. If he began a civil war at this moment, just before being evacuated, it could be seen as a criminal
act. There was an additional factor. If he opened fire, Fort Sumter
would probably be pounded to pieces long before a relief expedition might arrive. Using Sumter's cannon now would certainly
feel momentarily satisfying and quite heroic, but at what cost?

Anderson had labored long, at the cost of much of his remaining health, to prevent civil war. He decided he would wait a bit
longer. He sent Seymour and Snyder over to Morris Island to find
out what had happened. After speaking to the commander there,
they rowed out to the *Shannon,* still anchored at the bar, and spoke
to her harebrained skipper. They were able to piece together most
of the story. When the *Shannon* had waddled out of the fog and
across the bar, Beauregard's gunners at the nearby batteries,
under orders to find out the nature of any such ship, fired across
her bow. Captain Marts believed they were simply asking for his
nationality, so he immediately raised the American flag from the
masthead.

Had Marts stood in a bullring and flapped a cloth before an agitated *toro*, he would have achieved about the same result. For all the men at the island batteries knew, the *Shannon* might be leading a Black Republican armada into their midst. They began to shoot directly at the vessel. Luckily for Captain Marts and his crew, their aim was appallingly bad. One shot did puncture a sail, but that was about it. The skipper, totally confused by this greeting, had moved off a bit and anchored out of range of the guns, several of which continued unsuccessfully to try and sink her. When Seymour and Snyder arrived at the *Shannon*, they explained to Marts that, no, this was not Savannah, and they suggested he ought to move on. He did so. (During the shooting a touching incident occurred at one of the batteries. A Captain Alexander F. Warley, recently of the U.S. Navy, as he gave orders to fire, burst into tears. He had served long beneath that flag, he said, and it broke his heart to shoot at it now.)

Seymour and Snyder's report of this comic opera failed to ease the tension among the officers. Doubleday had never trusted Major Anderson and Foster had had several ugly run-ins with him. Davis, a natural hothead, was choleric at the insult to the flag. Talbot, Crawford, and Hall each liked and admired the major, but on this issue they were convinced he was wrong. The mood at Sumter that evening oozed with rage and disdain.

The following morning Anderson called his officers together. He wanted to explain to them, he said, his rationale of the day before. He wanted them to hear the orders from Washington he was merely obeying, ordering him to do nothing unless attacked, "to act strictly on the defensive." Up to this moment he had not revealed to them why he had permitted the Carolinians to build their obnoxious battery emplacements, why he had accepted so many insults, to his nation and to himself. He told them he had repeatedly asked Washington to give him advice about what exactly to do, especially now with their provisions almost gone, but that the government had remained mum. He also told them he was sending another message to Washington, describing the *Shannon* incident, this one to be hand-carried by Talbot himself, who should have been up there anyway. He said he was ordering Snyder to

Charleston to complain to Pickens and Beauregard about this and other recent irritants.

In truth Anderson felt personally humiliated and depressed, sensing that most of his officers were unsatisfied with his explanation. His message to Washington seemed to them bureaucratically cautious, containing none of their righteous anger. His complaints to Charleston seemed only more of the same. Yet pride kept him from revealing to his officers that he also told Washington how pained he was that he "did not feel at liberty to resent the insult thus offered to the flag of my beloved country."

Talbot and Snyder departed for Charleston. Talbot took the afternoon train northward and Snyder delivered his message. Beauregard and Pickens listened and promised to look into the issues in question. As it turned out, however, that day's irritations were not yet over. While Lieutenant Snyder was at Pickens's office, the four enlisted men who had rowed him and Talbot across were busy purchasing whatever they could, especially tobacco, tasty food, and intoxicants. Policemen had arrived, however, decided to expropriate the items, then left. The four enlisted men were now without their money, as well as the things they had bought. Their anger later spread to Sumter's other enlisted men. Nor would the tone at the fort be improved by Snyder's report when he returned. Although Pickens had been civil enough, Snyder said, the governor had explained to him that he had just received cables from both Washington and Montgomery, urging an immediate suspension of all future provisions bound for Fort Sumter. Three days later, Pickens would make it official: The garrison would be permitted to receive its mail, but no more food. Snyder also told the other officers that he had noticed a plan of Fort Sumter lying on Pickens's desk. It seemed not a good sign.

Tensions at Sumter kept rising. The garrison noticed work accelerating on the island batteries. More patrol boats scouted around the mouth of the harbor. On April 5 Anderson wrote once more toward the silent maw of Washington. His tone was becoming a bit scratchy. "I cannot think," he said, "that the Government would abandon, without instructions and without advice, a command which had tried to do all its duty to our country." He hoped, he continued, that if Washington did finally accept the fact of disunion, that it would not attempt to make it seem like it was his fault. Anderson was hardly naïve in the ways of government. He had a sinking feeling that the administration — which *still* had yet to contact him — might allow him to run out of food, thereby putting him in the position of surrendering Fort Sumter, then dishonoring him, even court-martialing him for it. He trusted, he said, obviously thinking about the dishonorable Twiggs, that the administration would not "compel me to do an act which will leave my motives and actions liable to misconception." Then he added a cry wrenched from his honorable heart, this son of a famous Revolutionary War hero: "After thirty odd years of service I do not wish it to be said that I have treasonably abandoned a post and turned over to unauthorized persons public property entrusted to my charge. I am entitled to this act of justice at the hands of my Government, and I feel confident that I shall not be disappointed." When General Scott read this note from his old friend several days later he saw in it only a bit of "nervous irritability," missing the desperate pain and fear of that lonely warrior at Fort Sumter, terrified at being flung onto history's trash heap with the likes of Benedict Arnold and Judas Iscariot.

The next day Anderson wrote another official note, this time much calmer. He described the growing work they could observe at the batteries. He had still heard nothing from his superiors and he could not forbear closing that the "sooner we are out of this harbor the better." As he saw it, an explosion here was inevitable, and he could do nothing to prevent it, or win it when it occurred. "God grant," he said, "that neither I nor any other officer in our Army may be again placed in a position of such mortification and humiliation."[4] One hears in Anderson's tone the haunting echoes of so many later frustrated American soldiers in similar predicaments — in Berlin and South Korea, Beirut and Vietnam, in all those places that become pawns in larger games. Soldiers like Robert Anderson are often, tragically, necessary tools of realpolitik.

A review of events in Washington during these days is not comforting. Some of the most talented, mentally nimble leaders in

American history were acting in ways somewhere between slap-dash and daft. Orders were being given, then contravened, then countermanded. Rumors were washing about that the city was soon to be assaulted by a large force of Virginians. A British cor-respondent, William Howard Russell, arrived in town and was bemused by the gaggle of these geese. He spoke to the commis-sioners from Montgomery, still hanging about the city to work out Sumter's transfer, and they convinced him that the Union had truly ceased to exist. It would be helpful, of course, they assured him, if Great Britain recognized the Confederacy. The cotton ties between the two were as intertwined as fine fabric. The next day Russell spoke to Secretary Seward, who pooh-poohed the whole thing. A tempest in the proverbial teapot, my good man, a mere spasm of madness. Russell decided to travel South to see for him-self. On April 11 he went over to Winfield Scott's to share, along with several cabinet members, one of the general's renowned repasts. As he arrived that evening Russell saw a crowd of soldiers outside the door, cheering for the general. The old man came out and said a few words to them, words that Russell disdainfully con-sidered tripe, things about "the old flag of our country," and "ral-lying about," and "dying gloriously." During dinner a telegram arrived for the general. Russell noticed that Seward seemed a trifle "agitated" when he read it, and that Attorney General Bates, also there, grunted oddly when he saw its message. The English-man had no inkling that a few hours later, a few hundred miles to the south, war would begin before the morrow's dawn.[5]

During several crucial days, beginning April 4, men in Washing-ton and in Montgomery moved their chessmen about the board, jockeying into position. The stakes were hardly just Forts Sumter and Pickens. They were Virginia and Kentucky, Britain and France, Boston and New Orleans. Union or disunion. Leaders on both sides were new in their positions, inexperienced at such weighty matters. Lincoln and Davis, General Beauregard, Gov-ernor Pickens, General Bragg, Lieutenant Slemmer, Major An-derson. The moment was pregnant, distended with coming battle.

Louis Wigfall had finally got around to leaving Washington. He and his wife, ironically, had sent their daughters to stay near

Boston to be safe, then traveled to Charleston, where he was greeted warmly. He found lodging at the crowded Mills House, and soon became one of Beauregard's official aides. Wigfall swelled with excitement at the delicious prospect of war. He strutted about town with a red sash around his waist and a sword clutched in his hand.

So did young Roger Pryor, congressman from Virginia (who had officially resigned his seat on March 3). He, too, had just arrived in town; as a well-known secessionist from that critical sister state, he also was placed on Beauregard's growing staff of politician-soldiers. On his first evening in Charleston Pryor was pressed to provide a crowd with an impromptu speech. Standing on the balcony of the Charleston Hotel, he told them he knew no more about war "than a spinster," but he assured the throng that as soon as blood was shed, his state of Virginia would join the great cause. Pryor was cheered mightily, then he retired for the night. A friend of Mary Chesnut, who had watched the oration, told her acerbically that the Virginian actually said nothing new, "but he made a great play with that long hair of his, which he is always tossing aside."[6]

On April 4 Lincoln read Major Anderson's April 1 message. It pushed the president into motion. He had been attempting for days to avoid precipitate action. He had been receiving much advice, most of it contradictory, all of it expressed with vivid urgency. The president kept hoping that soon the fog of uncertainty would lift, and that then he could be more confident in his steps. The government, he had thought, still had several days to see in which direction the frog might jump. But Anderson's letter changed things. It was the one where he'd specified that they would run out of food in about a week, or even sooner if Pickens did not permit the laborers to leave the fort. Lincoln could not know whether Pickens had or had not given his permission to the workmen, but in either case, the frog had hopped. The president's time had run out. A flutter of messages hurled out of Washington like a flock of startled turkeys, awakened from slumber.

The most important one went to Fort Sumter, signed by Simon Cameron, secretary of war. It opened stating that the April 1 message from Sumter "occasions some anxiety to the President."

Lincoln had been led to believe by Captain Fox that the garrison could hold out until at least April 15, but now the president, hoping that the garrison could last till April 12, was ordering the *immediate* launching of a relief force. If the American flag still flew over Fort Sumter when it arrived, it would attempt to send in provisions. If South Carolina made any attempt to stop it, the fleet would try to land reinforcements as well. "You will therefore hold out, if possible, till the arrival of the expedition." The president was confident, the message went on rather thanklessly, "that you will act as becomes a patriot and soldier, under all circumstances." On the other hand, if the major, "in your judgment, to save yourself and your command, [feel that] capitulation becomes a necessity, you are authorized to make it." Since this message was actually from the president, and was probably even written by him, its tone reveals Lincoln's concern that Anderson might—like Twiggs—betray his government. The letter was, at the very least, uncharitable. Anderson had stood for months, holding up the flaking pillars of the nation, while Lincoln had whiled away his time, first in Springfield, then in Washington, making postmaster appointments and telling whimsical stories. This April 4 message raised subtle questions about Anderson's honor and courage— and added an ugly whiff of something else, something later generations would smell far too often in politics. Lincoln was covering his backside. He was still placing the ultimate responsibility for surrender in Anderson's hands. The major was permitted to capitulate if, in *"your* judgment," it would be the only way to "save *yourself* and *your* command."[7] The Abraham Lincoln that would evolve over the next four years would become far too empathetic, far too estimable an individual to again stoop so low.

Anderson received this message on April 7. He was aghast. He had worked so diligently to maintain peace, and now he believed he was about to witness it crumble. He was positive that the "relief expedition" would certainly initiate hostilities. He had spent months watching South Carolina build and rebuild her batteries to stave off just such an attempt. His acquaintances in Charleston, friends like Robert Gourdin, had convinced him that any effort to bring supplies to Fort Sumter would trigger war.

Anderson felt bilious, as bleak and joyless as Sumter's walls. On April 8 he wrote Washington his next official report—No. 96—announcing that the garrison could observe greater activity among the work crews at the island batteries. It was a short note, concluding with a hope that God would find some way to "avert the storm."

Then he did something quite out of character, something that would haunt him the rest of his days. He added a second letter along with his short, official one. All these weeks he had tried to maintain a cool, professional demeanor. He was about to lose it. Not in public—that would not be proper. But he wanted to spill out some of the feelings that were rising to the lip of his cup. As a commander, he could not speak entirely candidly to his officers. Civilians could not understand—not even Eba. For months he had been jotting messages to the Adjutant General's Office. From there, he knew, each would be handed to the appropriate person. He had been writing such notes since he was a young man. Each letter was supposed to contain a certain professional tone, detached, gentlemanly. "I have the honor to report," each was to begin, and would close, "very respectfully, your obedient servant," followed by the writer's name. He had written thousands of these messages, ninety-six since he had first arrived at Fort Moultrie last November. Yet now he felt he had to speak to someone who might understand his pain, an old soldier like himself. He decided to pour out his heart to his friend Lorenzo Thomas, up in Washington at the office of the adjutant general. He asked Thomas to read his "heart-felt prayer" as a friend, then to destroy it.

Anderson could not know that the bag of Sumter's mail with this letter in it would be scooped up at the Charleston post office and deposited on Pickens's desk. The authorities in Charleston had heard that Washington was sending an expedition, had concluded that war was at hand and that stopping the mail was permissible. Actually opening letters, however, turned out to be an act of greater emotional power than had at first seemed likely. A gentleman did not do that sort of thing, and, besides, it was a federal offense. In Pickens's office at that moment were the governor, his aide, Andrew Gordon Magrath, and General Beauregard.

Each of them had worked for the United States government only a few months earlier: one in the foreign service, the second a judge, the third a soldier. For a moment the bag sat there, like some unclean thing. Pickens stared at it, and suggested that Magrath open it. Magrath said he could not do it in good conscience, and proposed that General Beauregard would be the proper person. "Certainly not," replied Beauregard. "Governor, you are the proper person to open these letters." Pickens picked up a letter from the pile, muttering something about the others being far too fastidious, but he held the envelope in his hand a long time, looking at it. Finally the strain grew too much for Magrath, who said, "Go ahead, Governor, open it." Pickens roughly, clumsily broke the seal. That is how Anderson's private letter soon became public knowledge.[8]

In this note Anderson admitted he had been stunned by Washington's April 4 message about the relief expedition. "I fear that its result cannot fail to be disastrous to all concerned." He dreaded to think of the numbers of Fox's own men who would die on Sumter's rocks as they struggled to bring in supplies. He did not, he told Thomas, even have enough oil to keep a lantern lit for a single night; how could Fox's boats see their way into the harbor. He said with justifiable bitterness, "I ought to have been informed that this expedition was to come." Then he closed with a sentiment that many, such as Abner Doubleday, would use against him forever: "I frankly say that my heart is not in the war which I see is to be commenced."[9] In retrospect the phrase seems so like the man. He had come to hate all wars, and given his background could hardly be expected to enthuse childishly about a civil war among Americans. He felt the sadness of a poet who understood war. In this he was close to that other native of Kentucky, the Abraham Lincoln of the war's latter months, who would speak of malice toward none.

His note never left Charleston. Instead, the Confederate authorities decided to release this private, sad letter to the public. Major Anderson, they knew, was a hero to many Americans, North and South. Beauregard and Pickens hoped that it would dilute enthusiasm for war in critical regions like Kentucky. All it accomplished was to embarrass poor Anderson. Once a war had begun, especially in the first excited flush of delightful rage, anyone speaking of war without enthusiasm seemed perhaps a bit soft on the enemy.

Anderson's more immediate problem involved preparing Fort Sumter for what was about to come. Everyone at Sumter was put on half-rations. Shortly, each man was down to two crackers a day, then one, finally merely a few pieces. They still had enough salt pork in barrels to satisfy their bodies' cry for basic sustenance. They ate their few remaining leftovers. A bit of rice, a potato, a few cups of tea or coffee. Anderson was frugal about their meals, but knew the importance to his men that they take in nourishment. He noticed one evening that Doubleday had left a crust of cracker on his plate and insisted the captain return and eat it. He was aware they would all soon need whatever strength they had. Fox's fleet could arrive at any hour, and a battle would then begin.[10]

Foster's workmen went outside the walls and built a platform of sorts where Fox's boats might land. They put ladders against it and slopes so supplies could be moved inside as fast as possible. They enlarged a nearby embrasure to permit barrels to be rolled through.[11]

Anderson told his officers to keep the fact of the expedition from the enlisted men, but that was impossible. The men saw the changes in their routine and immediately understood the implications. Rather than frighten them, however, the prospect of battle enlivened them. They sprang to their tasks with energy. They laughed, they whistled, they sang. The change startled the officers a bit, and pleased them. The men did not even complain when they were ordered to take their blankets and move into the dozens of stone and brick casemates that now became the sleeping quarters for everyone in the fort.[12]

As the prospect of fighting loomed, the garrison made some unpleasant discoveries. Beauregard's soldiers on Sullivan's Island knocked down a cottage, revealing a new and secret battery that Sumter had not expected. Then, the garrison saw that the Carolinians had moved the Floating Battery again, into a new position.

Both it and the previously hidden battery were craftily placed to permit direct fire onto most of Sumter's top-tier barbette guns. Gun crews on the parapet would have to face a terrible punishment. Few could survive there in the open. The garrison had spent months placing their best, their most powerful cannon up there, where they could fire against Fort Moultrie and other critical batteries about the harbor. Now, using these guns was in doubt. With sand bags they might build protective walls (*traverses*) along the open sides of each barbette gun, which would give the gun crews some protection, but they lacked such bags to fill with sand. Anderson, already despondent at his failure to keep the peace, realized that if he placed his men on the parapets where their guns might play real havoc on the Confederate batteries, it was likely much of his garrison would soon die. If he put them down below, in the lower tier, surrounded by thick walls on all sides, the guns there could do only slight damage to the enemy's positions. The caliber of the first-tier cannon was too small, and the only angle they could fire from was almost horizontal, fine against the hulls of ships but not very effective against well-constructed walls. Anderson at West Point had been a good artillery professor, and Beauregard had obviously absorbed the lessons well. The major was aware he was seeing the handiwork of his Creole friend. The coming battle would not have been an equal one in any case; now his tiny band of soldiers, weakened by their months of confinement, had no chance at all. The fact of complete failure and disaster was quite real. Crawford saw Anderson, walking alone through the casemates on the lower tier, pacing slowly among the guns. He seemed, the doctor recognized, inexpressibly melancholy.[13]

Anderson came to a decision. Using the barbette guns in a battle would be foolhardy. He did not have enough men to risk losing a number of them in fruitless tasks. That was simple logic, though maybe it was just that he had come to love his men too much to place them out to be slaughtered. Unlike most of the garrison, he had seen many battles. He felt no enthusiasm for the prospect of this one. He ordered everyone, once the enemy opened fire, to stay below, in the casemates. Even there, they would hardly be invulnerable. Dr. Crawford unpacked the hospital supplies he had boxed up when he thought they were leaving, and he laid out a spot in one casemate where he could perform amputations, setting aside the requisite surgical instruments.

Hundreds of miles to the south, at the mouth of Pensacola Bay, Lieutenant Adam Slemmer had also been waiting. He was less alone than Major Anderson since he had a fleet just to his back, and his garrison was unlikely to be starved out any time soon. Slemmer's tiny force, less than half the size of Anderson's, had neither the skill nor the manpower to do more than maintain a facade of preparedness, but the fleet still housed reinforcements for Fort Pickens and could quickly drop them off if the truce here was broken. Slemmer's main problem lay in the fact that it took far longer for him or the fleet to receive messages from Washington.

After Braxton Bragg's arrival in March, under orders from Jefferson Davis, the lieutenant could see the greater energy and tighter organization of the forces surrounding him. The Confederacy was shuttling thousands of men toward Pensacola. Bragg had considered the possibility of mounting landings on Santa Rosa Island, but had concluded his men were too inexperienced for such a disciplined maneuver. He decided instead on a simple mass assault with scaling ladders. This would lead to considerable bloodshed, but, as he cynically wrote Davis, his men were so eager, so ignorant, that they would leap at the opportunity. All he needed, he indicated, were his marching orders. Davis wrote him on April 3 to be a bit more patient, again explaining that it was in the best interests of the Confederacy to place Lincoln in the position of having to fire the first shot.[14]

On April 6 a young naval officer arrived in Washington all the way up from the squadron off Pensacola. He was tired and dusty from days on the road. He immediately went to the Navy Department and handed Gideon Welles the message from Captain Adams, head of the fleet down there. The bewigged Welles was aghast. Weeks earlier, Lincoln had ordered the squadron to drop the reinforcements off at Fort Pickens, but now Welles was holding Captain Adams's refusal. This meant that Fort Pickens might itself fall to an assault at any time. If Fort Sumter was lost, and it certainly seemed like it might be, and Lieutenant Slemmer was forced to surrender his fort, the double blow would greatly embarrass Lincoln's new administration — at the very least. It might have a terrible domino effect, causing a second wave of secession that could destroy any hope of maintaining the Union. Welles immediately spoke to the president, and within a few hours a lieutenant named John Lorimer Worden was rattling toward Pensacola with orders to Captain Adams to do as he was told, immediately. Under the best circumstances it would take Worden days to get there, and he might be stopped at any time by suspicious authorities along the way.[15]

Saturday, April 6, was market day in Charleston. Despite months of stress many citizens felt upbeat. Mary Pinckney wrote her brother Charley, "The danger has passed away, so I (& most people) believe." Even the sounds of artillery practice by the island batteries no longer bothered her: "We regard it no more than so many sneezes." The price of cotton was approaching an all-time high. Demand was strong, the wharves were jammed with hungry ships. It rained heavily that Saturday, but crowds gathered as usual beneath the roof of the vast Lower Market and strolled about the stalls, making their household purchases. Rich smells swirled about: newly butchered meat oozing blood, gardenias and wisteria, angel trumpet and azalea, the aroma of good earth wafting gently from yams and beans and kohlrabi.[16]

Sunday, April 7. The downpour continued. The mood in the city was less optimistic. All soldiers in town were told to gather, guns in hand, if the bells of St. Michael's began to peal. There had been a few rumors about discontent in some slave quarters, some worries that disgruntled servants might attempt arson. The mayor ordered the city's fire companies to keep a sharp eye out. Churches were packed. Ministers, rabbis, priests asked Providence to continue to bless their fair city, and all its worthy efforts. Some spoke of war, and strove for the proper homilies.

On Monday, after two days of rain, the Ashley and the Cooper were yellow and swollen with spring floods. South Carolina seemed to be flowing toward the city. Messages appeared on the bulletin boards with tales about an advancing fleet. The papers were sprinkled with war rumblings. Mary Chesnut read some reports and confided to her diary, "News *so* warlike I *quake.*"

Theodore Talbot and Robert Chew arrived in town by train and walked to the governor's headquarters, as uniformed men rushed by in all directions. Talbot, a professional soldier, remained calm enough, but Chew was a gentle fellow, a State Department clerk. Maybe it was the prospect of being pummeled to death in the streets; perhaps it was the weightiness of the piece of paper he held in his hand, but he was quite unnerved. He bowed to Governor Pickens, took the president's note from his pocket, read it aloud, his voice trembling slightly, then handed it to the governor. It was not a typical governmental message, no flowery introduction, no effusive, insincere closing remarks, not even a signature. But it was definitely clear. Lincoln hereby informed Francis Pickens that Washington was sending supplies to Fort Sumter. They would arrive soon. If there was no attempt at stopping them by anyone — South Carolina, the so-called Confederacy (the letter did not choose to dignify either one by name) — Washington would not send in reinforcements.

Here it was — *coercion* — after all these months of waiting. South Carolina had been preparing for this moment since well before secession. The Confederacy and Beauregard had merely refined what had been done. They had perhaps improved the military posture, but they had not altered the purpose or intensity of South Carolina's determination.

Pickens said he wanted to show the note to Beauregard. The general arrived almost immediately. The governor was affronted by the message's abruptness. He said something about formulating some reply. No, said Chew, no reply was expected, and in fact he was not authorized to accept one. Another slap.

While Pickens mulled over how he ought to react, Talbot turned to Beauregard. The tubercular Talbot had only come with Chew to introduce him to the governor, and by his presence indicate the validity of the dispatch. Now that he had fulfilled this obligation, would the general permit him to cross over to Fort Sumter and join his colleagues, to share their fate? Absolutely not, said Beauregard. In fact, he suggested that Talbot and Chew should leave the city, immediately. Robert Chew must have blanched at the thought of walking back across town, because Beauregard and Pickens arranged an escort for the two men to the station, who soon were on their way out of Charleston.[17]

The telegraph office got busy. Messages surged back and forth between Charleston and the outside world. Messengers raced about on foot and horseback. Excited men in uniform clambered into boats and set out across the harbor, clutching scraps of paper with orders to move units about.

Pickens and Beauregard somehow calculated that a Union army at least 2,600 strong, perhaps as many as 4,000, was coming toward their harbor. It would, they believed, land on Morris Island, out near where the Citadel cadets had placed their tiny battery in January. South Carolina — actually, now, the Confederacy — had less than 2,000 men spread from one end of that island to the other (though many more elsewhere throughout the harbor). In the coming battle many of these soldiers on Morris Island would have to man batteries facing Fort Sumter, so they would be terribly vulnerable on their right flank. Then there was Sullivan's Island. It was possible that Winfield Scott, who knew the terrain well, might thrust some or all of his attack force there rather than at Morris Island. The invaders could land out beyond the myrtle, then swoop down the island, past Moultrie House, and land in a great assault against the weak eastern wall of Fort Moultrie. After analyzing the condition of the tides, Pickens and Beauregard decided that the attack, wherever it came, would likely begin at six in the morning on April 10. This allowed them, they figured, less than thirty hours to call up all the available soldiers in the city, as well as reinforcements from the countryside. Railroads would have to rattle furiously about the state, plucking up units here and there, depositing them by the carload at the station in Charleston.[18]

At midnight the bells of St. Michael's rang out, calling up the city's reserves — and just to make sure, under orders from Pickens, seven guns at The Citadel fired an even more peremptory signal.

Lightning flickered Charleston's dark streets as men tumbled from doorways, adjusting their uniforms. They splashed through puddles and gathered with comrades, shouting out greetings and questions before tramping through the downpour toward their destinations. Wagons piled high with barrels of gunpowder clattered by them. The soldiers began arriving at the islands during that night and all the next day, flung helter-skelter into the entrenched encampments, bumping about, causing confusion and ill-temper till they situated themselves.

Mary Chesnut chatted with Robert Gourdin. Her husband James had just been named one of Beauregard's aides and had hurriedly left, wearing his official red sash and sword. Wigfall arrived, positively radiant, quoting a line from Lord Byron: "There was a sound of revelry by night." He was, Mary thought, "the only thoroughly happy person I see." After the men bustled out to perform their important, perhaps heroic, deeds, the women sat alone in the stillness. Mary's "heart beat so painfully," she told her diary. She and Charlotte Wigfall retired to Mary's room and spoke of civil war, finding nothing in it to remind them of Byron's "Childe Harold," just bloodshed and horror. Charlotte wept. She also gave Mary the creeps, asserting that *of course* the slaves would explode in rebellion, with all that that would mean. Mary did not sleep at all.[19]

Other women in South Carolina heard the news, and reacted. A young woman in Camden wrote in her diary her fears when a young man she loved left with his unit for Charleston — "among them Charlie. My pen falters as I write his name. What dangers await him?" Keziah Brevard, owner of several upcountry plantations, heard that an enemy fleet was on its way toward Charleston. Many local boys were being called down there. "How changeable my feelings are," she confided to her diary, "sometimes buoyed with a hope of good times (this is momentary), then I can see & hear nothing to hang my hopes on." The *Courier* printed a small, and perhaps apocryphal tale of a young Charleston mother whose husband was called up. As he prepared to leave several people gathered in their parlor. His wife sat in a chair, holding their child, and told him to do well in battle, but not to come home with a bullet in his back. Their little daughter, she said, would disown him if he revealed himself a coward. Then, as soon as he left, she fell from her chair, ghastly pale, onto the floor.[20]

Among the men, few were gleeful but many were excited. They were performing a necessary task, as they saw it, forced on them by an alien foe who hated them. Besides, battling Fort Sumter itself was not very frightening; in fact, to many young soldiers the prospect seemed almost a lark, an exciting game. Bloodshed would probably result, of course, but it would be heroic gore. One could admire Major Anderson and his doomed men. They could not really threaten Charleston, though they might throw a few cannonballs this way. Their position therefore was perfect for Charleston's spectators: heroic losers, tragic heroes, brought down by their loyalty to an unworthy Black Republican regime.

Major Anderson had come to represent the garrison, to personify the men out there. There was no way anyone in Charleston could hate him. His friendship with Robert Gourdin and others, who came and went to the fort and spoke to him, made him a well-known figure in the city. So much about Anderson was now well recognized: his open affection for the South, his sympathy for their concerns, his revulsion at the notion of civil war, his deep Christian devotion. Even his continued loyalty to the Union and his energetic efforts to strengthen Fort Sumter were recognized as manly qualities.

Charlestonians also knew many others at the fort. Foster, Talbot, Hall, and other officers — each had several close friends in the city. Lieutenant Davis's sister Annie still went to school here and corresponded with her brother from time to time. Sumter's enlisted men had friends here and family. The garrison was not a "foreign" force. A few months earlier they had been stationed on Sullivan's Island, where they had mixed socially with its residents and tourists who came out from the city. They had shopped in Charleston, eaten in its restaurants, drunk in its saloons, made love to its residents.

It was not the garrison, therefore, that was seen as the enemy, it was the advancing armada whose ships represented a far different, much more sinister foe — with attitudes and faces unknown to Charlestonians, therefore more frightening. The men who had sent them, moreover — Lincoln and his claque — were proclaimed enemies of all South Carolina stood for. The president's recent message had not specified when the fleet would arrive, how many ships or men it contained, where it would focus. Its unknown nature, therefore, allowed anyone to project on it the most hideous possibilities. If it arrived with a genuinely large force of soldiers — say, 4,000, along with horses and artillery — it might land on Morris Island, whip aside and slaughter the scattered young men of South Carolina who awaited them, whose families and friends awaited word in the city, eliminate the island batteries, then pounce upon Charleston like Visigoths, marauding, murdering, raping. The city's blacks — half the population — might rise up and join the Northern army in a spasm of dreadful African savagery.

"God only knows what will be the result," one man wrote. "I am ready for the issue at any moment but would be more satisfied if the women and children were in a place of safety." A plantation mistress living not far from Charleston confided to her diary that she was frightened. "There are six hundred Negroes perhaps prowling in our midst." Her husband and two sons were off soldiering. "They have all left me in this house alone, not a sound is heard." Her head ached with nightmare images. "What if Lincoln gain the advantage — & with sword in hand & [illegible] ravaging the land & destroying our firesides with ruthless revenge. It is horrible to think of."

A Charleston businessman wrote, "All business at a stand. Our shop may as well be closed." He also said, as an aside, he had heard that the tug, *Yankee,* carrying men and supplies, was expected that very evening, along with several men-of-war to protect her. (So much for Fox's plan of secrecy.) The cadet seniors at The Citadel took final exams but were allowed to skip commencement exercises. An amateur theater postponed its production because the manager of the company had been called to service at one of the islands. It was a time of waiting.

"The God of Battles," wrote one Charlestonian, "shall decide who is in the right."[21]

CHAPTER FIFTEEN

That Little Bridge

"Once across that little bridge the whole issue is with the sword."
— JULIUS CAESAR, CONTEMPLATING
CROSSING THE RUBICON

For days Jefferson Davis had been debilitated by blinding headaches. Never a jovial sort, he now looked especially grave. The dispatch he received from Beauregard on April 8 did not surprise him: "Authorized messenger from Lincoln just informed Governor Pickens and myself that provisions would be sent to Sumter peaceably, otherwise by force." Davis ordered him to prevent Sumter from getting those provisions. The fort, he said, "must be completely isolated."[1]

The following evening Davis met with his cabinet for some time to consider what to do at long last about Fort Sumter. He spoke wistfully, fondly, of his friend Robert Anderson. But on the issue of Fort Sumter the Confederate president was coldly determined. The meeting grew emotional, even stormy. Robert Toombs of Georgia found himself unable to sit down and so strode about the room. He had arrived late and found the others talking of sending Anderson an ultimatum. Toombs strongly disagreed (at least according to his own recollections — though Toombs would seldom be reluctant to embellish a tale). He said that such an ultimatum would result in a terrible civil war. Taking such a rigid position, he warned, would place them in a position of being aggressors, just the opposite of the stand they had been pursuing. If Lincoln chose "coercion," the Confederacy would appear the innocent victims. This would appeal to the Border States, and it would gain them important sympathy in the North. Worst of all, Toombs told those in the room, being rigid now "was unnecessary."[2] But the majority of them agreed with Davis.

Perhaps they recognized Davis's far greater knowledge of military affairs. Maybe they, like many in Charleston, had simply grown impatient with waiting. Rolling the dice can offer a powerful release. In fact "peace" is always conditional. War is seldom the result of simple rivalries and animosities. Wars begin when people consider that the state of "peace" that exists is no longer acceptable, that "war" would relieve their problems. And people tend to visualize "war" in terms of their impressions of previous conflicts. Davis and his cabinet could not possibly have understood the coming civil war. No American in a position of power had ever seen, or even read true accounts of, such a thing.

Early the next morning, the 10th, Leroy P. Walker, secretary of war, wired Beauregard: If the general was convinced Lincoln's messengers were not bogus, he must immediately demand Fort Sumter's evacuation. If Anderson refused this demand, "proceed, in such manner as you may determine, to reduce it."

Perplexingly, Beauregard did not immediately obey this order. He wired Montgomery that he would put off presenting an ultimatum until the next day, April 11, at noon. Walker and Davis were nonplussed. After their rancorous meeting their nerves were taut. They had made their decision, fully expecting to hear that the denouement of the drama would be revealed before nightfall; what was this about delay? They wired the general back: "Unless there are special reasons connected with your condition, it is considered proper that you should make the demand at an earlier hour." They received an enigmatic response from Beauregard within minutes: "The reasons are special for 12 o'clock." He did not clarify. Later, he sent another telegram, promising, "I am doing all in my power to prevent re-enforcements [note: not "provisions"] by barges to Sumter tonight or tomorrow night." Davis, perplexed, said okay. The politicians in Montgomery were forced to wait.

The same was true in Washington. Here, Lincoln was shut off from information. He had begun to receive some news from secret sources, which had tapped into telegraph lines, but the system was not yet sufficiently perfected to reveal what was going on.[3]

There has been some small debate about why Beauregard waited. He never publicly explained, but it would seem to have been a combination of three things. On April 9 a remarkable new cannon arrived. Called a Blakely and sent from London, it could fire with amazing accuracy. Instead of shooting toward a fort's walls, an artillerist could actually aim at the mouth of an opponent's cannon, or at least at its embrasure. Beauregard, recognizing the potential of this new weapon, wanted it in place when the battle began. Also, he knew that precious gunpowder was on its way from Augusta, Georgia; it arrived on the night of April 10 and still had to be parceled out to the batteries. Finally, General Beauregard was throwing many men quickly onto the islands. It was prudent to have his army reasonably in place before a battle began. Once the first gun went off, it would become far more complicated to move men and equipment about the harbor. Major Anderson's guns could see to that. Beauregard did not explain all this in detail, he simply stalled a bit.

By April 11 Beauregard was ready to take the critical step. He gave three aides an assignment: to carry to Robert Anderson a written demand to evacuate Fort Sumter. The three men were James Chesnut, sporting his new sash, Alexander Robert Chisholm, a planter from Beaufort who had been acting for days as a courier carrying messages on his skiff, and young Stephen Dill Lee, who would later be one of the last Confederate generals to surrender. When their boat bumped against Sumter's rocky wharf at 3:45 P.M., they were met by Lieutenant Davis, officer of the day, who had been watching them and their white flag approach. They told him they had a message they wished to give directly to Major Anderson. Davis suspected what was in the note. For days, they had been staring out to sea, looking for Fox's fleet; they had also been observing the recent hurried preparations on the islands for battle. Lieutenant Davis was civil enough. (Annie was still in the city.) He escorted the aides to the guardroom, just inside the gate's doorway. Here they spoke to Anderson.[4]

Anderson was, as always, courteous. He listened quietly, took the paper from them and read it, then excused himself. He sent orders to the other officers to join him in his quarters. He read to them Beauregard's demand. If they agreed to evacuate Fort Sumter, they would be provided with transportation to carry themselves, their private property, their "company arms and property" to any post (in the Union) they chose. "The flag," the note said, "which you have upheld so long and with such fortitude, under the most trying circumstances, may be saluted by you on taking it down." Anderson drew out another piece of paper he had never shared with them: his orders from December 21, 1860, written by Secretary Floyd. Buchanan had been acutely concerned that Anderson not believe he was expected to fight to the death, "the last extremity." Floyd had written Anderson that he was not "to make a vain and useless sacrifice" of himself and his men, over "a mere point of honor." If he was facing an overwhelming force and concluded that fighting would result only in "a useless waste of life, it will be your duty to yield to necessity, and make the best terms in your power." Floyd had ordered him to keep this note strictly confidential; he was not even to tell his officers, "without close necessity." Floyd's note had been referring to their position at Fort Moultrie, but the order had never been specifically altered by either Secretary Holt or Secretary Cameron, so it was still valid. Anderson could now decide that dueling with Beauregard's "circle of fire"—as that general called his batteries—was "a hopeless conflict" and "a useless waste of life," two things Anderson had been ordered to avoid. But if he evacuated now, after all they had done for so long, what had it all meant?

Anderson had tried so hard to prevent a war, but civil war had come to him, unbidden. What should he do? If he agreed to evacuate now, and Fox showed up in a day or so, did Floyd's orders cover that eventuality? Probably not. But the garrison, already on a fraction of an official day's "ration," was approaching its last morsels of food. In theory their salt pork might sustain them a week, maybe two, but the weakness of the men was becoming

evident. He could hardly expect them to fight for very long—
what with all the physical labor involved in battle—and continue
on desperately short rations. It was clear to him they had to refuse
Beauregard's demands, then try to hold out as long as they could.
Maybe Fox would show up, and somehow bring in extra supplies—but maybe not. Yet at least the garrison would have done
its best. He asked his officers if they supported his conclusion.
Yes, they emphatically said, all agreeing to reject the Confederate
ultimatum. The officers filed out, leaving Anderson to write an official reply. He thanked Beauregard for "the fair, manly, and courteous terms," but rejected the offer.

A few minutes later he appeared in the guardroom and handed
the three aides his response. It was sealed but he told them its gist.
As Beauregard's aides departed the fort, Anderson and Wylie Crawford walked as far as the gate with them. It was four-thirty, perhaps a few minutes after. Chisholm's boat was moored a few feet
away, where the wharf joined the Esplanade. The aides were stepping into it when Anderson blurted out a question, "Will General
Beauregard open his batteries without further notice to me?"

Chesnut, recently a senator, therefore perhaps the most senior
of them, seemed startled. The subject had not come up with Beauregard. Did they have the right to answer? Did they know the answer? "I think not," Chesnut said. Then, after a pause, "No, I can
say to you that he will not, without giving you further notice." He
and the others turned back to the boat. Anderson muttered something to them, but his words were muffled by the commotion of
their getting settled. They heard a few words but not everything.
Chesnut called out to Crawford, standing there. What did the
major say? he asked. The surgeon turned to the major and asked
him to repeat it. Anderson stepped forward and spoke again.

"Gentlemen, if you do not batter the fort to pieces about us,
we shall be starved out in a few days." Maybe Anderson was
simply musing aloud, but probably he was trying, one last time, to
prevent war. If Fox's fleet never showed up—and given the erratic
nature of Washington politics lately, to say nothing of the weather
over the Atlantic, this must have seemed possible—the two sides
could avoid shooting at each other. Robert Anderson was sophisticated enough to realize that as soon as guns opened fire, a ter-

rible civil war was inevitable. God, he believed, had kept them away from conflict thus far; maybe He would continue to do so. God's ways, reportedly, were mysterious.

Chesnut asked if he could relay this sentence to Beauregard — that is, was this just talk, or did the major consider his words a semiofficial "message"? Anderson said it was not really a "report," simply a fact, information that the general might want to have. Anderson, consciously or unconsciously, was attempting a final ploy.

The boat pushed off. This time it carried a red flag, not white.

The three aides realized the implications of what the major had just said. James Chesnut was deeply moved. He was a taciturn man. When Mary greeted him at home a while later and asked what had happened at Sumter, he replied that the conversation with Anderson had been "interesting." He said he wanted dinner; then, as an aside, he told Mary he felt deeply for Major Anderson.

Beauregard received Anderson's official reply — along with his informal statement — at five-thirty. While the general pondered what to make of the words, men throughout the harbor moved into action. The battle should begin quite soon, they thought, by seven o'clock that evening, maybe eight — a couple of hours away. The men on the islands made their final preparations for war. Hartstene's little navy pulled up a buoy in the main ship channel, then dragged three hulks, loaded with wood and resin, out to the bar and anchored them. If Hartstene's ships detected Fox trying to slip into the harbor, the hulks would be lighted, illuminating the water for miles.

At Fort Sumter the enlisted men knew about Beauregard's ultimatum, and Anderson's rejection of it. The garrison recognized that quite soon — hours? minutes? — they would be fighting. They became enthusiastic, energized. They had been, at long last, released from the torment of patience. They quickly grabbed powder kegs from the locked magazines and rolled them into place. They readied their guns.

In that era artillery work was grunt, blue-collar labor, all sweat and muscles. There was no poetry to it, and little romantic heroism. During years of service an artillerist's hands grew hard and callused from dealing with balky equipment. Fingernails became battered and broken, permanently marred by ridges and lumps. Cannonballs have a tendency to roll together, fingers get in the way.

Yet firing big guns took more than simple brawn and the capacity to accept discomfort and pain. An artillery team was an organic unit, each part meshing with another. A battery of several guns required disciplined teamwork between gun crews, and a single gun crew was virtually a living cell. Nothing in the army demanded more dedication to exacting precision. Whenever a gun crew fired its cannon, literally every step each man took had been choreographed far in advance, then practiced until each movement became rote. A single misstep could result in disaster, a premature explosion, killing them all. If a man moved to his left when he should have gone right he might easily bump against one of his companions, with unpleasant results. Each team, moreover, had to perform its tasks with precision while squinting through billowing smoke and haze, dodging enemy fire, all the while growing unimaginably weary as the battle continued.[5]

The army assumed that at a fort like Sumter each cannon would be fired by a five-man team. According to regulations, each member was given a precise number — 1, 2, 3, 4, 5. Each took a position near the cannon according to his number. Exactly what each man did varied with the gun in question. Artillery pieces in 1861 were defined by a bewildering variety of terms. Some guns were called *pounders*. (A 24-pounder fired a twenty-four-pound ball.) Other guns were referred to by the width of their bores — eight-inch, for instance. *Mortars* were short, stubby things that could aim their barrels upward to fling shells high in the air, so they were particularly effective shooting over walls.

To fully grasp the Battle of Fort Sumter, to sense what the soldiers on both sides went through, it is best to understand a few basic facts.

Originally, artillery was the result of a simple discovery. The Chinese had long known that if you lighted powder made from a mixture of sulfur, carbon, and saltpeter the substance disappeared instantly in a puff of smoke. It seemed quite a nifty magic trick. About the year 1200 someone realized that, if you contained the little puff, that expanding gas, giving it but a single exit from a container, it could push something — a round stone, an iron ball — in whatever direction you aimed.

But weapons using gunpowder had intrinsic problems. One involved igniting the gunpowder after it had been placed inside the barrel. For centuries, soldiers used a passage near the base of the gun called a vent hole. In early days some hapless artilleryman was assigned the unpopular duty of thrusting a lighted string or a hot poker into the hole, praying that this time the gun would not explode in his face. By 1860 standard practice was to use a *friction primer,* which acted very much like a large kitchen match. Its main component was a copper tube, about two inches long, filled with powder, which was far safer.

So far so good; but the explosion within the barrel, which hurled a cannonball, simultaneously recoiled the cannon backward, often quite far. A dozen feet or more was not unusual, and some howitzers sprang back as much as thirty feet. Recoils also twisted a cannon a bit left or right. A gun therefore had to be re-aimed after every shot. To counteract some of the effects of recoil, the barrels of fortress artillery were placed on wheeled *carriages,* each resting on a *chassis.* The carriage had two purposes. It could elevate or lower the cannon. Furthermore, when a gun was fired, recoiling the barrel, the carriage whipped backward on its wheels, bumping into special stops at the rear, and halted.

Now came the hardest physical work performed by a gun crew. Two of them sprang forward and cleaned out the barrel. They sponged it, using a long-handled device, often ten feet long. Both men, acting together, rammed the sponge in as far as it would go, turned it clockwise *exactly* three times, then pulled it out. This was to clean the barrel and cool it down enough to accept the next load of powder. During this operation the gunner, as head of the crew, stood next to the barrel with one of his fingers — protected with a thick pad attached to a glove — over the vent hole to prevent sparks from being flung about by the action of the sponge. (Sparks lingering within a vent hole could prematurely ignite the next batch of gunpowder.) Meanwhile, a fourth member of the crew picked up an empty pine box, walked over to a closed oaken barrel filled with cartridges, took one out and put it in the box, carefully closing the lid, and returned to the gun. This cautious process was designed to keep sparks from reaching any nearby loose powder. Originally gunners had poured powder into the mouth of a barrel, but *cartridges* meant that artillerists could be more certain of the amount of gunpowder they were using. The distance you intended to fire—the "range"—plus the weight of the cannonball determined the amount of powder one wanted to use. (Numbers were written down in complicated tables.) A cartridge was simply a bag of powder, preferably made of wool since wool tended to be consumed during the process of firing the cannon and did not leave behind dangerous bits of hot material. If absolutely necessary, one could construct cartridge bags of cotton or flannel, even paper.

Once the barrel had been sponged out, the two men who had performed that task took the cartridge from the pine box and loaded the gun with another long-handled tool, ramming the cartridge down as far as it would go. While they did this, another member of the team walked over to pick up a cannonball, which would then be rammed down into the gun until it rested on the cartridge.

By 1860 there were two main types of cannonballs: shot and shell. A *shot* was a solid iron ball. *Shells* were more complicated. As the name indicates, they were hollow. They could be filled entirely with powder or they could contain both powder and small metal balls. Each shell had some kind of fuse, permitting the gun crew to set it to explode at a certain range. Artillerists had to be very careful handling shells, because fuses were easily damaged and could become either worthless or dangerous to the crew.

Once a ball was rammed into place, the gunner stuck a wire deep into the vent hole and wiggled it around a bit until he had pricked a hole in the cartridge bag inside. He was now prepared to aim the cannon. He could elevate or lower its muzzle, but if he had to aim the gun left or right, the entire chassis had to be moved. This operation was hardly easy. Just the barrel of an eight-inch columbiad, for instance, weighed almost five tons, and a ten-incher weighed 15,400 pounds. The entire mechanism, counting the carriage and chassis, often weighed as much as ten tons. The gun crew of five men, straining every muscle, spun it around a post (a *pintel*), using large bars or handspikes, each about four feet long and weighing eighteen pounds. One can imagine the difficulty that even five large, well-rested, well-fed men would have performing this action. Fort Sumter's garrison had originally consisted of average-sized, slender men. It was now composed of almost exhausted, somewhat sickly, malnourished fellows. It is hard to visualize them shoving artillery pieces around inside Sumter's casemates, but they did.

The process of aiming a cannon was complicated. A gunner might think his gun was pointed correctly, but many factors could disabuse him. The powder in the cartridge, for example, could originally have been measured inexactly, or it might have become a trifle damp. A cannonball was seldom precisely round or perfectly balanced, so its center of gravity was usually off. Once a gun was fired, the inside of its barrel, its *bore*, grew fouled with powder residue, and sponging normally did not clean it completely. This tended to alter subtly the flight of the next ball. In addition the wind velocity and direction, temperature, the moisture content of the air, even the position of the sun, affected the flight of a cannonball. An accurate shot might be well off-target on the next round. Gunners had instruments that could give them guidance — quadrants and tangent scales and such — but often it came down to judgment, the experience of the gunner, his skill. He also had to be quite cool. It required self-control to aim a cannon properly during a battle while opposing gunners were firing directly at you. Excitement during battle, to say nothing of fear, is hard to control.

If you were firing solid shot at a wooden structure like a ship or a building, you could heat it first for over an hour in a special furnace. Moultrie had shot furnaces, so did Sumter. But a gun crew had to be extraordinarily careful while using one of these preheated balls, called *hotshot*. It required enormous caution merely to extract one from the furnace, a task requiring the efforts of three men other than the five-man gun crew.

When a cannon was ready to be fired, the gunner shoved the friction primer into the vent hole. He stepped to a position where he could see the target, so he could watch the exact flight of the ball. This was not as difficult a feat as it sounds since the ball would arc visibly toward the target for up to forty-five seconds. (During the coming battle both sides used spotters who would shout when they saw enemy cannonballs sailing toward them, and everyone would duck.) The gunner would give the command "Fire!" and one of the crew — in theory No. 3 — would yank the lanyard.

The sensory impact on the crew of each explosion, especially inside a casemate, was more than simply auditory. The floor beneath their feet shuddered, the walls and ceiling shook. The concussion of each explosion reached out and squeezed them, crushing against them for a moment. The incredible *BOOM* of the explosion often damaged eardrums. Most veteran artillerists grew noticeably deaf. The smoke of gunpowder filled the air about them. Within a casemate the smoke mixed with stone dust flying off the walls and the floor. Faces grew grimy. Sweat flowed, creating arroyos down men's cheeks and arms. Eyes grew raw.

A gun crew was expected to perform all its tasks crisply, in a well-organized ballet, to fire its gun every eight to ten minutes, and to do this while half-blinded from smoke and their own sweat, increasingly exhausted from the physical labor involved. To complicate matters further, they often changed from one kind of gun to another in the middle of a battle, from a columbiad to a howitzer to a mortar. Each gun had its own characteristics. They were supposed to know them all. This is why teams drilled hundreds of hours in preparation. One of the many inanities of Fox's expedition was his bringing raw recruits who had had no real training at artillery work. Even if, by pluck and luck, Fox had somehow gotten every one of those soldiers into Fort Sumter, what benefit could they have offered the fort's garrison? After the battle, Anderson would say that if he had had more men half would have died. He was being optimistic. Many of Fox's recruits would have been killed before they reached Sumter's gate, and those who staggered within would have served as a hindrance, stumbling about the unfamiliar environment, getting in the way of the professional artillerymen.

———

As soldiers on both sides readied their guns for battle, General Beauregard contemplated his options. He could begin the war immediately, given Montgomery's orders, but Anderson's offhand remark at the wharf made the general hesitate. He concluded that he would let Montgomery decide what to do. He wired them and asked for advice. A few hours later he had his reply. If Anderson would promise not to use his guns unless Sumter was fired on, and if he would state exactly when he would evacuate the fort, it would not be necessary "needlessly to bombard Fort Sumter." Beauregard examined this message, then sent it — carried by the same three aides — out to the major. Roger Pryor accompanied them, apparently just to witness this historic moment. They left Charleston about midnight. Mary Chesnut knew her husband James was out there somewhere in the harbor in a rowboat. She worried about him.

At Sumter most of the men were asleep. They had eaten little that night, beyond some salt pork and tea or coffee. They had stared out to sea, looking unsuccessfully for Fox's fleet. By eight o'clock daylight was fading and, except for a few sentries, they went to their bedrolls. Most fell asleep inside the casemates, but a few chose to lie that night beneath the sky. It might be their last opportunity to do so.

The officer of the day woke Anderson. A boat, carrying a white flag, was at the wharf; the same three men were at the gate. Pryor had chosen to remain in the boat. His state, Virginia, had not yet seceded, and he felt it improper to participate in official Confederate affairs. Anderson again went to the guardroom. He read their new message, then told the officer of the day to wake the other officers, as he wanted to speak with them in his quarters. By the time they arrived it was about one-thirty. He read them this latest dispatch. The key unacceptable phrase was its demand that they guarantee not to fire unless Sumter was shot at. The problem was Fox's fleet. When — or if — it arrived, Confederate guns would inevitably open fire on it. Anderson and his officers would not sit on their hands if that happened. They — or at least *he* — had not fired when the *Star of the West* was attacked, nor when beach batteries shot at the *Shannon*, just a week ago. Twice the American flag had been fired on without response from Fort Sumter. No more. They were in agreement.

But suppose Fox never showed up? Or suppose the Confederates should themselves promise not to fire upon the American flag, what then? Anderson asked Crawford how long the men could hold out on their present level of sustenance. The doctor answered four days, possibly five. All right, Anderson said, suppose he wrote an official note stating that they would evacuate the fort at noon on April 15, almost four full days from now, assuming that no one on the other side fired on the American flag, and assuming that they had not received other instructions from Washington? The officers concurred. The major quickly jotted this down and carried it back to the three envoys, waiting impatiently in the guardroom. It was after three o'clock.

The aides read Anderson's message. It did not exactly reject Beauregard's latest offer, but neither did it accept it. James Chesnut, acting again as their spokesman, dictated their official reply, following Beauregard's express wishes. Young Stephen Lee wrote down the words. Chesnut said that the shore batteries would open fire in one hour. Anderson pulled a pocket watch out and looked at it. He wanted to be clear about the time. It was 3:20. "I understand you, sir, then," he said, "that your batteries will open in an hour from this time?"

"Yes, sir," Chesnut answered, "in one hour."

The recollections of both Lee and Chisholm about this moment agree that Anderson was visibly "much affected."

He walked out with them to their boat. It had begun to drizzle. He shook the hand of each, and said that if they never saw one another again in this world, he hoped they would meet again in a better one. Their boat pushed off.

Major Robert Anderson reentered the dark, silent fort. He must have been exhausted. An unwell, slight figure in his late fifties, he had hardly slept in days. He stumbled about the dark fortress, telling those he saw to expect an attack to begin in a few minutes. Those sleeping in the open he ordered inside. He reminded everyone that they would not be returning fire till dawn, no matter when the battle started. He even urged them to try and sleep.

He ordered someone to raise the American flag. It was still well before Reveille but he did not want anyone near the flagstaff once the shells started falling. The huge garrison flag had a rip in it so he had to be satisfied with the smaller storm flag.[6] This one would still be quite visible at a distance; it would serve. He wanted to be sure the flag was flying if Fox's fleet came soon. He wanted it waving above his post when the South Carolinians — now, finally, his enemy — opened fire.

He may have tried to sleep himself. He had done as much as he could.

CHAPTER SIXTEEN

A Mere Point of Honor

"Armament is an important factor in war, but not the decisive factor. . . . Man, not material, forms the decisive factor."
— MAO ZEDONG

lexander Chisholm's boat pulled away from Sumter's wharf, the rowers straining at the oars. Chisholm, sitting at the back, could have headed to Fort Moultrie or Cummings Point, both nearer. But all four aides wanted to hurry back to Beauregard's headquarters, where the general would be impatiently awaiting their report on what Anderson had said. Fort Johnson, a little over a mile away, was just a jog off a straight line back to the city; Chisholm steered through the misting rain toward it. He knew that nearby this old installation were mortars — one of which would have the honor of signaling the opening of civil war. Just before four o'clock the boat slithered onto the sand of James Island. The aides hopped out and asked directions to the local commander. They were pointed toward the quarters of Captain George S. James, in charge of the guns on this island.[1]

James's command consisted of two batteries, each with two mortars and a company of infantry, there to protect the gun crews if the island was somehow invaded. One battery was down near the beach; the other, called the Hill Battery, was back a few hundred yards, near some cottages owned by summer residents. The aides woke Captain James. One of his mortars, they said, was to fire the signal, and it would have to be done quickly. The aides had, they told him, given Major Anderson a deadline, and they wanted it met. James hustled. Within a few minutes he was standing by the beach battery. He wanted to make a good clean shot. The aides, Roger Pryor among them now, stood by him as he cracked out orders. James turned toward Pryor and asked the Virginian if he wanted to be the one to pull the lanyard. The tousled congressman, a young man, had been advocating Southern independence for years. But "secession" was an abstraction, far different from real war, from pulling lanyards. He visibly winced. No, he said, his voice husky with emotion, "I could not fire the first gun of the war." He stepped away and, along with the other three aides, got into the boat. The oarsmen pulled toward the city. It was about 4:15. They had almost two miles to go; it would be dawn before they arrived.

Captain James returned to the task at hand. He issued orders that all four mortars should get ready to fire. The battery up on the hill would have to destroy one of the nearby cottages to provide a clear shot at Sumter. He told its commander, Lieutenant Wade Hampton Gibbes, to go ahead and blow up the building. James stayed down by the beach battery, whose two guns were officially under the command of Lieutenant Henry S. Farley, standing nearby, watching his two gun crews. When his battery was ready, Farley stepped forward and inserted a friction tube into the vent hole of the gun nearest him. He took the lanyard in his left hand and peered toward Fort Sumter's black outline, just visible against the night sky. A few feet to his right waited Captain James, looking at his pocket watch. This was an historic moment. James, who would soon die in this war, had been told to fire at 4:30. He wanted to get it right.

Out in the harbor, several hundred yards away in the darkness, Chisholm told his rowers to stop for a moment. The aides turned to look back toward Fort Sumter.

In Charleston the night air was raw. A chill breeze blew in from the Atlantic, flinging mist into Charleston's dark streets. The birds of the city slept. It was very still.

———

Captain James peered at his watch again. When it read exactly 4:30, he told Farley to fire. The lieutenant pulled the lanyard, and a shell arced high toward the fort.

A mortar shell at night is very visible. Its fuse glows, and jets twinkle behind it as it moves through the air. James Chesnut and his colleagues, sitting in their boat, saw the shell rise in the sky, a remarkably beautiful thing in its way. It reached its apogee, then tumbled toward Sumter. The aim was perfect. It exploded just above the fort like a Fourth of July rocket, in red and orange sparkles. Witnesses disagree on the exact time of the first shot. Captain James's watch had indicated 4:30, but other people, looking at their timepieces, saw it as 4:25 or 4:27. Charleston was usually not all that meticulous about exactitude in matters involving time.

On James Island the soldiers continued to move briskly. As soon as their signal shell went up, Gibbes's hill battery blew up the nearby cottage, then fired the second shot of the war. This shell landed within Fort Sumter, somewhere in the parade ground, scattering hot, sharp shards of metal in all directions. Anderson had been right to order the garrison into the casemates. Doubleday, probably taking literary license, later described the first shot that hit Sumter that morning. He said he was drowsing in his bedroll when he was startled awake by a ball smacking against the outside wall of the very chamber where he was sleeping.

Batteries on the southeastern islands began to fire fairly methodically. Beauregard had given orders to maintain a very precise rhythm. The forty-three guns facing Fort Sumter were each to fire in turn, in a counterclockwise circle around the harbor, two minutes between each shot. He wanted to conserve ammunition since he had only enough for a forty-eight-hour bombardment. He knew the emotional high of battle would likely excite his amateur soldiers, so he wanted to keep them on a tight leash. Despite his orders the batteries inevitably fell into their own individual patterns, firing each gun as it got ready.

The most famous man to pull a lanyard that morning was Edmund Ruffin.[2] He had returned to Charleston because he had sensed that an historic event was about to occur here. Soon after his arrival he heard about Talbot's and Chew's visit to Pickens. He concluded this meant war and felt an uncontrollable itch. On April 9 he woke early, found a musket, and took the ten o'clock ferry to Cummings Point, where the prestigious Charleston company called the Palmetto Guard was stationed. They welcomed his appearance with three loud huzzahs. He was touched. He swept off his hat and bowed low, his long white hair cascading down. They asked him to dine with them, which he did, and to join them at the Iron Battery. This he declined. He knew he really could do nothing helpful with artillery; besides, he refused to be hidden underground like a mole when the battle began. He wanted to see it, the whole glorious panorama. He did, however, accept their offer to sleep in a nearby tent.

Ruffin was disgruntled the next day — the 10th — when nothing happened. He finally agreed to join the Palmetto Guard as a private, but only to stay with them for any fight. By the 11th Ruffin was positively antsy. He considered it critically important to attack Sumter *now*, before a fleet might arrive to reinforce it. He felt the hours of inactivity drag at him. He then learned Beauregard had sent out an ultimatum, and that Anderson had refused it. It should not be long now — according to solid rumors, eight o'clock that evening. After dinner he marched with the others out to the guns, but at eight o'clock they trooped back to their tents, assured that a battle was almost certain to begin before dawn the next morning. Ruffin slept in his clothes. He had been told the Guards wanted him to have the honor of firing their first gun. He did not want to miss this opportunity.

Before four o'clock they were roused from their blankets — about the time Beauregard's aides were landing at Fort Johnson a couple of miles to the west. Ruffin went to his gun, a large columbiad that fired a sixty-four-pound shell. Shortly after the signal shot exploded over Fort Sumter, he proudly pulled the lanyard. It was dark but he was rather sure the cannonball struck the corner of Fort Sumter. Ruffin, and, later, others, mistakenly believed he had fired the first real attack gun of the war. He was wrong, but the fervent old secessionist had indeed fired one of the first.

As he watched the bombardment progress, the only thing that bothered him was that Sumter failed to reciprocate. It worried him that if Anderson and his garrison squatted down behind their walls and refused to fire back, this "would have cheapened our conquest of the fort."

On the evening of April 11 rumors in Charleston had danced that the bombardment was about to begin. By seven o'clock spectators had drifted down to the harbor to see history. Mary Chesnut strolled there with Charlotte Wigfall, each thinking about her husband. Eight o'clock was supposed to be the critical moment, but that time came and passed. Nothing. The watchers drifted away.

Very early the next morning, at some of the expensive homes near the Battery, slaves, under instructions from their owners given the night before, arose in the darkness and slipped quietly up to the flat roofs, carrying lanterns to light their way. They spread out carpets and set out chairs and tables, then retreated to kitchens to prepare beverages and picnic baskets. The homeowners and a few guests soon arrived to sit and wait. They chatted with one another. One could hear low laughter from the roofs. Suddenly, about 4:30, there it was, the signal shell rising from Fort Johnson. It seemed oddly noiseless to the people on the roofs. Then, when the shell was reaching its highest point, the loud *thrump* the mortar had made rolled across the Battery.

Mary Chesnut was in bed. James was still out there in the harbor somewhere. She had had a restless night. When the first guns went off, she tumbled to the floor and fell on her knees. Mary was not a religious person, but she now prayed very hard, then dressed quickly and went to the roof to watch. Down below her the streets quickly filled as people surged toward vantage points where they could see the battle. Again, the Battery became a gathering point. Men and women hurriedly arrived, to stand in clumps, saying little. Small boys climbed the Battery's twenty-five-foot lantern, to tiptoe atop one of its several tiers, leaning forward to peer through the fog. They could make out the flight of the shells and see those that burst above the fort. In the first gray light of dawn they could sometimes detect when a solid ball hit the fortress walls, because brick dust would spray in the air. The sound of the explosions was noisy but not oppressive this far away, though those inside their houses could feel concussions shake their wooden walls.

In a sense, this was a marvelous spectacle — exhilarating, deliciously exciting. Nobody really thought Fort Sumter could win the contest, so it was just a matter of time. To be sure, there was a concern about the arrival of Fox's armada, but the ships seemed nowhere in sight. By mid-morning the rain fell harder. Most of the crowds drifted away. Ladies inside their houses tried to stay busy. Some put their nervous hands to work, stitching up cartridge bags. Some prayed. Others simply gossiped and waited for news. Self-important men would burst into parlors and announce the latest rumor, then leave. Wigfall bustled off to Morris Island on some errand. James Chesnut finally arrived home, wearing his uniform and red sash, and Mary thought he looked quite handsome. He ate a quick meal, then departed, returning to Beauregard's headquarters.[3]

They could also hear the guns far up in the interior of South Carolina, perhaps as far as Pineville, forty miles away. The Reverend Francis Mood was visiting one of his Methodist pastorates. Early in the morning one of his slaves woke him. The servant said he heard something like thunder coming from the direction of Charleston, and thought his master would want to know that a battle might be taking place there. The minister rose and boarded a train heading for the city; it was packed with soldiers going in the same direction. When Reverend Mood arrived at Charleston, the streets felt oddly deserted. It seemed like a Sabbath. He saw few vehicles on the road and all the stores appeared closed. (The owners of Wilbur & Son would print an announcement in the next day's *Courier* stating that they had temporarily postponed their furniture sale, "in consequence of the bombardment of the harbor by the renegade who commands Fort Sumter.")

During the bombardment's first hours many of Charleston's spectators were disturbed because Major Anderson's guns remained silent. All that silence from the hulking fort whose presence had frightened the citizenry so many months. Sumter now was like a great, ugly beast — a mastodon — being pummeled and stabbed to death, yet standing there mute. What did it mean?

Anderson's orders to the garrison to remain hidden had been sensible. The fort lacked any method of lighting casemates well enough to fire the guns accurately or safely. They would wait for daylight. Meanwhile, as their fort was being battered, they hunkered down in the darkness. At first light, a bit after six, roll call was officially taken; they were told to eat breakfast, then get ready for morning assembly. The major had made sure their routine remained normal. A professional soldier, he knew the importance of remaining calm.[4]

All they had left to eat was salt pork. One of the enlisted men later classified it as "rusty," a term meaning old and foul. The officers were a bit luckier. At their mess they also had some farina Crawford had dredged up from somewhere among the hospital supplies. Doubleday's recollections of that breakfast contain a startling sidelight. Sitting at their long mess table that morning, the officers were quite cheerful, but the man who served them was not. "We had," Doubleday recalled, "retained one colored man to wait on us." According to Doubleday, "He was a spruce looking mulatto from Charleston, very active and efficient on culinary occasions." Doubleday, the Republican abolitionist, found his behavior shameful. The man was "completely demoralized by the thunder of the guns and crashing of the shot around us. He leaned back against the wall, almost white with fear, his eyes closed, and his whole expression was one of personal despair." Anderson, the ex-slaveholder, kindly urged the fellow not to expose himself to any danger. Anderson's empathy and compassion seem today far finer qualities than Doubleday's militant politics and abstract idealism.

After eating, the garrison broke into groups and prepared to fight. The musicians and some of the workmen assisted the gun crews, carrying things about, but otherwise they stayed out of the way. Except for one brief time when some laborers got caught up in the spirit and fired a cannon, apparently most of the "noncombatants" truly acted as noncombatants — with the exception of Wylie Crawford, who would command one of the gun crews, and one Charles Hall, listed as a "musician" with Company E, whose energy and courage were later noted. Lieutenant Meade, the Virginian and engineer, did command a gun crew as part of Seymour's shift. What Foster and Snyder did during the fight is unclear.

Anderson told his two company commanders to work shifts. Doubleday and Company E would open the battle, followed a few hours later by Seymour and Company H. Each would work their guns, then take time to rest.

Fort Sumter had been under attack for over two hours. The Confederates had already fired about two hundred cannonballs.

It was just after six-thirty when the garrison started to participate in the battle. They pulled the heavy shutters away from four embrasures and began. Doubleday's crew used the cannon in the angle facing the Iron Battery on Cummings Point and the new Blakely. When the battle was over the garrison agreed that the Blakely was the most frightening Confederate gun, because it was the most accurate. Most of the guns on Cummings Point fired first at the Gorge wall, but without much success. They smacked its sides and chipped its bricks, but for the most part did little other damage. The Blakely, however, with its rifled barrel could aim with remarkable precision. Doubleday found this out when the Blakely's shots began to chip away at the embrasure of the gun he was using. One of the Blakely's shots broke off chunks of stone and spun them around the interior of the casemate, wounding almost the entire gun crew. Three of the men had rather minor cuts, but a fourth, Sergeant Thomas Kirnan, a Mexican War veteran, received a severe thumping and was knocked to the ground, dazed and bleeding from his face and head. When revived, Kirnan reportedly said he was all right. "I was only knocked down temporarily," he said, and got back to work. Fortunately, the Blakely lacked enough proper ammunition and ceased firing after a short while.

Doubleday's first round flew entirely over the Confederate emplacement and skipped into the marsh beyond. He corrected his aim and fired again. His sixth shot struck the heavy slanted roof of the Iron Battery, glanced off harmlessly, and ricocheted into the distance, a peanut thrown against a tile floor. His gun was too small, the angle of its shooting too flat. He also had a problem maintaining any sort of accuracy. He was a competent artillerist, but all the gun crews lacked the right equipment for proper firing. The materials they left behind by mistake at Fort Moultrie were now sorely missed. Anderson's officers had devised two methods to aim the guns. During the weeks before the battle began, gun crews had shot balls in the direction of specific island targets — Fort Moultrie, for example — purposely using insufficient amounts of gunpowder. Once satisfied they would have hit a particular target if they had used the correct weight of powder, they would mark a line and the name of the target precisely on the iron rail that arced behind that gun. This allowed them during the battle to turn their gun left or right with some confidence. As to the cannon's elevation, that was more complicated. The guns had no breech sights. Doubleday and Seymour had rigged up a couple of notched sticks that they could place next to the gun's barrel and estimate roughly how much to raise or lower it, but the system was clumsy at best. It mattered little, of course, since their lower-tier guns would have done small damage, even with the most sophisticated equipment, but they would have felt better.

Their most serious deficiency was in the most mundane of articles: empty cartridge bags. When they had arrived at Fort Sumter they had plenty of gunpowder. They lacked, however, enough bags. They had brought hundreds with them — Crawford himself recalled placing armloads of them in a boat — but these were not nearly enough. New bags had to be carefully hand-sewed to a particular size, depending on the distance one wanted to shoot. Every senior cadet at West Point was taught how to produce cartridge bags, and since Lieutenant Meade had recently graduated from there, he was put in charge. In the months before the bombardment he cut up extra cloth found around the fort to make the bags, but the fort did not contain much superfluous cloth.

By late March the garrison had on hand about five hundred cartridges. They had only six needles available, and some laborers were put to work. But it was slow going (as the ladies of Charleston knew well). It was also probably a matter of expedience; it may not have seemed all that important until April 8 or so for

Meade to drive his sewing workmen to greater effort. Crawford later estimated that, when the battle opened, they had a total of seven hundred cartridges. If he was correct in his calculation, they had made two hundred bags in the previous seventeen days — which comes out to a dozen a day, two cartridges per needle wielder. Meade's men were obviously not working too furiously. An additional problem was that the fort probably did not have accurate scales for measuring powder, which would have forced Meade to estimate the proper size.[5] They had to make do.

A Sumter crew, firing toward the western end of Sullivan's Island, faced the two batteries, recently revealed to them, that so threatened the barbette guns — the Floating Battery and what was called the Enfilading Battery (the one previously hidden behind a cottage). Shortly after the contest opened, when Crawford saw he had no patients to care for, he was put in charge of this crew. The army had just lost a surgeon — but it had gained a warrior who would eventually serve as one of its better battlefield generals. By mid-morning Crawford recognized that he had been unable to do damage to either the Floating or the Enfilading Batteries, since both were well entrenched and he was unskilled at aiming a cannon with precision. He moved his crew over to guns aimed at Fort Moultrie and took on that structure with more satisfying results. Moultrie's walls were now well-padded and almost indestructible, but, like Sumter, its interior buildings were vulnerable. Crawford elevated his guns and whaled away. In fact, Sumter's gun crews moved about throughout the day, searching for better targets or leaving casemates that had become too dangerous.

By late morning Major Anderson realized that at their present rate they would run out of cartridges entirely by late afternoon. They would then be defenseless. He ordered them to use fewer guns. The fort had only twenty guns on the lower tier facing Confederate positions, and at some point during the battle most were used, but the garrison was too small to man more than a portion of these at any time. At mid-morning — when some of Seymour's crews could not resist jumping into the fight — the garrison was simultaneously firing nine, maybe ten; Anderson reduced this number to six.

Another worrisome problem was the danger of fires. The fort's exterior walls were fireproof, since they were made of rock and brick, but the three interior buildings, constructed mostly of wood, were especially vulnerable because their peaked roofs and chimneys jutted above the walls and served as natural targets. The roofs were sheathed in slate, but these tiles lay atop a timber base and were flung quickly aside by the barrage, which opened up the interior of the buildings. It was a serious design flaw, because the buildings either housed or abutted important parts of the fort like the ammunition storage rooms and the stairwells. If the Confederates began throwing hotshot at the roofs — and eventually it would dawn on a professional like Ripley to do so — the preheated cannonballs would lodge in the timbers and start fires. The flames and the heat would lick about the fort, searching out vulnerable corners. Early during the battle Anderson was seen examining the magazines in concern.

On three occasions that first day major fires broke out in one or another of the fort's buildings, especially the large one against the Gorge wall, the one that had served, among other things, as the officers' quarters. Luckily, the Confederate cannon fire also destroyed several of the huge water cisterns in the corners of the buildings. This doused the flames. The garrison saw Peter Hart, the New York policeman who had come to the fort with Eba in January, attacking some fires, putting them out. Governor Pickens, it will be recalled, had only permitted Peter Hart to go to Sumter if he guaranteed not to act there as a soldier, and he kept his promise, though his raw courage revealed itself often during the bombardment.

The large view of any battle might be found in generals' reports and history books, but the people who actually participate in them have a worm's-eye view, and their memories are so scattered they later have difficulties piecing together what they did and where they were at any particular time. The men of the garrison could hear the sounds of breaking windowpanes and bricks being flung about, of slivers of metal spattering across the parade ground, but these were just impressions, not exactly memories. Afterward, the best they could usually do was to say that at some point they themselves had done this thing or had seen that. Those reading a variety of accounts can manufacture a reasonable portrait of a battle, but some incidents refuse to be nicely placed. For example, there is the story of Sergeant John Carmody who ignored Anderson's strict orders and snuck up to the barbette guns, where several of the fort's largest guns were already loaded and aimed at the foe. He fired them, one by one, at Morris Island.

Two other stories involved enlisted men from Company E. Two sergeants snuck off during the day and went upstairs to the parapet, where sat a ten-inch columbiad. It was already loaded and aimed at the Iron Battery, so they simply pulled its lanyard. The large ball just skimmed over the entrenched gun emplacement. If it had actually hit it, they concluded, the weight of this large ball might have done real damage, so they decided to try again. But since there were just the two of them, although they could load the gun they did not have the strength to move it forward again from its recoiled position. One went to get help while his comrade lay low and held on to the lanyard. The Confederates, however, had turned their attention to his position out in the open and shells began to explode about him. Finally, he could not stand it and yanked the lanyard. The great cannon recoiled backward and flipped out of its chassis, part of it tumbling into the stairwell, just missing his companion, the other sergeant, who was running back up. The two scuttled away quickly, before any officers could find them out, pleased with their efforts; the second shot had very nearly hit the target.

Another incident involved a crew firing at Sullivan's Island. They noticed that several hundred yards farther down the beach, in front of the Moultrie House, stood a crowd of people observing the battle as though it were an entertaining spectacle. The soldiers in Sumter, sweaty and tired, grew annoyed at the casualness of those people. When Doubleday and the other officers were out of sight, some of them, led by two sergeants, snuck over to two unused 42-pounders off to the side. They loaded and aimed them at the crowd and fired. They missed, but one of the balls landed in front of the spectators and skipped over their heads, crashing into the second floor of the Moultrie House. They were pleased to note the crowd leaping in all directions. Later on, Doubleday would claim credit for the shot, saying wryly, when asked about it by a Southerner, that he chose to hit the hotel because he had once been given an unsatisfactory room there; the Southerner considered that a capital answer.[6]

It was important to those on both sides of this battle, especially the officers, to appear nonchalant. Schoolboys on the playing fields of Eton. Stories would later be recited about clever witticisms uttered by them, chipper bons mots, so cherished by those raised on British war literature.

Late that first morning, when Seymour came to relieve Doubleday, Seymour was insouciant. "Doubleday," he said, "what in the world is the matter here, and what is all this uproar about?" Doubleday, becoming caught up in Seymour's sangfroid lingo, said, "There is a trifling difference of opinion between us and our neighbors opposite, and we are trying to settle it." "Very well," Seymour answered, "do you wish me to take a hand?" He did so.

The men at the Confederate batteries also strove hard to appear casual. It was said that at Fort Moultrie, when one of its protective cotton bales was knocked down by shots from Sumter, someone shouted out, "Cotton is going down." And when a cannonball struck the oven in the courtyard scattering loaves about, someone called out, "Foodstuff is going up."[7]

After the battle Charleston's newspapers told wonderful tales of bravado; some true, others dubious. It was a fact, for example, that a young man at the Iron Battery, who had gone outside the enclosure at dawn to plant a Palmetto flag atop the parapet, was doing so when Doubleday's first shot buzzed by his head. He waved the flagstaff about, then scurried back to cover as his comrades cheered. Another accurate tale involved a twelve- or thirteen-year-old boy, Paul Lalane, who had before the battle gone to visit his brother, a member of the Palmetto Guard. When the bombardment began he stayed and was allowed to fire the guns. Thus, with Edmund Ruffin and Paul Lalane among them, the Palmetto Guard had the youngest and oldest warriors on hand during the bombardment.

Such stories indicate a kind of innocence in these first hours of war. Their jocularity would have seemed too far-fetched, however, in a few months.

During the afternoon something occurred that momentarily made both the Confederate soldiers and civilians of Charleston less nonchalant. Fox's fleet began to arrive.

In the morning Anderson had placed a lookout at one of the embrasures opening toward the Atlantic to keep an eye out for any sign of Fox's arrival. About one o'clock the lookout thought he spied it and came to tell the major. Some of the men nearby gave out a cheer. Anderson ordered the fort's flag dipped once, a signal to Fox that Sumter was still holding out. The signal was premature; the fleet was having complications of its own.

A gale storm off the coast had tossed the fleet about.[8] The *Harriet Lane,* an armed revenue cutter, had arrived first, sometime the day before. (She was spotted by a pilot boat, which informed Hartstene's patrols, which had then sent word to Beauregard. This meant the general knew well before the battle that Fox's fleet had indeed begun to arrive.) Gustavus Fox, aboard the unarmed steamer *Baltic,* encountered the *Harriet Lane* at the rendezvous point, ten miles outside the mouth of Charleston Harbor, at three o'clock in the morning of April 12 — a few minutes before Beauregard's aides shook Anderson's hand at Sumter's wharf and set off for Fort Johnson. Just after dawn the warship *Pawnee* arrived. Fox went over to it and told its captain that he would use her until the others arrived. Oh, no, Captain Stephen C. Rowan replied, he was under orders to await the *Powhatan* (presently steaming for Florida because Lincoln had confused its name with the *Pocahontas*). Fox, growing increasingly frustrated, boarded the *Harriet Lane* and proceeded toward the harbor. This is when he discovered that Sumter was under attack. He sped back to tell Captain Rowan. Hearing of the battle, the captain changed his mind. He was ready for a fight. The three vessels closed up and hove to just outside the bar. They did not know where the three tugs were, nor the *Powhatan* nor the *Pocahontas,* and they contemplated whether to use what they had on hand, the *Pawnee's* launches. After some debate they agreed that the two armed ships would anchor near the bar, that the *Baltic* would stay out by the rendezvous point looking for the others. If the rest had not arrived by the next morning, they would make an attempt to aid Fort Sumter with their rowboats.

Throughout the harbor people watched this confused scene of ships coming and going—including a large merchant steamer, *Nashville*, which arrived by chance as the battle was erupting and stayed beyond the bar, waiting. At Sumter they wondered what was going on out there. Why were United States naval vessels staying calmly out of range during a battle? Did they intend to break toward Sumter's wharf after dark? Anderson assumed so. He seemed of two minds about the prospect. He had opposed any such attempt for months, but that was partly because he knew it would cause a war. Now that fighting had started, the apparent unwillingness of the fleet to dirty its hands was vexing.

In Charleston they could see the ships outlined against the skyline. Their first arresting appearance sent a ripple of alarm through the watching masses. What the city had feared for so long had arrived at the mouth of the harbor. But as time went by and the ships made no apparent effort to come to Sumter's aid, the attitude of the crowds changed. People began to shout that the ship captains were timid and spineless; some outraged citizens began to hiss and boo and shake their fists at the ships.

On the outer islands Beauregard's soldiers were also quite aware of Fox's arrival. Most were not concerned that the ships would attack them right away, but maybe would so after dark. Because of the strong winds, the surf was too heavy to permit small boats much of a landing, but during the night, when the tide was up, it seemed possible. The officers on Morris Island held a meeting and agreed that the enemy would likely move in and attack their positions this night, probably between seven and eight when the tide was at its highest. They wrote Beauregard and begged for reinforcements. As darkness arrived Hartstene ignited the three hulks in the channel.

Many Confederate infantrymen, up to this moment mere witnesses of the bombardment, looked forward to action. A young man, stationed at the far end of Sullivan's Island, wrote in his diary, "We have hopes they will land and give us a brush." Another soldier on Morris Island called Lincoln's sailors "miserable cowards" for not joining the fight. "The execrations of our men," he confided to his diary, "are loud against them."[9]

By seven o'clock it was growing dark. Anderson ordered his gun crews to cease firing till the following morning. The garrison closed the shutters of the open embrasures, ate some more rancid pork, and tried to rest. Sentries were placed in key places and told to watch for boats landing somewhere outside the walls, perhaps from Fox's fleet, perhaps a Confederate assault force. With the howling winds and the harsh rain, with both foes speaking English, Anderson decided to assume any arrivals were the enemy unless they provided immediate proof they were not. Meade kept men sewing more cartridges until midnight.

Anderson was concerned about the flagstaff. Shell fragments had clipped the halyards enough that the flag could no longer be moved. If the fort wanted to signal the fleet it would not be able to do so.

Beauregard's guns almost ceased, except for two batteries of mortars, which maintained a nagging fire every quarter hour just to frazzle nerves.

Late that night Snyder and Crawford wandered about outside the walls to inspect the damage. They saw that the Gorge wall was especially badly pockmarked, but except for superficial scars the fort had held up quite well. The men inside were all right, too. Only four were hurt, all with relatively minor wounds.

Americans outside South Carolina gradually learned about the battle in Charleston as the news spread across the land by telegraph line. By evening people were talking excitedly about it in major cities and small hamlets. At the White House messengers rushed in with the latest reports. Had Southern leaders like Jefferson Davis been aware of it, the reactions were ominous for the Confederacy. Northerners who had shrugged at secession a few days earlier felt a different and strange emotion when confronted by the reality of the Confederacy's attack on Major Anderson's tiny band. During the past months the plight of Robert Anderson and his few score men had become well known. This attack on them instantly turned them into martyrs. When even the spectators on Charleston's waterfront came to cheer every time one of Sumter's pitiful guns went off, indicating there were men alive inside and that they were still fighting, when people on the Battery shouted "three cheers for Major Anderson," it is hardly surprising Northerners were praising his name from New England to Iowa. Words like "secession" and "Confederacy" and "Union" are abstractions. "Major Anderson" and "Fort Sumter" gave them meaning. Other men, other battlefields, would soon replace them. But for this moment they symbolized important things to many people — something to fight for.

Crawford had presciently written his brother about this prospect back in February: "The first gun fired at our fort will call the country to arms. The bugle that sounds that attack on us will echo along the slopes of the Alleghenies amid the granite hills of the North, along the shores of the Great Lakes, and far away on the rolling prairies of the West — and the earth will shake with the tread of armed men."

In Montgomery few foresaw this. About nine o'clock the first telegram arrived from Charleston: The deed was done! The local telegraph office announced it by raising a flag outside. Men threw up their hats and cheered. Cannon fired eight shots — the first seven for each state of the Confederacy, the eighth to honor General Beauregard. Smiling people hugged one another in genuine happiness. As a Montgomery paper stated, "The agony is over." About midnight a throng of more than a thousand people milled outside the Exchange Hotel and shouted that they wanted to see Jeff Davis.

Inside, the Confederate president was quite ill, lying on a couch in his parlor much of the day, smoking cigars. Maybe he gave a thought to his good friend Robert Anderson, whose life he might have just snatched away. Certainly he regretted firing the first shot. Like Francis Pickens, he would always later claim that it was the fault of the other side — Lincoln and that ilk — but the weight of this moment seemed, just now, to bear him down.

The crowd shouted insistently for some words, and eventually Secretary of War Walker stepped out and gave a little speech. Unfortunately for his cause, in the excitement of the moment he used some ill-chosen phrases. No one, he said, could know exactly what would happen, but he prophesied that the great Confederate flag would be flying over the Capitol in Washington in less than three months — and maybe, he added, even Faneuil Hall in Boston. The cheering grew ecstatic.[10] (Since the South's leaders had been trying desperately for months to appear the *victims* of Black Republicanism, Walker was unwise to suggest the possibility of an aggressive military campaign against the North. In coming weeks his words would be quoted often to stir up sentiment in the North.)

A footnote about the evening following the war's first day: At Pensacola Bay Lieutenant Adam Slemmer had become convinced that General Braxton Bragg's large army was preparing to assault Fort Pickens — "at any moment," he wrote that day to the commander of the American fleet, still hovering outside the bay. He had even read about a coming attack in the local newspaper, the Pensacola *Observer.* Slemmer believed that the only thing that had kept them back the last few days was a recent spate of bad weather.

By chance, these same heavy winds had held up the mission of Lieutenant John L. Worden. He had been on the road since the stern and bewigged secretary of the navy, Gideon Welles, had told him to travel immediately to the fleet outside the bay. He had arrived on the morning of April 11 and gotten Braxton Bragg's permission to go out to the fleet. He had boarded a boat, but the weather prevented it from moving. The next day he reached the fleet at noon and handed his dispatch to its commander, Captain Adams.

War had already begun hundreds of miles away in Charleston, but here they had no way of knowing. That afternoon, Bragg received a message from Montgomery to prevent any person named "Worden" delivering a message to the fleet. It was too late.

After dark, Adams dropped the reinforcements onto Santa Rosa Island. Fort Pickens was saved. It had been a very close thing. Had it not been for some stiff breezes, Lieutenant Worden would have reached Captain Adams a day earlier, and Slemmer might have been reinforced on April 11. Had Bragg decided to attack, the Civil War might have begun here instead of in Charleston. As it was, strong winds in Florida had guaranteed that Charleston and Fort Sumter—both doomed—would meet their fate. It was appropriate.[11]

At the Brevoort in New York Eba Anderson also heard the news. Many people stopped in to see her. She was unwell. She was not receiving any visitors.

CHAPTER SEVENTEEN

Ashes and Dust

Edmund Ruffin slipped into his tent, tried to sleep, then gave up and stood outside with others in the drizzle to stare out toward where the Union ships had recently been, trying to peer through flashes of sheet lightning to see if Lincoln's navy would use the blackness of this night to swoop in — either toward Sumter or to the beaches of Morris Island. Ruffin could detect nothing, and after a bit he went back to bed. About midnight he was wakened by a rattle of musket fire and explosions from nearby cannon. It must be the expected attack, he thought, for why else would muskets be firing? He crept into the night. Through the murk he could detect a commotion far down the beach. He heard shouting, a twenty-four-pound howitzer belching out grapeshot, more shouts. Then quiet. It took a while to piece together what had just happened.

Two civilian fishermen had dropped off some soldiers at Cummings Point, had stopped for a few intoxicating draughts of pick-me-up, then started uncertainly back toward Charleston. But the swells were high and the tide was running rapidly out. The fishermen were just sober enough to think it a good idea to head into shore, but when their vessel appeared out of the darkness a sentry spotted it and gave an alarm. Guns went off, and the fishermen dropped below their gunwales to hide. They shouted out — "Friends, Southern Confederacy, don't shoot for God's sake" — but their voices, at the bottom of their boat, were muffled by the crashing of the surf. Meanwhile, their boat, no longer under control, bobbed along the shoreline. More men became involved. Some waded into the water to grab the boat, then were forced to scurry back when their own cannon tried to blow the vessel out of the water. The boat continued to slip along the beach. More guns went off. "Don't shoot," the drunks pleaded again, "we are friends." Soldiers wading into the waves finally took hold of the boat. The two men slurred out their tale, and were allowed to sleep it off at the encampment.[1]

The clumsiness of the soldiers on Morris Island, the wildness of their fire, which left two sodden scamps unscathed after countless shots, suggests that Fox's optimism might not have been ill placed — at least so far as his chances of successfully dropping off the recruits and supplies, especially if he had had the use of the sailors and boats from the *Powhatan*.

Out beyond the entrance to the harbor the array of ships was increasing. In addition to Fox's three ships — the steamer *Baltic*, and the two naval vessels, *Pawnee* and *Harriet Lane* — the number of commercial ships increased, each arriving in the normal course of events to make profits in trade. On Morris Island, as dawn broke, a fog lay atop the sea like a thick layer of meringue. A sentry rushed into headquarters and announced that a *vast* federal flotilla hovered just beyond the bar, and worse, that it had begun to form into a great line of battle in preparation to break into the harbor. The officers at headquarters leaped to their feet in excitement. Beat the long roll, they shouted, form the troops on the beach to repel any attempt by the enemy to land. They rushed a dispatch to Beauregard's headquarters, pleading for reinforcements.[2]

It soon became obvious, however, that the "enemy" had no immediate plan to invade Morris Island. Probably what the sentry had seen and misinterpreted was a movement by the *Baltic*. During the night the large steamer, being unarmed, had moved well back from the harbor's mouth. As morning approached, it slowly maneuvered through the swells toward the anchorage of its two companions, but in the fog its captain ran onto a shoal near Sullivan's Island and had slid to a stop in the sand. It appeared for a while she was stuck, but by desperate rocking she was able to back off.[3]

The second day of bombardment started just after daybreak, slowly, methodically, adagio, following Beauregard's orders. At Sumter the garrison once again spent the first hours hidden inside their casemates. They ate their pork breakfast, then got to work. They had few cartridges left, so Anderson told them to focus only on targets on Sullivan's Island, especially Moultrie, and to take their time. For the next hour the battle, such as it was, continued in slow motion, like two exhausted fighters pawing at each other in the late rounds. Then something happened.

About 7:30 A.M. a mortar shell went through one corner of the officers' quarters' roof, then exploded. It seems to have begun a conflagration, probably by breaking a large hole in the weakened roof, opening up some smoldering embers to a rush of fresh oxygen. Foster later said he suspected that a fire from the day before had never quite gone out, or that perhaps a hotshot had pressed for an entire day against a timber, finally causing it to flame up. The morning sky was clear and blue. An April breeze whipped across the fort from the west.

The buildings were still damp from yesterday's heavy rains and the waters that had gushed from the broken cisterns. Dampened joists caught fire; black smoke poured from the roofs of the Gorge, then from the barracks to its left. About eight o'clock watchers on both sides of the harbor saw giant clouds of smoke billowing from the fort. A major fire was blazing. Spontaneously, guns from all sides, ignoring Beauregard's demands for frugality, poured shot and shell into the fort. Colonel Ripley at Fort Moultrie ordered more cannonballs heated in Moultrie's furnaces, then fired them into Sumter's roofs. Ripley and the others realized this was no time for pinchpenny prudence. A great and dangerous beast had just revealed a weakness. Best attack her with all one's might right now before she had a chance to heal herself. Great gouts of flame erupted toward the sky, visible for miles. The fire raced from one end of the building to the other, then sprang voraciously upon the barracks on both sides. "Indestructible" Fort Sumter seemed an inferno. The batteries around the harbor increased their assault, anxious to kill her now before she could recover.

Captain Fox and Commander Rowan, captain of the *Pawnee*, became desperate to do something, but, although the sky was clear, the waves were still too high to hazard entering in small boats. They were forced to watch the conflagration from afar, choleric with rage. By noon Rowan could no longer bear the frustration. He decided to grab one of the civilian ships that huddled outside the harbor. He chose a schooner, just arrived from Boston, bound for Charleston's wharves with a load of ice. He fired some shots near her until her captain reluctantly came about and anchored. Rowan sent across a lieutenant and five men, all well armed. They seized her and placed her crew aboard the *Pawnee*. It was an act of piracy, but Rowan was desperate. He justified his actions by claiming he thought the ship a Charleston vessel loaded with munitions. When her captain expostulated, noting that he was obviously carrying ice, Rowan offered him $500 for the use of the schooner. Rowan's plan was to put Fox, the supplies, and the 200 recruits aboard the schooner, then send them to Fort Sumter after dark. Fox agreed, though he felt sure they would all be blown apart before they could accomplish the mission. He now could admit that his entire premise had been wrong: Even had he succeeded in depositing the men and provisions at Sumter, it would only have lengthened Anderson's tenure there but a few days. He blamed this logical flaw on unnamed army men—presumably Scott—who had led him to believe that reinforcements and more food would have made the fort impregnable. As it was, none of this made any difference. The garrison's sojourn at Fort Sumter was almost over.[4]

When the upper story of the officers' quarters began to smoke early that morning, Anderson told those not directly involved in firing back at Moultrie to go up there and try to smother it, or at least to use axes and cut down the heavy wooden moldings to see if that might contain the blaze. It was dangerous work because of the barrage of shells being flung now into the building from all sides of the harbor. When the bombardment grew too fierce and the flames too high, he changed his mind and ordered them to leave it alone. It was obvious they would lose this main building and one of the barracks. They might save the other, maybe not. The voracious fire found the main gate and the wooden shutters covering the sally ports and embrasures, and devoured them. The heat cracked and crumbled the thick brick wall Foster's men had built inside the gate as a backup. Many wooden gun carriages on the parapet went up in flames. Those cannon facing Sumter's wharf were now useless. Fort Sumter was wide open to an assault by infantry.[5]

The most immediate danger to the garrison was their three hundred barrels of gunpowder. Although stored in a magazine with a thick metal door, loose powder trailed everywhere nearby. During the previous night the men sewing cartridges in the darkness had spilled powder about. Crews had not always been as careful when moving cartridges to the cannon as they might. When the fire grew fierce, it spat burning flakes of timber into the air. The wind whipped these cinders about, flinging them into nooks and niches throughout the fort. Men's skin and clothing were getting burned and scorched. Inevitably, one of these sparks would find a trail of gunpowder, and then shoot along it till it found the magazine.

Men raced to the barrels of powder and started to roll them to places that seemed safer, then covered them with wet blankets. Later, no one could agree on how many they had moved — somewhere between forty and a hundred. They then slammed shut the heavy copper door of the magazine and dug a trench in front of it, filling the trench with water, hoping this would keep flames from licking underneath. (A chance shot from the enemy soon afterward crashed into the door, denting it in such a way that it could no longer open.) Anderson decided that the blanket-covered barrels were bound to explode, so he had all but four of them taken to nearby embrasures and thrown out. Some failed to fall far enough from the fort to land in the water and lay in a pile on the stones, where a Confederate shell found them. The result was a large explosion, but because the barrels were in the open and away from the wall the resulting damage to the fort was negligible.

Inside the walls the garrison staggered about in a world of fierce madness. Shot and shell crashed about them. A hotshot from Moultrie landed on the parade and bounded into one of the open casemates where it came to rest against a soldier's bedding, lighting it afire. A shell, bursting just above the ground, slashed against the legs of one of Foster's Baltimore masons, John Schweirer, wounding him badly. The inferno roared and screeched. Timbers collapsed, brick and mortar and granite cracked and fell from fifty feet above. Fire found the hundreds of nine-inch grenades piled away in the stairwells, and they went up with a great *whuff*, throwing white smoke into the air, mixing with the black smoke of the pine timbers. Explosions blocked off one of the stairwells and nearly destroyed another. At one point, when Anderson asked Crawford to go check on the status of Fox's fleet — whether it was on its way in or not — the surgeon had a hard time scrambling his way up to the parapet to peer out.

Physically, the worst aspect of the morning was the smoke. The powerful west wind blew the thick haze down inside the fort. The men choked and coughed. They covered their faces with damp handkerchiefs. They pressed themselves against the ground. A few, Doubleday among them, crawled out of embrasures to breathe the clear outside air. They all grew painted with soot. Luckily, about noon the wind changed direction and the men could breathe more easily.

Through it all, there was Anderson, "his head erect as if on parade," as Sergeant James Chester saw him, calmly reminding his gun crews to maintain a slow, steady fire on Moultrie, walking here and there about the fort, checking on its status, seeing how the men were faring.

Charleston's citizens again came out to watch the battle. Since the morning was clear it was easier to see the two sides, though the wind blowing toward Fort Sumter erased all sounds of battle. The whole panorama seemed to take place in pantomime. Puffs of silent smoke rose from batteries on Morris Island, the Floating Battery, Fort Moultrie. Occasionally, solitary little puffs appeared from only one side of the great fort out in the harbor. It was a strangely arresting sight. Anna Brackett, the schoolteacher, was there. "Women of all ages and ranks of life look eagerly out with spyglasses and opera glasses. Children talk and laugh and walk back and forth in the small moving space as if they were at a public show." Then the crowd spotted the black smoke billowing above the Gorge, and the awful flames. Spectators shouted out the news — first with glee. Brackett heard a boy shout, "Now you'll see that old flag go down." After a while, however, some spectators felt growing concern for the fort's surviving occupants. A few days later a woman described her feelings to her children: "We forgot our people, we forgot everything, for a few moments, but the gallant band within the burning crater." Even tough Edmund Ruffin felt moved as the flames rose above the fort. Sumter had long ceased firing toward Morris Island and its dunes crowded with soldiers, who emerged from their holes to gape in awe, Ruffin among them. "I looked on," he wrote, "with my feelings of joy and exultation at our now certain prospect of speedy success mixed with awe and horror of the danger of this terrible calamity, & pity for the men exposed to the consequences — & with high admiration for the indomitable spirit of the brave commander."[6]

About one o'clock the flagstaff fell. Thus began a series of events, some serious, some farcical, that would end all this.

Inside Fort Sumter's parade ground, near its westernmost flank, stood its immense flagstaff, as tall as a ten-story building. The fort's builders had propped up the staff with four long struts angled outward like flying buttresses, because otherwise Atlantic gale winds would have snatched greedily against any large flag and whipped it and its pole to the ground. Since the flagstaff flew so high above the fort's walls, it served as a perfect bull's-eye. When the bombardment began, gun crews throughout the harbor had used the flag as a sighting device to aim their shots at the fort. Some gunners simply aimed at the staff itself, trying to knock it and the flag to the ground. In the afternoon of the second day the huge mast finally crashed, falling like a tall forest pine, disappearing into the smoky ruin of the fort. In the city, on Sullivan's Island, on Morris Island the watchers gave out a great hurrah. "Then arose the loudest & longest shout of joy," said Ruffin from his position with the Palmetto Guard, "— as if this downfall of the flag, with its cause, was the representation of our victory."[7]

In Sumter men scrambled to erect the flag again. Hall ran into the courtyard and snatched it up, somehow disentangling it from its halyards before the flag burst into flames. Peter Hart found a useful spar from somewhere, probably one of the flagstaff's four legs, broken off when it fell. Seymour and Snyder, plus one or two others, helped search for a good place to reraise the flag. They had to rush; they did not want the enemy to think they had surrendered. Through the smoke and bursting shells, carrying the long and heavy pole, the men stumbled up the cluttered stairs to the parapet — no mean feat. They dashed to one of the gun carriages on the Moultrie side. Hart hurriedly nailed the flag to the spar and they fastened the stick to the side of the carriage, then ran back down to the safety of the casemates. They did all this in fifteen minutes.

On nearby Cummings Point, when the flag first toppled, the men wondered what to make of this. The command immediately ordered their batteries to cease firing and discussed among themselves their next step. Among them were Brigadier General James Simons, commanding the entire island, and four of Beauregard's aides. Three of the aides had just arrived a few minutes earlier. At mid-morning Beauregard had sent James Chesnut and ex-governor John L. Manning off to Morris Island to check on things. The planter Chisholm had taken them in his skiff, the same one that had carried Chesnut out to speak to Anderson before the battle. The three had just come up to Simons when they heard a shout that Sumter's flagstaff was down. Beauregard's fourth aide, there at that moment, was Colonel Louis Trezevant Wigfall. He had arrived the day before on a similar mission, and had decided to stay. He had found a horse and ridden around, ordering infantry units about in the name of the general, commanding them to defend the island against any assault, stopping on at least one occasion to tell a battery to quicken its fire on the fort. He had written his wife in Charleston that "all is well." But on this second day of the bombardment he had become restless. He also began to feel an admiration for Robert Anderson and his garrison, and a growing concern as he watched the flames shooting upward. "Anderson is a damned rascal to hold out against us as he does," an acquaintance of his described Wigfall's feelings, "but he is brave & he has shown pluck."[8]

Beauregard's aides and General Simons conferred hurriedly and agreed that a boat should immediately go over. Wigfall volunteered and he and Chisholm rushed back toward the creek behind them to find Chisholm's vessel. On the way they saw an enlisted man with the Palmetto Guards standing at the creek's edge while a rowboat prepared to pull away from shore. His name was William Gourdin Young, a nephew of the Gourdin brothers. At that moment Private Young was thirty years old, married, tired, and, like Wigfall, more than a bit bored. He had been asking some passersby in a boat for news when Wigfall and Chisholm scampered up and examined the craft. It was a small rowboat and leaky, and Chisholm peered at it suspiciously and declared it unseaworthy. His own vessel was just up the creek a few minutes away, and they could use that. No, said Wigfall, who had run out of patience, the boat seemed fine to him; Anderson and his men might be dying in the fort right now, there was not a moment to spare. He said that if he could find someone to go with him — looking at Private Young — he would take this very rowboat right now. When Young noted he had no authorization to leave his post, Colonel Wigfall pooh-poohed such a trivial matter, that he was an aide to Beauregard, which should be sufficient. Nearby clustered a group of slaves who had been ordered to wait out of the line of fire during the battle (to keep them — valuable commodities — out of harm's way). Wigfall instantly chose three slaves to come with him, and he ordered them into the boat. The slaves were reluctant to go, but Wigfall gave them no choice. He put two in charge of rowing, and the third was assigned to continuously bail out the bottom. He and Private Young jumped in. Off the five men went, toward Fort Sumter.[9]

Wigfall was in such a state of ecstasy or excitement that he failed to hear shouts from Morris Island that Sumter's flag had just gone up again, nor could he see that particular corner of Fort Sumter from the boat, and so his leaky vessel kept moving. On the harbor's northern side, however, the flag's reappearance was quite evident. So was the presence of Wigfall's boat. At Fort Moultrie Colonel Ripley told his gunners to fire a warning shot toward it. A moment later a 32-pounder ball splashed uncomfortably near, followed by others, including a shell that burst close to them. The slaves, feeling no attachment to secession or the Confederacy, had a powerful itch to return to Morris Island, but Wigfall insisted they continue to pull toward the fort. At one point Young asked Wigfall how he expected to signal the fort since he had forgotten to bring a flag. Good point, responded Wigfall, and he reached into his pocket and whipped out an enormous white handkerchief. Private Young, using strips from his shirtsleeve, tied it to Wigfall's ceremonial sword, and Wigfall stood up to wave it aloft. A swell bumped against the boat's side and the colonel plopped back down again.

They approached the fort as shots hitting its parapet scattered pieces of brick upon them. They tried shouting through the burning gate to attract attention from those within, but received no response. It was as if they had arrived at Beau Geste's fortress of dead men. They steered toward its wharf, but discovered it far too littered with wall chunks to land safely, so finally Wigfall and Young clambered out, splashing through the water till they were standing on the island. They stood, examining the smoky fortress. The only sounds were the crash of cannonballs. Behind them, bobbing in the waves, were the three unhappy slaves, who began to move the boat off. Young saw what they were doing, abandoned Wigfall, and rushed back with his pistol out. He ordered the three out of the skiff and into the water.

As these four were standing amid the waves Major Anderson, who'd been told someone was outside the fort, stepped through the smoking remnants of the main gate, Snyder by his side. The scene must have seemed curious: one white man and three blacks hovering in the water near the wharf, an old rowboat bobbing up and down next to them, while a battle raged around their ears. What, he asked Young, are you doing here? Young said he had escorted an officer to the fort under a flag of truce; the officer had come to speak with the major and had gone around the side looking for some way in. This, too, may have struck Anderson as odd since he himself had just come out the gate. Why couldn't the emissary have entered that way? The major ordered Snyder to look around the outside walls, while he spun on his heel and went back inside. He was gone but a few moments, then reappeared, saying suspiciously he had found no one matching Young's description. Anderson declared he wanted the young man to come with him right now. Young, fearing the slaves would depart, refused to abandon his post unless someone from the fort came out to watch them. The three slaves pleaded with the major, for God's sake, to help them find a safer spot, away from falling shells. Anderson quietly suggested that where they were right now was about the safest place anywhere on the island. At this moment, an officer from the fort rushed through the gate and announced that an emissary was indeed inside, asking to speak to Major Anderson. Thus, Private Young was relieved of his predicament. He remained by the boat, eyeing the three slaves.

Wigfall had been having his own problems.[10] After leaving Young, he had started off down the Esplanade, looking for some way to enter the fort. In his hand he waved aloft his sword, white handkerchief still attached. In a few moments he arrived at the far edge of the Gorge wall, and stepped cautiously beyond it onto the rugged rocks that skirted the fort's wall. He came to the first open embrasure, the one Doubleday had first used the morning before, now badly gouged by the Blakely. He stood several feet below it, shouting up, "Who is there? I want to come in." Someone peered out and said, "Who is there?" It was John Thompson, an Irish-born enlisted man from Company E. Thompson and James Digdam had been standing a few paces back from the embrasure, putting out a fire. Wigfall shouted his name to Thompson and said that he wished to come in and speak to Anderson. No, said Thompson, you can stay right there while I get the major, and he disappeared toward the parade ground. It was Thompson who first told Anderson about the intruder — which information had caused Anderson and Snyder to go out the gate looking for him.

As soon as Thompson departed, Wigfall, still outside, looked hastily around for some way to boost himself through the embrasure. He found a good-sized piece of timber on the rocks and leaned it against the wall to form a step. He looked up through the embrasure and saw Private Digdam watching him. Again he pleaded to come in, this time more anxiously, as shots struck around him. No, Digdam said, not until the major appeared. Another nearby shot brought another plea from Wigfall. Okay, said Digdam—the same pugnacious chap who had spent much of 1860 in confinement at Moultrie, in chains and on bread and water—but only if you first hand me your sword. Wigfall handed up the sword, white flag attached, and started drawing his bulbous hips up with the help of Digdam. At this very moment Snyder came up below him on the rocks. Snyder yelled at Wigfall that Anderson was now at the main gate. The Confederate emissary merely continued to shinny his way in through the embrasure, using one hand to pull at the mouth of what had been Doubleday's cannon. Snyder followed quickly after. Digdam handed Wigfall his sword and white flag.

Meanwhile, out in the harbor, halfway between Charleston and the fort, was a vessel carrying three *authentic* messengers from General Beauregard, who had sent them to find out what the fallen flag meant, and to offer the garrison assistance to put out the fire. They were not carrying any offer to make peace. They had just begun the long passage from the city when they saw the flag raised again. As soon as they noticed this, they stopped, and waited, wondering what all this meant.

Inside the fort, Lieutenant Snyder escorted Wigfall down the row of casemates to where several officers stood: Foster, Meade, and Davis. The Confederate colonel excitedly said he was from Beauregard with a request that they stop fighting. "Let us stop this firing," he said. "You are on fire, and your flag is down. Let us quit."

"No, Sir," Davis calmly replied, "our flag is not down." He pointed out the back of the casemate to the parade ground. "Step out here and you will see it waving over the ramparts."

Wigfall realized his whole mission had been based on a misconception, but he was not to be dissuaded at this point. "Let us quit this," Wigfall said again. "Here is a white flag," and he waved his handkerchief about, "will anybody hoist this?" Wigfall, unsophisticated in military subtleties, most likely did not understand that he was asking them to indicate their surrender. None of the officers moved. "That is for you to do," one of them said, "if you choose." In this case the use of a white flag could have meant that firing should cease while a parley was going on.

Wigfall asked whether it would be all right if he did so, and went over to the casemate's embrasure. As he stepped into its opening he was facing directly toward Ripley's guns at Moultrie. He whipped the white flag back and forth. At this sign of Wigfall's sincerity Davis stepped forward, and told Corporal Charles Bringhurst, standing nearby, to take it from the emissary and try waving it himself.

The enlisted man had hardly put his head and handkerchief out the embrasure when a shot landed quite near. He sprang angrily back in. "God damn it," he said, "they don't respect this flag. They are firing on it."

"They fired at me two or three times," Wigfall snorted. "I stood it, and I should think you might stand it once."

At this point Anderson arrived. Wigfall introduced himself, and added, "General Beauregard wishes to stop this."

Robert Anderson was exhausted and worn. In the past few months he had lost considerable weight, and his hair had thinned and grown almost white. His face and clothes were smudged. He knew the fort had only four small barrels of gunpowder left and, at that moment, but three cartridges. His guns could fire only three more times, at least until the garrison had sewed a few more cartridges. He and the others had eaten only some bad pork today and had washed it down with water, with the prospect for future meals being the same. They might have held out five or six more days, but his men were already weak and he could see that some were growing sick. They had been moving the last two days on sheer energy, but their candles were burning very low. Fox's fleet had not moved. If Beauregard sent an assault force after dark, it would mean a slaughter. Up to this moment no one at the fort, except the workman Schweirer, had been badly wounded. Anderson was a profoundly religious man, and Wigfall's appearance may have seemed providential. God must have protected them all for some reason. They were whipped, and Anderson knew it. Now, here was a messenger claiming to represent Beauregard, suggesting that General Beauregard was offering some sort of *truce,* not demanding a *surrender.* To many civilians the difference might appear slight, but Major Anderson understood the remarkable implications. A truce meant that he and his garrison had not been defeated. One of his officers later remarked that when Wigfall said these words, Anderson stiffened a bit, rose up on his heels, then came down with a clack and said, simply, "Well, Sir!"

"You have defended your flag nobly, Sir," Wigfall said. "You have done all that it is possible to do, and General Beauregard wants to stop this fight. On what terms, Major Anderson, will you evacuate this fort?"

Anderson must have noticed that Wigfall used the critical word "evacuate," not "surrender." He instantly responded, "General Beauregard is already acquainted with my only terms." He had told them to Chesnut two days earlier. They would involve leaving the fort with their belongings and company property, that they would be supplied some sort of transportation north, and, equally important, perhaps, that they could salute their flag as they lowered it.

"Do I understand you, Major Anderson, that you will evacuate this fort upon the terms proposed to you the other day?" Wigfall was understandably confused by the military delicacies involved.

"Yes, Sir, and on those terms only."

"Then, Sir, I understand, Major Anderson, that the fort is to be ours?"

"On those conditions only, I repeat."

"Very well," Wigfall said. "That is all I have to do. You military men will arrange everything else on your own terms." He said he would "return to General Beauregard," and departed. He crossed the parade ground, sidled through the gate, and climbed back into his rowboat, much to the relief of Private Young and the three slaves. Wigfall had been inside the fort less than fifteen minutes, but it had seemed much longer to the four men waiting for him. The slaves had been suggesting to Private Young that clearly Wigfall had been killed inside, so they should push off right now. Then the colonel appeared, and the five of them happily departed. One of the slaves admitted aloud that he had been quite afraid, but that now the danger was over, he was glad he had come. "It will be a good thing to tell my wife," he said proudly.

At some point during the past minutes — and, amazingly, no one there could later recall when — Wigfall's white handkerchief was raised over Fort Sumter and the American flag brought down. This signal of the white flag was seen by Beauregard's three messengers still in the harbor, somewhere in transit back to Charleston. They were now completely baffled. They turned and started back toward the fort. The firing from all the island batteries ceased.

In Charleston spectators saw the white flag and cheered hysterically. Men on horseback raced about the streets shouting the tidings. One woman in town, peering at Fort Sumter through a spyglass, saw men there staggering out onto the ramparts and the wharf. She could not guess why it was. (They were in fact coming out to get some cool, clean air. Their battle was done, their ordeal was over. Exhaustion quickly set in. By evening the garrison sat around listlessly — silent and reserved.)

Wigfall approached Cummings Point. A great crowd awaited him on the sands. They could clearly see the white flag flying over Sumter behind him. The ex-senator stood up in the boat, waved his hat back and forth, and gave out three mighty cheers. "Sumter is ours!" he yelled. Men on the beach rushed out into the surf and grabbed his boat even before it landed. They hugged both Wigfall and Young and scooped them up on their shoulders. They screamed out their joy. Hurrah for South Carolina! Hurrah for the Palmetto Guards! (No one paid any attention to the three slaves.) Someone jumped on a horse and raced out to the farthest companies to tell them the wonderful news. The shoreline rang with the voices of thousands of happy Confederate soldiers. They threw their hats into the air, they shook hands, they pounded one another on the back, they clasped one another. Some looked around for something alcoholic with which to celebrate, and were lucky enough to find some on hand.

By this time Wigfall had given General Simons his report, and the general sent him, along with Private Young, James Chesnut, and the other aides, to tell Beauregard about the conversation with Anderson. As they passed by Fort Sumter, Wigfall, a brave man if nothing else, could see some of the garrison standing outside now, and he persuaded Chisholm to dip his skiff's flag in honor of their courage. When the aides arrived at Charleston's wharf, the city went mad. Once again, Wigfall was carried on people's shoulders, off to Beauregard's headquarters. Young was forced to follow along, pressed on by the crowd. His shirt was torn, his pants had shrunk from his time in the salt waters of the harbor, his face was grimy. All he wanted was to go home and see his wife and family, but he had been ordered to see the general. At headquarters Wigfall went in to report. As he was trying to explain to Beauregard his recollections of his conversation with Anderson, outside the building a mob pounded at the door demanding a speech to describe the good news. Beauregard became annoyed at this racket, walked out to the anteroom, and ordered Private Young to go out and say something to quiet it. A few minutes later, after a few words to the crowd, Young made good his escape. He spent the evening at home.[11]

Out at Fort Sumter things had grown more complicated. Beauregard's genuine emissaries had arrived at the wharf. They were Stephen D. Lee, who had been there two days earlier with Chesnut; Porcher Miles, one-time mayor of Charleston; and Roger Pryor, late of Virginia. Pryor had not considered it proper to wear a Confederate uniform, but he did want to seem military, so he had donned a colored shirt and large spurs, had found and carried a sword, a revolver, and a bowie knife. As the three were getting out of their boat, sputtering, an officer from within Sumter approached. He escorted them to Anderson. They told him they had been sent by Beauregard to offer assistance with the fire. Anderson thanked them but said the fire seemed under control. It apparently then struck him as odd that they had come from Beauregard's headquarters. He told them he had just spoken to Colonel Wigfall, who had indicated *he* had come from the general, and that Wigfall and he had made arrangements to evacuate the garrison. Impossible, they replied, Wigfall has not seen the general in the last two days.

Anderson was furious, and embarrassed. He had been put, he felt, in an awkward position. He gestured with his hand toward Moultrie and said, "Very well, gentlemen, you can return to your batteries." As for himself, he was going to raise the American flag and start firing. The aides were stunned. They went off into a corner to confer, then came back and asked Anderson if they could parlay with him. For more privacy the four retreated to another casemate, which Crawford and Foster had been sleeping in. It had a couple of tables and camp beds. It retained a certain degree of order, therefore seemed a place to hold a reasoned discussion. The aides asked Anderson to write down precisely his conversation with Wigfall. They said they would carry it to the general in Charleston, and he might accept it. Anderson went over to a small table in a corner and began to write.

The inside of Fort Sumter was still decidedly warm, the air filled with smoky residue. The light in the casemate was murky because its doorway had been partly blocked to keep the room relatively shell-proof. Recently, Dr. Crawford had felt ill, perhaps with urinary problems, hardly surprising given his recent diet. He had prescribed himself tiny doses of iodide of potassium, and had kept a bottle of it by his bed. Pryor was thirsty. He noticed a bottle of liquid nearby, and a glass next to it. Thinking it was water, he poured himself a large dollop, threw back his head, and downed it. Instantly he knew he had made a mistake. He yelped at Anderson for assistance, and Crawford was sent for. When the surgeon ran in, Pryor admitted he had just swallowed a large amount of that liquid, pointing toward it. The surgeon told him he had doubtless just poisoned himself. The Virginian begged Crawford to do something for him, "for I would not have anything happen to me in this fort for any consideration." Crawford hurried him down to a casemate designated as the fort's dispensary, found a stomach pump, shoved a tube down the Virginian's gullet, and cleared out the poor man's belly. That night, when a crowd in Charleston gathered outside Pryor's hotel, demanding a speech on this wonderful occasion, he staggered out, looking wan, and with a scratchy voice said he was too unwell to say more than that the victory was great, then disappeared quickly back into his bedroom.

At his makeshift desk Anderson finished jotting down his recollections of his earlier conversation with Wigfall. While everyone waited for Pryor to return from his purging, Anderson asked about Confederate casualties. The aides replied that a few of their men had received minor wounds, but not one man had been killed. Anderson felt vast relief. "Thank God," he said, and meant it. He would always consider it, as he later said, one of his proudest moments, because he had not "taken the life of another human being." "There has been a higher power over us." How else, he wondered, could one explain two days of ferocious bombardment — about a thousand shots fired by Sumter and 3,341 by the island batteries — yet no one killed on either side, except a single horse stabled behind Moultrie?

As to the casualties on the Confederate side, Doubleday would always remain convinced that many men had been killed at Moultrie, a fact, he believed, that had been suppressed. In his own account he cited stories about attempts to hush up the matter. For example, someone told him that a number of bodies had been secretly buried in an obscure graveyard north of Charleston. On the other hand, the after-battle reports from Confederate officers were clear and specific; they described only "four trifling contusions," all at Fort Moultrie. To be sure, these reports referred only to *soldiers*. The island encampments were packed with civilian laborers, especially slaves. Some of them might have been killed and their deaths gone unreported.[12]

While Anderson was chatting with Beauregard's aides, two more aides arrived from the city. Beauregard had sent these men as soon as he'd heard about the white flag. One was David R. Jones, a West Point classmate of both Foster and Seymour, who was the general's closest adjutant and therefore in the best position to speak confidently. When Beauregard had sent Jones that afternoon, the general had known nothing of Wigfall's adventure. Beauregard, Jones said, was prepared to make Anderson an offer. If the garrison would evacuate the fort, they could do so under the same conditions he had offered two days previously — with one key exception: They would not be permitted to salute their flag. Jones now read what Anderson had just written about the Wigfall conversation. Jones said he was authorized to agree with everything but the salute, then asked if that would be a deal breaker. Anderson said no, he would not insist on it, though his men would be extremely gratified to salute the flag they had "so gallantly defended." On that note all five aides left the fort.

David Jones returned that evening with the news that Beauregard, in the general's own words, "cheerfully agreed to the salute, as an honorable testimony to the gallantry and fortitude with which Major Anderson and his command had defended their post." According to his calculation they could salute their flag the next morning, then take a Charleston steamboat from the wharf out to their waiting fleet.[13]

This second day of the Civil War was almost over. Beauregard sent a surgeon and the city's fire chief out with fire engines to see if the garrison needed any assistance. The offer was gracefully refused.

In Charleston and out on the islands there still lingered a concern about the fleet. Robert Rhett, Jr., wired Secretary Walker in Montgomery that Sumter had fallen, but added, "Fight expected on Morris Island tonight." Captain Hartstene was also uneasy. He sent Beauregard a dispatch saying that he planned to go out to the mouth of the harbor after dark to keep an eye open for any attempt by the armada to slip in. He would signal if he saw anything.

The men of Fox's fleet pondered the meaning of the sudden silence in the harbor. At 2:30 they sent a lieutenant in a rowboat to find out what was going on, directing him to go to Moultrie where they thought Beauregard was stationed. As the boat moved past Morris Island, one of the island batteries fired two warning shots. The first was a blank cartridge, but the second hit close enough to spray water across the boat's occupants. The nearby sand dunes were crowded with lounging soldiers who cheered the accurate shooting. The boat turned toward Cummings Point, its lieutenant frantically waving a white flag. Eventually, he found General Simons. Had Major Anderson surrendered? Yes, unconditionally. Could the ship, the *Pawnee*, come in — under a clear flag of truce — and take the garrison off? If not, could the unarmed merchant steamer *Baltic* do so? Simons said he would relay these questions to Beauregard in Charleston; the lieutenant could return in the morning for the general's response.

By the way, asked Simons, would the lieutenant promise that Fox's fleet would not try an attack tonight? Yes, said the lieutenant, he guaranteed it. He would be back early tomorrow.[14]

That evening Eba received two telegrams, one from her mother in Savannah, the other from her brother, Bayard, in Charleston. They both told her Fort Sumter had fallen, and that Robert had survived. She visited with a few friends.[15]

At Sumter the garrison slept soundly.

It was dark, well before dawn, when Captain Hartstene arrived at Sumter's wharf. Accompanied by several of Beauregard's aides, he had come to pick up Lieutenant Snyder and take him out to the fleet. It was nine by the time they returned.

The garrison had been awake for hours, bustling about, getting ready to leave. According to Beauregard's agreement they could take with them all their personal belongings, plus the "company property," which meant the few remaining barrels of food, hospital supplies, kettles, tables. This was a lot of stuff to be moved by tired men. Tentatively, they were to depart in early afternoon.

Hartstene entered the fort and spoke briefly to Major Anderson. Would it be all right with the major to use the small steamer *Isabel* to transport his men and goods? Anderson assented. Hartstene handed him a Sumter mailbag with letters that had piled up the past six days at the Charleston post office. Anderson was happy, probably for the first time in quite a while, and smilingly distributed the mail.

The weather was glorious, the sort of day when Charleston really is the center of the universe. Mild breezes spread the scent of spring flowers from the city's courtyards. It was a Sunday and had been declared "A Day of National Fasting, Thanksgiving, and Prayer." God was certainly on their side. By late morning happy citizens found vessels to take them about the harbor so they could watch the proceedings of the American flag being lowered and the Confederate and South Carolina flags being raised. Folks brought picnic baskets. Women carried parasols to protect them from too much sunlight. Ferrymen made a handsome living that day. The harbor seemed a vast regatta, boats of all sizes sporting colorful bunting and twirling about Sumter's somber pile of stone and bricks, smoke still drifting above its walls.

Lieutenant Davis went in to Charleston to pick up Annie, but Beauregard decided that the lieutenant should not be permitted to enter the city. Later that day Beauregard's aide Chisholm brought her to the fort. Davis thanked him emotionally. Chisholm and Annie asked him about the experience of the bombardment. He tried to tell them, then broke down weeping. Tension and exhaustion require a toll.

In late morning the *Isabel* anchored seventy yards off the wharf, because of the shallowness of the waters there, and a smaller boat carried the garrison's things out to her. It was a cumbersome process and took longer than had been planned. Some of the enlisted men signaled to passing Carolinians that they were quite interested in inebriates. A generous citizen gave them some brandy, and it was rapidly consumed. Anderson handed an agent from Beauregard several keys to the fort, most useless now since the doors they had fit had been devoured by fire. The keys to the magazines still worked, but when Anderson showed the man the main magazine, its copper door was still too hot to touch. The major shook the man's hand and said, "Pray present to General Beauregard my compliments and thanks for the many acts of courtesy and kindness that he extended to me and my command."

At 2:30 the fort's guns were ready to give their final salute to the American flag. Several of the garrison had worked furiously that morning sewing cartridges. The proper number was a delicate question. Someone asked Anderson if he planned to fire a thirty-four-gun salute, ignoring the fact of secession, and he replied, "No, it is one hundred, and those are scarcely enough." He broke into sobs.[16]

Lieutenant Hall had the assignment of firing the salute. He took several gun crews to the parapet and chose some serviceable cannon on the side facing the Atlantic. The teams piled cartridge bags near the carriages, loaded the guns, and announced they were ready. The rest of the garrison stood below on the parade ground along with the workmen, all of them standing more or less where they had on December 27. The American flag, raised one last time this day, pressed by a strong breeze, floated back toward the city.

The gun crews began firing the cannon methodically but quickly. The hour was getting late. If they did not board the *Isabel* within thirty minutes the tide would have dropped too much, and they'd be stuck in this harbor another night.

Not far away, Governor Francis Pickens and a large party of dignitaries waited with General Beauregard for this process to be completed so they could go to Sumter and initiate their ceremonial celebrations. The general was growing impatient. He was seen to count the number of shots being fired. When the number passed twenty-seven he grimaced in annoyance, thinking that Anderson was choosing to insult them by ignoring the Confederacy. When the number of shots passed thirty-four, he relaxed again. Just before the count reached fifty there was an explosion from the fort, followed a few minutes later by three more salutes, then silence. Fifty in all, not a hundred.

On the parapet an accident had taken place. One of the guns had fired prematurely. Private Daniel Hough was in the process of ramming a cartridge bag into its muzzle, when the blast ripped off his right arm at the shoulder and flung him to the ground. A chunk of something hot whammed into a pile of nearby cartridges, which exploded, flinging about the detritus of the recent battle: broken brick and slate, lead and pieces of wood. Every member of the gun crew was wounded.

When poor Hough had enlisted in 1849, naming his occupation as "farmer," he was twenty-three, but his hair had grown noticeably gray. In 1857, while stationed in Florida, he had shown signs of emotional problems. His commanding officer wrote the Adjutant General's Office that Private Hough, "is so crazy as to be unmanageable and I would respectfully recommend that he be sent to the Insane Asylum." He had always been a quiet person, and his condition was new. According to a medical examiner, Hough suffered some sort of emotional seizures during which he became uncontrollably "violent and unruly, assaulting anyone that might be in his way." In the summer of 1857 the army ordered Private Hough to Washington for treatment at St. Elizabeth's Hospital for the Insane. In September the hospital staff concluded Hough was fit for service, and they returned him to his regiment. He may not have been completely cured—his records show that he was sentenced to Moultrie's guardhouse in April 1860—but for some reason the army had kept him on. Daniel Hough now became the first soldier officially "killed" in this war. (Those South Carolinians who had died earlier—the soldiers killed in accidents or by disease—these did not count since war had not yet begun. Those workers and slaves who may have been killed in the bombardment were not soldiers.) Before two hours passed Hough was buried in the sandy soil of the parade ground. A minister from Charleston, a grizzled ex-sailor named William B. Yates, performed the service, watched by members of the garrison and also by some of the Palmetto Guard, who had arrived to participate in the later ceremonies. Edmund Ruffin and some others placed a makeshift cross over the grave.

Private Edward Gallway was also injured in the explosion. Born in Cork, Ireland, he was perhaps the youngest soldier of the garrison. He was taken quickly to a hospital in Charleston, but he died that night and was buried in a Charleston cemetery. Private George Fielding, born in Waterford, Ireland, also badly wounded in the accident, was taken to a hospital facility in Charleston. Here he lingered for six weeks until sufficiently recuperated that Beauregard permitted him to leave for the North without waiting for an exchange. Three other members of the gun crew who were also seriously wounded were put on mattresses and placed aboard the *Isabel,* where Crawford supervised their care.

Why did the accident occur? It is impossible to know. Exhausted men make mistakes. Maybe they did not swab out the gun properly after the previous shot, maybe a man forgot to put his thumb down on the vent hole, maybe the cartridge itself had been sewed too loosely and some powder had dribbled out. It had been almost miraculous that some such accident had not happened before, either at Fort Sumter or on the island batteries manned by amateur soldiers.

The explosion and the follow-up added an extra hour or two, and it was almost 4:30 when the garrison marched out through the blackened gate. Six men held aloft Peter Hart's tall, heavy spar with the American flag attached. Their clothes were ragged. A month earlier Foster had written a friend, asking for thread. He had wanted to patch his uniform, "for I swear I am in tatters." Now they looked like remnants from Valley Forge. As they started toward the ship, their band struck up "Yankee Doodle." It seemed right somehow. (For some reason they followed that with "Hail to the Chief.")

Due to the delay, the *Isabel* was stuck on the shoal, just a few yards from Fort Sumter, and Anderson's garrison had to listen all night to the sounds of speechifying inside the fort and revelry throughout the harbor. Captain Hartstene, an empathetic man, sensed their discomfort. He raised their flag over his ship so they might feel less alienated.

The next morning, April 15, 1861: The tide rose and the *Isabel* headed toward the fleet. As the steamer passed Cummings Point the soldiers of the Marion Artillery, led by Captain J. Gadsden King, saw it coming. They silently took off their caps and stood at attention on the sands, in honor of their gallant foe.[17]

Mystic Chords of Memory:
A Postscript

F ort Sumter's battered garrison wended northward three days on the *Baltic*. On April 18 they arrived, still ex hausted, at New York's harbor. It was a fine spring day. Doubleday and Seymour ordered the two companies drawn up in full uniform on the quarterdeck. Major Anderson, enshrouded against chillier northern temperatures in a heavy overcoat, stood above them at the wheelhouse. They had no way of knowing what sort of reception they would receive. They had, after all, just been beaten in a battle. From the *Baltic*'s foremast waved Fort Sumter's giant garrison flag, weathered and faded. Lashed to the ship's mizzenmast was the spar from Sumter's flagstaff, and the storm flag that had withstood the island batteries for two days.

As the ship entered New York Harbor, suddenly all about them they saw scores of ships and thousands of people on the banks. Then the batteries along the harbor's mouth opened up in salute, ships around them rang bells and tooted their horns, men and women on boats and on the shoreline waved flags and screamed out love. They were being welcomed . . . home.

At noon the steamer anchored off Sandy Hook. In his cabin, An derson dictated his official statement of the battle. His face had deep lines, and his voice was still hoarse from damage wrought by the recent heat and smoke. He was too exhausted to put pen to paper coherently so Gustavus Fox offered to take dictation for him. He wanted this message sent to Simon Cameron, secretary of war:

> Sir — Having defended Fort Sumter for thirty-four hours, until the quarters were entirely burned, the main gates destroyed by fire, the gorge wall seriously injured, the magazine surrounded by flames, and its door closed from the effects of the heat, four barrels and three cartridges of powder only being available, and no provisions but pork remaining, I accepted terms of evacuation offered by General Beauregard, being the same offered by him on the 11th inst., prior to the commencement of hostilities, and marched out of the fort Sunday afternoon, the 14th inst., with colors flying and drums beating, bringing away company and private property, and saluting my flag with fifty guns.
>
> Robert Anderson, Major, First Artillery

It was but a single sentence, long, awkward, packed with facts . . . and with emotion.

A few minutes later he departed the *Baltic.* As he did, the men of the garrison and even the last of Foster's workmen came out to say farewell. They stood by the bulwarks and on the hurricane decks and bellowed out their cheers. He raised his cap to them, tears rolling down his cheeks, then spun quickly and left.

Wherever his carriage went that afternoon crowds on the sidewalks shouted to see the Hero of Fort Sumter. He tried to smile and raise his hat in the constant recognition. Eventually, he reached the Brevoort. When he entered he saw his eldest daughter, Eliza, now fifteen, run down the stairs. He leaped forward and caught her before she reached the bottom and clasped her to him. The two disappeared up the stairs. Half an hour later, the shouts from a throng of perhaps a thousand people brought him out to a balcony to raise his hat once again in silent salute.

Anderson's next few days were much like that. He was weary but felt that his duty, as well as good manners, demanded that he acknowledge the support he was receiving. A shy man, he may have felt secret pleasure receiving such amazing adulation — the most striking example of which took place the second day after his arrival. He agreed to come to Union Square, with the flags he still kept with him, to participate in a patriotic meeting of some sort. Early in the day he met some politicians, and they escorted him to a grandstand in the square. The police estimated the massive mob at between 150,000 and 250,000; in either case, the police said, it was the largest gathering in the history of the city.

Peter Hart was also there, and he hung the garrison flag from a high tree above the grandstand; he lay the storm flag, still attached to its spar, across the arms of George Washington, whose equestrian statue graced the square. Before Anderson arrived, Hart, the New York City policeman, agreed to say a few words. "I see here," he said, "a great many patriotic hearts before me, who on each day [down there] we were wishing were with us at Fort Sumter when we were sustaining the flag of our country and our laws." The ovations for Hart—and for the flags—rolled across him. The cheers for Major Anderson when he arrived grew tumultuous. George Templeton Strong, a diarist in New York, wrote, "The city seems to have gone suddenly wild and crazy."[1] Robert Anderson and his confreres were, for the moment, superstars.

In a few days the excitement was over. Other events, farther south, captured the public's attention.

Foster's workmen disembarked from the *Baltic* and disappeared from history. The garrison's two companies, E and H, settled for some weeks at the army base where their families had been quartered, then were sent off to the Shenandoah Valley to participate in the new, great war. The officers spread out in various directions.

Virginia had seceded while the *Baltic* steamed toward New York. Lieutenant Meade resigned his commission to serve his native state and would die before the year was up. Snyder fought at Bull Run in July, but died in Washington in November. Talbot died in the same city a few months later. The garrison's other officers survived the war, each rising rapidly in rank. But their health was impaired, perhaps triggered by their months at Fort Sumter. Though none was actually killed in battle, all ten officers were either dead by 1874 or had retired for medical reasons.

———

On April 17, 1861, a band of ninety Texans slipped up to the *Star of the West* while it was docked in Galveston and captured her. She became part of the Confederate navy.

Louis Wigfall became a Confederate politician. His exploit of April 13 remained his most famous single act. He served for a time as an aide to Jefferson Davis, though he came to believe, like many, that the Confederate president was responsible for most of the South's disasters. At the end of the war he eluded notice by shaving his head and wearing a private's uniform. He fled to London, stayed there a few years, and returned to die in Texas in 1874.

Roger Pryor went to New York after the war, studied law, and became a respected lawyer, ending his career on New York's supreme court.

P. G. T. Beauregard had a relatively distinguished career as a Confederate general. He won the first big battle of the war at Bull Run in July 1861. He saved the Southern army at Shiloh in 1862. After that, he served with distinction at Charleston and elsewhere, but he never quite received the respect he believed due him. The civilians of Charleston and New Orleans adored him, but he often annoyed politicians like Jefferson Davis and his fellow generals. He spent his postwar years, like too many on both sides, defending each move he had made during the war.

Jefferson Davis — who soon rid himself of his incompetent secretary of war Leroy Walker — was a strong leader of his Cause, perhaps too strong for a people who resented authority enough to secede from its prospect. For two years following the war he was imprisoned in a dank and unhealthy prison cell, but after his release he survived long enough to write his memoirs.

Edmund Ruffin committed suicide at the end of the war.

Charleston and Fort Sumter each felt the wrath of war.

After the great fort fell to the South Carolinians, things in Charleston calmed down for a while. Within a few days dozens of merchant ships were again each day arriving and leaving. Most of the batteries on Morris Island were dismantled. Many of South Carolina's soldiers were permitted to leave service after Fort Sumter's fall. Two entire regiments were disbanded. A third was sent north to Virginia to join the large Confederate army gathering near a railroad station at Manassas, near the stream called Bull Run.

Eventually, federal ships began a blockade of Charleston, but energetic merchants found it easy at first to elude it. Things became gradually more difficult after a Union army captured the Beaufort region seventy miles to the south, using it as a base of operations for blockaders. Even then, it took a while before Charleston's economy felt much pinch, well into 1862. After that things went downhill. Prominent families began to move away, a few at a time. Mary and James Chesnut had long since departed for Richmond.

As to Fort Sumter, the efforts of hundreds of slaves and white laborers made the fort usable again, and it served to hold off Lincoln's forces trying to take Charleston from the sea. As long as it held out, no Union fleet could enter the harbor unscathed. Charleston would remain relatively safe unless the fort fell or unless a Union army came up behind the city from the state's interior.

There were those in the North who were determined that Charleston must be punished. They included Foster and Seymour, both of whom would lead attacks on the city during the war, but mostly it was Gustavus Fox, Lincoln's new assistant secretary of the navy, who was obsessed with Charleston. In 1863 both the U.S. Army and U.S. Navy made determined attempts to take Fort Sumter. A whole fleet, including ironclads, attacked the fort — but those at the fort beat them back. Meanwhile, thousands of Union soldiers died trying to secure Morris Island and Sullivan's Island. All attempts to reach the city failed. In an act of pure maliciousness, the army brought its biggest mortar to the islands, the Swamp Angel they called her. They used her to pitch shells into Charleston from a distance, simply to kill people and cause havoc.

All things considered, Charleston remained fairly unscathed. Of all the Southern states South Carolina was the best protected. She had Virginia and North Carolina to her north to act as buttresses, and Georgia and other states to the south. But when Savannah, only a hundred miles away, fell to Sherman's army late in 1864, the end loomed. More of the city's white population departed, including Confederate soldiers who burned the railroad station and hundreds of bales of cotton as they left, which set off piles of ammunition, killing hundreds of civilians, mostly impoverished people who had been using the station as a place to sleep. By the end of the war most of Charleston's population consisted of slaves—whose status was about to change. Even the Rhetts, father and son, had abandoned the *Mercury*; a black woman homesteaded its empty offices.

Columbia, South Carolina, fell first; then on February 17, 1865, Union troops marched into Charleston. They immediately went out to Fort Sumter and raised an American flag over it. The fort did not look like much now. Years of bombardment by Union artillery had reduced most of it to rubble. Almost 50,000 shells had been thrown against it. (Not all had exploded. In 1949, as part of the preparation for turning it into a national monument, soldiers carefully sifted through its soil; it took them eight days to locate all the live shells still buried beneath the sand and bricks.[2])

In May 1861 Robert Anderson was asked by Abraham Lincoln to come to Washington. The president personally thanked him for all he had done, and wanted him to go to Cincinnati to organize the vast numbers of state militia being raised by Midwestern governors. Lincoln was raising three separate armies: one in Washington and one beyond the Mississippi River; Anderson's would be the third. Lincoln understood the importance of keeping Kentucky from joining the Confederacy; having her favorite son—now Brigadier General Anderson—across the Ohio River should be helpful. Anderson, however, wanted nothing to do with this war; as he had already said, his "heart was not in it." Yet he was a soldier who did his duty, and he went. Then, in September, when Confederate troops raided Kentucky, and Union soldiers entered that state for the first time, Lincoln ordered General Anderson to move aggressively. Whether it was Anderson's natural pacifist reluctance to fight or his declining health, he asked out of this assignment and his wishes were granted. An army medical report cryptically described his condition as "softening of the brain." Could this have meant Alzheimer's, a touch of dementia? No, he was still giving eloquent speeches for years thereafter. There is no clear way of knowing what the report meant, but he was indeed weak and became easily tired. He had probably suffered from a weakened heart for years, and his many weeks at Fort Sumter had certainly exhausted him. (If the report was suggesting he was emotionally unstable, it was likely correct. In fact he may have suffered a mild breakdown in the fall of 1861; the overpowering stressors of that year could have easily accomplished that.) He lingered in military sinecures for a while, then in 1863 he finally resigned for reasons of health.

Late in the war a soldier from Sherman's army, visiting New York, was approached at the Metropolitan Hotel by an elderly man with white hair. The old fellow, wearing a weathered army cape, handed over his card, which indicated he was Robert Anderson, major general. The young officer was one of Sherman's adjutants and Anderson just wanted to say hello to a subordinate of "Cump" Sherman — "one of my boys," Anderson called him.[3]

In 1865 Anderson was asked to perform one last service for his country. Secretary of War Stanton wanted to emphasize the symbolic nature of Fort Sumter. The fort had officially fallen to the Confederacy on April 14, 1861; Stanton decreed that on April 14, 1865, a special ceremony would be performed atop its sands. He wanted General Robert Anderson, who still had possession of Sumter's flags, to go back to Charleston and raise the exact flag he had taken down the day they had left, four years earlier. Stanton also invited numerous prominent dignitaries, including the famous abolitionist Henry Ward Beecher. William Lloyd Garrison also came; he would stand at Charleston's main slave market, step up on the block, and speak of freedom. In the crowd around him stood a number of African Americans, now free. Later, Garrison led a large crowd in the singing of "Roll, Jordan Roll," and "John Brown's Body."

Anderson agreed to go. Eba of course was too unwell and stayed home. He traveled by ship accompanied by his six-year-old son, arriving several days before the official ceremony. General Anderson, like most dignitaries, stayed aboard ship. The city had few public accommodations available — other than the Charleston Hotel, which was doing its usual, booming business. The city looked ill-used. All the paving had been taken up from the Battery's promenade to be turned into protective barriers. The Union siege and bombardment, which had lasted nearly six hundred days, had broken windows, caved in roofs, smashed up roads. Most of the lovely gardens had gone to seed and birds searched about curiously for their accustomed nectar. Many houses were deserted. Some had been expropriated for military use by order of the provost-marshal. The Race Course was a wreck. It had been used as a prison for Union prisoners of war, many of whom had died there.

On the morning of April 14, 1865, Charleston's great harbor was packed. Hundreds of vessels crowded it, all bearing banners and streamers. Thousands of people were there. Abner Doubleday was in attendance, as was Norman Hall. One of the ships in the harbor was *The Planter,* owned and captained by Robert Smalls. On this day his boat was crowded with African Americans, freed men and women who wanted to observe the great occasion.

Visitors arriving at Fort Sumter's rubble that morning stepped through two lines of soldiers, one white, one black, all sternly at attention. Between three thousand and five thousand celebrants crowded onto the acre or so of space. Several whispered to each other some news, just announced, that Robert E. Lee had surrendered to Ulysses S. Grant five days earlier. In the middle of what had been the parade ground they noticed a flagstaff nearly 150 feet high, erected just for this occasion.

The ceremonies opened with a prayer by old Reverend Matthias Harris, who had been the chaplain that day on December 27, 1860, and had given the prayer when they first raised their flag over Sumter. Someone read aloud Anderson's one-sentence summary of the bombardment, the one he had dictated to Fox. Its pounding short phrases still retained their dignity. Then Peter Hart stepped forward. In his hand he carried the garrison's battered old mailbag. Anderson had used it to store the flags all these years. When Hart pulled the scorched and ripped flag from the bag and held it dramatically up, an animal roar erupted from the crowd. Hart and three sailors attached it to the halyards, then stood aside and waited.

Robert Anderson stood up. He held his hat under his arm; his thin, white hair blew in the breeze. He stood there, very erect, for a long moment, obviously rattled by powerful emotions. He had not wanted to speak. He had thought the whole ceremony should have been a religious service, but Stanton had pressed him. He finally began speaking. "I am here, my friends, my fellow citizens and fellow soldiers, to perform an act of duty to my country. . . . After four long, long years of war, I restore to its proper place this dear flag." He took the halyards in his hands, and continued. "I thank God that I have lived to see this day, and to be here, to perform this, perhaps the last act of my life, of duty to my country. My heart is filled with gratitude to that God who has so signally blessed us, who has given us blessings beyond measure." He prayed that all nations would one day proclaim, "Glory to God in the highest, and on earth peace, good will to men." He tried to pull on the heavy ropes, but found the effort too taxing to do alone. With the help of Hart and the sailors the flag rose to its place. The band played "The Star-Spangled Banner." The thousands in the audience sprang to their feet. When they reached its closing lines, "Oh, long may it wave, O'er the land of the free, and the home of the brave," people wept and hugged one another. Following Stanton's orders, cannons boomed out from each of the old Confederate batteries that had fired on the fort, at least those still there. From Fort Johnson, from Cummings Point, from Fort Moultrie, and others came their roar. The guns of the ships throughout the harbor gave out their own salutes to Anderson's — and America's — old flag.

There were other speeches that day, lots of them. But the most moving was given that night, once again by Robert Anderson. After the flag-raising ceremony, he went to the Charleston Hotel to attend a dinner being given by the military district's commanding general. Following the meal there were many, many toasts. Doubleday stood and praised the enlisted men of Fort Sumter. Joseph Holt, Buchanan's last secretary of war, stood and praised Anderson. Finally Robert stood.

Four years later he would depart the United States to live in France, where he died in 1871. The French government gave him a military funeral, and his remains were returned to America to be interred in a cemetery at West Point. As a cadet, and in all his decades in the army, he had served the *whole* of the nation, not just a state or a region. During the Civil War he had come to recognize that that was how President Lincoln, another native Kentuckian, felt. He thought of that when he rose to present his toast. "I beg you now," he said, his glass in hand, "that you will join me in drinking the health of another man whom we all love to honor — the man who, when elected President of the United States, was compelled to reach the seat of government without an escort, but a man who now could travel *all* over our country with millions of hands and hearts to sustain him. I give you the good, the great, the honest man, Abraham Lincoln."[4]

It was a few minutes after ten o'clock. At almost that precise moment John Wilkes Booth put a gun to the head of the president of the United States and pulled the trigger.

Notes

T
hroughout this book I have occasionally altered the original manuscript text in slight matters involving punctuation and spelling, but only to modernize nineteenth-century usage.

For the sake of brevity, I have used the following shorthand notations in the footnotes:

AD   Abner Doubleday Papers, New-York Historical Society.

AL   *The Collected Works of Abraham Lincoln,* 9 vols., New Brunswick, NJ: Rutgers University Press, 1953–55.

BAL   *Battles and Leaders of the Civil War,* 4 vols.

ER   Edmund Ruffin, *The Diary of Edmund Ruffin,* edited by William Kauffman Scarborough, 3 vols., Baton Rouge: Louisiana State University Press, 1972–80.

FM   Archives, Fort Moultrie Museum.

GEN   Samuel Wylie Crawford, *The Genesis of the Civil War: Fort Sumter, 1860–1861,* 1887.

JD   Jefferson Davis, *The Papers of Jefferson Davis,* eds. Lynda Lasswell Crist et al., Baton Rouge: Louisiana State University Press, 1971–.

LSUP   Baton Rouge: Louisiana State University Press.

MIL   H. L. Scott, *Military Dictionary,* 1861.

OR   *The War of the Rebellion: A Compilation of the Official Records of the Union and Confederate Armies,* 1880–1901.

ORN   Official Records of the Union and Confederate Navies in the War of Rebellion, 1897–1927.

RA   Robert Anderson Papers, Library of Congress.

REM   Abner Doubleday, *Reminiscences of Forts Sumter and Moultrie in 1860–'61,* 1876.

SCHS   South Carolina Historical Society, Charleston, SC.

SCL   South Caroliana Library, University of South Carolina, Columbia, SC.

SWC   Samuel Wylie Crawford Papers, Library of Congress.

TT   Theodore Talbot Papers, Library of Congress.

UNCP   University of North Carolina Press, Chapel Hill, NC.

USC   University of South Carolina, Columbia, SC.

USCP   University of South Carolina Press, Columbia, SC.

Chapter One: Asunder

1. Thomas R. Waring, "Red-Light Reflections," *The* (Charleston) *News & Courier,* January 11, 1981; John G. Leland, "Early Taverns in Charleston, *Preservation Progress,* XVI (No. 3), pp. 1ff; Leland, "History of the Unholy City," *Charleston Magazine,* May/June 1991, pp. 19ff; "Charleston's Other Side," *Chicora Foundation Research,* VIII (No. 4), 1995, p. 5; "Prostitution" file, SCHS; William H. and Jane H. Pease, *The Web of Progress: Private Values and Public Styles in Boston and Charleston, 1828–1843,* New York: Oxford University Press, 1985, p. 102.

2. Calculated from the Records of Legare & Colcock, December 31, 1860, SCHS.

3. John C. Roberson, "The Foundation of Southern Nationalism: Charleston and the Low Country, 1847–1861," Ph.D. dissertation, USC, 1991, pp. 66–67; John P. Radford, "Culture, Economy and Urban Structure in Charleston, South Carolina, 1860–1880," Ph.D. dissertation, Clark University, 1974, pp. 126, 129; Peter A. Coclanis, *The Shadow of a Dream: Economic Life and Death in the South Carolina Low Country, 1670–1920,* New York: Oxford University, Press, 1989, pp. 118–19; Charleston Typographical Union No. 43, Southern Typographical Union No. 1, Records, 1859–1862, SCL.

4. D. E. Huger Smith, "A Charlestonian's Recollections: 1846–1913," Charleston: Carolina Art Association, 1950, p. 59.

5. ER, I, 517–18.

6. Jack Alexander Sutor, "Charleston, South Carolina during the Civil War Era, 1858–1865," master's thesis, Duke University, 1943, p. 27; Rosser H. Taylor, *Ante-Bellum South Carolina,* Chapel Hill, NC, 1942, pp. 168–69.

7. Sutor, pp. 64–65; Robertson, pp. 117, 121.

8. Bernard Edward Powers, Jr., "Black Charleston: A Social History, 1822–1885," Ph.D. dissertation, Northwestern University, 1972, pp. 48–57; Taylor, p. 185.

9. James D. Johnson to Henry Ellison, September 16, 1860; Michael P.

Johnson and James L. Roark, eds., *No Chariot Let Down: Charleston's Free People of Color on the Eve of the Civil War,* 1984, pp. 119–21, 144n.

10. Dorothy Sterling, *Captain of the Planter: The Story of Robert Smalls,* NY: 1958.

11. Jack Kenny Williams, *Vogues in Villainy: Crime and Retribution in Ante-Bellum South Carolina,* USCP, 1959, p. 31.

12. Ibid., p. 38. The rest of the Deep South was as violent as South Carolina, some states perhaps more so, but there is no way to compare tendencies toward violence with any confidence.

13. William Kingsford, *Impressions of the West and South during a Six Weeks' Holiday,* 1858: "What struck me particularly in Charleston," he said, "was the police organization. It is a perfect *gens d'armerie,*" p. 77; Edward G. Mason, "A Visit to South Carolina in 1860," *Atlantic Monthly,* February, 1884, LIV, 243.

14. *Courier,* September 14; October 11; October 18; October 27, p. 2; October 29, 1860.

15. John Berkley Grimball, December 17, 1860, Papers, Special Collections, College of Charleston; Henry William Ravenel, *The Private Journal of Henry William Ravenel, 1859–1887,* ed. Arney Robinson Childs, 1947, p. 34; Brevard, pp. 38–39, 43; Emma Holmes, *The Diary of Miss Emma Holmes, 1861–1866,* ed. John F. Marszalek, LSUP, 1979, p. 10; H. Pinckney Walker Papers, November 9, 1860, SCHS; Sally Baxter Hampton, *A Divided Heart: Letters of Sally Baxter Hampton, 1853–1862,* ed. Ann Fripp Hampton, Spartanburg, SC: The Reprint Company, 1980, p. 87; Chesnut, p. 25.

16. Jean Martin Flynn, *The Militia in Antebellum South Carolina Society,* Spartanburg, SC: The Reprint Company, 1991.

17. *Courier,* October 15 and 25, 1860; Roy F. Nichols, *The Disruption of American Democracy,* 1948, pp. 361–62; Ravenel, p. 31.

18. *Mercury,* November 6, 1860.

19. Schirmer Diary, November 17 and 22, 1860, Alfred Schirmer Papers, SCHS.

20. *Mercury,* November 12, 1860; Keziah Goodwyn Hopkins Brevard, *A Plantation Mistress on the Eve of the Civil War,* USCP, 1993, p. 49.

21. Lillian A. Kibler, "Unionist Sentiment in South Carolina in 1860," *Journal of Southern History,* August 1938, IV, 346–66.

22. Hammond to Marcus C. Hammond, November 12, 1860, *The Hammonds of Redcliffe,* ed. Carol Bleser, NY: Oxford University Press, 1981, pp. 88–89.

23. *Mercury,* November 21. Did Berry plan this himself? It seems doubtful. The sparse evidence seems to indicate that his employers, the owners of the shipping company, were behind it.

Chapter Two: A Gentle Man

1. Robert Anderson, *An Artillery Officer in the Mexican War, 1846–47: Letters of Robert Anderson,* NY, 1911, p. 93.

2. George Gordon Greenough, "Address Delivered at the U.S. Military

Academy," undated but presumably 1905, the centenary of Anderson's birth, pp. 9–10, Robert Anderson File, Archives, United States Military Academy.

3. Robert to Larz Anderson, August 5, 1832, RA.

4. William C. Davis, *Jefferson Davis: The Man and His Hour,* New York: Harper Collins, 1991, p. 50.

5. For information on both the Black Hawk War and the Seminole Wars, see Francis Paul Prucha, *The Sword of the Republic: The United States Army on the Frontier, 1783–1846,* Lincoln: University of Nebraska Press, 1969.

6. Ibid., pp. 192–193, 229.

7. Anderson, *Artillery Officer,* pp. 81, 91, 179.

8. Ibid., pp. 312–317; W. Marshall Anderson, "A Sketch of Major Robert Anderson," privately printed in Ohio, 1861, pp. 5–6.

9. Anderson to "Sister," February 11, 1827, RA.

10. Anderson, *Artillery Officer,* pp. 30, 56, 103, 124.

11. Ibid., p. 117.

12. Sarah to Robert, January 5, 1842, RA.

13. Ibid.; Larz Anderson to Robert, July 3, 1829; Robert to Maria, July 1, 1834; Robert to Maria, August 24, 1834, RA.

14. Robert to Maria, May 22, 1834, RA.

15. Robert to mother, November 21, 1835, RA.

16. Robert to Scott, January 16, 1841, RA.

17. Duncan Lamont Clinch to Anderson, January 9, 1842, RA.

18. Rembert W. Patrick, *Aristocrat in Uniform: General Duncan L. Clinch,* Gainesville, FL, 1963.

19. April 21, 1857, RA; Frank Moore, ed., *The Rebellion Record,* 1861, I, 129. Another source says, with no attribution, that he did not order the sale of the slaves until after the fall of Fort Sumter in April 1861, which would have been very different from selling them a year earlier: Gary R. Baker, *Cadets in Gray,* Columbia, SC: Palmetto Bookworks, 1989, p. 9n.

20. Robert to Clinch, March 7, 1842, RA.

21. Anderson, *Artillery Officer,* pp. 63–64, 105, 132.

22. May 5, 1858, RA.

23. Robert to Eba, July 8, 1857, RA.

24. Anderson, *Artillery Officer,* p. 207.

25. Ibid., pp. 71, 300.

26. Henry Barton Dawson, "The Story of Fort Sumter," *Historical Magazine,* (January 1872), I, 38.

27. OR, I, 72, 73.

Chapter Three: Salad Days

1. ER, I, 490.

2. Truman Seymour, "Forts Moultrie and Sumter: 1860, 1861," *The History of the First Regiment of Artillery,* 1879, p. 470.

3. Otto Eisenschiml and E. B. Long, "'The Big Ifs' at Fort Sumter," *American Mercur* (April 1956), LXXXII, 95.

4. James Chester, "Inside Sumter in '61," BAL, I, 50–51n.

5. Theodore Talbot to sister, August 14, 1859, TT.

6. Robert Anderson to Maria, July 1, 1834, RA.

7. Talbot to sister, November 20, 1860, TT.

8. Talbot to sister, May 4, 1859, TT.

9. Robert M. Utley, *Frontiersmen in Blue: The United States Army and the Indian, 1848–1865*, New York, 1967, pp. 40–41.

10. MIL, p. 161.

11. Leslie D. Jensen, "The Fort Sumter Flags: A Study in Documentation and Authentication," typescript, U.S. Department of the Interior, National Park Service, Harpers Ferry Center, 1982, pp. 26, 48, 82, and 330–31.

12. MIL, pp. 454–57.

13. James L. Morrison, Jr., *"The Best School in the World": West Point, the Pre–Civil War Years, 1833–1866*, Kent, OH: Kent State University Press, 1986, p. 20. Morrison miscalculates a colonel's salary by $6 a month; in either case the comparison is apt.

14. Edward M. Coffman, *The Old Army: A Portrait of the American Army in Peacetime, 1784–1898*, New York: Oxford University Press, 1986, p. 139.

15. Ibid., pp. 140, 175.

16. Extracted from the "Registers of Enlistments in the United States Army, 1798–1914," Microcopy No. 233, rolls 24–28, National Archives; FM.

17. OR, I, 70.

18. See, for example, David Morgan Ramsey, "The 'Old Sumpter Hero': A Biography of Major-General Abner Doubleday," Ph.D. dissertation, Florida State University, 1980, pp. 11–21.

19. Abner Doubleday, mss., Archives, United States Military Academy; John S. McCalmont, "Abner Doubleday," *Annual Reunion, 1893*, West Point, pp. 88–101; George W. Cullum, *Biographical Register of the Officers and Graduates of the U. S. Military Academy*, 3d ed., Boston, 1893, pp. 132–34.

20. McCalmont, p. 89.

21. Doubleday, reel #24, p. 53. It is unclear when he wrote these notes, but internal evidence indicates it was before 1858.

22. Ibid., p. 13.

23. Ibid., p. 53.

24. For some of the details of Mary Doubleday's life, see McCalmont, pp. 98–99.

25. Doubleday, Reel #24, pp. 38–39.

26. REM, pp. 22–23.

27. Company E, 1st Artillery, Records, FM; Jefferson C. Davis, "Charleston Harbor, 1860–1861: A Memoir from the Union Garrison," *South Carolina Historical Magazine*, ed. James P. Jones, July 1961, LXII, 148–150; Lloyd Lewis, *Sherman: Fighting Prophet*, New York, 1932, pp. 348–49.

28. Talbot to sister, October 22, 1860, TT.

29. He became a captain on November 22, 1860; throughout the crisis his rank placed him just below Doubleday.

30. P. T. Turnley, "Truman Seymour," *Annual Reunion, 1892*, West Point, pp. 35–37.

31. Cullum, pp. 271–72; *Dictionary of American Biography*; *Harper's Weekly*, March 23, 1861, p. 190.

32. REM, p. 23.

33. Talbot to sister, August 14, 1859, TT.

34. Talbot to mother, January 30, 1861, TT.

35. Talbot to mother, February 16, 1861, TT.

36. Norman Hall, mss., Archives, United States Military Academy; Cullum, pp. 726–27; Morris Schaff, *The Spirit of Old West Point, 1858–1862*, Boston, 1908, pp. 69–70.

37. Samuel W. Crawford to his brother, March 4, 1861, SWC.

38. Ibid.

39. Ibid., February 24, 1861, SWC.

Chapter Four: The Fulcrum

1. Seymour, p. 469; Doubleday, p. 25; Theodore Talbot to sister, October 22, 1860, TT.

2. REM, p. 21.

3. Foster to Lewis Robertson, March 26, 1861, Samuel Wylie Crawford, diary, "notes," SWC.

4. Noyes, p. 18; see also Cullum, p. 260, which contains almost the same description.

5. Cullum, pp. 638–39.

6. Dennis Hart Mahan, *A Complete Treatise of Field Fortification*, New York 1836, p. 258. See also William E. Birkhimer, *Historical Sketch of the Organization, Administration, Matériel and Tactics of the Artillery, United States Army*, Washington, DC, 1884.

7. *Mercury*, December 12 and 13, 1860.

8. REM, p. 19, 31–32; George H. Gordon, "Major Anderson at Fort Sumter," *Papers of the Military History of Massachusetts*, 1912, IX, 5.

9. OR, I, 67–68; Foster, p. 6.

10. OR, I, 68–69.

11. Crawford, diary, undated but probably November 9, 1860, SWC. He suspected that a man named Maynard was the one who slipped over to Charleston with the information.

12. Ibid.; GEN, pp. 57–58, has a slightly different account, perhaps not quite as accurate; OR, p. 69.

13. ER, I, 488.

14. *Mercury*, December 19, 1860. Ruffin had always distrusted democratic passions (which might explain his fear of abolitionism and his loathing for what he considered the culture of the North).

15. Humphreys, November 12, 1860, OR, I, 72; Crawford, diary, November 16, 1860, SWC.

16. OR, I, 73.

17. Crawford, diary, undated, but between November 12 and 15, 1860, SWC; Jefferson C. Davis, "Charleston Harbor, 1860–1861: A Memoir of the Union Garrison," *South Carolina Historical Magazine,* July 1961, LXII, 149; REM, p. 40.

18. OR, I, 70–72. According to Porter, it was Humphreys, the arsenal's storekeeper, not the officers at Moultrie, who wanted them to take the ammunition — "in case of negro insurrections." Yet Humphreys's own note on the matter, OR, I, 69, makes no mention of this, and whines that his hands were tied by the "peremptory" nature of Gardner's demands. One may surmise that Porter was supplied this version of events by Gardner, who would have wanted to cover up his connection to the incident when the aqffair went sour.

19. Ibid.; George W. Cullum, "Robert Anderson," *Third Annual Reunion, 1872,* West Point, 1872, p. 30.

20. JD, I, 216; Jefferson Davis to Robert Anderson, December 3, 1860, RA.

21. November 16, 1860, TT.

22. MIL, pp. 75, 240.

23. His daughter, Eba Anderson Lawton, who wrote a loving recollection of her father's experiences at this time, *Major Robert Anderson and Fort Sumter, 1861,* says that he was unacquainted with any other officer at Moultrie, but it would seem she was incorrect (New York, 1911, p. 3).

24. Theodore Talbot to sister, November 20, 1860, Talbot to mother, November 26, 1860, TT.

25. OR, I, 75, 79.

26. Henry Barton Dawson, "The Story of Fort Sumter," *Historical Magazine,* January 1872, XXI, 40.

27. OR, I, 74–76.

28. Ibid., 78–79.

29. Henry Gourdin to Robert, November 19, 1860, RA.

30. REM, p. 42.

31. Rhoades, p. 14; Huger to Robert, December 10, 1860, RA.

32. OR, I, 92–93.

33. Ibid., 81.

34. REM, p. 50.

35. Richard K. Meade, Jr., Papers, Archives, United States Military Academy.

36. GEN, p. 96; OR, I,191.

37. Mary Doubleday to sister, December 11, 1860, reprinted from the New York *Post* by the *Courier,* December 18, 1860; REM, pp. 43–44, 47. The author of the Park Service's official guide to Fort Moultrie has adopted Doubleday's error: Jim Stokeley, *Fort Moultrie: Constant Defender,* Washington, DC: U.S. Department of Interior, 1985, p. 44.

38. OR, p. 82.

Chapter Five: *Twilight of the Old Union*

1. See William Henry Trescot, "Narrative of William Henry Trescot," *American Historical Review*, XIII (1908), 531–56; Robert Nicholas Olsberg, "A Government of Class and Race: William Henry Trescot and the South Carolina Chivalry, 1860–1865," Ph.D. dissertation, USC, 1972; Robert Nicholas Olsberg, "William Henry Trescot: The Crisis of 1860," master's thesis, USC, 1967.

2. Trescot, p,. 532.

3. A. Howard Meneely, *The War Department, 1861,* New York, 1928, pp. 25–26.

4. Ibid., pp. 43–49; Mark W. Summers, *The Plundering Generation: Corruption and the Crisis of the Union, 1849–1861,* New York: Oxford University Press, 1987, pp. 242–46, 259.

5. David Potter, *The Impending Crisis, 1848–1861,* New York: Harper & Row, 1976, pp. 517–18; Trescot, pp. 533–34. There is a discrepancy between these sources, and Trescot's recollections about dates were often a bit awry.

6. Ibid., pp. 534–36. James Buchanan, *The Works of James Buchanan,* ed. John Bassett Moore, New York, 1910, IX, 5.

7. December 22, 1860, AL, IV, 160.

8. Lincoln to William Kellogg, December 11, 1860, ibid., 150; Lincoln to Elihu B. Washburne, December 13, 1860, ibid., 151. Still the best book on Lincoln during these months is David M. Potter, *Lincoln and His Party in the Secession Crisis,* LSUP, 1995, with an introduction by Daniel W. Crofts.

9. Margaret McLean, "When the States Seceded," *Harper's Magazine* (January 1914), CXXVIII, 283–84.

10. *Frank Leslie's Illustrated Weekly,* January 12, 1861, p. 114.

11. GEN, p. 16n.

12. Agnes Sara Pryor, *Reminiscences of Peace and War,* New York, 1908, p. 110.

13. OR, I, 125–128.

Chapter Six: *Commanders and Chiefs*

1. GEN, p. 72.

2. Ibid., p. 74.

3. Ibid., p. 73.

4. OR, I, 89–90.

5. GEN, pp. 72n, 74.

6. OR, I, 103.

7. December 6 and 22, 1860, ibid., pp. 87–88, 105–06.

8. December 6, 1860, ibid., p. 87.

9. Anderson to Gourdin, December 11, 1860, quoted in GEN, p. 69.

10. *Mercury,* December 12, 1860; Crawford to his brother, December 12, 1860, SWC.

11. *Mercury,* December 21, 1860.

12. December 9, 1860, OR, I, p. 89.

13. Ibid., pp. 83–86.

14. December 13, 1860, ibid., p. 90–91; John G. Foster, *Report of Major General John G. Foster to the Committee on the Conduct of the War,* Washington, DC, 1866, II, 6.

15. Ibid.; OR, I, 100–01.

16. For the documents on this affair, see ibid., pp. 94–103; Foster, p. 6; William Henry Trescot, "Narrative of William Henry Trescot," *American Historical Review* (1908), XIII, 539.

17. James Buchanan, *Mr. Buchanan's Administration on the Eve of the Rebellion,* 1866, p. 104; George Ticknor Curtis, *Life of James Buchanan,* New York, 1866, II, 297; French Ensor Chadwick, "Fort Sumter, 1861," *Decisive Battles of the Civil War,* New York, 1909, pp. 236–37.

18. Winfield Scott, *Memoirs of Lieut.-General Scott, NY, 1864,* 1864, I, 615–17; Roy Franklin Nichols, *The Disruption of American Democracy,* New York, 1948, p. 410.

19. *Journal of the Convention of the People of South Carolina, Held in 1860–'61,* 1861, pp. 4–5.

20. Anna C. Brackett, "Charleston, South Carolina, (1861)," *Harper's New Monthly Magazine* (May 1894), LXXXVIII, 946.

21. Robert N. Rosen, *Confederate Charleston,* USCP, 1994, p. 44.

22. Louisa McCord Smythe, "Recollections," typescript, Smythe Papers, SCHS; ER, I, 512–13; *Mercury,* December 21, 1861; W. F. G. Peck, "Four Years under Fire at Charleston," *Harper's New Monthly Magazine,* August 1865, p. 358; Lacy K. Ford, Jr., *Origins of Southern Radicalism: The South Carolina Upcountry, 1800–1860,* New York: Oxford University Press, 1988, p. 303.

Chapter Seven: Slim Pickens, Stout Fort

1. *Journal of the Convention of the People of South Carolina, Held in 1860–'61,* 1861, pp. 36, 58–59, 70–72. See also, Ellison Capers to Samuel Wylie Crawford, August 3, 1883, Capers Papers, and Charles Cotesworth Pinckney, Jr., to "Charley," December 23, 1860, Pinckney Papers, SCL.

2. *The Record of Fort Sumter,* Charleston, 1862, pp. 7–8.

3. Ibid., pp. 9–11.

4. William Henry Trescot, "Narrative of William Henry Trescot," *American Historical Review* (1908), XIII, 542.

5. *Mercury,* November 28, 1860, and December 18, 1860.

6. H. D. Kennedy to Pickens, December 20, 1860, F. W. Pickens Papers, SCL.

7. Crawford, p. 89; Pickens to W. S. Pettigrew, May 18, 1864, RA.

8. OR, I, 101–02.

9. Ibid., p. 106.

10. Ibid., p. 105. See, also, John G. Nicolay and John Hay, *Abraham Lincoln: A History,* NY, 1915, III, 48n.

11. GEN, p. 89.

12. Pickens to W. S. Pettigrew, May 18, 1864, RA; Pickens, "Report to South Carolina Legislature," November 5, 1861. See also, REM, p. 49; GEN, pp. 88–89.

13. Crawford, p. 90; ER, I, 514.

14. Morrison, *"The Best School in the World,"* p. 10; MIL, p. 444.

15. REM, pp. 35–36. This story has some holes. Doubleday provides no specifics about the name of the sergeant or the exact date. An examination of the present archives at Fort Moultrie's museum reveals no match for Doubleday's tale.

16. South Carolina, *Statutes at Large of South Carolina,* V, 501.

17. For the history of the development of Fort Sumter, see Frank Barnes, "Fort Sumter: December 26, 1860," typescript, 1950, FM; "Fort Sumter: Anvil of War," Department of the Interior, National Park Service, 1984; Samuel Wragg Ferguson, "Fort Sumter," typescript, undated, SCHS; GEN, pp. 2–4; W. G. Sheppard, *Story of Fort Sumter,* Charleston, 1938.

18. Elise Rhett Lewis, *Fort Sumter: The Key of Charleston Harbor,* 1896, p. 3.

19. U.S. War Department, *Annual Report of the Secretary of War,* 1856, pp. 15–16; Joseph G. Totten, *The Effects of Firing with Heavy Ordnance from Casemate Embrasures, Papers on Practical Engineering,* Number 6, Engineering Department, 1857, pp. 137–39.

Chapter Eight: Eventide

1. *Mercury,* December 25, 1860; C. Patton Hash, "A Lowcountry Christmas," *Carologue* (Winter 1993), IX, 24.

2. Crawford, diary, December 24, 1860, SWC; *Mercury,* December 25, 1860; "Beleaguered Charleston: Letters from the City, 1860–1864," eds. Martin Abbott and Elmer L. Puryear, *South Carolina Historical Magazine* (April 1960), LXI, 63.

3. Crawford, diary, undated, but written on either December 24 or 25, 1860, SWC; REM, p. 56.

4. Truman Seymour, "Forts Moultrie and Sumter: 1860, 1861," *The History of the First Regiment of Artillery,* 1879, p. 473; Crawford, diary, undated. Crawford to brother, undated but written in late December or early January, SWC.

5. Charles S. Bull to "Theodore," December 19, 1860, Charles S. Bull Papers, SCL; Morrison, *"The Best School in the World,"* p. 126; GEN, p. 91.

6. Theodore Talbot to sister, December 25, 1860, TT; Henry Barton Dawson, "The Story of Fort Sumter," *Historical Magazine* (January 1872), I, 48.

7. Printed in the *Boston Journal,* undated, reprinted in *Mercury,* January 7, 1861; printed in *Harper's Weekly,* January 12, 1861, pp. 17–18.

8. Crawford to brother, undated, but its context indicates late December 1860 or early January 1861, SWC.

9. Much of his scheming can be found in a letter that Robert Anderson wrote to Eba, late December 1860, printed in John G. Nicolay and John Hay, *Abraham Lincoln: A History,* New York, 1915, III, 47–48n; Dawson, p. 49.

10. Crawford to brother, December 12, 1860, SWC. As a surgeon, he may have misunderstood the planning of the other officers. On December 19, 1860, Foster reported that he was placing mines *outside* the fort; these could be triggered from within if it came to an attack. OR, I, 98.

11. Anderson's official report, sent from Fort Sumter at 8:00 P.M., December 26, 1860, OR, I, 2.

12. Hall's recollections, Crawford diary, notes, December 26, 1860, SWC; Anderson to Eba, late December, Nicolay and Hay, I, 48n.

13. REM, p. 67; *Courier,* February 5, 1861.

14. What actually happened was not this neat, though it was certainly better than Robert had a right to expect. Piecing the story together is complicated, probably because so many participants have left us detailed accounts — unfortunately, not in agreement. History, like life, is a matter of connecting the dots, of extracting the facts, or the options, and deciphering from them the most plausible pattern.

15. *Harper's Weekly,* February 9, 1861, p. 87.

16. Miss A. Fletcher, *Within Fort Sumter,* 1861, p. 11 — almost certainly fictional.

17. Eba Anderson Lawton, *Major Robert Anderson and Fort Sumter, 1861,* pp. 8–9.

18. REM, p. 67.

19. Henry B. Dawson to Crawford, February 24, 1872, Henry B. Dawson Papers, SCL; "Thomas Williams," Company E, 1st United States Artillery Regiment, FM.

20. GEN, p. 91.

21. Chester, p. 52.

22. ER, I, 516.

23. Published originally in an undated *Troy Daily News,* reprinted in the *Courier,* January 8, 1861.

Chapter Nine: Dueling Flags

1. December 27, 1860, unsigned note to Samuel Wylie Crawford, Notes, I, SWC; E. Milby Burton, *The Siege of Charleston, 1861–1865,* USCP, 1970, p. 11.

2. OR, I, 213; Frank Barnes, "Fort Sumter, December 26, 1860," U.S. Department of the Interior, National Park Service, File No. 845, 1950; the Davis quotation is among Crawford's "Notes" for December, SWC; Crawford's medical preparations are in an undated letter he sent his brother late in December, ibid.

3. GEN, pp. 109–11; REM, pp. 79–80.

4. Henry Wager Halleck, *Elements of Military Art and Science,* 3d ed., New York, 1863, p. 405.

5. Leslie D. Jensen, "The Fort Sumter Flags: A Study in Documentation and Authentication," U.S. Department of the Interior, National Park Service, Harpers Ferry Center, 1981, typescript.

6. Both accounts were dated January 26, 1861, but appeared almost two weeks earlier, exactly the same, word for word. *Frank Leslie's* states that the story

came from "a Baltimore gentleman who was also present," pp. 145–46; *Harper's*, p. 49. Who was the source of the story? *Frank Leslie's* also claimed that it had the only "news artist" in Charleston. A number of the mechanics were from Baltimore, and so was Foster's brother-in-law, Edward Moale of Baltimore. On that very day *Harper's* wrote Anderson, asking him to supply them with information, but there is no evidence he did so: *Harper's* to Anderson, December 27, 1860, RA. But Crawford, Hall, and Seymour did send things, especially drawings, to that magazine, and were paid to do so: see, e.g., Crawford to his brother, February 21, 1861, SWC; *Harper's Weekly*, March 23, 1861, p. 190.

7. Crawford, diary, December 27, 1860, SWC.

8. Ibid.; *Courier*, December 28, 1860.

9. Alfred Ford Ravenel, Ravenel Papers, SCL; Jacob F. Schirmer, diary, SCHS; Mary Hort, Mary Hort Papers, SCL.

10. Mary Chesnut, *Mary Chesnut's Civil War*, ed. C. Vann Woodward, New Haven, CT: Yale University Press, 1981, p. 48.

11. *Journal of the Convention of the People of South Carolina, Held in 1860–'61*, Charleston, 1861, pp. 114, 118.

12. *Mercury*, January 30, 1861; Mary Chesnut, *The Private Mary Chesnut*, eds. C. Vann Woodward and Elizabeth Muhlenfeld, New York: Oxford University Press, 1984, p. 6.

13. *Mercury*, December 31, 1860.

14. Edward McCrady, Jr., to Crawford from Charleston, Letters, I, December 27, 1860, SWC; letter from Pickens to W. S. Pettigrew, May 18, 1864, RA. Pickens's official orders refer only to the Washington Light Infantry and Meagher Guards (OR, I, 12), but Crawford's note states that the Carolina Light Infantry also went; the *Courier*, December 28, 1860, also lists all three companies. It is possible that this unit arrived later.

15. REM, p. 73.

16. Crawford, diary, notes, December 27, 1860, drawing from Meade's recollections of that day, SWC; Henry Barton Dawson, "The Story of Fort Sumter," *Historical Magazine* (March 1872), I, 152–53n.

17. *The Record of Fort Sumter*, Charleston, 1862, p. 12.

18. *Courier*, December 28, 1860; Burton, *The Siege of Charleston, 1861–1865*, p. 14; Crawford Papers, recollections of Lieutenant Norman C. Hall, December 28, 1860, SWC. Sergeant Williams was released; he apparently tried to sneak over to Sumter and failed, then left for Washington: *Courier*, January 11, 1861.

Chapter Ten: The Wolf at the Door

1. William Howard Russell, *My Diary North and South*, ed. Eugene H. Berwanger, New York: Alfred A. Knopf, 1988, p. 87; "The Diary of a Public Man," *North American Review*, 129, 131; Margaret McLean, "When the States Seceded," *Harper's Magazine*, 128 (January 1914), 285; *The Congressional Globe*, 36th Cong., 2d sess., December 12, 1860, pp. 74, 76.

2. William Henry Trescot, "Narrative of William Henry Trescot," *American Historical Review* (1908), XIII, 543–44; see Nichols, *The Disruption of American Democracy*, p. 428, for a slightly different account.

3. GEN, pp. 148–49; Crawford's source is a letter he received from James L. Orr, one of the commissioners; on Adams's wire: REM, pp. 83–84.

4. OR, I, 115–18.

5. Ibid., 114.

6. Ibid., 252.

7. Curtis, *Life of James Buchanan*, 445–49, 544; James Buchanan, *National Intelligencer*, October 28, 1862; Scott, *Memoirs of Lieut.-General Scott*.

8. Buchanan, *Mr. Buchanan's Administration on the Eve of the Rebellion*, pp. 120–25.

9. Ibid., p. 189.

10. *The Record of Fort Sumter*, compiled by W. A. Harris, 1862, pp. 14–21.

11. Gwynn to Pickens, December 30, 1860, Walter Gwynn Papers, Archives, Duke University; *Courier*, January 7, 1861; *Mercury*, January 3, 1861.

12. OR, I, 5–9.

13. On their supplies and the officers' wives: OR, I, 120; SWC, recollections of Lieutenants Snyder and Hall, December 28, 1860, Diary, January 5, 1861, letter, Crawford to brother, January 5, 1861, SWC; GEN, pp. 117–19; REM, pp. 85–86, 95–100; McLean, pp. 284–85.

14. Larz to Robert, December 28, 1860, RA; *Mercury*, January 4, 7, 9; Crawford, diary, January 6, 1861, SWC; REM, p. 100; McLean, pp. 284–85.

15. OR, I, 120, 133; Talbot to mother, January 6, 1861, TT.

16. Diary, January 8, 1861, SWC.

17. The *Star* incident drawn from issues of the *Mercury* and *Courier*; *New York Evening Post*, January 12, 1861; REM, pp. 102–03; GEN, pp. 139, 174–84; Crawford, diary, January 9, 1861, SWC; *Frank Leslie's Illustrated Weekly*, January 26, 1861, pp. 151, 155; OR, I, 9–10, 128–32, 253; ORN, pp. 219b, 221; H. M. Clarkson, "Story of the Star of the West," *Confederate Veteran* (May 1913), XXI, 234–36; Baker, *Cadets in Gray*, pp. 16–24; Holmes, *The Diary of Miss Emma Holmes*, pp. 2–3; A. M. Vanderhorst, diary, January 7, 1861, SCHS.

18. Bank of Charleston, *Daily Ledger*, Vol. VI, Special Collections, College of Charleston.

19. Fletcher, *Within Fort Sumter*, pp. 14–15 — most likely fictional.

20. *Congressional Globe*, 36th Cong., 2d sess., p. 1373.

Chapter Eleven: Hostages

1. Letter to brother, SWC.

2. Eba Anderson Lawton, *Major Robert Anderson and Fort Sumter, 1861*, p. 9.

3. The story of this meeting and both Hall's and Talbot's subsequent trips to Charleston: Crawford, diary, January 9, 1861, SWC; GEN, pp. 187–91; OR, I,

134–36; *Courier*, January 10, 1861; James Chester, "Inside Sumter in '61," BAL, I, 61.

4. *Mercury*, January 10, 1861.

5. GEN, pp. 191–97; *The Record of Fort Sumter*, 1862, pp. 28–32.

6. Lord Lyons to Lord Russell, quoted in "Secession," Case Program: C14-86-435T, Kennedy School of Government, Harvard University, 1983; *Mercury*, January 12, 1861.

7. Benson J. Lossing, *The Pictorial History of the Civil War*, New York, 1866, I, 313. The source of the story was probably Snyder.

8. Kenneth M. Stampp, *And the War Came: The North and the Secession Crisis, 1860–1861*, LSUP, 1970, pp. 83–98; *Courier*, January 11, 1861; McLean, "When the States Seceded," 287.

9. Schaff, *The Spirit of Old West Point, 1858–1862*, pp. 68–69, 188–89; Company E, 1st U.S. Artillery, Records, Archives, Fort Moultrie; *Frank Leslie's Illustrated Weekly*, February 16, 1861, p. 208f.

10. February 7, 1861, TT.

11. Crawford, diary, March 7, 1861, SWC.

12. Permit for visit for someone named "Murphy," signed D. J. Jamison, March 7, 1861, RA; February 27, March 1, 6, 7, 1861, Diary, SWC; Talbot to mother, January 26, 1861, TT.

13. Robert Gourdin to Anderson, January 12, Mathias Harris to Anderson, February 1, Lynch to Anderson, January 10, 1861, RA; OR, I, 176; Talbot to mother, February 24, 1861, TT; REM, pp. 94–97.

14. OR, I, 143, 158; Crawford, diary, January 17, 27, 28, February 1, 2, 3, 19, 26, 1861, SWC; Henry Missroon to Truman Seymour, January 30, 1861, Adjutant General to Fort Hamilton, NY, February 2, 1861, D. Stinson to Eba, February 13, 1861, RA; *Courier*, January 26, March 1, 1861; *New York Times*, February 7, 1861; *Frank Leslie's Illustrated Weekly*, February 23, 1861, p. 212.

15. Crawford, diary, March 9, 1861, Medical record, undated, but written in early April, Crawford to his brother, March 14, 1861, SWC; OR, I, 139, 227, 232, 247–48; Doubleday to Mary, April 2, 1861, quoted in David C. Mearns, *The Lincoln Papers*, 1948, p. 473.

16. MIL, pp. 543–44; OR, I, 195; February 27, March 14, 24, 1861, diary, SWC; *Courier*, February 6, 1861.

17. REM, pp. 86–87; Crawford, diary, January 23, Crawford to brother, February 2 and 24, 1861, SWC; Talbot to mother, January 30, 1861, TT.

18. MIL, p. 544.

19. BAL, I, 56; OR, I, 150, 173.

20. Crawford to brother, January 24, 29, 1861, and diary, January 31, February 10, 25, 1861, SWC; Robert Gourdin to Anderson, February 2, Anderson to Henry Gourdin, February 16, 1861, RA; GEN, pp. 201–04.

21. Talbot to mother, March 15, 1861, TT; REM, pp. 130–31.

22. For details about their activities, see, for example: OR, I, passim; GEN; REM; James Chester, "Inside Sumter in '61," BAL, I.

23. Crawford, diary, February 13, 24, 25, 1861, SWC; Foster, "Report of Major General John G. Foster to the Committee on the Conduct of the War," vol.

11, 1866; Dawson, "The Story of Fort Sumter." REM, p. 126, claims Anderson openly said that all federal property in the Deep South should have been turned over to the states to avoid war, and that if Kentucky had seceded he would have fled to Europe, which seemed dubious, though, if said, it might have been the kind of thing people under pressure say but do not mean, or at least do not carry out.

24. Crawford to brother, January 17, 24, 1861, SWC; *New York Herald*, April 5 (this "letter" may have been bogus, since its author—one Private Johnson McNeill—was not on Sumter's rosters, but there was a Johnson, a Magill, and a Neilan, and uncertain handwriting might have led to an error); Talbot to mother, February 21, 1861, TT.

25. Talbot to mother, January 21, 1861, TT; Crawford, diary, January 19, 1861, SWC; Robert to Eba, January 20, 1861, RA.

26. OR, I, 136–37, 140.

27. Drawn mostly from the Anderson Papers, January through March, 1861, RA; otherwise: *Mercury*, January 8, 26, 31, 1861; *Courier*, January 31, February 12, 23, 1861; John Titcomb Sprague to Crawford, January 23, 1861, Crawford Papers, Special Collections Library, Duke University.

28. *Frank Leslie's Illustrated Weekly*, February 16, 1861, pp. 193–94.

29. Crawford to brother, February 5, 10, 1861, diary, February 5, 8, 9, 1861, SWC; Talbot to mother, February 6, 1861, TT; Eba to Anderson, February 7, 1861, RA; Baltimore *Sun*, February 7, 1861; John Thompson, "A Union Soldier at Fort Sumter, 1860–1861," *South Carolina Historical Magazine* (April 1966), LXVII, 99.

30. Crawford to brother, February 24, 1861, SWC; *Courier*, February 23, 1861; Samuel Wells Leland, journal, February 22, 1861, SCL. It should be noted that Texas had not officially joined the Confederacy, which still only consisted of six states. Also, Kansas had entered the Union on January 30, and Anderson had carefully incorporated this fact in his counting.

31. Crawford, diary, February 28, March 11, 17, 19, 1861, Foster to Lewis Robertson, March 26, Crawford, diary, notes, SWC; OR, I, 195; *Courier*, March 20, 1861.

32. John A. Hamilton, handwritten account, dated 1890, Hamilton Papers, SCL; published, somewhat altered, in *Southern Historical Society Papers*, IX (1881), 265–67.

33. Curtis, *Life of James Buchanan*, II, 495–97, 533, 537.

34. Caroline Baldwin Darrow, "Recollections of the Twiggs Surrender," BAL, I, 33–39; Talbot to sister, March 3, 1861, TT; Crawford to brother, March 4, 1861, SWC; Charles Anderson to Robert, March 20, 1861, Eba to Robert, February 5, 25, 1861, RA.

Chapter Twelve: The Boys on the Beach

1. Russell, *My Diary North and South*, p. 85.
2. Stephens Calhoun Smith to his brother, January 30–31, 1861, S. C. Smith Papers, Duke University.

3. *Courier,* February 23, April 18, 1861; T. W. Martin Papers, SCHS; Russell, p. 85.

4. Hampton, *A Divided Heart,* pp. 89–90; Chesnut, *Mary Chesnut's Civil War,* pp. 36–37.

5. John McLaren McBryde, speech made about 1923, Papers, SCL; *Courier,* March 23, 1861, *Mercury,* March 22, 1861; F. G. de Fontaine, "The First Day of Real War," *The Southern Bivouac* (July 1886), II, 78; A. Toomer Porter, *Led On! Step by Step,* New York, 1898, p. 123; Holmes, *The Diary of Miss Emma Holmes, 1861–1866,* pp. 2–3.

6. *Courier,* January 25, March 8, 1861; *Journal of the Convention,* 1861, p. 36; Margaret Adger Smythe to Augustine Smythe, Jr., February 20, 1861, Smythe Papers, SCL; Ripley to George James, February 5, court-martial record, February 20, 1861, Ripley Papers, SCL.

7. *New York Weekly Tribune,* March 30, 1861.

8. Jacob F. Schirmer, diary, January 7, 9, 1861, SCHS; Crawford, diary, early January 1861, SWC; *Mercury,* April 12, February 14, January 30, 1861; OR, I, 158–59; *Courier,* February 13, 1861; McBryde Papers.

9. Crawford, diary, March 8, 1861, SWC.

10. Anderson note to "Officer Commanding," March 8, 1861, RA; Crawford, Diary, March 8, 1861, SWC; OR, I, 273; *Courier,* March 9, 1861.

11. *Mercury* and *Courier,* passim; ER, I, 531; Walter Gwynn to S. R. Gist, January 14, 1861, Gwynn Papers, Duke; J. R. Cheves to Langdon Cheves, January 15, 1861, Langdon Cheves Papers, SCHL; OR, I, 276, 278–79, 281, 284; T. W. Martin to "Tommie," March 2, 1861, Martin Papers, SCHS.

12. *Courier,* March 12, April 1, 1861; Fontaine, p. 74.

13. Margaret Adger Smythe to Augustine, February 24, 1861, Sue to Augustine, February 23, 1861, Augustine T. Smythe Papers, SCL; Talbot to mother, February 28, 1861, TT; Burton, *The Siege of Charleston, 1861–1865,* pp. 22–23; *Frank Leslie's Illustrated Weekly,* February 16, pp. 193–94, March 30, pp. 289, 292, April 27, 1861, p. 360; OR, I, 224, 227; *New York Herald,* April 13, 1861.

14. Ravenel, *The Private Journal of Henry William Ravenel, 1859–1887,* pp. 51–52; JEC, pp. 38, 40–41; J. W. Forest, "Charleston under Arms," *Atlantic Monthly* (April 1861), VII, 502–03; Pickens to Adjutant General, March 2, 1861, Pickens Papers, SCL.

15. Stephens Calhoun Smith to his brother, January 30–31, 1861, Smith Papers.

16. "Sketches of Camp Life during the Civil War," August 4, 1885, Mechanics Union of Charleston Papers, SCL; Ripley, Report, February 7, 8, 1861, Ripley Papers, SCL; OR, I, 264–65.

17. A. M. Vanderhorst, diary, February 6, 1861, Vanderhorst Papers, SCHS; Sally Baxter Hampton to Wyllis Baxter, in Hampton, *A Divided Heart,* pp. 105–06.

18. JD, VII, 23–25; Davis, *Jefferson Davis,* p. 294; *The Record of Fort Sumter,* 1862, p. 49.

19. OR, I, 254–57; John B. Edmunds, Jr., *Francis W. Pickens and the Politics*

of Destruction, UNCP, 1986, p. 161; Charles Edward Cauthen, *South Carolina Goes to War, 1860–1865,* UNCP, 1950, p. 118.

20. Emory M. Thomas, *The Confederate Nation: 1861–1865,* New York: Harper & Row, 1979, pp. 38–40; William C. Davis, *"A Government of Our Own": The Making of the Confederacy,* LSUP, 1994, pp. 22–43; *Mercury,* February 26, 1861.

21. *Courier,* February 9, 1861; *Mercury,* February 8, 1861; OR, I, 175.

22. OR, I, 177, 179–81, 183–84, 257 (oddly, Foster wrote his superiors on February 23, "there is no great vigor exhibited in hurrying forward the work," 178); Robert L. Cooper to Thomas B. Cooper, February 23, 1861, T. B. Fraser Papers, SCL; Pickens to Lucy, February 23, 1861, quoted in Edmunds, pp. 162–63; Burton, p. 27. The Peace Convention disbanded on February 25.

23. OR, I, 258–60.

24. JD, VII, 38; Alfred Roman, *The Military Operations of General Beauregard,* New York, 1884, I, 18–22; T. Harry Williams, *P. G. T. Beauregard: Napoleon in Gray,* LSUP, 1955, pp. 49–50.

25. OR, I, 191, 282–83; Samuel Wragg Ferguson, "Fort Sumter," typescript, undated, SCHS.

26. *Mercury,* March 16, April 1, 1861; *Courier,* April 1, 1861; ER, I, 573–74.

Chapter Thirteen: *Takes Two to Tango, But One Can Do the Twist All Alone*

1. AL, IV, 137, 139–40, 150–52, 155, 157, 159–60, 170, 172–73.

2. Ibid., pp. 195, 215–16, 237, 240–41; Crawford, to brother, February 24, 1861, SWC; Richard B. Duane to Anderson, February 21, 1861, RA.

3. Talbot to sister February 17, Talbot to mother, February 24, 26, 1861, TT; Crawford, diary, February 17, 25, Crawford to brother, February 21, 1861, SWC; Anderson to B. D. Silliman, February 19, 1861, in *South Carolina Historical and Genealogical Quarterly* (July 1905), XXVI, 133, Anderson to J. Hal. Elliot, February 20, 1861, in *Courier,* March 5, 1861.

4. Margaret Leech, *Reveille in Washington, 1860–1865,* New York, 1941, pp. 37–38.

5. Ben: Perley Poore, *Perley's Reminiscences of Sixty Years in the National Metropolis,* New York, 1886, I, 64–65; Robert Gray Gunderson, *Old Gentlemen's Convention: The Washington Peace Conference of 1861,* Westport, CT: Greenwood Press, 1961, pp. 84–85; Richard N. Current, *Lincoln and the First Shot,* 1963, pp. 34–35. On the question of whether Lincoln was serious, see Potter, *Lincoln and His Party in the Secession Crisis,* pp. xlviii, 352–58.

6. OR, I, 261.

7. Holmes, *The Diary of Miss Emma Holmes, 1861–1866,* p. 11; *Mercury,* March 5, 1861; *Courier,* March 5, 1861; Crawford, diary, March 5, 6, 1861, SWC; Eba to Anderson, March 15, 1861, RA.

8. OR, I, 202–03; Crawford, diary, February 28, 1861, SWC. Oddly, Crawford's "notes" on that day contain slightly different figures, though the pattern was the same.

9. GEN, pp. 284–85.

10. David Morgan Ramsey, "The 'Old Sumpter Hero': A Biography of Major-General Abner Doubleday," Ph.D. dissertation, Florida State University, 1980, pp. 82, 88–89; REM, p. 130; OR, I, 179.

11. AL, IV, 277–79.

12. ORN, pp. 90, 109–10; Grady McWhiney, "The Confederacy's First Shot," *Civil War History* (March 1968), XIV, 7–8.

13. Bates, Edward, *The Diary of Edward Bates, 1859–1866*, Washington, DC, 1953, p. 177; AL, IV, 279; OR, I, 198–200, 232–35. Totten also did not think that Fort Pickens could hold out against a determined attack because he assumed Montgomery could focus an immense army against it. What Totten overlooked was the fact that Jefferson Davis had to consider a number of trouble spots and could not afford to congregate a huge army against a single one. Totten, like most of the other professional soldiers on both sides, saw and emphasized his own weaknesses and overlooked his foe's. Bragg at Pensacola, for example, was deeply troubled by the raw indiscipline of his troops: McWhiney, pp. 8–9.

14. James C. Welling, "The Proposed Evacuation of Fort Sumter," *The Nation* (December 4, 1879), XXIX, 383–84; Albert Castel, *Fort Sumter: 1861*, Eastern Acorn Press, 1976, p. 25; *Courier*, March 11, 12 and *Mercury*, March 12, 1861; OR, I, 195, 196, 273; Crawford, diary, March 12, 13, 21, 1861, SWC.

15. *Courier*, March 16, 18, 1861; ER, I, 569; Crawford to brother, March 19, 1861, SWC; T. W. Martin to [illegible], March 24, 1861, Martin Papers, SCHS.

16. AL, IV, 284–85; OR, 196–203.

17. Stephen A. Hurlbut, *Between Peace and War: A Report to Lincoln from Charleston*, NY, 1953, pp. 4–11.

18. Ward Hill Lamon, *Recollections of Abraham Lincoln*, New York, 1895; GEN, pp. 374–75; Crawford, diary, notes, March 25, 1861, Crawford to brother, February 27, March 23, 1861, SWC; OR, I, 221–22, 230, 237, 276, 279; Robert Gourdin to Anderson, February 2, Eba to Anderson, March 1, 1861, Scott to Anderson, March 29, Anderson to Scott, April 1, 1861, RA; *Courier* and *Mercury*, March 26, 1861; *New York Daily Tribune*, March 30, 1861.

19. Crawford, diary, March 29, 30, 1861, SWC.

20. Davis to Bragg, April 3, 1861, quoted in McWhiney, p. 11.

21. ER, I, 562; Eba to Anderson, February 7, March 1, 1861, RA; OR, I, 163, 272.

22. OR, I, 203–08; Scott, *Memoirs*, 1864, II, 620; Ari Hoogenboom, "Gustavus Vasa Fox and the Relief of Sumter," *Civil War History* (Winter 1963), IX, 383–84; *Confidential Correspondence of Gustavus Vasa Fox*, Washington, DC, 1918, I, 1–10; William Ernest Smith, *The Francis Preston Blair Family in Politics*, New York, 1933, II, 11–12. GEN, p. 249, says that Fox's plan could have succeeded if initiated in early February, but, like Scott's estimate, he offers no proof; nor does he consider the longer-range implications about (a) immediate war; (b) the status of the Border States; or (c) the fact that soon Sumter would need more provisions. Some unanswerable questions linger. Actually, the president's orders, given through Secretary of War Cameron, were to Scott: "The President

requires accurate information in regard to the command of Major Anderson in Fort Sumter, and wishes a competent person sent for that purpose. You will therefore direct some suitable person to proceed there immediately." It is apparent Lincoln had Fox in mind, but if so, why not specify him? If the choice was truly Scott's, why would the general choose a man who fervently wanted the very thing Scott had been opposing, an armed expedition to Sumter? One must assume, therefore, that Scott understood Lincoln's unspoken order: It was to be Fox. Another curious aspect of the trip is that phrase Fox used with his wife when he told her his orders were to examine the real situation at the fort, in light of "its final evacuation." Nothing, not a word, about sending provisions or reinforcements. Yet there was no reason why Fox would not have crowed to his wife about his coup if that had been his understanding at that time. His official orders were only to go to the fort and return with "accurate information" about the status of the garrison. Assuming it was Lincoln who indirectly designated Fox as the emissary, the president's purpose, therefore, remains enigmatic.

23. GEN, p. 372n; REM, p. 132.

24. OR, I, 299–300.

25. OR, I, 209, 211, 230, 292, 294; Crawford, diary, notes, March 22, 1861, Crawford to brother, March 23, 1861, SWC; GEN, pp. 370–73; Hoogenboom, 385–86; Smith, 11–12.

26. Foster to Lewis Robertson, March 26, 1861, in Crawford, diary, notes, SWC.

27. OR, I, 235–36; Lincoln quoted in Smith, II, 12.

Chapter Fourteen: The Yellow Brick Road

1. OR, I, 209, 232; *Mercury,* April 1, 1861; Talbot to mother, March 26, April 1, 1861, TT; Doubleday to Mary, April 2, 1861, quoted in Philip Van Doren, *Prologue to Sumter,* New York, 1961, p. 473; Crawford to brother, March 14, Crawford, diary notes, April 1, 1861, SWC.

2. Talbot to sister, April 2, 1861, TT; OR, I, 211 (this document mistakenly lists the garrison as having three boxes of "candles"; Hall's own note, March 21, 1861, Hall Papers, SCL, says "carrots"), 228, 230–32, 243.

3. The *Shannon* incident: OR, I, 236–39; REM, pp. 135–36; *Mercury,* April 4, 1861; *Courier,* April 6, 1861; John McLaren McBryde, typescript of 1923 speech, McBryde Papers, SCL; GEN, pp. 375–82; Crawford, diary, April 3, 4, 1861, SWC.

4. OR, I, 241, 245; Scott quoted in Richard N. Current, *Lincoln and the First Shot,* New York, 1963, p. 114.

5. Russell, *My Diary North and South,* pp. 58–68.

6. On Wigfall's pugnacious appearance: John R. Moffett to R. B. Cain, April 10, 1861, Cain Papers, SCL; on Pryor's speech: *Courier,* April 11, 1861; Chesnut, *Mary Chesnut's Civil War,* p. 47.

7. OR, I, 235.

8. GEN, p. 384n.

9. Ibid., pp. 293–94.

10. Crawford, diary, notes, April 10, 11, 1861, SWC.

11. OR, I, 70.

12. REM, p. 138; OR, I, 7.

13. GEN, p. 398.

14. Slemmer's and Bragg's situations: see especially, ORN pp. 97–142 and OR, I, 331–473; Davis's letter to Bragg is quoted in Grady McWhiney, "The Confederacy's First Shot," *Civil War History* (March 1968), XIV, 10–12.

15. Gideon Welles, *Diary of Gideon Welles*, New York, 1911, I, 30–31; Welles, "Fort Sumter," *Galaxy*, November 1870, p. 632.

16. Mary to Charley, March 29, 1861, Charles Cotesworth Pinckney, Jr. Papers, SCL. For impressions of these last prewar days, see, e.g., both the *Mercury* and *Courier*; ER, I, 577ff; Mary Chesnut, *The Private Mary Chesnut*, New York: Oxford University Press, 1984, pp. 54ff.

17. AL, IV, 324n.

18. OR, I, 292–93, 300, 302–03.

19. Chesnut, *Civil War*, pp. 43–44, 47; Chesnut, *Private Mary Chesnut*, pp. 56–58; Wigfall to Davis, JD, VII, 100.

20. Sue McDowell, journal, April 10, 1861, SCL; Keziah Goodwyn Hopkins Brevard, *A Plantation Mistress on the Eve of the Civil War*, USCP, 1993, pp. 113–14; *Courier*, April 16, 1861.

21. A. M. Vanderhorst, diary, SCHS; John R. Moffett to R. W. Cain, April 10, 1861, Cain Papers, SCL; A. Robertson to R. F. W. Alston, April 11, 1861, Vanderhorst Papers, SCHS; Baker, *Cadets in Gray*, p. 34; *Courier*, April 11, 1861.

Chapter Fifteen: That Little Bridge

1. OR, I, 289–91.

2. For events in Montgomery this week, see Davis, *"A Government of Our Own,"* pp. 304ff; OR, I, 289ff.

3. AL, IV, 326–28.

4. The next few hours of meetings at Sumter: OR, I, 12–16, 59–60, 103, 302–05; Crawford, diary, April 11, 1861, SWC; GEN, pp. 422–26; Alexander Robert Chisholm, Journal, Special Collections Library, Duke University; A. R. Chisholm, "Notes on the Surrender of Fort Sumter," BAL, I, 82–83; Stephen Dill Lee to "Sis," September 29, 1904, Special Collections, Dartmouth College Library; Stephen D. Lee, "The First Step in the War," BAL, I, 74–81; Chesnut, *The Private Mary Chesnut*, pp. 58–59; *Mercury*, April 26, 27, 1861.

5. See, e.g., MIL, passim; Robert Anderson et al., *Instruction for Heavy Artillery*, Washington, DC, 1857; Mahan, *A Complete Treatise on Field Fortification*.

6. Leslie D. Jensen, "The Fort Sumter Flags: A Study in Documentation and Authentication," U.S. Department of the Interior, National Park Service, 1982, pp. 88–89.

Chapter Sixteen: A Mere Point of Honor

1. The first shot: Robert Lebby, "The First Shot on Sumter," *South Carolina Historical and Genealogical Magazine* (July 1911), XII, 141–45; Lebby Family Papers, SCL; Lee, "The First Step in the War," BAL, I, 76–77; Alexander Robert Chisholm, Journal, Special Collections Library, Duke University; OR, I, 60.
2. ER, I, 583ff.
3. The first hours, from the civilian point of view: Chesnut, *The Private Mary Chesnut*, pp. 58–59, and Chesnut, *Mary Chesnut's Civil War*, pp. 46–47; Louise Wigfall Wright, *A Southern Girl in '61*, New York, 1905, pp. 37–38; Caroline Howard Gilman, "Letters of a Confederate Mother," *Atlantic Monthly* (April 1926), CXXXVII, 506–07; Francis Asbury Mood, "Autobiography," p. 117, typescript, SCL; Brackett, "Charleston, South Carolina (1861)," 947–48; *Courier* and *Mercury*.
4. The morning at Sumter: REM, pp. 141–55; GEN, pp. 428–32; James Chester, "Inside Sumter in '61," BAL, I, 66–70; *New York Tribune*, April 19, 1861; Frank Barnes, "Fort Sumter: April 12, 1861," typescript, U.S., Department of the Interior, National Park Service, 1950.
5. Cartridge bags: OR, I, 18, 212, 215.
6. REM, p. 161; *Mercury*, April 15, 1861; E. Milby Burton, *The Siege of Charleston, 1861–1870*, USCP, 1970, p. 57.
7. Ibid., p. 45.
8. The fleet: ORN, I, passim; Gustavus Vasa Fox, *Confidential Correspondence of Gustavus Vasa Fox*, NY, 1918, I, 26–44; Albert Bigelow Paine (B. S. Osbon), *A Soldier of Fortune: Personal Memoirs of Captain B. S. Osbon*, New York, 1906, pp. 116–27, probably fictional; *New York Tribune*, April 19, 1861; OR, I, 304, 307.
9. Thomas W. Chadwick, ed., "The Diary of Samuel Edward Burges, 1860–1862," *South Carolina Historical and Genealogical Magazine*, April 1947, p. 155; Francis L. Parker, "Battle of Fort Sumter As Seen from Morris Island," typescript, FM.
10. Montgomery *Advertiser*, April 13, 1861; Montgomery *Mail*, April 13, 1861; Davis, *"A Government of Our Own,"* pp. 313–16.
11. ORN, pp. 114–23, passim; *Mercury*, April 18, 20, 1861.

Chapter Seventeen: Ashes and Dust

1. ER, I, 592; Francis L. Parker, "Battle of Fort Sumter As Seen from Morris Island," typescript, FM; *Courier*, April 20, 1861.
2. OR, I, 313–14.
3. John McLaren McBryde, mss., SCL; Fox, *Confidential Correspondence of Gustavus Vasa Fox*, I, 31–36; ORN, 244–45.
4. Fox, pp. 34–41; *Courier*, April 18, 25, 1861; *New York Tribune*, April 19, 1861.

5. The fire: OR, I, 21–23; Thompson, "A Union Soldier at Fort Sumter, 1860–1861," 102–03; Chester, "Inside Sumter in '61," I, 71–72; REM, pp. 156–59; GEN, pp. 435–37.

6. OR, I, 44–48; Gilman, "Letters of a Confederate Mother," 507; ER, I, 596–97; Brackett, "Charleston, South Carolina (1861)," 948–49.

7. ER, I, 597. The falling flag: Chester, p. 71; REM, p. 159; GEN, p. 438. A minute analysis is in Leslie D. Jensen, "The Fort Sumter Flags: A Study in Documentation and Authentication," U.S. Department of the Interior, National Park Service, 1982, pp. 109–14.

8. OR, I, 57, 60–61; Mrs. D. Giraud Wright, *A Southern Girl in '61*, pp. 38–40; H. Lescone to Adele, April 16, 1861, R. W. F. Alston Papers, Vanderhorst File, SCHS.

9. Young's wry account is quoted in, May Spencer Ringold, "William Gourdin Young and the Wigfall Mission — Fort Sumter, April 13, 1861," *South Carolina Historical Magazine* (January 1972), LXXIII, 27–36.

10. Wigfall's adventure: The best account consists of the diary notes, dated April 13, 1861, SWP, made by Crawford that day, after speaking to several of the witnesses and getting two of them to write down their recollections. The surgeon wanted his contemplated book to be accurate on this crucial event. As soon as the garrison survivors arrived in New York they gave a brief news conference, the best resulting accounts of which were the *New York Times* and the *New York Tribune*, both April 19, 1861. See also, Thompson, p. 104; GEN, pp. 438–40; Chester, pp. 72–73; report by Seymour, dated April 18, 1861, RA; Wright, p. 42; and OR, I, 23, 61.

11. The reactions to the news: Bessie to Mamma, April 13, 1861, R. W. F. Alston Papers, Vanderhorst File, SCHS; Young; *Mercury*, April 14, 1861; Francis L. Parker, "Battle of Fort Sumter As Seen from Morris Island," manuscript, FM; ER, I, 597.

12. REM, pp. 168–69; OR, I, 42, 66, 311; James Harrington Powe, *Reminiscences and Sketches of Confederate Times*, Columbia, SC, 1909, p. 11.

13. GEN, pp. 441–43; OR, I, 32–33; Chester, p. 73; Stephen D. Lee, "The First Step in the War," BAL, I, 78; *New York Tribune*, April 15, 1861; *Mercury*, April 17, 1861.

14. OR, I, 309–10, 313; John McLaren McBryde, typescript, SCL; Parker; *New York Tribune*, April 19, 1861.

15. *Courier*, April 19, 1861.

16. The morning: *Courier* and *Mercury*, April 15–18, 1861; Alexander Robert Chisholm, Journal, Special Collections Library, Duke University; Thomas Smythe, "The Battle of Fort Sumter: Its Mystery and Miracle," SCL; Samuel Wragg Ferguson, "Fort Sumter," typescript, SCHS.

17. The afternoon and departure: OR, I, 56; REM, pp. 171–72; GEN, p. 446; William Marvel, "The First to Fall," unpublished typescript, 1986, FM; Jensen, pp. 118f; *Mercury* and *Courier*, April 15–23, 1861. Foster's letter: *New York Herald*, April 6, 1861.

Mystic Chords of Memory: A Postscript

1. First days in New York: *New York Tribune,* April 19, 1861; *New York Herald,* April 19, 21, 23, 1861; *New York Evening Express,* April 18, 1861; *Frank Leslie's Illustrated Weekly,* April 30, 1861, p. 370. Strong's quotation: *The Diary of George Templeton Strong,* NY, 1952, II, 117–18.

2. *Life,* September 5, 1949, pp. 61–64.

3. Lewis, *Sherman,* p. 518.

4. William A. Spicer, *The Flag Replaced on Sumter: A Personal Narrative,* Providence, RI, 1885; Justus Clement French, *The Trip of the Steamer* Oceanus *to Fort Sumter and Charleston, South Carolina.,* Brooklyn, NY, 1865; Edward Davis Townsend, "Address," May 28, 1865, SCL; Lee, "The First Step in the War," BAL, I, 81n; G. A. Follin to mother, September 9, 1863, Gustavus Augustus Follin, Jr., Papers, SCL; Eugene T. Haines, Papers, SCL.

Bibliography

The materials on aspects of this story are formidable. On the topic of secession alone, there are bulky scholarly libraries devoted to this or that opinion. The amount of information about Lincoln, about slavery, about the South is intimidating. The following list, therefore, is purposely limited in its scope to those things that seemed especially helpful to understanding the human side of this tale.

Manuscripts

University of South Carolina
    Allen, Charles H.
    Alston, William Algernon
    "Annual Commencement of the Polytechni . . . March 28, 1861"
    Barnwell, Edward H.
    Bellinger, E. C.
    Bird, Pattie A.
    Bryan, W. H.
    Bull, Charles S.
    Burns, J. H.
    Cain Family
    Capers, Ellison
    Carolina Light Infantry
    Carstens and Company ("Receipt Book")

Charleston Club
Charleston Typographical Union No. 43
Crawford, Samuel Wylie
The 1860 Association
Faber, John Christopher
Follin, Gustavus Adolphus
Gignilliat Family
Hagood, James R. ("Memoirs of the First South Carolina . . .")
Haines, Eugene T.
Hall, Norman J.
Hamilton, John A.
Hatch, Lewis. (Anderson, Charles. "An Hour with Major Anderson in 1860.")
Hort, Mary
Jamison, David Flavel
Kelley, Henrietta A. ("Wild Flowers")
Lebby Family
Leland, Samuel Wells
Lynch, David
McBryde, John McLaren
McDowell, Sue
Moffett, John R.
Mood, Francis Asbury ("Autobiography")
Petigru & King
Pickens, Francis Wilkinson
Pinckney, Charles Cotesworth, Jr.
Ravenel, Alfred Ford
Ravenel, Edmund
Ripley, Roswell Sabine
Ryan, John S.
Sale, W. W.
Siegling, Henry
Smyth, Augustine T.
South Carolina Engineer Bureau File
South Carolina Militia File
Steinmeyer, J. H. ("Marion Rifles")
Townsend, Edward Davis
Wade, Theodosia

South Carolina Historical Society
Allston, R. F. W.
Charleston Club
Cheves, Langdon
Dunovant, R. G. M.
Ferguson, Samuel Wragg ("Fort Sumter")

Harleson, John
John Fraser & Company
Kirk, Caroline
Legare & Colcock
Lord, Louisa
Louis Cohen Dry Goods Company
Martin, T. W.
Prostitution File
Schirmer, Jacob ("Diary")
Sloan, Alice Witte
Smythe, Louisa McCord ("Recollections")
"The Southern Flag"
Vanderhorst/Caroline Carson Family
Vanderhorst, A. A.
Vanderhorst, A. M.
Walker, Henry Pinckney

College of Charleston
Bank of Charleston ("Records," "Daily Ledger")
Glennie, Alexander
Grimball, John Berkley
Gwynn, Walter
Middleton, Nathaniel Russell
Porcher, Philip A.

Duke University
Chisholm, Alexander Robert ("Journal")
Crawford, Samuel Wylie
Holmes, Emma E.
Gwynn, Walter
Jamison, David Flavel
Jeffords, Robert J.
Palmer, John S.
Pinckney, Charles Cotesworth, III ("The Order of ...")
Ripley, Roswell Sabine
Smith, Stephens Calhoun
Spicer, William Arnold

Fort Moultrie, South Carolina
Barnes, Frank ("Fort Sumter, April 12, 1861," "Fort Sumter, December 26, 1860")
Census of 1860
Company E File
Company H File
Hough, Daniel File
Parker, Francis L. ("Battle of Fort Sumter")

Library of Congress
Anderson, Robert
Crawford, Samuel Wylie
Talbot, Theodore

Miscellaneous
Anderson Family: National Archives
Doubleday, Abner: New York Historical Society
Grimball, Meta Morris ("Diary"): University of North Carolina
Lee, Stephen Dill: Dartmouth University
Medical Society of Charleston ("Minutes"): Medical University of South Carolina, Waring Historical Library
Military Records. Archives. West Point
Willis, F. Milton. "Replacing the Flag upon Sumter from a Narrative of An Eye Witness": Carlisle Barracks, Pennsylvania

Documents

The Congressional Globe. 36th Cong., 2d sess.
Executive Documents No. 2. "Correspondence and Other Papers Relating to Fort Sumter." Charleston, 1861
Fort Sumter: Anvil of War. U.S. Department of the Interior. National Park Service, 1984.
Foster, John G. *Report of Major General J. G. Foster to the Committee on the Conduct of the War.* Vol. II. 1866
Jensen, Leslie D. "The Fort Sumter Flags: A Study in Documentation and Authentication." U.S. Department of the Interior. National Park Service. Harpers Ferry, WVA. 1982
Journal of the Convention of the People, South Carolina, Held in 1860–61. Charleston, 1861
Magrath, A. G. *Executive Documents.* 1861
Stokeley, Jim. *Fort Moultrie: Constant Defender.* U.S. Department of the Interior. National Park Service. 1985
Thomsen, Fonda Ghiardi. "Technical Study of the Flags of Ft. Sumter." U.S. Department of the Interior. National Parks Service. 1982
U.S. Secretary of War. "Defences of the Harbor of Charleston, and the Distribution of Arms." January 9, 1861. House of Representatives. 36th Cong., 2d sess.
Walter C. McCrone Associates. "Microscopical Analysis of the Ft. Sumter Flags." 1982

Theses

Angell, Harold V. "A Partial Analysis of Henry Ward Beecher's Use of Invention in the Speech 'Raising the Flag over Fort Sumter.'" MS. St. Cloud MN State Teachers' College, 1956

Bellows, Barbara Lawrence. "Tempering the Wind: The Southern Response to Urban Poverty, 1850–1865." Ph.D. University of South Carolina, 1983

Bright, Samuel R. "Coast Defense and the southern Coast before Fort Sumter." MA. Duke University, 1958

Greb, Gregory Allen. "Charleston, South Carolina Merchants, 1815–1860: Urban Leadership in the Antebellum South." Ph.D. University of California, San Diego, 1978

Keel, Edward H., Jr. "Francis Wilkinson Pickens, Governor of South Carolina, 1860–1862." MA. University of South Carolina, 1961

Murray, Gail S. "Poverty and Its Relief in the Antebellum South. Perceptions and Realities in Three Selected Cities: Charleston, Nashville, and New Orleans." Ph.D. Memphis State University, 1991

Olsberg, Robert Nicholas. "A Government of Class and Race: William Henry Trescot and the South Carolina Chivalry, 1860–1865." Ph.D. University of South Carolina, 1972.

———. "William Henry Trescot: The Crisis of 1860." MA. University of South Carolina, 1967.

Powers, Bernard Edward, Jr. "Black Charleston: A Social History, 1822–1885." Ph.D. Northwestern University, 1982.

Radford, John Price. "Culture, Economy, and Urban Structure in Charleston, South Carolina, 1860–1880." Ph.D. Clark University, 1974.

Ramsey, David Morgan. "The 'Old Sumter Hero': A Biography of Major-General Abner Doubleday." Ph.D. Florida State University, 1980.

Roberson, John C. "The Foundation of Southern Nationalism: Charleston and the Low Country, 1847–1861." Ph.D. University of South Carolina, 1991.

Stavisky, Leonard Price. "The Negro Artisan in the South Atlantic States, 1800–1860: A Study of Status and Economic Opportunity with Special Reference to Charleston." Ph.D. Columbia University, 1958.

Sutor, Jack Alexander. "Charleston, South Carolina during the Civil War Era, 1858–1865." MA. Duke University, 1943.

Books

Alexander, E. P. *Military Memoirs of a Confederate.* NY, 1907.

Allston, Joseph Blythe. *Sumter.* Charleston, 1874.

Anderson, Frank Malloy. *The Mystery of "A Public Man": A Historical Detective Story.* Minneapolis, MN, 1948.

Anderson, Robert. *An Artillery Officer in the Mexican War, 1846–47: Letters of Robert Anderson,* NY, 1911.

Anderson, Thomas McArthur. *The Political Conspiracies Preceding the Rebellion.* NY, 1882.

Anderson, W. Marshall. *Major Anderson.* 1861.

Auchampaugh, Philip Gerald. *James Buchanan and His Cabinet on the Eve of Secession.* 1926.

Baker, Gary R. *Cadets in Gray.* Columbia, SC: Palmetto Bookworks, 1989.

Baker, Samuel T. *Fort Sumter and Its Defenders.* Buffalo, NY, 1891.

Barney, William A. *The Abolitionist Impulse: Alabama and Mississippi in 1860.* Princeton, NJ: Princeton University Press, 1974.

Basso, Hamilton. *Beauregard: The Great Creole.* NY, 1933.

Bates, Edward. *The Diary of Edward Bates, 1859–1866.* Washington, DC, 1933.

The Battle of Fort Sumter and First Victory of the Southern Troops, April 13th, 1861. Charleston, 1861.

Birkhimer, William E. *Historical Sketch of the Organization, Administration, Matériel and Tactics of the Artillery, United States Army.* Washington, DC, 1884.

Blainey, Geoffrey. *The Causes of War.* NY, 1973.

Bleser, Carol (ed.). *The Hammonds of Redcliffe.* NY: Oxford University Press, 1981.

Brevard, Keziah Goodwyn Hopkins. *A Plantation Mistress on the Eve of the Civil War.* USCP, 1993.

Brice, Martin. *Forts and Fortresses.* NY: Facts on Files, 1990.

Browning, Orville Hickman. *The Diary of Orville Hickman Browning.* 2 vols. Springfield, IL, 1925, 1933.

Buchanan, James. *Mr. Buchanan's Administration on the Eve of the Rebellion.* NY, 1866.

———. *The Works of James Buchanan.* NY, 1910.

Burton, E. Milby. *The Siege of Charleston, 1861–1865.* Columbia, SC: University of South Carolina Press, 1970.

Cardozo, Jacob Newton. *Reminiscences of Charleston.* Charleston, 1866.

Cauthen, Charles E. *South Carolina Goes to War, 1860–1865.* Chapel Hill, NC, 1950.

Chesnut, Mary. *Mary Chesnut's Civil War.* New Haven, CT: Yale University Press, 1981.

———. *The Private Mary Chesnut.* NY: Oxford University Press, 1984.

Coclanis, Peter A. *The Shadow of a Dream.* NY: Oxford University Press, 1989.

Coffman, Edward M. *The Old Army: A Portrait of the American Army in Peacetime, 1784–1898.* NY: Oxford University Press, 1986.

Coker, P. C., III. *Charleston's Maritime Heritage, 1670–1865.* Charleston: Coker-craft Press, 1987.

Crawford, Samuel W. *The Genesis of the Civil War: The Story of Sumter, 1860–1861.* 1887.

Cullum, George W. *Biographical Register of the Officers and Graduates of the U.S. Military Academy.* (various editions and dates.)

Current, Richard N. *Lincoln and the First Shot.* NY, 1963.

Curtis, George Ticknor. *Life of James Buchanan.* 2 vols. NY, 1883.

Davis, Jefferson. *The Papers of Jefferson Davis.* Baton Rouge, LA: Louisiana State University Press, 1971–.

Davis, William C. *"A Government of Our Own": The Making of the Confederacy.* Baton Rouge, LA: Louisiana State University Press, 1994.

———. *Jefferson Davis: The Man and His Hour.* NY: HarperCollins, 1991.

Doubleday, Abner. *Reminiscences of Forts Sumter and Moultrie in 1860–'61.* NY, 1876.

Dowdey, Clifford. *The Land They Fought For.* Garden City, NY, 1956.

Dumond, Dwight Lowell. *Southern Editorials on Secession.* NY, 1931.

Edmunds, John B. Jr. *Francis W. Pickens and the Politics of Destruction.* Chapel Hill, NC: University of North Carolina Press, 1986.

Evans, Clement A., *et al. Confederate Military History.* The Blue and Grey Press, nd.

Fletcher, Miss A. *Within Fort Sumter.* 1861.

Flynn, Jean Martin. *The Militia in Antebellum South Carolina Society.* Spartanburg, SC: The Reprint Company, 1991.

Foote, Henry S. *Casket of Reminiscences.* 1874.

Ford, Lacy K., Jr. *Origins of Southern Radicalism: The South Carolina Upcountry, 1800–1860.* NY: Oxford University Press, 1988.

Fox, Gustavus Vasa. *Confidential Correspondence of Gustavus Vasa Fox.* 2 vols. NY, 1918.

Fraser, Walter J., Jr. *Charleston! Charleston!: The History of a Southern City.* Columbia, SC: University of South Carolina Press, 1989.

French, Justus Clement. *The Trip of the Steamer* Oceanus *to Fort Sumter and Charleston, South Carolina.* Brooklyn, NY, 1865.

Gibbon, John. *The Artillerist's Manual.* (reprint.) Westport, CT: Greenwood Press, 1971.

Grant, A. F. *Fort Sumter, or, The Opening Guns of War.* NY, 1884.

Guenter, Scot M. *The American Flag, 1777–1924.* Rutherford, NJ: Fairleigh Dickinson University Press, 1990.

Gunderson, Robert Gray. *Old Gentlemen's Convention: The Washington Peace Conference of 1861.* Westport, CT: Greenwood Press, 1961.

Halleck, Henry Wager. *Elements of Military Art and Science.* 3d ed. NY, 1863.

Hampton, Sally Baxter. *A Divided Heart: Letters of Sally Baxter Hampton.* Spartanburg, SC: The Reprint Company, 1980.

Harris, W. A. (comp.). *The Record of Fort Sumter.* Columbia, SC, 1862.

Hendrickson, Robert. *Sumter: The First Day of the Civil War.* Chelsea, MI: Scarborough House, 1990.

Hesseltine, William B. *Lincoln and the War Governors.* NY, 1948.

Heyward, DuBose. *The Battle of Fort Sumter.* 1932.

History of the First Regiment of Artillery, The. Portland, ME, 1879.

Hitchcock, Ripley. *Decisive Battles of America.* NY, 1909.

Holmes, Emma. *The Diary of Miss Emma Homes, 1861–1866.* Baton Rouge, LA: Louisiana State University Press, 1979.

Holt, Joseph. *Treason and Its Treatment.* NY, 1865.

Hughes, Quentin. *Military Architecture.* NY: St. Martin's Press, 1974.

Hurlbut, Stephen A. *Between Peace and War: A Report to Lincoln from Charleston, 1861.* NY, 1953.

Johnson, Michael P., and James L. Roark (eds.). *No Chariot Let Down: Charleston's Free People on the Eve of the Civil War.* Chapel Hill, NC: University of North Carolina Press, 1984.

Jomini, Antoine Henri. *The Art of War.* NY, 1862.

King, Alvy L. *Louis T. Wigfall: Southern Fire-eater.* Baton Rouge, LA: Louisiana State University Press, 1970.

King, Horatio. *Turning on the Light.* Philadelphia, 1895.

Knoles, George H. (ed.). *The Crisis of the Union, 1860–1861.* Baton Rouge, LA, 1965.

Lamon, Ward Hill. *Recollections of Abraham Lincoln.* NY, 1895.

Lawton, Eba Anderson. *Major Robert Anderson and Fort Sumter, 1861.* NY, 1911.

Leech, Margaret. *Reveille in Washington, 1860–1865.* NY, 1941.

Lewis, Elise Rhett. *Fort Sumter: The Key of Charleston Harbor.* Charleston, 1896.

Lewis, Emanuel Raymond. *Seacoast Fortifications of the United States.* Washington, DC, 1970.

Lewis, Lloyd. *Sherman: Fighting Prophet.* NY, 1932.

Life in Charleston in Quiet Times. NY, 1861.

Lincoln, Abraham. *The Collected Works of Abraham Lincoln.* 9 vols. New Brunswick, NJ, 1953.

Lossing, Benson J. *The Pictorial History of the Civil War.* NY, 1866.

Mahan, Dennis H. *A Complete Treatise on Field Fortification.* NY, 1836.

McPherson, Edward. *The Political History of the United States of America during the Great Rebellion.* Washington, DC, 1865.

McPherson, James. *What They Fought For, 1861–1865.* NY: Doubleday, 1994.

Meneely, A. Howard. *The War Department, 1861.* NY, 1928.

Meredith, Roy. *Storm over Sumter.* NY, 1957.

Moore, Albert Burton. *A New Nation.* (reprint.) 1965.

Moore, Frank (ed.) *The Rebellion Record.* NY, 1861.

Morrison, James L., Jr. *"The Best School in the World": West Point, the Pre–Civil War Years, 1833–1866.* Kent, OH: Kent State University Press, 1986.

Newbrough, J. B. *The Fall of Fort Sumter.* NY, 1867.

Nichols, Roy Franklin. *The Disruption of American Democracy.* NY, 1948.

Nicolay, John G. *The Outbreak of the Rebellion.* NY, 1881.

Nicolay, John G., and John Hay, *Abraham Lincoln, A History.* Vols. I–III, NY, 1904–15.

Noyes, Frank Gardner. *Biographical Sketch of Major-General John G. Foster.* Nashua, NH, 1890.

Official Records of the Union and Confederate Navies in the War of Rebellion, 1897–1927. Washington, DC, 1927.

Paine, Albert Bigelow. *A Soldier of Fortune: Personal Memoirs of Captain B. S. Osbon.* NY, 1906.

Patrick, Rembert W. *Aristocrat in Uniform: General Duncan L. Clinch.* Gainesville, FL, 1963.

Pease, William H., and Jane H. Pease. *The Web of Progress: Private Values and Public Styles in Boston and Charleston, 1828–1843.* NY: Oxford University Press, 1985.

Poore, Ben: Perley. *Perley's Reminiscences of Sixty Years in the National Metropolis.* 2 vols. NY, 1886.

Porter, Anthony Toomer. *Led On! Step by Step.* NY, 1898.

Porter, David D. *Incidents and Anecdotes of the Civil War.* NY, 1885.

———. *The Naval History of the Civil War.* (reprint). Secaucus, NJ: Castle, 1984.

Potter, David. *The Impending Crisis, 1848–1861.* NY: Harper & Row, 1976.

———. *Lincoln and His Party in the Secession Crisis.* 2d ed. Baton Rouge, LA: Louisiana State University Press, 1995.

Powe, James Harrington. *Reminiscences and Sketches of Confederate Times.* Columbia, SC, 1909.

Pryor, Agnes Sara. *Reminiscences of Peace and War.* (reprint). Freeport, NY, 1970.

Ravenel, Henry William. *The Private Journal of Henry William Ravenel, 1859–1887.* Columbia, SC, 1947.

The Record of Fort Sumter. Charleston, 1862.

Rhoades, Jeffrey L. *Scapegoat General: The Story of Major General Benjamin Hunger, C. S. A.* Hamden, CT: Archon Books, 1985.

Ripley, Warren. *Artillery and Ammunition of the Civil War.* NY, 1970.

Roman, Alfred. *The Military Operations of General Beauregard.* NY, 1884.

Rosen, Robert N. *Confederate Charleston.* Columbia, SC: University of South Carolina Press, 1994.

Rosengarten, Theodore. *Tombee: Portrait of a Cotton Planter.* NY: William Morrow, 1986.

Russell, William Howard. *My Diary North and South.* NY: Alfred A. Knopf, 1988.

Ruth, David R. *A Guide to the Manuscript Collection of Fort Sumter National Monument.* Fort Sumter National Monument, SC, 1983.

Schaff, Morris. *The Spirit of Old West Point, 1858–1862.* Boston, 1908.

Schultz, Harold S. *Nationalism and Sectionalism in South Carolina, 1852–1860.* Durham, NC, 1950.

Scott, H. L. *Military Dictionary.* NY, 1861.

Scott, Winfield. *Memoirs of Lieut.-General Scott.* NY, 1864.

Severens, Kenneth. *Charleston: Antebellum Architecture and Civic Destiny.* Knoxville, TN: University of Tennessee Press, 1988.

Sheppard, W. G. *Story of Fort Sumter.* Charleston, 1938.

Smith, William Ernest. *The Francis Preston Blair Family in Politics.* 2 vols. NY, 1933.

Snowden, Yates, and H. G. Cutler. *History of South Carolina.* NY, 1920.

Spicer, William Arnold. *The Flag Replaced on Sumter: A Personal Narrative.* Providence, RI, 1885.

Stampp, Kenneth M. *And the War Came: The North and the Secession Crisis, 1860–1861.* 2d ed. Baton Rouge, LA: Louisiana State University Press, 1970.

State Board of Agriculture of South Carolina. *South Carolina: Resources and Population, Institutions and Industries.* Charleston, 1883.

Stern, Philip Van Doren. *Prologue to Sumter.* Greenwich, CT, 1961.

Summers, Mark W. *The Plundering Generation: Corruption and the Crisis of the Union, 1849–1861.* NY: Oxford University Press, 1987.

Swanberg, William A. *First Blood: The Story of Fort Sumter.* NY, 1957.

Taylor, Rosser H. *Ante-Bellum South Carolina.* Chapel Hill, NC, 1942.

Thomas, Emory M. *The Confederate Nation: 1861–1865.* NY: Harper & Row, 1979.

Thomas, John Peyre. *The History of the South Carolina Military Academy.* Charleston, 1893.

Thompson, Robert Means, and Richard Wainwright. *Confidential Correspondence of Gustavus Vasa Fox.* 2 vols. NY, 1918.

Tilley, John Shipley. *Lincoln Takes Command.* (reprint.) Nashville, TN: Bill Coates, 1991.

Tower, Roderick. *The Defense of Fort Sumter.* NY, 1938.

Utley, Robert M. *Frontiersmen in Blue: The United States Army and the Indian, 1848–1865.* NY, 1967.

Van Deusen, John G. *Economic Bases of Disunion in South Carolina.* NY, 1928.

Wallace, David Duncan. *The History of South Carolina.* 4 vols. NY, 1934.

Walther, Eric H. *The Fire-Eaters.* Baton Rouge, LA: Louisiana State University Press, 1992.

War of the Rebellion: A Compilation of the Official Records of the Union and Confederate Armies, The. DC, 1880–1901.

Welles, Edward L. *A Sketch of the Charleston Light Dragoons.* Charleston, 1888.

Welles, Gideon. *Diary of Gideon Welles.* 3 vols. NY, 1911.

West, Richard S., Jr. *Gideon Welles, Lincoln's Navy Department.* NY, 1943.

Williams, Jack Kenny. *Vogues in Villainy: Crime and Retribution in Ante-Bellum South Carolina.* Columbia, SC, 1959.

Williams, T. Harry. *P. G. T. Beauregard: Napoleon in Gray.* Baton Rouge, LA, 1955.

Wooster, Ralph A. *The Secessionist Conventions of the South.* Princeton, NJ, 1962.

Wright, Louise Wigfall. *A Southern Girl in '61.* NY, 1905.

Articles

Abbott, Martin, and Elmer L. Puryear (eds.). "Beleaguered Charleston: Letters from the City, 1860–1864." *South Carolina Historical Magazine,* 61 (April 1960), 61–74.

Anderson, Robert. Letter to B. D. Silliman, February 19, 1861. *South Carolina Historical and Genealogical Magazine,* 6 (July 1905), 133.

Anderson, W. Marshall. "A Sketch of Major Robert Anderson." Ohio, 1861.

Brackett, Anna C. "Charleston, South Carolina (1861)." *Harper's New Monthly Magazine.* 88 (1894), 941–50.

Bristoll, William Merrick. "Escape from Charleston." *American Heritage.* 26 (April 1975), 9ff.

Capers, Ellison. "South Carolina." *Confederate Military History.* 5 (1899), 2–28.

Castel, Albert. "Fort Sumter: 1861." *Civil War Times Illustrated.* 15 (1976), 6f.

Chadwick, French Ensor. "Fort Sumter, 1861." *Decisive Battles of the Civil War.* NY, 1909, 232–73.

Chepesiuk, Ron. "Eye-Witness to Fort Sumter: The Letters of Private John Thompson." *South Carolina Historical Magazine.* 85 (October 1984), 271–79.

Chester, James. "Inside Sumter in '61." In *Battles and Leaders of the Civil War.* I, 50–73.

Chisholm, A. R. "Notes on the Surrender of Fort Sumter." In *Battles and Leaders of the Civil War.* I, 82–83.

Clarkson, H. M. "Story of the Star of the West." *Confederate Veteran.* 21 (May 1913), 234–36.

Current, Richard N. "The Confederates and the First Shot." *Civil War History.* 7 (1961), 357–59.

Dawson, Henry Barton. "The Story of Fort Sumter." *Historical Magazine.* 21 (January and May 1872), 34ff.

de Fontaine, F. G. "The First Day of the Real War." *The Southern Bivouac.* 2 (July 1886), 73–79.

———. "The Second Day of the War." *The Southern Bivouac.* 2 (September 1886), 201–07.

"The Diary of a Public Man." *North American Review.* 129, pp. 125ff.

Doubleday, Abner. "From Moultrie to Sumter." In *Battles and Leaders of the Civil War.* I, 40–49.

Eisenschiml, Otto, and E. B. Long. "Big Ifs at Fort Sumter." *American Mercury.* 82 (April 1956), 94–98.

"Flags of Fort Sumter, The." *South Carolina Historical and Genealogical Magazine.* 6 (July 1905), 134.

Gilman, Caroline Howard. "Letters of a Confederate Mother." *Atlantic Monthly.* 137 (April 1926), 503–15.

Gordon, George H. "Major Anderson at Fort Sumter." *Papers of the Military Society of Massachusetts.* 9 (1912), 1–52.

Grimball, John Berkley. "Diary of John Berkley Grimball." *South Carolina Historical Magazine.* 56 (April 1955), 92–107.

Hall, W. L. "Lincoln's Interview with John B. Baldwin." *The South Atlantic Quarterly.* 13 (1914), 260–69.

Hamilton, John A. "An Incident of Fort Sumter." *Southern Historical Society Papers.* 9 (1881), 265–67.

Hash, C. Patton. "A Lowcountry Christmas." *Carologue.* 9 (Winter 1993), 8ff.

Hoogenboom, Ari. "Gustavus Fox and the Relief of Fort Sumter." *Civil War History.* 9 (Winter 1963), 383–98.

Hunt, David R. "Restoring the Flag at Fort Sumter." *Sketches of War History, 1861–1865.* Vol. V. Cincinnati, 1903.

Johnson, Ludwell H., III. "'The Few Brave and Hungry Men': Another Look at the Fort Sumter Crisis." *South Atlantic Quarterly.* 84 (Winter 1985), 81–88.

———. "Fort Sumter and Confederate Diplomacy." *Journal of Southern History.* 26 (November 1960), 441–57.

Jones, James P. (ed.). "Charleston Harbor, 1860–1861: A Memoir from the Union Garrison." *South Carolina Historical Magazine.* 62 (July 1962), 148–50.

Kibler, Lillian A. "Unionist Sentiment in S. C. in 1860." *Journal of Southern History.* 4 (August 1938), 346–66.

Klingsberg, Frank Wysor. "James Buchanan and the Crisis of the Union." *Journal of Southern History.* 9 (1943), 455–74.

"Last Shots of Civil War." *Life.* 27 (September 5, 1949), 61–64.

Lebby, Robert. "The First Shot on Fort Sumter." *South Carolina Historical and Genealogical Magazine.* 12 (July 1911), 3ff.

Lee, Stephen D. "The First Step in the War." In *Battles and Leaders of the Civil War.* I, 74–81.

Lee, Stephen D., and Julian M. Ruffin. "Who Fired the First Gun at Sumter?" *Southern Historical Society Papers.* 11 (1883), 501–04.

Magruder, Allen B. "A Piece of Secret History." *Atlantic Monthly*. 35 (April 1875), 438–45.

Mason, Edward G. "A Visit to South Carolina in 1860." *Atlantic Monthly*. 53 (February 1884), 241–50.

McGinty, Brian. "Robert Anderson: Reluctant Hero." *Civil War Times Illustrated*. 31 (May 1992), 45ff.

McLean, Margaret. "A Northern Woman in the Confederacy." *Harper's Magazine*. 128 (February 1914), 440–51.

———. "When the States Seceded." *Harper's Magazine*. 128 (January 1914), 282–88.

McWhiney, Grady. "The Confederacy's First Shot." *Civil War History*. 14 (1968), 5–14.

Meigs, M. C. "Diary, March 29–April 8, 1861." *American Historical Review*. 26 (January 1921), 285–303.

Morehead, Charles S. "Fort Sumter Again." *Mississippi Valley Historical Review*. 28 (June 1941), 63–73.

Peck, W. F. G. "Four Years under Fire at Charleston." *Harper's New Monthly Magazine*. 59 (August 1865), 358–66.

Pressley, J. G. "The Wee Nee Volunteers of Williamsburg District, South Carolina, in the First (Gregg's) Regiment — Siege and Capture of Fort Sumter." *Southern Historical Society Papers*. 13, 48–96.

Radford, John. "The Charleston Planters in 1860." *South Carolina Historical Magazine*. 77 (October 1976), 227–35.

Ramsdell, Charles W. "Lincoln and the First Shot." *Journal of Southern History*. 3 (August 1937), 259–88.

Reid, Brian Holden. "The Crisis at Fort Sumter in 1861 Reconsidered." *History*. 77 (February 1992), 3–32.

Ringold, May Spencer. "Robert Newman Gourdin and the '1860 Association.'" *Georgia Historical Quarterly*. 55 (1971), 501–09.

———. "William Gourdin Young and the Wigfall Mission — Fort Sumter, April 13, 1861." *South Carolina Historical Magazine*. 73 (January 1972), 27–36.

"Robert N. Gourdin to Robert Anderson, 1861." *South Carolina Historical Magazine*. 60 (January 1960), 10–13.

Roberts, Chalmers. "The Glorious Flag of Fort Sumter." *The Illustrated American*. February 19, 1898, pp. 233–35.

Seymour, Truman. "Forts Moultrie and Sumter: 1860, 1861." *The History of the First Regiment of Artillery*. Portland, ME, 1879.

Smyth, Thomas. "The Battle of Fort Sumter: Its Mystery and Miracle: God's Mastery and Mercy." Columbia, SC, 1861.

Spaulding, Oliver Lyman. "The Bombardment of Fort Sumter, 1861." American Historical Association. *Annual Report*. 1 (1913), 177–203.

Steen, Ivan D. "Charleston in the 1850s: As Described by British Travelers." *South Carolina Historical Magazine*. 71 (1970), 36–45.

Thompson, John. "A Union Soldier at Fort Sumter, 1860–1861." *South Carolina Historical Magazine*. 67 (April 1966), 99–104.

Trescot, William H. "Narrative of William Henry Trescot." *American Historical Review.* 13 (April 1908), 531–556.

Vandiver, Frank E. "The South Carolina Ordnance Board." *The Proceedings of the South Carolina Historical Association.* (1945), pp. 14–22.

Waldron, Webb. "If Lincoln Had Yielded and Withdrawn Major Anderson in 1861." *The Century Magazine.* (June 1927), pp. 151–56.

Welles, Gideon. "Facts in Relation to the Expedition Ordered by the Administration . . ." *Galaxy.* (November 1870), pp. 613–37.

———. "Narrative of Events." *American Historical Review.* 31 (April 1926), 484–94.

Welling, James C. "The Proposed Evacuation of Fort Sumter." *Nation.* 29 (December 4, 1879), 383–84.

Williams, Frank B., Jr. "From Sumter to the Wilderness . . ." *South Carolina Historical Magazine.* 63 (January 1962), 1–12.

Woodford, Steward L. "The Story of Fort Sumter." In *Personal Recollections of the Rebellion.* NY, 1891.

Young, Rogers W. "Castle Pinckney: Silent Sentinel of Charleston Harbor." *South Carolina Historical Magazine.* 39 (April 1938), 51–67.

Index